Copyright © 1996 Sheffield Academic Press

Published by Sheffield Academic Press Ltd
Mansion House
19 Kingfield Road
Sheffield S11 9AS
England

Printed on acid-free paper in Great Britain
by Bookcraft Ltd
Midsomer Norton, Bath

British Library Cataloguing in Publication Data

A catalogue record for this book is available
from the British Library

ISBN 1-85075-558-2

Disciples of the Beloved One

The Christology, Social Setting and
Theological Context of the
Ascension of Isaiah

Jonathan Knight

Journal for the Study of the Pseudepigrapha
Supplement Series 18

JOURNAL FOR THE STUDY OF THE PSEUDEPIGRAPHA
SUPPLEMENT SERIES
18

Editors
James H. Charlesworth
Lester L. Grabbe

Editorial Board
Randall D. Chesnutt, Philip R. Davies, Jan Willem van Henten,
Judith M. Lieu, Steven Mason, James R. Mueller,
Loren T. Stuckenbruck, James C. VanderKam

Sheffield Academic Press

Contents

Preface	7
Abbreviations	8

Chapter 1
AN INTRODUCTION TO THE *ASCENSION OF ISAIAH* 11

Chapter 2
THE CHRISTOLOGY OF THE *ASCENSION OF ISAIAH* 71

Chapter 3
THE SETTING OF THE *ASCENSION OF ISAIAH* 186

Chapter 4
THE *ASCENSION OF ISAIAH* AND THE NEW TESTAMENT
LITERATURE 274

Bibliography	315
Index of References	336
Index of Authors	350

Preface

This book is the result of several years' work. It emerged from a doctoral dissertation which I submitted to the University of Cambridge in 1991, although the work has acquired a substantially different form in the course of revision. Many people have helped me with the assembly of ideas which are presented here. In particular, I must mention Professors Christopher Rowland (my supervisor), Martin Hengel and Richard Bauckham. It continues to surprise me that, during the decade and more in which I have been engaged in study of the *Ascension of Isaiah*, relatively little has been published on this important apocalypse. I hope that this situation will change with the publication of the new edition. As is the way of the world, the new edition to which I allude was received in the period between the submission of the manuscript and the correction of the proofs. The work referred to is, P. Bettiolo with A. Giambelluca Kossova, C. Leonardi, E. Norelli and L. Perrone (eds.), *Ascensio Isaiae: Textus* (Corpus Christianorum, *Series Apocryphorum* 7; Bripoli: Turnhout, 1995). It was clearly impossible for me to incorporate this substantial advance in my work, much as I should like to have done so.

Translations of the *Ascension of Isaiah* and of the other pseudepigraphal literature are reproduced in this book from the collection edited by James H. Charlesworth, *The Old Testament Pseudepigrapha* (2 vols.; London: Darton, Longman & Todd, 1983, 1985), except where stated. I have used the United Bible Society version of the Greek New Testament, and a number of English translations of the Bible. Where no specific English translation is indicated I have used the Revised Standard Version.

I must acknowledge the financial assistance of the British Academy, the Tyndale Fellowship and the Trustees of the Sir Henry Stephenson Fellowship at Sheffield University for their sponsorship of the work which has now acquired its finished form.

The book is dedicated to my family, in this world and the next, and especially to my Mother.

ABBREVIATIONS

ABD	D.N. Freedman (ed.), *Anchor Bible Dictionary*
AJA	*American Journal of Archaeology*
ANRW	*Aufstieg und Niedergang der römischen Welt*
ASNU	*Acta seminarii neotestamentici upsaliensis*
ATANT	*Abhandlungen zur Theologie des Alten und Neuen Testaments*
BA	*Biblical Archaeologist*
BAGD	W. Bauer, W.F. Arndt, F.W. Gingrich and F.W. Danker, *Greek–English Lexicon of the New Testament*
BHT	*Beiträge zur historischen Theologie*
Bib	*Biblica*
BJRL	*Bulletin of the John Rylands University Library of Manchester*
BT	*The Bible Translator*
BZ	*Biblische Zeitschrift*
BZAW	*Beihefte zur ZAW*
CBQ	*Catholic Biblical Quarterly*
CrSt	*Cristianesimo nella Storia*
ExpTim	*Expository Times*
EvT	*Evangelische Theologie*
Fthst	*Frankfurter Theologische Studien*
GAP	Guides to the Apocrypha and Pseudepigrapha
HSM	Harvard Semitic Monographs
HTR	*Harvard Theological Review*
HUCA	*Hebrew Union College Annual*
IEJ	*Israel Exploration Journal*
JAAR	*Journal of the American Academy of Religion*
JBL	*Journal of Biblical Literature*
JewEnc	*The Jewish Encyclopedia*
JJS	*Journal of Jewish Studies*
JNES	*Journal of Near Eastern Studies*
JSJ	*Journal for the Study of Judaism in the Persian, Hellenistic and Roman Period*
JSNT	*Journal for the Study of the New Testament*
JTS	*Journal of Theological Studies*
LCL	Loeb Classical Library
MBT	*Münsteriche Beiträge zur Theologie*
NCB	New Century Bible

Abbreviations

NovT	*Novum Testamentum*
NovTSup	*Novum Testamentum*, Supplements
NTAbh	Neutestamentliche Abhandlungen
NTS	*New Testament Studies*
OrChr	*Oriens christianus*
PG	J. Migne (ed.), *Patrologia graeca*
PVTG	Pseudepigrapha Veteris Testamenti graece
RB	*Revue biblique*
Rel	*Religion*
RevQ	*Revue de Qumran*
RHR	*Revue de l'histoire des religions*
RSR	*Recherches de science religieuse*
SBLDS	SBL Dissertation Series
SBLSCS	SBL Septuagint and Cognate Studies
SBS	Stuttgarter Bibelstudien
SBT	Studies in Biblical Theology
SCS	Septuagint ad Cognate Studies
SJT	*Scottish Journal of Theology*
SNTSMS	Society for New Testament Studies Monograph Series
ST	*Studia theologica*
SUNT	Studien zur Umwelt des Neuen Testaments
SVTP	Studia in Veteris Testamenti pseudepigrapha
TDNT	G. Kittel and G. Friedrich (eds.), *Theological Dictionary of the New Testament*
TS	*Theological Studies*
TSK	*Theologische Studien und Kritiken*
TT	*Teologisk Tidsskrift*
TU	Texte und Untersuchungen
TZ	*Theologische Zeitschrift*
VTSup	*Vetus Testamentum*, Supplements
WMANT	Wissenschaftliche Monographien zum Alten und Neuen Testament
WUNT	Wissenschaftliche Untersuchungen zum Neuen Testament
ZAW	*Zeitschrift für die alttestamentliche Wissenschaft*
ZNW	*Zeitschrift für die neutestamentliche Wissenschaft*
ZTK	*Zeitschrift für Theologie und Kirche*
ZWT	*Zeitschrift für wissenschaftliche Theologie*

Chapter 1

AN INTRODUCTION TO THE *ASCENSION OF ISAIAH*

This book is a study of the early Christian apocalypse which is called the *Ascension of Isaiah*.[1] This text was written in the early second century CE and contains a wealth of material to interest scholars of primitive Christianity. It enshrines traditions about Jesus that have affinities with Matthew's Gospel,[2] including extra-canonical traditions;[3] and it offers

1. The *Ascension of Isaiah* exists in full only in an Ethiopic translation (E) but there are other partial versions: two Latin (L1, L2), Slavonic (S), some incomplete Greek fragments (Gk), a medieval Greek recasting called the Greek Legend (GL), and a Coptic version. There is an edition of the text by R.H. Charles, *The Ascension of Isaiah* (London: A. & C. Black, 1900), (see also C.F.A. Dillmann's *Ascensio Isaiae* [Leipzig, 1877]), but further manuscripts of E have since been discovered since these were published. An Italian research team is preparing a new edition of the apocalypse but this has not yet been published. I shall cite the apocalypse throughout this book in M.A. Knibb's English translation, which is found in J.H. Charlesworth (ed.), *The Old Testament Pseudepigrapha* (London: Darton, Longman & Todd, 1985), II, pp. 156-76. The most recent scholarship on the *Ascension of Isaiah* is mainly in Italian. See M. Pesce (ed.), *Isaia, il Diletto e la Chiesa* (Brescia: Paideia, 1983), the published proceedings of a conference on the apocalypse which was held in Rome in April 1981; A. Acerbi, *Serra Lignea: Studi sulla Fortuna della Ascensione di Isaia* (Rome: Editrice AVE, 1984); *idem*, *L'Ascensione di Isaia: Cristologia e Profetismo in Siria nei primi decenni del II Secolo* (Milan: Vita a Pensiero, 1989) and a number of articles in the Italian journal *Cristianesimo nella Storia*. For an English introduction to the *Ascension of Isaiah* see J.M. Knight, *The Ascension of Isaiah* (GAP, 2; Sheffield: Sheffield Academic Press, 1995).
2. The date proposed for the apocalypse makes it likely that the author knew Matthew. This case has been argued by J. Verheyden, 'L'Ascension d'Isaïe et l'Évangile de Matthieu', in J.-M. Sevrin (ed.), *The New Testament in Early Christianity* (Leuven: Leuven University Press, 1989), pp. 247-74. The question of what sources lie behind the description of the life of Jesus in 3.13-18 and 11.2-22 must be distinguished from the issue of what New Testament literature the author knew. R.J. Bauckham thinks that these two passages derived from a 'kerygmatic summary' of the kind which also resourced the early speeches in Acts and which

early interpretation of the New Testament, notably of passages such as 1 Pet. 3.22; 1 Cor. 2.8; 2 Thess. 1.7 and Col. 2.15.[4] The *Ascension of Isaiah* was well known to the Church Fathers, who cited its account of Isaiah's death, and it anticipates some of the themes of Gnosticism.[5] The apocalypse further offers important evidence for the history of Christianity in Syria in the period after the martyrdom of Ignatius. Specifically, the author notes the demise of prophecy in the church (3.21-31) and the problem of relations with the Roman administration (4.1-13) as issues which caused concern at this time. It will be argued in this book that this person had come to hear of the test of loyalty to the state which Pliny had used against the Christians of Bithynia in 112 CE and that the apocalypse represents a response to that development.[6] This early origin of the work means that the *Ascension of Isaiah* constitutes post-

---

was related to the oral tradition (in an unpublished paper, 'Gospel Traditions in the Ascension of Isaiah'). This case is apparently also argued in an unpublished paper by E. Norelli. It seems a plausible hypothesis given the *differences* from Matthew in 3.16-17 and 11.14a. I shall examine this issue in Chapter 4.

3. For example the statement about the absent midwife in 11.14a. There is a parallel to this idea in *Odes* 19.9.

4. The author's use of the New Testament literature is an important conclusion of my research. I argue this case throughout the book and especially in ch. 4.

5. For the patristic usage see e.g. Origen, *Epistula ad Julium Africanum* 9.25; and Jerome, *Commentarius in Isaiam* 64.4-5. There is an assessment of it in Acerbi, *Serra Lignea*, pp. 13-67. The *Ascension of Isaiah* also holds material about Isaiah in common with rabbinic literature. Rabbinic accounts of Isaiah's death are reported by L. Ginzberg, *The Legends of the Jews* (Philadelphia: Jewish Publication Society of America, 1947), IV, pp. 277-80, and VI, pp. 370-76. The two major sources for the legend are *b. Yeb.* 49b and *y. Sanh.* 10.2 (others are listed below). The problem of the work's relation with Gnosticism will be discussed in Chapters 2 and 3. The point must be made here that the *Ascension of Isaiah* displays significant differences from Gnosticism which cast doubt on any attempt to present it as a fully 'Gnostic' apocalypse. It seems rather to represent a form of Christianity which stands midway between the New Testament and the Gnostic literature.

6. The significance for the exegesis of the *Ascension of Isaiah* of the correspondence between Pliny and Trajan was mentioned to me by Professor M. Hengel who read an earlier draft of this book. Pliny (*Ep.* 10.96) told Trajan of the measures which he had taken against the Christians in his province. These measures included the demand to offer incense before the statues of the emperor and the gods and to curse Christ as a sign of Christian loyalty to the state. This procedure is called 'the sacrifice test' in this book. It was upheld by Trajan in his reply to Pliny (see Pliny *Ep.* 10.97). My belief is that the *Ascension of Isaiah* is a neglected response to this situation.

1. An Introduction to the Ascension of Isaiah

apostolic literature of the greatest importance. It ought (like the better-known *1 Clement*, the *Didache* and Ignatius) to be studied by everyone who is interested in the history of the New Testament period and the formation of Christian doctrine.

The *Ascension of Isaiah* has not always received such careful attention from scholars, however. The apocalypse has been neglected for much of this century despite the efforts of people like Burkitt and Werner to rehabilitate it.[7] Only in 1981 was a whole conference devoted to the work; three further monographs have now appeared, together with some articles.[8] This history of neglect is reflected in the state of textual studies at present. The standard critical edition remains that of R.H. Charles which was published in 1900 and which is based on manuscript evidence that is now outdated.[9] A successor to this has only recently been published (and was not available in the preparation of this book). *Ascension of Isaiah* studies are in a state of flux until it appears; scholarship must work with incomplete evidence in the meantime. This uncertain textual basis is problematic, but it must not deter scholars from doing what they can to interpret the apocalypse now. This is a field which will be widened and shown to be significant when the new edition appears.

What, then, is the *Ascension of Isaiah* and why should it be valued so highly? A glance at the text helps to answer these questions. The apocalypse falls into two halves. Chapters 1–5 (specifically 1.1–3.12; 5.1-16) record some traditions about Isaiah's death which the Italian scholar, Pesce, thinks were derived from Jewish oral tradition (and not from a written 'Martyrdom of Isaiah' which is what Charles and other scholars believed).[10] We must add that the present form of this material clearly

---

7. F.C. Burkitt, *Jewish and Christian Apocalypses* (London: British Academy, 1914), pp. 45-47, 73-74; M. Werner, *Die Entstehung des christlichen Dogmas* (Bern: Verlag Paul Haupt, 2nd edn, 1954 [Bonn, 1941]). There is an abridged English translation of this second book by S.G.F. Brandon (*The Formation of Christian Dogma* [London: A. & C. Black, 1955]).

8. This took place in Rome on 9–10 April 1981. Its proceedings are reported by Pesce in his edited collection, *Isaia*. The three further monographs are those by Acerbi and my own introduction to the apocalypse.

9. Charles, *Ascension of Isaiah*. The current manuscript evidence is set out by Knibb in Charlesworth (ed.), *Old Testament Pseudepigrapha*, II, p. 144. Knibb's translation is invaluable in the present state of *Ascension of Isaiah* studies because he has had access to more manuscripts than Charles (but still not the complete range) and has made a fresh collation of that evidence.

10. M. Pesce, 'Presupposti per l'utilazzione storica dell'*Ascensione di Isaia*:

serves the purposes of the Christian apocalyptist who was concerned to ward off harassment from the Roman government and to sustain the prophetic tradition in the church.

These traditions about Isaiah provide the setting for a Christian eschatological prophecy (3.13–4.22, which is called the 'First Vision' in this book). This Vision takes the form of an apocalyptic historical review (a device which is found as early as the book of Daniel[11]). The author presents the time of Jesus and of the apostles as a golden age that had been lost to history (3.13-20). He offers a pessimistic account of life in the post-apostolic church (3.21-31). He comments on the ethical laxity of the church leaders and mentions the decline of prophecy at the time of writing.[12] Chapter 4 includes a mythological description of the demon Beliar's incarnation as Nero. The author uses this form of mythology to criticize the Roman government for its attitude towards the Christians (4.1-13).[13] The First Vision climaxes in the hope for the imminent

Formazione e tradizione del testo; genere letterario; cosmologia angelica', in his edited collection *Isaia*, pp. 13-76 (see especially pp. 28, 40-45). The denial of a written Martyrdom of Isaiah exercises an important effect on theories about how the *Ascension of Isaiah* was composed. The structure of chs. 1–5 is examined by Acerbi, *L'Asensione di Isaia*, pp. 8-42; see also P.C. Bori, 'L'estasi del profeta: *Ascensio Isaiae* 6 e l'antico profetismo cristiano', *CrSt* 1 (1980), pp. 367-89 (who has a particular interest in a proposed patristic redaction of the apocalypse).

11. Daniel's use of this device is examined by J.J. Collins, *The Apocalyptic Vision of the Book of Daniel* (HSM, 16; Missoula, MT: Scholars Press, 1977), pp. 158-62; see also *idem*, *Daniel: A Commentary on the Book of Daniel* (Philadelphia: Fortress Press, 1993), pp. 166-70. Daniel exercised a significant impact on the author of the *Ascension of Isaiah* (see 4.12, 14), perhaps because both apocalypses were addressed to situations of religious crisis.

12. See further J.H. Charlesworth, 'Christian and Jewish Self-Definition in Light of the Christian Additions to the Apocryphal Writings', in E.P. Sanders (ed.), *Jewish and Christian Self-Definition*, II (London: SCM Press, 1985), pp. 27-55 (especially pp. 41-46). Charlesworth notes the ethical basis of the criticism and the absence of any evidence that the author of the *Ascension of Isaiah* was combatting false teaching. The *Sitz im Leben* of *Asc. Isa.* 3.21-31 is analyzed also by Acerbi, *L'Asensione di Isaia*, pp. 210-33; and by Pesce in his *Isaia*, pp. 52-62.

13. There is a fusion of mythology in 4.1-13 which is discussed by Charles, *Ascension of Isaiah*, pp. li-lxvii, who reviews the work of Wilhelm Bousset (*The Antichrist Legend* [ET London: Hutchinson, 1896]); and by Acerbi, *L'Ascensione di Isaia*, pp. 87-98. The author of the *Ascension of Isaiah* took up the identification of Nero as Beliar which is found in *Sib. Or.* 3.63-74 and he combined it with the notion of the demon's descent from heaven which I think he derived from the New Testament literature (see Lk. 10.18; Rev. 12.7-12). The notion of Satan's fall from

1. *An Introduction to the Ascension of Isaiah*

parousia (4.14-18). This was the time when the 'Beloved One' (as the heavenly Christ is called in the *Ascension of Isaiah*)[14] would appear from heaven to drag Beliar (who inspired the Romans) to Gehenna (4.14). The Beloved One would then commence his earthly reign with the saints until their final translation to heaven (4.15-17). The structure and the content of the First Vision show that the hope for imminent change was a prominent feature of the author's expectations. He had the strong conviction of living in 'the last generation' (see 11.38), and interpreted the Christian eschatological tradition to deal with the problem of difficult relations with the Romans which troubled him as he wrote.[15]

The second half of the *Ascension of Isaiah* (chs. 6–11, which are called the 'Second Vision' in this book) has a self-contained character, but the material is related thematically to the earlier chapters.[16] Like the First Vision, the purpose of this section was to provide assurance that Beliar had been made subject to the Beloved One. This assurance offered readers a new perspective on their difficult situation. Demonology is an important feature of this part of the apocalypse (as of the earlier chapters). The author presents Beliar as the chief demon in the firmament (the 'sky' or intermediate region between the heavens and earth). Beliar struggled with his angels there; the author hints at a correspondence between angelic strife and his own experience of conflict (7.9-12; cf. 4.4-12).[17] He states that Beliar had refused to acknowledge the true

---

heaven was itself a Christianized version of Jewish legends about the descent of the Watchers in Genesis 6 which had become a popular theme in Jewish apocalyptic literature.

14. 'Beloved One' was a Jewish messianic title which was carried over into early Christianity (see ch. 2). The Beloved One in the *Ascension of Isaiah* is a divine being who appears on earth as Jesus (3.13-18; 11.2-22). The work's Christology rests on the belief that Jesus is the temporary epiphany of the heavenly mediator in this way. The hidden descent is thus made a key theme in the apocalypse. This represents a development of the earlier christological tradition.

15. The history of Christian millenarianism is examined by H. Bietenhard, 'The Millenial Hope in the Early Church', *SJT* 6 (1953), pp. 12-30. The *Ascension of Isaiah* reworks the New Testament view by allowing for subsequent heavenly immortality (4.17).

16. S and L2 reproduce chs. 6–11 in isolation from the rest of the apocalypse. This causes problems in the study of the *Ascension of Isaiah*. It is generally accepted that these versions represent a redaction of the lost Greek original which the E text (supported by the Coptic fragments) reproduces more exactly (but not with total accuracy).

17. Beliar was a traditional opponent of the righteous in Jewish apocalyptic

God and had proclaimed himself the supreme cosmic authority (10.12-13; cf. 4.6). Chapter 10 predicts that the demon will be 'judged and destroyed' through the Beloved One's intervention (10.7-16). The crucial moment in this destruction, so it seems, is the crucifixion (10.14-15; see Col. 2.15).[18] The second half of ch. 10 describes how the Beloved One descends through the heavens disguised as an angel; he appears on earth in the form of Jesus by entering Mary's womb (11.2). The Beloved One dies on the cross and rises from the dead. Finally, he casts aside his disguise and ascends through the heavens (11.23-33). The angels then recognize and worship him because his disguise has been left behind (11.23-31). The first angels to do this are the rebellious ones in the firmament (11.23-24).[19] This offering of worship signifies that they have been subjugated in the way that the Second Vision describes. At the conclusion of the apocalypse the Beloved One occupies his throne at the right hand of God's throne. The Holy Spirit is said to be seated on the left (11.32-33).[20]

Despite this language about Beliar's defeat, the *Ascension of Isaiah* addressed a situation in which the demon was recognized to be powerful

literature (see for example *Jub.* 1.20; *T. Dan.* 1.7; *Liv. Proph.* 17.2; CD 16.5; 1QM 13.11; and 1QS 2.19). This demon has a variety of names in the *Ascension of Isaiah* (for example Sammael, Satan, Matanbukus) but all of them identify the same opponent. This point was made by V. Burch, 'Material for the Interpretation of the *Ascensio Isaiae*', *JTS* 21 (1920), pp. 249-65; see also Knibb in Charlesworth (ed.), *Old Testament Pseudepigrapha*, II, pp. 151-52, who discusses the different titles. N. Forsyth has argued that 'Satan' was displacing the other names in the apocalypse but that it still appears alongside them (*The Old Enemy* [Princeton, NJ: Princeton University Press, 1987], p. 211).

18. *Asc. Isa.* 10.14 states that the Beloved's victory over Beliar will be complete by the time of the resurrection (which it calls '[ascension]...from the gods of death'). The decisive moment must therefore be the cross.

19. There is a textual problem in *Asc. Isa.* 11.23-24 (see below), but the likelihood is that the angels in the firmament are the first to worship the Beloved One (cf. 10.13-15). This is a sign of their defeat.

20. The description of the Beloved One's ascension and enthronement was aided by a knowledge of 1 Pet. 3.22 which the author evidently knew. Werner argued that knowledge of Isa. 6 also resourced the portrait of the enthroned deity who was attended by two subordinates. This matter is examined also by J. Daniélou, *The Theology of Jewish Christianity* (ET London: SCM Press, 1964), pp. 134-40. For the view that the *Ascension of Isaiah* enshrines more than one Trinitarian understanding see M. Simonetti, 'Note sulla cristologia dell'*Ascensione di Isaia*' in Pesce (ed.), *Isaia*, pp. 185-209.

1. An Introduction to the Ascension of Isaiah

in the readers' experience. This is why the apocalypse was written. Readers had fallen foul, or expected to fall foul, of the Romans, who harassed the Christians in the form of the 'sacrifice test' in the second century, as we know from Pliny's correspondence with Trajan. The First Vision presents the Beloved One's parousia as the remedy for this situation. This would be the moment when a new world order was introduced. The Second Vision presents an 'apocalyptic' response to the crisis which offers 'revealed knowledge' about it and explains Beliar's true position as an insubordinate demon who had been defeated by the Beloved One. This knowledge helped to provide a positive attitude towards the situation by changing readers' thoughts about it through the description of the divine intervention. The two Visions offer complementary ways of viewing the crisis, and they were written to sustain hope.

This brief guide helps to answer the questions that I posed. The *Ascension of Isaiah* is to be valued for the light that it sheds on second-century Christian soteriology, Christology, eschatology, demonology and apocalypticism, and on the early interpretation of the New Testament (not to mention Trinitarianism and Mariology). In its theology the *Ascension of Isaiah* demonstrates the binitarianism (belief in two divine powers) which distinguished Christianity from Judaism. The work also takes steps in a Trinitarian direction which anticipates later reflection, particularly that which was founded on exegesis of Isa. 6.1-4 (see especially *Asc. Isa.* 9). The author's portrait of the Beloved One makes use of material which derived from Jewish angelology, but the apocalypse leaves no doubt that the mediator was *distinguished* from the angels through his inclusion in the worship of God (for example in 7.17).[21] The *Ascension of Isaiah* also shows that belief in the imminent parousia and in the messiah's earthly kingdom still held currency at the time of writing. This was combined with the promise of heavenly immortality (see for example 4.17) which seems to represent a development from the New Testament eschatology. The detailed description of the Beloved One's descent in chs. 10–11 represents the beginnings of a dogmatic interest in Christian theology. All of these areas are of great importance in the study of early Christianity. In view of what it contains, it is surprising to learn that the *Ascension of Isaiah* has been neglected for so long by researchers. Such neglect is most definitely a reflection of

---

21. See Chapter 2 for the elucidation of this point. The worship of Jesus was the hallmark of primitive Christianity.

18   *Disciples of the Beloved One*

scholarly interests rather than of the intrinsic merits of the apocalypse. The *Ascension of Isaiah* deserves to be re-established as a second-century source of great value for historians and theologians alike.

The Scope of this Book

This book is an attempt to redress that scholarly neglect of the *Ascension of Isaiah* by examining three aspects of its interpretation which have yet to be fully explored in research. These are the work's Christology, its setting and its relevance for the study of the New Testament.

After an introduction to the apocalypse (the rest of this chapter), I shall examine the Christology of the *Ascension of Isaiah* (Chapter 2). The origins of beliefs about Jesus have long aroused interest among scholars. Several have identified the Jewish Wisdom tradition as a source for Christology but have been sceptical that angelology could have exercised a similar influence.[22] It has been suggested, either that the Christians turned away from angelology because it failed to express Christ's unique position in heaven,[23] or else that angelology was simply peripheral as a means for expressing what was believed about him.[24] The *Ascension of Isaiah* recommends a different evaluation of this issue. I shall argue that the apocalypse makes a new and creative use of material that derived from angelology. The author used angelology to present the Beloved One as a divine being and the subordinate of God in a context in which his inclusion in the cult and reception of worship, and thus his *transcendence* of the angels, were dominant factors. This use of angelic material to describe Christ as different from the angels will be called 'angelomorphic Christology' in this book.[25] This form of belief differs

---

22. See for example J.D.G. Dunn, *Christology in the Making* (London: SCM Press, 1980), p. 158: 'No New Testament writer thought of Christ as an angel'. Dunn summarizes the angelic background to Christology in a mere ten pages.
23. This position is adopted by C.H. Talbert in his article, 'The Myth of the Descending-Ascending Redeemer in Mediterranean Antiquity', *NTS* 22 (1976), pp. 418-40.
24. This view is expressed by M. Hengel in his book, *The Son of God* (ET London: SCM Press, 1976), p. 85.
25. The significance of angelomorphic Christology is examined by Daniélou, *Jewish Christianity*, pp. 117-46; and by R. Longenecker, *The Christology of Early Jewish Christianity* (SBT, 17; London: SCM Press, 1970), pp. 26-32. The theological significance of worship addressed to Jesus in early Christianity is explored by R.J. Bauckham, 'The Worship of Jesus in Apocalyptic Christianity', *NTS* 27 (1980–81),

markedly from what has been called 'angel-Christology', which I take to be the presentation of Christ quite literally as an angel. There is no such 'angel-Christology' in the *Ascension of Isaiah*, where the Beloved's appearance in angelic likeness (as in human likeness) is said to be the result of transformation and not of nature (see ch. 10). The evidence of the apocalypse indicates that angelology was *not* abandoned as a source for Christology, but that it was developed by this second-century author who prepared the way for later literature in this respect.

At least two strands of angelology must be considered in this assessment of the work's Christology. A number of Jewish apocalyptic texts elevate a subordinate figure to a position of prominence in heaven (for example Dan. 10.5-6 and 11QMelch). This development of an exalted angel in apocalyptic literature influenced several early Christian descriptions of Christ, including that found in Rev. 1.13-14 and the Synoptic transfiguration narrative (Mk 9 and parallels). My belief is that the author of the *Ascension of Isaiah* drew on this strand when he described the Beloved in angelomorphic language (see the Ethiopic text of 7.7-8 and 9.27-28) and insisted that he must worship God (9.40) despite the fact of his divinity. Moreover, the notion of an angel's appearance on earth ('an angelophany'), which is exemplified by the portrait of Raphael in the book of Tobit (second century BCE) and by other texts, helped to shape the description of the hidden descent which is found in *Ascension of Isaiah* 10 and 11 (cf. also *Asc. Isa.* 3.13). This strand of angelology allowed the author to suggest that the Beloved One could appear on earth in human form. My belief is that these two strands of angelology together contributed to the formation of the *Ascension of Isaiah* Christology. They allowed the author to present Jesus as the earthly appearance of the Beloved One in a context in which his hidden descent through the seven heavens and his transformation into human likeness are made major themes.

Chapter 3 examines the setting of the apocalypse. The First Vision seems to be the work of an author who was ill at ease with other people. These others include the Jews (3.6-10; 4.21-22), who had become long-standing opponents of the Christians by the second century CE; fellow Christians, in this case principally over the issue of prophecy in the church (3.21-31; see also 2.7-11; 6.14, 17); and the Roman government, who were persecuting Christians in Bithynia and possibly elsewhere at

pp. 332-41; and by L.W. Hurtado, *One God, One Lord* (London: SCM Press, 1988), pp. 93-124.

the time. The Second Vision is a narrative of Beliar's defeat which hardly disguises the fact that the Romans had the power to harass the author and his friends. The *Ascension of Isaiah* enshrines an ethical and cosmological dualism whose purpose was to reassure an isolated group who felt displaced in their 'world' by describing the superiority of their heavenly patron.

Previous studies have identified the model of a prophetic circle as a helpful way to describe the author and his friends. Pesce believes that they were a school of prophets who collected and interpreted prophetic oracles in the way that the *Ascension of Isaiah* reveals. Hall presents them in conflict with other Christians over the issue of the Beloved One's descent and ascension.[26] This book agrees with this broad approach but develops the emerging portrait in two different ways. First, the evidence which the apocalypse offers for the demise of prophecy in the second century will be explored through a reading of other literature including the *Didache* and the letters of Ignatius. Secondly, the state of relations between the Romans and the Christians at that time will be examined to find an explanation for the strong polemic against Rome which is found in *Asc. Isa.* 4.1-13. This will lead to the suggestion that the work's setting was among a Syrian Christian community which included prophets who found themselves increasingly marginalized in the church and who feared that the Romans would demand profession of obedience as Pliny had done in Bithynia.

Chapter 4 considers the relevance of the *Ascension of Isaiah* for the early use of the New Testament literature. This too is a neglected area in research. The author of the *Ascension of Isaiah* knew and exegeted some of the New Testament documents but without acknowledgment. His apocalypse shows how certain passages, especially christological ones, were interpreted to meet the demands of Christian belief at this early period of exegesis. The author developed the diverse christological tradition into a new and more coherent whole under the demands of his soteriology. He made reflection about the Beloved's past achievement the central feature of chs. 6–11, which represent a sustained account of Christology. This observation shows both the distance at which the *Ascension of Isaiah* stands from the New Testament literature and also the importance which the author attached to the New Testament

---

26. Pesce in his *Isaia*, pp. 52-56; R.G. Hall, 'The *Ascension of Isaiah*: Community Situation, Date, and Place in Early Christianity', *JBL* 109.2 (1990), pp. 289-306.

1. An Introduction to the Ascension of Isaiah

documents. This evidence makes for a fascinating study as we ask which of the New Testament documents the author knew and how he used the material that was available to him in this way.

This book was written before the new edition of the apocalypse was published. It remains to be seen how many of my conclusions will need to be revised in the light of an authoritative text. I hope, of course, that much will be able to stand. The areas which are discussed here, however—Christology, social setting and contact with the New Testament—are crucial ones and will continue to form the backbone of *Ascension of Isaiah* studies even when the new edition appears. I hope that my work can be integrated into wider scholarship and that further research will lead in due course towards a consensus about the different aspects of the text's interpretation.

The Critical Basis of Ascension of Isaiah Studies

Difficult critical problems surround all serious study of the *Ascension of Isaiah*.[27] These problems must be considered before embarking on research.

A major difficulty is that of establishing the original text of the apocalypse. The *Ascension of Isaiah* was written in Greek, but only a fragmentary Greek text (Gk) has survived.[28] We must rely for the bulk of the apocalypse on the evidence of later translations, of which the Ethiopic (E) is the most extensive. The Greek fragment was discovered by Grenfell and Hunt in a papyrological collection at the beginning of the present century. It covers *Asc. Isa.* 2.4-4.4 with occasional lacunae.[29]

---

27. See Pesce's discussion of this matter in his *Isaia*, pp. 13-35; and Knibb in Charlesworth (ed.), *Old Testament Pseudepigrapha*, II, pp. 144-49.

28. A Greek original is commonly assumed by those who work on the apocalypse; see Knibb's comments in Charlesworth (ed.), *Old Testament Pseudepigrapha*, II, pp. 146-47.

29. B.P. Grenfell and A.S. Hunt, *The Amherst Papyri...Part I: The Ascension of Isaiah and Other Theological Fragments* (London: Oxford University Press, 1900). The Greek text is printed in Charles, *Ascension of Isaiah*, pp. 84-95; and in A.-M. Denis, *Fragmenta Pseudepigraphorum Graeca*, (PVTG, 3; Leiden: Brill, 1970), pp. 108-13 (but Denis concludes his citation at *Asc. Isa.* 3.12). The Greek text has been re-edited for the new critical edition by E. Norelli (see Pesce in his *Isaia*, p. 30). An important lacuna in Gk is in 3.16 where Grenfell and Hunt believed that the name 'Gabriel' for the Holy Spirit had accidentally been omitted. There is a

The Greek text comprises some of the Isaiah traditions (2.4-3.12) and more than half of the First Vision (3.13-4.4). It allows us to test the reliability of E in these places, where it emerges as a faithful but at times rather wooden translation.[30]

In addition to Gk, there is a medieval Greek rewriting of the apocalypse which is called the 'Greek Legend' (GL). The GL begins with an abbreviated version of *Ascension of Isaiah* 1 but then places a reworked version of the Second Vision before the material that is found in *Ascension of Isaiah* 2–5.[31] The GL clearly alters the original: it resolves the chronological problem in E (see 1.1; 6.1) and shows signs of conformity to the New Testament in some of its readings.[32] Like Gk, however, the GL is of value since it allows us to test the reliability of E in crucial places. This is a useful facility because in parts of the apocalypse (for

discussion of this matter in Charles, *Ascension of Isaiah*, pp. 19-20 n.16 (and see also Verheyden, 'L'Ascension d'Isaïe', pp. 270-74).

30. There are occasions, however, where the E translator is guilty of error and inaccuracy. An example of this is 9.3 which Knibb translates: 'Who is this one who turned to me that I might go up?' There L2 has *Quis est praecipiens mihi ascendere?* and GL 2.24 τίς ἐστιν ὁ ἐπιτρέπων μοι ἀναβαίνειν. The E translator has misunderstood the sense of ἐπιτρέπων and assumed that it means 'turned to me'; see Knibb in Charlesworth (ed.), *Old Testament Pseudepigrapha*, II, p. 169, note c. On Ethiopic Bible translations generally see E. Ullendorff, *Ethiopia and the Bible* (London: British Academy, 1968), pp. 31-59, especially pp. 55-59; and J. Hofman's article in B.M. Metzger, *The Early Versions of the New Testament* (Oxford: Oxford University Press, 1977), pp. 240-56.

31. The GL was discovered in a twelfth-century Greek manuscript (Paris Cod. Gr. 1534) and it was published by O. von Gebhardt, 'Die *Ascensio Isaiae* als Heiligenlegende', *ZWT* 21 (1878), pp. 330-53. It can now be found in Charles, *Ascension of Isaiah*, pp. 141-48 and in E. Tisserant, *Ascension d'Isaïe* (Paris: Letouzey et Ané, 1909), pp. 217-26. There has been a further manuscript discovery (Vatic. Palat. of the 11th century) which is noted by A.M. Denis, *Introduction aux Pseudépigraphes grecs d'Ancien Testament* (SVTP, 1; Leiden: Brill, 1970), p. 172, and by Pesce in his *Isaia*, pp. 20, 30-31. E. Norelli has written an unpublished paper on this new discovery: 'Collazione del testo della Leggenda greca pubblicata da O.v. Gebhardt dal ms. Paris Gr. 1534 con il testo del ms. Vat. Pal. Gr. 27' (this paper is mentioned by Pesce in his *Isaia*, p. 20 n.12). See also Denis, *Fragmenta*, pp. 105-14 for a discussion of the GL.

32. For an example of such conformity see GL 2.25 ὁ κύριος τῆς δόξης, ὁ υἱὸς τοῦ θεοῦ τοῦ ζῶντος (its version of *Asc. Isa.* 9.5). The GL has emended E's reading ('this is your LORD, the LORD, the LORD Christ, who is to be called in the world Jesus'; L2 *filius Dei*) to conform with Mt. 16.16. GL 2.37 nevertheless supports E in 10.7 by including the proper name 'Jesus' against S and L2.

1. *An Introduction to the Ascension of Isaiah*

example, 5.1-16) E is our *only* textual witness, and it shows major differences from S and L2 in the Second Vision (see below). It is reassuring to know that E does not contain wild idiosyncrasies in those places where it can be tested against a Greek version (but this is not to say that it is accurate at every point).

The Ethiopic translation was made in the fourth or fifth century CE.[33] It is known through seven manuscripts. The first three were available to Charles and all but the last two to Knibb. These manuscripts are:

A (Bodleian MS Aeth. d. 13, 15th century, fol. 95–115),
B (British Library Or. 501, 15th century, fols. 62–69),
C (British Library Or. 503, 18th century, fols. 57–62),
D (Vatican Library, Eth. 263, 14–15th century, fols. 85–104),
E (fragment covering 1.4–2.2 from the Abba Garima Codex, microfilm in Hill Monastic Manuscript Library. Ms E closely resembles D),
F (15th century),
G (Vatican Library, 14–15th century).

D is an important discovery. It often agrees with A, as apparently does G, but it sometimes supports the readings of B and C which more often agree with F. Perrone shows that the manuscript tradition has two stems, ADEG on the one hand and BCF on the other. He thinks that both of these derived from a common archetype.[34]

We possess two Latin translations of the *Ascension of Isaiah* (L1 and L2). These are of quite different character and scope. L1 covers 2.14–3.13 and 7.1-19 and it has close affinities with E. It was found in a Vatican palimpsest (Vatic. Lat. 5750) and has recently been re-edited by

---

33. The text is printed in Charles, *Ascension of Isaiah*, pp. 83-139. This, however, is based on incomplete manuscript evidence. There are (similarly problematic) versions of the Ethiopic text by R. Laurence, *Ascensio Isaiae Vatis* (Oxford, 1819) and Dillmann, *Ascensio*. L. Perrone has re-edited E for the new edition (see his 'Note critiche [e "autocritiche"] sull'edizione del testo etiopico dell'*Ascensione di Isaia*' in Pesce [ed.], *Isaia*, pp. 77-93; and the brief comment by Pesce in the same volume, p. 29).

34. Perrone in Pesce (ed.), *Isaia*, pp. 89-91. Perrone reproduces Norelli's view of chs. 1–5 on pp. 90-91 of this volume. He adds his own study of chs. 6–11 on p. 91. Norelli's view is taken from his unpublished paper, 'Studio sul rapporto tra i. mss. etiopici di AI, limitamente ai capp. 1–5', which is mentioned by Pesce in his *Isaia*, p. 31, n.32. See also Knibb in Charlesworth (ed.), *Old Testament Pseudepigrapha*, II, p. 144.

24   *Disciples of the Beloved One*

C. Leonardi.[35] Despite some differences between them E, Gk, and L1 all represent essentially the same textual tradition.[36] This is obvious in 7.1-19 where E and L1 usually agree together against S and L2 in reporting the early stages of Isaiah's ascension.

L2 is quite different from L1.[37] It was published in 1522 by the Venetian printer A. de Fantis from a manuscript that is now unknown,[38] and republished by Gieseler in 1832.[39] L2 covers only chs. 6–11 ('The Second Vision') which it introduces with the title *Visio, quam vidit Isaias propheta, filius Amos*. The Slavonic translation (S) also reproduces only *Ascension of Isaiah* 6–11 and has a similar introduction.[40] L2 often

---

35.   L1 forms part of the original writing of this palimpsest. It comes from the fifth or sixth century CE (see Knibb in Charlesworth [ed.], *Old Testament Pseudepigrapha*, II, pp. 144-45). It was originally published by A. Mai in his *Collectio Nova Scriptorum Veterum* (Rome, 1828), 3.2, pp. 238-39. The fragments were identified by B.G. Niebuhr and republished by I. Nitzsch, 'Nachweisung zweier Bruchstücke einer alten lateinischen Übersetzung vom *Anabatikon Esaiou*', *Theologische Studien und Kritiken* 3 (1830), pp. 209-246. L1 is printed also in Dillmann, *Ascensio*, pp. 83-85; *PL* 13, cols. 629–32; Charles, *Ascension of Isaiah*, pp. 87-92, 102-108; Tisserant, *Ascension d'Isaïe*, pp. 100-109, 142-54 and (2.14–3.12 only) in Denis, *Fragmenta*, pp. 111-13. For the re-editing of L1 see C. Leonardi, 'Il testo dell'AI nel Vat. lat. 5750', *CrSt* 1 (1980), pp. 59-74 (and Pesce in his *Isaia*, pp. 29-30).
36.   This broad agreement is recognized by Knibb in Charlesworth (ed.), *Old Testament Pseudepigrapha*, II, p. 145; and by Pesce in his *Isaia*, p. 22. Pesce summarizes an unpublished paper by Norelli, 'Studio sui rapporti tra testo etiopico, frammento greco, antica versione latina, versione copta sahidica, con esame e critica delle testi di Charles sulla storia del testo di AI 1-5' (in his *Isaia*, p. 31 n. 32).
37.   Text in Dillmann, *Ascensio*, pp. 76-83; and Charles, *Ascension of Isaiah*, pp. 98-139 (see also Knibb in Charlesworth (ed.), *Old Testament Pseudepigrapha*, II, pp. 145-46). It has been re-edited for the new edition by Leonardi (see Pesce in his *Isaia*, pp. 29-30).
38.   A. de Fantis, *Opera nuper in lucem prodeuntia* (Venice, 1522); see further Acerbi, *Serra Lignea*, pp. 145-75. L2 was evidently lost when Laurence prepared his edition but he knew about it through a reference in the work of Sixtus of Siena (see Knibb in Charlesworth (ed.), *Old Testament Pseudepigrapha*, II, p. 145; and Laurence, *Ascensio*, p. 151).
39.   J.C.L. Gieseler, *Programma quo Academiae Georgiae Augustae prorector et senatus sacra pentecostalia anni MDCCCXXXII pie concelebranda indixerunt* (Göttingen, 1832).
40.   The lost parent of L2 and S probably underwent patristic redaction; see Acerbi in Pesce (ed.), *Isaia*, pp. 277-98. S and L2 were used by the medieval Cathari; see Acerbi, 'La Visione di Isaia nelle vicende dottrinali del catarismo

1. An Introduction to the Ascension of Isaiah

agrees with S against E, most obviously in ch. 11 where both omit E's traditions about Jesus, but there are important differences between these versions which should not be minimized.[41]

The Slavonic version comes from the eleventh century CE. It exists in two forms, the second of which is an abbreviation of the first.[42] The complete version is known from a twelfth-century Russian manuscript and from other later manuscripts.[43] The Slavonic version can be found in Bonwetsch's Latin translation which is printed in Charles's edition, but Vaillant has noticed some unfortunate inaccuracies in this.[44] The relation between S and L2 has been a matter of dispute.[45]

---

lombardo', *CrSt* 1 (1980), pp. 59-74; and *idem*, *Serra Lignea*, pp. 103-148.

41. As evidently in 7.8 (see below).

42. See Knibb in Charlesworth (ed.), *Old Testament Pseudepigrapha*, II, pp. 145-46. S has been re-edited for the new edition by Kossova and Danti (this is mentioned by Pesce in his *Isaia*, p. 30).

43. There is an edition of the Russian manuscript, with variants from a 14th century Serbian manuscript, by A. Popov, *Opisanie rukopisei i katalog knigi tserkovnoi pechati biblioteki A.I. Khludova*, (Moscow, 1872). There is a further edition of the Russian manuscript by A.A. Sachmatov and P.A. Lavrov, *Sbornik XII věka Moskovskago Uspenskago Sobora, I* (Moscow, 1899).

44. N. Bonwetsch in Charles, *Ascension of Isaiah*, pp. 98-139; A. Vaillant, 'Un apocryphe pseudo-bogomile: La Vision d'Isaïe', *Révue des Études Slaves* 42 (1963), pp. 109-121.

45. See Knibb's summary of this problem in Charlesworth (ed.), *Old Testament Pseudepigrapha*, II, pp. 145-46. J. Ivanov in his *Bogomilski knigi i legendi* (Sofia, 1925) argued that L2 was copied from a Slavonic text, but E. Turdeanu thinks that S was subjected to Bogomil editing (see his article 'Apocryphes bogomiles et apocryphes pseudo-bogomiles', *RHR* 138 [1950], pp. 213-18). Vaillant then argued that the differences between S and L2 indicated independent use of a common Greek original which had been revised to make it more 'orthodox' in outlook ('Un apocryphe pseudo-bogomile', p. 110). On S see also A. Giambelluca Kossova, 'Osservazioni sulla tradizione paleoslava della Visione di Isaia: coincidenze e divergenze con la tradizione testuale dell'Ascensione di Isaia' (this is noted by Pesce in his *Isaia*, p. 30 n. 29); A. Vaillant, *Textes Vieux-slaves* (Institut d'Études slaves; Paris: Imprimerie Nationale, 1968) I *Textes et Glossaire*, pp. 87-98; II *Traduction et Notes*, pp. 72-82; E. Kozak, 'Bibliographische Übersicht der biblisch-apokryphen Literatur bei den Slaven', *Jahrbücher für Protestantischer Theologie* 18 (1892), pp. 127-58 (138-39); N. Bonwetsch in A. von Harnack, *Geschichte der altchristlichen Literatur* (Leipzig, 1893), 1.2, p. 916; W. Lüdtke, 'Beiträge zu slavischen Apokryphen', *ZAW* 31 (1911), pp. 218-35; and E. Turdeanu, *Apocryphes slaves et roumaines de l'Ancien Testament* (SVTP, 5; Leiden: Brill, 1981), pp. 1-74, 145-72, together with the additional notes on pp. 436-39.

Fragments of the apocalypse are found also in the Sahidic and Akhmimic dialects of Coptic.[46] The Coptic translation, like the Ethiopic, preserves all eleven chapters of the apocalypse. This encourages us to suppose that that was its original form.

This evidence yields the agreed scholarly conclusion that the textual tradition of the *Ascension of Isaiah* has two distinct branches: that represented by E, L1 and Gk on the one hand and by S and L2 on the other. The relation between E and S and L2 in the Second Vision is a major difficulty for researchers. S and L2 reproduce *only* chs. 6–11 as if this material at one time circulated independently of the rest. These versions also have a marked tendency towards abbreviation. P.C. Bori has examined this problem in the case of *Ascension of Isaiah* 6. He shows that, where E goes into considerable detail about Isaiah's ascension, S and L2 shorten the description as if mystical prophecy were viewed with suspicion when their parent was composed.[47] Bori concluded from this that S and L2 represent a *redacted* version of the lost original and that E more accurately reproduces the Greek in that chapter. He suggested that S and L2 suppressed the identification of prophecy with ecstasy because their parent was influenced by the mainstream reaction against the Montanist movement after c. 175 CE. This is an important point for determining when the patristic redaction was made. It comes in all probability from the third century CE or perhaps from the early fourth.[48]

The tendency of L2 and S towards abbreviation can be seen again in ch. 11. S and L2 omit the passage which describes the life of Jesus (11.2-22 [E]) and replace it with a short summary of the Beloved One's earthly appearance. The Ethiopic version of 11.2-22 is, however, similar in tone to the material about Jesus which is found in *Asc. Isa.* 3.13-19, where E is supported by Gk and initially by L1. This means that the Jesus traditions cannot easily be held to be the insertion of the E

46. The Sahidic fragments were published by L.T. Lefort, 'Coptica Lovaniensia', *Le Muséon* 51 (1938), pp. 24-30; the Akhmimic were also published by Lefort, 'Fragments d'apocryphes en copte-akhmîmique', *Le Muséon* 52 (1939), pp. 7-10. There is a more complete version of these by P. Lacau, 'Fragments de l'Ascension d'Isaïe en copte', *Le Muséon* 59 (1946), pp. 453-67. The Coptic text has been re-edited for the new edition by P. Bettiolo (see Pesce in *Isaia*, p. 29). Its value as a source for the apocalypse as a unified work is noticed by Pesce in *Isaia*, pp. 28-29.

47. Bori, 'L'estasi del profeta' pp. 370-38.

48. Jerome cited the conclusion of the apocalypse in the L2 version (*Comm. in Is.* 64.4).

1. *An Introduction to the Ascension of Isaiah*

translator.[49] This tends to confirm Bori's suspicion that S and L2 represent a redaction of the Greek original and that E is the more reliable tradent of that text. As in ch. 6, dogmatic considerations account for the omission of 11.2-22 in these later versions. Their parent evidently wanted to remove E's docetism and its author excised the whole section as a consequence. I suspect that he also omitted chs. 1–5 because of their millenarian tendencies. Although L2 and S thus have a secondary character, this should not lull us into supposing that they are without value. The opposite is in fact the case. On occasion they reveal the true text where the E translator nods or errs (for example in 9.3).

Another difficulty for researchers (at the time of writing) is that of deciding which text or translation of the *Ascension of Isaiah* to use for study. Until the new edition, scholarship had to rely on outdated editions of the Ethiopic together with a number of translations. Editions of the Ethiopic include those of Laurence (1819), Dillmann (1877) and Charles (1900). Several new manuscript discoveries have since been made which had not previously been included in a published text. It is clearly desirable to have access to the best possible text. Curiously, the best way to do this in the absence of the new edition was to use an English translation of the *Ascension of Isaiah*. English translations currently available are those by Charles, Barton, Hill and Knibb, and there is a French translation by Tisserant.[50] *All* are based on incomplete manuscript evidence, but there were reasons for preferring Knibb's work to its rivals. Charles used only three Ethiopic manuscripts. Barton's translation is no more than an updating of Charles, and Hill's was made from the German of Flemming-Duensing. Knibb by contrast used all but two of the seven Ethiopic manuscripts and he made a new collation of that evidence. He corrects the Ethiopic with reference to the other versions and includes footnotes which detail the manuscript variants. His work offers an approach to the text which is not matched by the other

---

49. But 11.2-22 has sometimes been seen as a later interpolation: as by F.C. Burkitt in his *Jewish and Christian Apocalypses*, p. 46.

50. Charles, *Ascension of Isaiah*; and *idem*, *The Apocrypha and Pseudepigrapha of the Old Testament* (Oxford: Oxford University Press, 1913), II, pp. 155-62; J. Barton's revision of Charles' work in H.F.D. Sparks (ed.), *The Apocryphal Old Testament* (Oxford: Clarendon Press, 1984), pp. 775-812; D. Hill's translation of Flemming-Duensing's German original in E. Hennecke, with W. Schneemelcher and R.McL. Wilson (eds.), *New Testament Apocrypha* (ET London: SCM Press, 1963–65), II, pp. 642-63; Knibb, in Charlesworth (ed.), *Old Testament Pseudepigrapha*, II, pp. 156-76; and E. Tisserant, *Ascension d'Isaïe*, pp. 85-215.

translations and which will continue to serve a need even now that the new edition has appeared. I have used his translation throughout this book (although I sometimes cite the other versions).

The Sources of the Apocalypse

We have seen that the *Ascension of Isaiah* contains more than one strand of material. There has been uncertainty in previous scholarship about what to call the different parts of the *Ascension of Isaiah*. Charles promoted the theory that the Isaiah traditions were known to the author in the form of a text called the 'Martyrdom of Isaiah'.[51] This view is repeated by Knibb.[52] The existence of a written 'Martyrdom of Isaiah' was however challenged by Pesce at the 1981 Conference.[53] Pesce used rabbinic evidence to argue that the Isaiah material derived more plausibly from Jewish oral tradition. He showed that reports about Isaiah's death circulated in two different forms early in the Common Era.[54] *B. Yeb.* 49b describes how Manasseh sentenced Isaiah and sawed

51. Charles, *Ascension of Isaiah*, Introduction, p. xliii.
52. Knibb in Charlesworth (ed.), *Old Testament Pseudepigrapha*, II, p. 143. On this putative document see also G. Beer in E. Kautsch, *Die Apokryphen und Pseudepigraphen des Alten Testaments*. II. *Die Pseudepigraphen des Alten Testaments* (Tübingen, 1900), pp. 119-27, who translates 2.1-15 and 5.2-14; P. Riessler, *Altjüdisches Schrifttum ausserhalb der Bibel* (Heidelberg: F.H. Kerle Verlag, 2nd edn, 1966), pp. 481-84; Denis, *Introduction*, pp. 170-76, and *Fragmenta*, pp. 105-114 (who argues that the Martyrdom corresponds to *Asc. Isa.* 1.1-5, 3.13, 6.17, 6.1-6, 1.7-13, 2.12, 5.1-14); E. Hammershaimb, 'Das Martyrium Esajas', in W.G. Kümmel *et al.* (eds.), *Jüdische Schriften aus hellenistisch-römische Zeit* (Gütersloh: Gerd Mohn, 1973) II, pp. 15-34; and *idem, De Gammeltestamentlige Pseudepigrapher* (Copenhagen: Gads Forlag, 1976), I, pp. 303-15; J.H. Charlesworth, *The Pseudepigrapha and Modern Research* (Missoula, MT: Scholars Press, 2nd edn with Supplement, 1981), pp. 125-30; E. Norelli, 'Il Martirio di Isaia come *testimonium* antigiudaico?', *Henoch* 2 (1980), pp. 37-57; L. Rost, *Einleitung in die alttestamentlich Apokryphen und Pseudepigraphen einschliesslich der grossen Qumran Handschriften* (Heidelberg: Quelle & Meyer, 1971), pp. 112-14 and E. Katz, 'Das Martyrium Isaias', *Communio Viatorum* 11 (1968), pp. 169-74. A. Caquot also comments on the Isaiah narrative in his 'Bref Commentaire du Martyre d'Isaïe', *Sem* 23 (1973), pp. 65-93.
53. Pesce (ed.), *Isaia*, pp. 28, 40-45. See also the publication, 'Il *Martirio di Isaia* non esiste. L'*Ascensione di Isaia* e le tradizioni giudaiche sull'uccisione del profeta' in *Atti del III Convegno di studi giudaici* (Rome: Associanze Italiana per lo Studio del Giudaismo, 1984); this is mentioned by Pesce in his *Isaia*, p. 27 n. 22).
54. Pesce in his *Isaia*, pp. 40-45. Pesce also has an unpublished paper,

1. An Introduction to the Ascension of Isaiah

him in two after a trial which consisted of formal charges. *B. Sanh.* 103b says only that Manasseh slew Isaiah, and cites 2 Kgs 21.16 to the effect that the king shed innocent blood in Jerusalem. The Yebamot version, Pesce argues, describes a legal process but the Sanhedrin report is tantamount to murder. Pesce shows that the *Ascension of Isaiah* combines elements from both versions of the Isaiah legend. It describes first a formal trial before Manasseh (3.6-12) and then the king's unwarranted rage which led to Isaiah's martyrdom (5.1-16). This fusion of sources convinced Pesce that the author was familiar with more than one legend about Isaiah, which he adapted to suit his purposes, but not with a written document. This view is accepted by at least one later commentator (Hall)[55] and has yet to be challenged in research.

Charles called *Asc. Isa.* 3.13–4.22 the 'Testament of Hezekiah'. He argued that this passage reflects the warning which Hezekiah gave to Manasseh in *Ascension of Isaiah* 1.[56] Charles came to this view through reading the medieval chronicler George Cedrenus who cited *Asc. Isa.* 4.12 as from the 'Testament of Hezekiah'.[57] Charles then linked 3.13–4.22 with 1.1-2 and assumed that it reported what was said by Hezekiah. This view is intrinsically suspect. *Ascension of Isaiah* 3.13–4.22 is neither testamentary in form nor ascribed to Hezekiah as author. It is by contrast a Christian eschatological prophecy that is attributed pseudonymously to Isaiah. Pesce especially criticized Charles's assumption that Cedrenus had *only* 3.13–4.22 before him.[58] He observed that, since Cedrenus alludes to the martyrdom tradition as well, the Byzantine had

---

'Tradizione giudaiche utilizzate in AI 1-5 e il genere letterario di AI', which he notes in *Isaia*, p. 35 n. 39. The relevant rabbinic material is *b. Yeb.* 49b, *y. Sanh.* 10.2 (f. 28c), *b. Sanh.* 103b, *Pes. R.* 4.3, and the Isaiah Targum to Isa. 66.1 (on the last of these see P. Grelot, 'Deux toséphtas targoumiques inédites sur Isaïe LXVI', *RB* 79 (1972), pp. 511-43). There is an account of rabbinic Isaiah traditions in Ginzberg, *Legends*, IV, pp. 277-81; VI, pp. 370-76.

55. Hall, 'Ascension of Isaiah'.
56. Charles, *Ascension of Isaiah*, Introduction, pp. xl-xliii.
57. Cedrenus' evidence is discussed by Charles, *Ascension of Isaiah*, Introduction, pp. xiii-xiv; 2, 29. His significance is examined by Pesce in *Isaia*, pp. 25-27; see also Acerbi, *Serra Lignea*, p. 64; C. de Boor, 'Weiteres zur Chronik des Skylites', *ByzZ* 14 (1905), pp. 425-33; K. Schweinburg, 'Die ursprüngliche Form des Kedrenechronik', Byzantinischer Zeitschrift 30 (1929–30), pp. 68-77; M.E. Colonna, *Gli Storici bizantini dal IV al XV secolo, I: Storici profani* (Naples: Casa Editrice Armani, 1956), pp. 13-14 and G. Moravcsik, *Byzantinoturcica* (2nd edn, Budapest, 1958), I, pp. 273-75, 325-41.
58. Pesce, *Isaia*, pp. 22-28.

very likely read the whole apocalypse.[59] This makes it unlikely that Cedrenus knew only part of the *Ascension of Isaiah* under the title 'The Testament of Hezekiah'.

This dispute explains why I have introduced my own title for this passage in this book. I shall call 3.13–4.22 the 'First Vision'. This section can no longer be called the 'Testament of Hezekiah' in the wake of Pesce's paper. Care must also be taken to distinguish it from the later vision of Isaiah which begins in ch. 6. I hope that 'the First Vision' readily identifies this material without offering a preconceived view of its origin and place in the *Ascension of Isaiah*.

Difficulties also surround the title of chs. 6–11. The Slavonic version and L2 call this section 'The Vision of Isaiah', but that title causes problems because of the earlier vision of Isaiah which is recorded in chs. 3 and 4. In any event their title for chs. 6–11 derives from the patristic redaction and not from the original *Ascension of Isaiah*. I shall call chs. 6–11 the 'Second Vision' to provide uniformity with my title for *Asc. Isa.* 3.13–4.22 and to avoid the ambiguity which is introduced by L2 and S when the apocalypse is read in its longer form. The time has come to resolve these difficulties inherited from the past and to avoid approaches to the apocalypse which are over-complicated and inherently confusing. I hope that my titles do this. I must emphasize that they are not intended to advocate the return to any 'documentary' hypothesis about the origin of the apocalypse.

How the apocalypse achieved its present form, must now be considered. Charles argued that the *Ascension of Isaiah* was in effect written by an editor who fused the 'Martyrdom of Isaiah' with the 'Testament of Hezekiah' and the 'Vision of Isaiah'.[60] Charles thought that the last two of these works were written in the first century but he argued that the present form of the *Ascension of Isaiah* belongs to the late second or even the third century CE.[61] Charles also posited a single Greek archetype (G) for the 'Vision of Isaiah' and suggested that this was known to Epiphanius in the fourth century (*Adv. Haeres.* 67.3) and perhaps to Ignatius (*Eph.* 19) and the authors of the *Protevangelium of*

---

59. Bori also argued against the existence of a 'Testament of Hezekiah'. He argued that chs. 1–5, for all their difficulties, have a uniform purpose; see his 'L'estasi del profeta', p. 378.
60. Charles, *Ascension of Isaiah*, pp. xxxvi-xliii.
61. Charles, *Ascension of Isaiah*, pp. xxliv-xlv.

1. *An Introduction to the Ascension of Isaiah* 31

James and the *Acts of Peter* in the second century.[62] According to his view two people edited G independently of each other at an early date. Both made their own additions and abridgments. Charles called these two recensions G1[63] and G2.[64] He also thought that chs. 1–5 circulated in the two forms represented by E and L1 and by Gk.[65] This theory established a link between Gk and S and L2, for Gk represented G2 in chs. 1–5 and S and L2 did so in chs. 6–11.

This view about the nature and extent of Gk was also criticized by Pesce at the Rome Conference.[66] Pesce showed how Charles linked the Gk of chs. 1–5 with G2, the supposed Greek parent of S and L2 in chs. 6–11. Yet he also believed that the two halves of the apocalypse underwent *separate* redactions, that in S and L2 a deliberate abridgement[67] when Gk displayed merely 'the errors and variations incidental to the process of transmission'.[68] There is clearly a contradiction in this. Gk must either represent the pre-abridged form of S and L2 (and thus have contained chs. 6–11 as well) or else have derived from a source other than the parent of S and L2. Pesce argues the first case. He thinks that Gk contained the whole of the *Ascension of Isaiah*. This view is supported in an unpublished paper by E. Norelli.[69]

The upshot of this research is that Charles's literary-critical views must be considered difficult to sustain. They represent a period of scholarship when it was fashionable to break texts into sources and to expose their literary seams. The present trend is to see the author as a creative individual who shaped his apocalypse from a variety of sources (which must be duly acknowledged) but who cannot be considered an editor who soldered earlier documents. This is the approach which I shall follow in this book. I accept that there were sources for the *Ascension of Isaiah*— the Isaiah legend and the New Testament literature are only two of these—but I shall concentrate in my research on the final form of the text, which E suggests went back to the original author. The two Visions have an essential coherence which I have found difficult to break. I think

---

62. Charles, *Ascension of Isaiah*, pp. xxxi-xxxiii.
63. Represented by E and L1; he believed that the text was used by the author of the GL.
64. Represented in chs. 6–11 by S and L2 and allegedly used by Jerome.
65. Charles, *Ascension of Isaiah*, pp. xxxi-xxxiii.
66. See Pesce, *Isaia*, p. 22.
67. Charles, *Ascension of Isaiah*, pp.xxiv, xxxi.
68. Charles, *Ascension of Isaiah*, p.xxxi.
69. Norelli, 'Studio sui rapporti tra testo etiopoco'.

that the work can and should be interpreted as it stands, despite some awkward transitions.

Acerbi and Hall have both accepted Pesce's criticism of a written 'Martyrdom of Isaiah' but argued for more formal written sources behind *Asc. Isa.* 3.13–4.22. Acerbi believes that 3.13b–4.1 was interpolated into this section.[70] Hall thinks that 4.1-13 came from an 'emperor worship source' which the author freely interpolated.[71] I cannot pause to discuss these suggestions in detail except to say that I regard 4.1-13 as quite central to the author's purpose in the apocalypse. This is the view on which my own interpretation is based. The way in which the *Ascension of Isaiah* was composed will doubtless prompt further discussion. My belief is that the apocalypse can satisfactorily be interpreted in the form represented by E. This conclusion has the effect of thrusting the material about Rome to the forefront of the interpreter's attention.

The sources of the Second Vision are more difficult to discover. This part of the *Ascension of Isaiah* bears comparison with Paul's reported experience in 2 Corinthians 12 and with Jewish mystical writings like *2 Enoch* and *Hekhaloth Rabbati*. Jewish influences are easy to discern, like the belief in seven heavens and the vision of God as an enthroned deity. We should not ignore the possibility that the Second Vision draws on real experience of mysticism even if this point is difficult to prove in practice.[72] Meditation on Isaiah 6 doubtless played a part in shaping this section, as did a knowledge of the New Testament literature.[73] Behind the work stand three centuries of Jewish and Christian apocalyptic activity. I suspect that research on the psychology of apocalypticism, notably the tendency towards the elaboration of earlier material, has much to contribute to our knowledge of the *Ascension of Isaiah*.

---

70. *L'Ascensione di Isaia*, p. 261.
71. Hall, 'Ascension of Isaiah', pp. 289-92.
72. Hall is surely right to set mystical praxis at the heart of this prophetic community ('The Ascension of Isaiah'). Bori, too, comments on their ecstatic activity ('L'estasi del profeta'). On the other hand I cannot agree with Hall's more recent article ('Isaiah's ascent to see the Beloved: an ancient Jewish source for the Ascension of Isaiah', *JBL* 111.3 [1994] pp. 463-84) that 'the Vision of Isaiah...does not seek primarily to reveal the saving actions of the Beloved' (p. 476). I accept that the Second Vision anticipates the immortal life of the seventh heaven (see 4.17) but this is surely connected with the theme of the Beloved One's journey so that Christology is an essential element in the soteriology.
73. See further Daniélou, *Jewish Christianity*, pp. 134-40.

1. An Introduction to the Ascension of Isaiah

The Date and Provenance of the Ascension of Isaiah

A major reason why the *Ascension of Isaiah* demands attention from scholars arises out of its origin in the early second century. The apocalypse was probably written between 112 CE and the death of Hadrian in 138 CE. This sets it in the crucial period midway between the New Testament and the Gnostic literature.

This early date has not always been recognized in research. The belief that the *Ascension of Isaiah* was a composite text led Charles to date it in the late second or early third century CE (although he accepted that the constituent elements were earlier).[74] Helmbold thought that the Second Vision showed affinities to Gnosticism and he dated this part of the apocalypse to around 150 CE.[75] At the other end of the scale stand Richard Laurence and J.A.T. Robinson, both of whom believed that the *Ascension of Isaiah* was written before the fall of Jerusalem (70 CE). This view seems impossibly early, not least because of the particular form which the Nero mythology has acquired in the *Ascension of Isaiah*.[76] The consensus of research is now to set the *Ascension of Isaiah* in the early second century CE.[77] This is the position which is adopted in this book. The work's evidence of impending conflict with the Romans (ch. 4) and its author's sense of distance from the apostolic age (3.21) both support a date around this time. I shall argue in what follows that the letters exchanged between Pliny and Trajan in 112 CE illuminate the setting of the *Ascension of Isaiah* and that this evidence dates the apocalypse after that time.

The Isaiah traditions in the apocalypse are Jewish in origin. Knibb connects them with the Antiochian Crisis in the second century BCE.[78]

---

74. Charles, *Ascension of Isaiah*, pp. xliv-xlv.
75. A.K. Helmbold, 'Gnostic Elements in the Ascension of Isaiah', *NTS* 18 (1971–72), pp. 222-27.
76. Laurence, *Ascensio Isaiae Vatis*; J.A.T. Robinson, *Redating the New Testament* (London: SPCK, 1975), p. 239n.
77. This is the conclusion of Hall, 'Ascension of Isaiah', pp. 300-306; of the Italian scholars as expressed in Pesce (ed.), *Isaia*, p. 299; and of Acerbi, *L'Ascensione di Isaia*, pp. 277-82. This view was anticipated by Burkitt in *Jewish and Christian Apocalypses*, p. 46.
78. Knibb in Charlesworth (ed.), *Old Testament Pseudepigrapha*, II, pp. 149-50. The 'Antiochian Crisis' was the time when Antiochus Epiphanes IV desecrated the Jerusalem Temple (167–64 BCE). It provided the backcloth for the book of Daniel.

Their present form owes much to the Christian author, and it is difficult to distil a satisfactory version of the Jewish legend from the Christian accretions. This is why the most recent scholarship has rejected the theory of a written 'Martyrdom of Isaiah'. The orientation of much of the narrative shows that it was composed with recent events in the author's mind. The fact that Heb. 11.37 alludes to the legend of Isaiah's death is to be explained with reference to the wide circulation of this legend in Jewish tradition, and it cannot be held to support a first-century date for the *Ascension of Isaiah* (or to indicate that the author of the apocalypse knew Hebrews).[79]

The Nero section (ch. 4) anticipates a posthumous return by the emperor. Speculation about Nero's return was a feature of the months and years which followed his suicide in 68 CE, but it did not fade away for a considerable time.[80] Like the Nazi Holocaust it became embedded in the Jewish imagination and surfaced again in the reign of Hadrian (see *Sib. Or.* 5.101-04), some sixty years after Nero had died.[81] This evidence confirms the point that the *Ascension of Isaiah* cannot be restricted to a first-century date because of its legendary material.

The polemic against Rome which is found in ch. 4 makes a comparison with the situation of the Bithynian Christians in 112 CE appropriate.[82] The year 112 CE is a significant date in church history because for the first time (so far as we know) the 'sacrifice test', which had originally been used by the Romans against the Antiochene Jews in 67 CE, was employed against the Christians.[83] There is evidence to this effect in the letters of Pliny, the *legatus pro praetore* of Bithynia (*Ep.* 10.96-97).[84] Pliny wrote to Trajan for instructions about what to do with the Christians who had come to notice in his province (10.96). There seem to have been two stages in Pliny's process of investigation of the Christians. At first, a few people were accused. Later, and once it was recognized that the charge was being accepted, an unsigned paper gave the names of many Christians. Pliny reported that he had never taken

79. I discuss this matter further in Chapter 4.
80. According to Tacitus, *Hist.*, 2.8, 9; Dio Cass., 64.9. See also Suetonius, *Nero*, 57.
81. See my discussion of this material in Chapter 3.
82. On the Bithynian situation see W.H.C. Frend, *Martyrdom and Persecution in the Early Church* (Oxford: Basil Blackwell, 1965), pp. 217-22.
83. The Antioch incident is described by Frend, *Martyrdom*, pp. 135-37.
84. The correspondence is conveniently accessible, with a commentary, in J. Stevenson (ed.), *A New Eusebius* (London: SPCK, 1957), pp. 13-16.

1. An Introduction to the Ascension of Isaiah 35

part in trials of Christians and he asked the emperor whether they were to be investigated for secret crimes or merely for holding to 'the name' (of Christ). He states that he had investigated certain people whom he had asked three times whether they were Christians. Those who persisted in their admission were executed for 'obstinacy and unbending perversity', except for citizens, who were sent to Rome. Those who denied that they were Christians were spared punishment provided that they underwent what I have called the 'sacrifice test'. This involved the recital of a prayer to the gods, the offering of wine and incense before the imperial statue and the cursing of Christ and was something which Pliny noted (no doubt accurately) that true Christians would refuse to do.

Trajan's reply (Pliny, *Ep.* 10.97) commended Pliny for his course of action but said that a general rule could not be made to deal with the situation. The emperor insisted that the Christians were not to be sought out nor to be made the object of anonymous denunciation. Nevertheless, he ordained that those who stubbornly persisted in their beliefs must be punished for their obduracy. The test of worshipping the gods was upheld, whatever past life a person might have led, with the possibility of release or punishment as Pliny had defined it.

The legal basis of Pliny's procedure against the Christians has provoked a considerable discussion.[85] His exchange with Trajan implies that the open profession of Christianity was regarded as an offence, but Trajan's reply indicates that he had no intention of legislating against Christians specifically as Christians. The test of sacrifice to the Roman gods which Trajan upheld suggests that the familiar charge of 'atheism' loomed large in the background of the crisis. A possible solution to the difficulty, one which is discussed by Frend,[86] takes the view that Pliny regarded Christians as belonging to an illegal Jewish *collegium* and that he believed in consequence that they were inclined towards conspiracy. *Collegia* were held in deep suspicion in Bithynia. Both Pliny and Trajan regarded them as responsible for the bad state of the province at the

---

85. See A.N. Sherwin-White, 'Early Persecutions and Roman Law Again', *JTS* 3 (1952), pp. 199-213; G. de Ste Croix, 'Why were the Early Christians Persecuted?', *Past and Present* 26 (1963), pp. 6-38; A.N. Sherwin-White, 'Why were the Early Christians Persecuted?—an Amendment', *Past and Present* 27 (1964), pp. 23-27; and de Ste Croix, 'Why were the Early Christians Persecuted? A Rejoinder', *Past and Present* 27 (1964), pp. 28-33.

86. Frend, *Martyrdom*, pp. 221-22.

time.[87] This theory would explain the unsystematic nature of Pliny's measures against the Christians which Trajan upheld. It probably also supplies the reason for the martyrdom of Ignatius, as the known head of an illegal college, which on my date for the apocalypse had taken place not many years before the writing of the *Ascension of Isaiah*.

The author's projected knowledge of the Bithynian situation does much to explain the form of material in *Ascension of Isaiah* 4–5. There are clear references to Rome's arrogance in 4.1-13 which the sacrifice test illumines. On this view Beliar's demand for worship (*Asc. Isa.* 4.6-7) reflects the demand for obeisance to the statues produced in court, as do the references to 'sacrifice' in 4.8 and to the erection of the imperial statue in 4.11. The reference in 4.6 (see 10.12-13) to Beliar calling himself 'Lord' might reflect the epithet *dominus* which had earlier been attributed to Domitian. It is difficult to find a better setting for *Ascension of Isaiah* 4 in the known history of early Christianity, but this situation suits the chapter very well.

A culture in which Christians might be subjected to sporadic investigation, including occasional martyrdom, also explains the form taken by *Ascension of Isaiah* 5. This chapter describes how Isaiah was put on trial and executed for what was effectively discipleship to Jesus. His trial and demise calls to mind the death penalty which Pliny imposed on the Bithynian Christians. It is possible that the author was thinking also of the martyrdom of Ignatius as a recent example of what conflict with the Romans might bring. He advocated caution in 5.13, as I understand that reference, to those who were moved to follow the bishop's example, by warning against the phenomenon of voluntary martyrdom.

My conclusion is that the Bithynian situation makes for a plausible exegesis of the *Ascension of Isaiah* and that this sets the text after 112 CE. I think that it was written to address the fear of persecution among Christians in Syria who had heard about the events in Bithynia. It is not certain that the author's circle had suffered investigation like their Bithynian counterparts (but not impossible that they had). It is more likely that they feared they would and that their refusal to offer sacrifice would provoke a similar reaction from the Romans. Trajan's reply had established the sacrifice test as the norm for Roman governors who were confronted by the problem of the Christians.[88] The author and his

---

87. See Pliny, *Ep.* 10.33 on the subject of the Nicomedian fire brigade (and see also Frend, *Martyrdom*, p. 232 n. 93).

88. As we know from the *Martyrdom of Polycarp*, where the bishop was

friends would have heard about it on the Christian grapevine. The *Ascension of Isaiah* was written to deal with this problem. This it did by asserting the theme of Beliar's defeat by the Beloved One which the author used to deny the basis of Roman authority to people who stood to suffer at the hands of the Romans.

In support of a second-century date is the observation that 3.21 (which claims to describe the period 'after' the apostolic age) firmly places the apocalypse beyond the New Testament period. This verse laments the fact that the apostolic age had passed and that it had been succeeded by an inferior time. *Ascension of Isaiah* 4.13 has sometimes been taken to imply that some of the original Christians were still alive at the time of writing, but this is impossible given my date for the apocalypse. This verse does not in fact preserve a link with the past so much as assert that few of those who had seen Jesus would be left in the last days 'as his servants' in view of the apostasy which is anticipated by 4.9. Although the reference to 'seeing' Jesus is a little awkward in this context, 4.13 on its own must not be allowed to determine a first-century date given the other material in the *Ascension of Isaiah*. This passage may in any event have been inserted from a source. In its context it is a virtual admission that none of the original eyewitnesses of Jesus were still alive. There is a strong sense of distance from the apostles in the *Ascension of Isaiah* (see especially 3.21) which cautions against setting the work in the first century.

To evaluate the *terminus ad quem* of the *Ascension of Isaiah* we must consider some significant differences from the Gnostic literature displayed by the apocalypse.[89] These conspire to set the *Ascension of*

---

asked to swear by the gods and to curse Christ. Polycarp is said to have withdrawn to an isolated farm (which makes for an important parallel with *Asc. Isa.* 5.13). Recent studies of the *Martyrdom of Polycarp* include B. Dehandschutter, *Martyrium Polycarpi: Een literair-kritische Studie* (Leuven: University Press, 1979) and S. Ronchey, *Indagine sul Martirio di San Policarpo: critica storica e fortuna agiografica di un caso giudiziario in Asia Minore* (Rome: Instituto Palazzo Borromini, 1990).

89. I use the term 'Gnosticism' in this book in the sense that was proposed by the 1966 conference on Gnostic origins which met at Messina: 'The Gnosticism of the Second Century sects involves a coherent series of characteristics that can be summarized in the idea of a divine spark in man, deriving from the divine realm, fallen into this world of fate, birth and death, and needing to be awakened by the divine counterpart of the self in order to be finally reintegrated' (cited from U. Bianchi [ed.], *Le Origini dello Gnosticismo* [Leiden: Brill, 1967], p. xxvi).

Isaiah before the earliest Nag Hammadi texts which were written c. 150 CE.[90] I shall examine these differences from Gnosticism in Chapter 2 and summarize them briefly here. Foremost among them is the absence of any mythological cosmogony in the *Ascension of Isaiah*. The apocalypse excludes Beliar from the heavens (7.9-12) and offers no speculation about the event of creation. *Asc. Isa.* 7.9-12 more closely resembles the notion of the aerial powers in Ephesians, worked up to accommodate a seven-storied universe, than the mythological world of the *Apocryphon of John*. There is no notion of a pre-mundane fall in the *Ascension of Isaiah*. This silence determines the nature of the soteriology, which anticipates the future millenarian kingdom (4.14-16) that the Gnostics rejected. The work's optimism about life in the flesh and its understanding of Isaiah's martyrdom are also different from the Gnostic literature. Moreover, incarnation as such is absent from Gnostic writings but the *Ascension of Isaiah* describes the appearance of the Beloved One as the human Jesus.[91] These points are vital to the assessment of the question of how the *Ascension of Isaiah* relates to Gnosticism. They combine to place the apocalypse intellectually before the writing of the Gnostic apocalypses in the middle of the second century. This suggests that the *Ascension of Isaiah* was written in the first third of the second century rather than in its middle or its second half.

It remains uncertain whether the material which predicts the fall of Jerusalem (*Asc. Isa.* 3.6-10) looks back on the events of 70 CE or much more closely on those of 135 CE. Lampe observes that, of the two calamities, the one in 135 ultimately exercised the greater effect on the Christian imagination.[92] Passages such as Lk. 21.20, however, show that

---

90. Some of these differences were explored by U. Bianchi at the Rome Conference; see his 'L'*Ascensione di Isaia*: Tematiche Soteriologiche di *descensus/ ascensus*' in Pesce (ed.), *Isaia*, pp. 155-83. I discuss this matter in Chapter 2 below.

91. This point is made by L. Schotroff, *Der glaubende und die feindliche Welt: Beobachtungen zum gnostische Dualismus und seiner Bedeutung für Paulus und der Johannesevangelium* (WMANT 37; Neukirchen–Vluyn: Neukirchener Verlag, 1970), p. 280: 'an incarnation is not reported for Gnostic figures'. There is an early anticipation of this Gnostic view in *Asc. Isa.* 10.7-16, which in a prediction of the descent makes no explicit reference to the Beloved One's appearance as Jesus. The wider context of the apocalypse, however, shows that an appearance as Jesus is presupposed in the *Ascension of Isaiah* so that this passage is exceptional. *Asc. Isa.* 10.6-17 nevertheless shows the developing Christian mediatorial interest which partly fuelled the origins of Gnosticism.

92. G.W.H. Lampe, 'AD 70 in Christian Reflection', in C.F.D. Moule and

1. An Introduction to the Ascension of Isaiah

the first destruction of Jerusalem was regarded as divine punishment in at least some first-century literature. On the balance of probability I think that *Asc. Isa.* 3.6-10 refers to the events of 70 CE. Perhaps more would have been made of the second destruction of Jerusalem in 135 CE and the banishment of the Jews from their homeland had the author known about them. I regard the death of Hadrian (138 CE) as the latest date for the *Ascension of Isaiah* but the apocalypse is probably somewhat earlier than this. I have in mind a date c. 120 CE as a provisional working hypothesis to allow both for the spread of reports about the sacrifice test and for the important differences between the *Ascension of Isaiah* and Gnosticism.

The provenance of the *Ascension of Isaiah* is Syria.[93] The work shows traces of Syrian views such as the seven-storied cosmology and the understanding of the Beloved One's descent as a mystery revealed to the elect.[94] Bori thinks that the *Ascension of Isaiah* came from Asia Minor because of the similarities with Montanism; but Jewish traces like the 'Beloved One' title and the description of the Spirit as an angel better suit a setting in the eastern Mediterranean.[95] The *Ascension of Isaiah* shows the development of a distinctively Christian apocalyptic in that region in the period after the death of Ignatius.

The Contents of the Ascension of Isaiah

I shall now provide a more detailed guide to the contents of the apocalypse.

The *Ascension of Isaiah* opens with some traditions about Isaiah which the author derived from Jewish tradition. The early verses of ch. 1 describe a meeting between Hezekiah and Manasseh.[96] In his 'twenty-sixth' regnal year the king summons his son to teach him some visionary oracles (1.1).[97] Two different visions are mentioned. The first, which is

E. Bammel (eds.), *Jesus and the Politics of his Day* (Cambridge: Cambridge University Press, 1984), pp. 153-71.
    93. Thus Knibb in Charlesworth (ed.), *Old Testament Pseudepigrapha*, II, p. 150.
    94. See Daniélou, *Jewish Christianity*, p. 15.
    95. Bori, 'L'estasi del profeta', pp. 387-88.
    96. Our knowledge of ch. 1 is derived from E, the Coptic fragments and the GL; Gk begins in 2.4 and L1 not until 2.14.
    97. GL 1.1 has the 'twenty-fifth' year and the Coptic the 'sixteenth'. *Asc. Isa.*

evidently attributed to Hezekiah on his sick-bed,[98] concerns 'the eternal judgements, and the torments of Gehenna, and the prince of this world, and his *angels*, and his *authorities*, and his *powers*' (1.3-4). The italicized nouns demonstrate a precise verbal contact with 1 Pet. 3.22 (but only partial similarities with other New Testament passages).[99] The second visionary report is also attributed to Hezekiah.[100] It claims that the king foresaw 'the judgment of the angels...the destruction of this world...the robes of the saints and their going out, and...their transformation and the persecution and ascension of the Beloved' (1.5).[101] These summaries set the agenda for the *Ascension of Isaiah*. The apocalypse is said to describe the defeat of the 'prince of this world' (that is, Beliar) and his angels through the Beloved One's intervention. Isaiah confides this vision to Josab his son (1.6),[102] but warns that it will have no effect on Manasseh. He predicted that Manasseh will put him to death (1.7), despite Hezekiah's concern (1.12).

Chapter 2 describes what happened when Manasseh acceded.[103] The new king more than fulfilled all that had been predicted of him. The apocalypse comments on the lawlessness of his régime and on its harsh

---

6.1 sets the Second Vision in Hezekiah's 'twentieth' year. This causes a chronological problem (but explains the Coptic reading).

98. Hezekiah's sickness is described in the Old Testament in 2 Kgs 20.1-11, Isa. 38 and 2 Chron. 32.24. There are historical problems as to whether Manasseh functioned as co-regent at this time. These problems are examined by E.R. Thiele, *The Mysterious Numbers of the Hebrew Kings* (Grand Rapids: Eerdmans, 1983), pp. 64, 174, 176. The *Ascension of Isaiah* says nothing about any co-regency.

99. This indicates that the author knew 1 Peter. His knowledge of this text is confirmed by *Asc. Isa.* 11.23-33 (see below).

100. This is suggested by the phrase 'what he himself had seen' (1.5). *Asc. Isa.* 1.6, however, says that 'in the twentieth year of the reign of Hezekiah Isaiah had seen the words of this prophecy'. This causes confusion about who saw the vision.

101. There is a manuscript problem in this passage. The Ethiopic text refers the 'going out' and 'transformation' to the saints through the use of a plural suffix but GL 1.2 assigns it to the Beloved One. E should be corrected, as has been done by Knibb, on the basis of the GL and 3.13 (E) where the nouns 'going out' and 'transformation' are referred to the Beloved One.

102. Caquot, 'Bref Commentaire' p. 70, links *Asc. Isa.* 1.6 with the events recorded in 2 Kgs 20.12-19: the arrival of ambassadors from the Babylonian king Merodach-Baladan.

103. On the sources for this story see Pesce in his *Isaia*, pp. 28, 40-45. There is no trace of the sympathetic attitude towards Manasseh which is found in 2 Chronicles 33.

treatment of opponents. Manasseh's behaviour is attributed to demonic influence: 'Sammael dwelt in Manasseh and clung closely to him. And Manasseh abandoned the service of the LORD of his father, and he served Satan, and his angels, and his powers' (2.2). This passage establishes a dualism which has both ethical and cosmological implications. The *Ascension of Isaiah* incorporates a seven-storied cosmology which asserts that the earth is encircled by seven regions of increasing transcendence and that the heavens are separated from the earth by the firmament or sky.[104] Beliar inhabits the firmament (4.1-4; 7.9-12) and so is designedly excluded from the heavens. Ethics are related to cosmology in the *Ascension of Isaiah* inasmuch as which heavenly power people worships (the Beloved One or Beliar) is reflected in their behaviour (see 7.9-12). The author says that Manasseh 'served Satan' (2.2). This explains in terms which the author wished his readers to understand why the king did bad deeds, as if the king were inspired by hostile cosmic powers. The dualism comes to a head in ch. 4, where Beliar is said to have incarnated himself in Nero, which makes the point that the Romans were similarly inspired by malevolent beings. There is a strong hint in the *Ascension of Isaiah* (especially in 2.7-11) that *only* the prophets were righteous at the time of writing, which does much to explain the author's isolated outlook on the world. The prophets are said to have maintained the faith of the Beloved One when other Christians had turned from apostolic ways (3.21) and were even tempted to follow Beliar (cf. 4.9). This is an indication of the pious and prophetic nature of the circle from which the *Ascension of Isaiah* came.

The vices which Manasseh permitted are said to include sorcery, magic, divination, fornication, adultery,[105] and 'the persecution of the righteous' (2.5); 2.6 alludes to others besides. They have a pronounced effect on Isaiah, who leaves the capital to settle in Bethlehem (2.7). He

104. Seven was the number of heavens in rabbinic cosmology according to *b. Ḥag.* 12b (which records a dispute about this issue). The *Ascension of Isaiah* cosmology is examined by H. Bietenhard, *Die himmlische Welt im Urchristentum und Spätjudentum* (WUNT, 2; Tübingen: Mohr, 1951), pp. 215-19; and by Acerbi, *L'Ascensione di Isaia*, pp. 138-48. The *Ascension of Isaiah* cosmology has the social function of reassuring alienated disciples of the Beloved One by emphasizing the superiority of their patron in the cosmic system.

105. The Greek text omits 'adultery'. The hostility towards divination and sorcery reflects existing Jewish concerns: W. Horbury has shown that the charge of false prophecy was familiar in early Christianity ('1 Thess. ii.3 as Rebutting the Charge of False Prophecy', *JTS* 33 [1982], pp. 492-508).

finds the same problems there and withdraws further to dwell 'on a mountain in a desert place' (2.8).[106] There he founds an ascetic community. This is described in a passage of great importance in the apocalypse:

> And Micah the prophet, and the aged Ananias, and Joel, and Habakkuk, and Josab his son, and many of the faithful who believed in the ascension into heaven, withdrew and dwelt on the mountain. All of them were clothed in sackcloth, and all of them were prophets; they had nothing with them, but were destitute, and they all lamented bitterly over the going astray of Israel. And they had nothing to eat except wild herbs [which] they gathered from the mountains, and when they had cooked [them], they ate [them] with Isaiah the prophet. And they dwelt on the mountains and on the hills for two years of days (2.9-11).[107]

This passage holds together the themes of prophecy, poverty, penance and mystical experience. It presents Isaiah's community as a pious group who retreat from the world and engage in ecstatic practices.[108] It would be mistaken to interpret the passage as an *allegory* of the author's circle, or to see apocalyptic as the prerogative of the marginalized alone,[109] but this description evidently represents ideals which the author and his friends espoused (and perhaps to which he directed them). The narrative encouraged those who knew themselves to be vulnerable under Beliar's oppression and in this context it upholds the validity of mystical prophecy. The statement that the prophets believed in 'the ascension into heaven' confirms the point that the author's view of prophecy had an ecstatic dimension. *Asc. Isa.* 2.7-11 should be compared with 4.13-14

106. Knibb notes the possible influence of the Elijah story, 1 Kgs 19.1-8, at this point (see Charlesworth [ed.], *Old Testament Pseudepigrapha*, II, p. 158 n. l).

107. Only Micah in fact was a contemporary of Isaiah; see Knibb in Charlesworth (ed.), *Old Testament Pseudepigrapha*, II, p. 158 n. m, who has a theory about the origin of this passage. Pesce in his *Isaia*, p. 54, links *Asc. Isa.* 2.7-11 with the portrait of displaced Christians that is found in 4.13.

108. D. Flusser, ('The Apocryphal Book of *Ascensio Isaiae* and the Dead Sea Sect', *IEJ* 3 [1953], pp. 30-47 [esp. pp. 30-34]) interpreted the apocalypse with reference to the history of the Qumran sect. A Qumran provenance for the *Ascension of Isaiah*, is however, extremely doubtful. The text comes from a second-century Christian author who worked after the Qumran settlement had fallen into disuse.

109. P.D. Hanson's thesis (which was advanced in his book, *The Dawn of Apocalyptic* [Philadelphia: Fortress Press], 1975) that apocalyptic originated in the displacement of a visionary group has been criticized by later scholars. See for example, K.J.A. Larkin, *The Eschatology of Second Zechariah: A Study of the Formation of a Mantological Wisdom Anthology* (Kampen: Kok, 1994) on the 'mantological' quality of Deutero–Zechariah's oracles.

1. *An Introduction to the Ascension of Isaiah*

which states that the faithful must inhabit the desert for an ordained period of time in anticipation of the millenarian kingdom.

A Samaritan named Belchira discovers where the community live and visits them there (3.1).[110] Following a digression (2.12-16, 3.2-5),[111] *Asc. Isa.* 3.6-10 relates several charges which this man lays against Isaiah. He accuses the prophet of speaking against Jerusalem and its territory and of predicting that the king will be captured in chains (3.6).[112] Belchira next alleges that Isaiah 6 represents a claim to mystical prowess beyond what Moses had allowed in the Pentateuch:

> And Isaiah himself has said, 'I see more than Moses the prophet'. Moses said, 'There is no man who can see the LORD and live'. But Isaiah has said, 'I have seen the LORD, and behold I am alive'. Know, therefore, O king, that they (are) false prophets [113] (3.8-10).

This passage sets Exod. 33.20b against Isaiah 6 and significantly prefers the evidence of the prophetic text to that of the Torah. Later in this book I shall argue that it represents a Christian version of an existing scriptural comparison through which the author granted the prophets a genuine vision of God in repudiation of what the rabbis thought about

---

110. The form of this man's name causes problems. In Gk he is known variously as Belicheiar, Melcheira, and Belchira; in L1 as Bechira; in E by a variety of titles, notably Belkira, Balkira, Melkira, and Malkira; in the Coptic, as Belch[ira]; and in the GL as Melchias or Becheiras. This problem is examined by Knibb in Charlesworth (ed.), *Old Testament Pseudepigrapha*, II, pp. 151-52 who argues that the name in Hebrew was originally *behî-ra'* (= 'the elect of evil') which was transliterated into Greek as Becheira, and that all the different forms can be explained on the basis of two alternatives, Belch(e)ira or Becheira, and Melcheira. Knibb holds that the second of these is a corruption of the first. This book follows Knibb in reading 'Belchira'. The meaning of his name is discussed also by D. Flusser, 'Apocryphal Book', p. 35; and by Caquot in 'Bref Commentaire', p. 75.

111. There are considerable difficulties in this section which only detailed commentary can unravel. Knibb notes that 'underlying vvs 13b-16 is an otherwise unknown tradition about the fate of Micaiah in the reign of Ahaziah, but many details are obscure' (in Charlesworth [ed.], *Old Testament Pseudepigrapha*, II, p. 159, n. x). Micaiah's death (2.16), however, undoubtedly foreshadows that of Isaiah; see Pesce's location of this episode within the structure of the *Ascension of Isaiah* in his *Isaia*, p. 39. The textual problems are described also by Caquot, 'Bref Commentaire', pp. 79-81.

112. The prophecy against Manasseh recalls 2 Chron. 33.11; Charles shows on the basis of Gk that it is independent of the LXX (*Ascension of Isaiah*, p. 17, n.6).

113. In Gk, L1, 'that he is a liar'.

this issue.[114] Then Belchira denounces Isaiah as a false prophet who had compared the situation in Jerusalem to Sodom and its rulers to the people of Gomorrah (3.10). Since Sodom was the city said to have been destroyed by God in Genesis 19, this passage contains an implicit reference to the destruction of Jerusalem.[115] As a result of these charges, Isaiah is arrested and brought before the king (3.12).

The First Vision

The 'First Vision' begins at this point (3.13). The author uses the device of the historical review to describe four periods of history before the Beloved One's return from heaven and the establishment of his earthly kingdom. These periods are: (1) the ministry of Jesus (3.13-18); (2) the apostolic age (3.19-20); (3) the post-apostolic period (3.21-31); and (4) the appearance of Beliar in Nero (4.1-13). The parousia and millenarian kingdom (including the promise of heavenly immortality) are then described as a fifth element—the antithesis or climax—in 4.14-18.

Asc. Isa. 3.13-18 describes the Beloved One's appearance as Jesus. In this passage the author fuses the myth of the Beloved One's descent (which he had derived in essentials from first-century Christology but substantially elaborated) with some traditions about Jesus which stemmed from the oral tradition that stood behind the Gospels. Similar and more detailed material about Jesus is found in 11.2-22 (E text only). The author says in 3.13 that the Beloved One descended from the seventh heaven and that he was 'transformed' into the likeness of the human Jesus. This makes the hidden descent the framework for the description of Jesus, and it specifically introduces the language of 'transformation' into the existing christological tradition.

The Beloved One's transformation into human likeness is followed by his persecution and tormenting by the 'sons of Israel' (3.13);[116] the coming of the twelve disciples; the teaching;[117] his crucifixion 'before

114. See Chapter 3.
115. This criticism is based on Isa. 1.10. Sodom was a familiar term of comparison in early Christian literature (see for example, Mt. 10.15; Rom. 9.29; Jude 7). Calling Jerusalem 'Sodom' is strong rhetoric indeed.
116. L1 ceases in 3.13 after the phrase *et contumeliam quam patere(tur)*. The phrase 'sons of Israel' occurs in the NT in Lk. 1.16; 2 Cor. 3.7, 13; and Mt. 27.9 (see Schweizer, 'υἱός κτλ', in *TDNT*, VIII, p. 365). Here it describes the Jewish role in opposing Jesus.
117. In the Gk, 'the teaching of the disciples'.

1. An Introduction to the Ascension of Isaiah 45

the sabbath';[118] his crucifixion with wicked men; his burial in the grave (all 3.13); the offence of the twelve (3.14);[119] the stationing of guards at the tomb (3.14);[120] and the descent from heaven of the 'angel of the church' (3.15).[121] 3.16-17 preserves an account of the resurrection that has no parallel in the Gospels: 'And that the angel of the Holy Spirit and Michael, the chief of the holy angels, will open his grave on the third day, and that Beloved, sitting on their shoulders, will come forth.'[122] The passage demonstrates the Beloved's superiority to the angels in that the two principal angels escort a greater being from the tomb. It presents the Beloved in the enthroned position which had been reserved for God in the biblical theophanies as if the Beloved were understood as an analogous though subordinate being. The Risen One sent out his twelve[123] disciples (3.17) who taught 'all nations and every tongue' the resurrection of the Beloved (3.18).[124] 'Those who believed in his cross' would be saved, according to 3.18.[125] The Beloved One's appearance on earth concludes with his ascension to the seventh heaven 'from where he came' (3.18).[126]

This material about Jesus is followed by a short description of the apostolic age (3.19-20). This is presented as a time when the Christians spoke with the Holy Spirit and when signs and miracles abounded. It contrasts strongly with the author's presentation of his own time (3.21-31). This was a very different period: 'And afterwards, at his approach,

118. This detail agrees with the Synoptic chronology: notably with Mk 15.42.
119. See Mt. 27.31.
120. See Mt. 27.62-66.
121. On the meaning of this phrase see Daniélou, *Jewish Christianity*, p. 298. The author assumes that the church existed as a heavenly body before its earthly manifestation.
122. The Greek text has a lacuna before 'the angel of the Holy Spirit' which Grenfell and Hunt restored with 'Gabriel'. On this passage see Charles, *Ascension of Isaiah*, p. 19, n. 16; Norelli, 'La Resurrezione di Gesù nell'*Ascensione di Isaia*', *Cr St* 1 (1980), pp. 315-66; and Verheyden, 'L'Ascension d'Isaïe', pp. 272-74. A similar description of the resurrection is found in *Gos. Pet.* 39 where two angels support Jesus from the tomb. The passage probably reflects the influence of Jewish *merkabah* mysticism.
123. Gk omits the figure 12. Is this a correction in E?
124. This seems to be an allusion to Mt. 28.19 (see also 1 Tim. 3.16).
125. The meaning of this phrase is given by ch. 10; see below.
126. Knibb notes that Gk has ἀνάβασις but that E uses a word which is normally translated 'resurrection' (in Charlesworth [ed.], *Old Testament Pseudepigrapha*, II, p. 160 n. x).

his disciples will abandon the teaching of the twelve apostles, and their faith, and their love, and their purity (3.21)'.[127] No christological heresy is mentioned in this section, but 3.21 sets 'the teaching of the twelve apostles' at the head of the list and it is possible that, given the willingness of many Christians to benefit from the existing order (3.25), scepticism about the parousia in the wider church (and perhaps in his own circle) was an issue which the author confronted.[128] *Asc. Isa.* 3.21-31 has no precise parallels in other Christian literature and in my view it represents the author's own understanding of the church in his day. This observation emphasizes the value of this section, particularly since it comes from a marginalized and obsolescent group in the church.

The author states that there was contention (Gk αἱρέσεις)[129] on the eve of the Beloved One's return. He complains that many loved office but lacked the wisdom needed to discharge it (3.23). This directs the blunt of the criticism to the office-holders or institutional leaders in the church. *Asc. Isa.* 3.24 complains that these 'wicked elders and shepherds' had wronged their sheep.[130] *Asc. Isa.* 3.25 laments that they were what the author calls too 'worldly' in their ambitions. They had: 'exchange[d] the garments of the saints[131] for the robes of those who loved money. There will be much respect of persons in those days,[132] and lovers of the glory of the world.' This reveals a difference between people known to him which the author explains in terms of money, social climbing and ambition. Presumably, those who engaged in such behaviour must have regarded the existing order as sufficiently

127. Pesce notices the difficulties which the author of the *Ascension of Isaiah* experienced with institutional Christianity (see his *Isaia*, pp. 52-54). Acerbi has a section on the same theme (*L'Ascensione di Isaia*, pp. 217-33). I shall explore this issue in Chapter 3.

128. Like the author of 2 Pet. 3 (see also 1 Clem. 23).

129. The term αἵρεσις in early Christian literature is an interesting one. It can mean 'school' in a neutral sense (for example, Acts 5.17, see Justin *Dial.* 17.1) but it more often means 'division' pejoratively. H. Schlier comments helpfully: 'The basis of the Christian concept of αἵρεσις is to be found in the new situation created by the introduction of the Christian ἐκκλησία. Ἐκκλησία and αἵρεσις are mutual opposites' ('αἵρεσις', *TDNT*, I, pp. 182-83). This comment suggests that the *Ascension of Isaiah* (at least in the Greek version) uses a loaded term to deny the authority of recognized Church leaders.

130. The language implies that they were like the wicked shepherds of Ezek. 34.

131. Perhaps an early indication of a distinctive Christian form of dress (see Knibb in Charlesworth *Old Testament Pseudepigrapha*, II, p. 161, n. d2).

132. Compare the situation outlined in Jas 2.1-7.

permanent to believe that they could benefit from it. The people cultivated in this way were perhaps the Roman administration (see 4.9); the sycophants were no doubt the church leaders or other prominent Christians.

Asc. Isa. 3.26 details slander (E 'slanderers')[133] and vainglory on the eve of the parousia and says that the Holy Spirit will withdraw from many (the future tense is explained by the pseudonymous setting). This is a strong comment whose meaning is given by 3.27. That verse notes the disappearance of reliable prophets except 'one here and there in different places' (see 2.7-11). The demise of prophecy in the church was a major issue for this author and it is expressed in several different ways in the apocalypse.[134] *Asc. Isa.* 3.28 lists among the reasons for it 'the spirit of error and of fornication, and of vainglory, and of the love of money among those who are said to be servants of that One'. According to 1 Corinthians 12–14 prophecy was a universal gift in first century Christianity. The author of the *Ascension of Isaiah* by contrast addressed a situation in which the prophets had become hard to find and which he describes in terms of the withdrawal of the Spirit from 'many' in the church. This marks a substantial difference from the apostolic age, as he himself notes (3.19-21). The author regarded himself as one of the faithful few who kept prophecy alive at this time (see 2.7-11 again).

Asc. Isa. 3.30 anticipates 'great jealousy' in the last days as each person 'spoke what he pleased' (as opposed no doubt to genuine inspiration by the Spirit—the prerogative of the prophets alone). *Asc. Isa.* 3.31 specifies a deliberate attempt to silence the prophets. 'Isaiah' speaks in the first person of opposition which he had experienced: 'And they will make ineffective[135] the prophecy of the prophets who were before me, and my visions also...they will make ineffective, in order that they may speak what bursts out of their heart.' At this point I think that the pseudepigraphy recedes to reveal the voice of the author himself. The verse represents a Christian prophet's complaint that people had spurned his oracles and opposed him personally (or at least familiar members of his own circle). *Asc. Isa.* 3.31, when seen in company with 3.26-27 and 2.7-11, shows that the prophets were being repressed in the

---

133. An example of a mistake in E; see Knibb in Charlesworth (ed.), *Old Testament Pseudepigrapha*, II, p. 161 n. e2.

134. See Bori, 'L'estasi del profeta'; and 'L'Esperienza profetica nell'*Ascensione di Isaia*', in Pesce (ed.), *Isaia*, pp.133-54.

135. Gk 'neglect'.

situation for which the apocalypse was written. The author relates this fact to the power struggles which he says took place among the church officials at the time.

Confrontation with the Romans

These problems in the church were accompanied by further and more pressing difficulties.[136] Chapter 4 anticipates that Beliar will descend from the firmament to incarnate himself in Nero. Where 3.21-31 is the author's own creation, 4.1-13 reworks a variety of imagery to address a new situation of conflict with the Romans in the early second century. This passage alludes to the myth of Nero's return (often called the myth of Nero *redivivus*) which circulated throughout the Mediterranean world in the decades after the emperor's death.[137] What the *Ascension of Isaiah* says about Nero at this point has parallels with the Jewish Sibylline Oracles. *Sib. Or.* 3.63-74 identifies Nero with Beliar. *Sib. Or.* 5.101-104, which reached its final form in the reign of Hadrian,[138] anticipates Nero's return as a way of expressing antipathy to Rome at the time of the Second Revolt. The *Ascension of Isaiah* thereby uses existing mythology about Nero to express dissatisfaction with the Roman administration in what appears to have been a critical situation for the author's circle.

The view which I have taken is that the *Ascension of Isaiah* was written with a knowledge of the situation in Bithynia where Christians had been obliged to participate in the sacrifice test after 112 CE. I think that the author found a specific reason for writing in the fear that conflict with the Romans would also emerge in Syria. He elevated this problem to the level of a grand cosmic contest between Beliar and the Beloved One in which the Beloved proves victorious. He developed the Nero mythology by the suggestion that Beliar would descend from the

---

136. For the first four verses of the chapter E can be tested against Gk. From then on E is our only witness besides the GL until ch. 6.

137. Evidence for this myth is examined by Charles, *Ascension of Isaiah*, pp. lvii-lxi. See also A.Y. Collins, *Crisis and Catharsis: the Power of the Apocalypse* (Philadelphia: Westminster Press, 1984), pp. 99-104; and J.J. Collins, *The Sibylline Oracles of Egyptian Judaism* (SBLDS, 13; Missoula, MT: Scholars Press, 1974), pp. 80-95.

138. The Hadrianic date is noted by M. Hengel, 'Messianische Hoffnung und politischer "Radikalismus" in der "jüdisch-hellenistischen Diaspora"', in D. Hellholm (ed.), *Apocalypticism*, pp. 668-74.

1. An Introduction to the Ascension of Isaiah

firmament. This involved the view, which was a familiar one in the Christian eschatological tradition,[139] that demonic forces would become active on earth as the final opponents of the faithful. The description is allusive, but the author's use of mythology should not be allowed to mask the point that he employs such ideas to make a specific point on the real human level of conflict.

Asc. Isa. 4.3 looks back to the Neronian Persecution (64 CE) to describe the current situation: '[He will] persecute the plant which the twelve apostles of the Beloved will have planted; some of the twelve will be given into his hand'.[140] The year 64 CE makes for an appropriate comparison since it was the last time that numbers of Christians had been put to death by the Romans.[141] *Asc. Isa.* 4.4 anticipates that: 'This angel, Beliar, will come in the form of that king, and with him will come all the powers of this world, and they will obey him in every wish'. This passage receives its full meaning when the Second Vision is read. It then becomes clear that in the author's perspective Beliar had descended to earth because his defeat had been made obvious in the heavens. In the First Vision, however, the descent signifies a temporary increase in Beliar's power of which the author was very much aware. The Second Vision as I have explained it has the social function of limiting the Romans' authority by offering a new perspective on their source of power, and it corrects the perspective of Beliar's dominance which is introduced initially by the First Vision.

Asc. Isa. 4.5 mentions Beliar's mastery over the sun and moon,

---

139. See for example 2 Thess. 2 and Rev.13, 17 for other evidence of this view.

140. The Greek text apparently states that *one* of the twelve would be delivered to Nero, an important difference from E (but the text is corrupt and it has been restored by Grenfell and Hunt. See Charles, *Ascension of Isaiah*, p. 95). *Asc. Isa.* 4.3 represents important evidence for the martyrdom of Peter in 64 CE. On this matter see C. Clemen, 'Die Himmelfahrt des Jesaja, ein ältestes Zeugnis für das römisches Martyrium des Petrus', *ZWT* (1896), pp. 388-415; E. Zeller, 'Die Märtyrtod des Petrus', *ZWT* (1896), pp. 558-68; C. Clemen, 'Nochmals der Märtrytod des Petrus in der *Ascensio Jesaiae*', *ZWT* (1897), pp. 455-65; and K. Heussi, 'Die *Ascensio Isaiae* und ihr vermeintliches Zeugnis für ein römisches Martyrium des Apostels Petrus', *Wissenschaftliche Zeitschrift der Friedrich-Schiller-Universität, Jena*, 12 (1963), pp. 269-74. The reference to earlier martyrdom(s) served to delineate the current situation in which some had died, as we know from the Pliny–Trajan correspondence (and from the martyrdom of Ignatius).

141. It is disputed whether there was a formal persecution of Christians under Domitian; see Chapter 3.

which will rise at unnatural times.[142] According to 4.6, the demon will have absolute sway in the world and he will act and speak like the Beloved One. He will claim, in words which are parodied from Isa. 45.18, that 'I am the LORD, and before me there was no one'.[143] This strong statement reflects what was seen as Roman blasphemy in the demand for obeisance, and also perhaps the title *dominus* which had been attributed to earlier emperors. *Asc. Isa.* 4.8 mentions the offering of sacrifice to Nero. This recalls the offering of incense before the imperial statue which had been required of the Bithynian Christians by Pliny. *Asc. Isa.* 4.9 expects that Nero–Beliar will turn the majority of Christians apostate.[144] We know from Pliny's letter that some Christians had recanted and that others had confessed (to being Christians) under torture, so that this author's fear of apostasy (and martyrdom) was a realistic one. *Asc. Isa.* 4.10-11 anticipates the power of Beliar's miracles in every city and district. It is possible that this is an early indication of the widespread use of the sacrifice test against the Christians. *Asc. Isa.* 4.11 refers to the erection of the imperial statue 'in every city'.[145] *Asc. Isa.* 4.12, however, limits Beliar's rule to 'three years and seven months and twenty-seven days'.[146] This passage interprets the eschatological

---

142. See *Sib. Or.* 3.63-5; 4 *Ezra* 5.4. The suggestion is that Beliar's miracles went against the natural order as if to demonstrate the demon's destructive character.

143. Isa. 45 is one of the great Old Testament declarations of monotheism. The author of the *Ascension of Isaiah* used it ironically to mock the demon's claims to sovereignty. Gnostic literature later attributed the words to the Demiurge (for example, *Ap. John* 11.18-21). This is another example of the way in which an idea that is found in the *Ascension of Isaiah* was used in a different sense in Gnosticism.

144. See Mk 13.20-22; Mt. 24.24.

145. The aura surrounding the emperor's person in the ancient world is assessed by L.R. Taylor, *The Divinity of the Roman Emperor* (Middletown, CT: American Philological Association Monographs, 1931). L.L. Thompson questions the theory that Domitian himself demanded to be called *dominus atque deus* at the end of the first century. Thompson believes that this was attributed to him by flatterers such as Martial who wished to join his circle. See Thompson, *The Book of Revelation: Apocalypse and Empire* (Oxford and New York: Oxford University Press, 1990), especially pp. 104-106.

146. *Asc. Isa.* 4.14 mentions a different figure: '[one thousand] three hundred and thirty-two days'. Knibb believes that 'three years and seven months and twenty-seven days' is the equivalent of the 1,335 days found in Dan. 12.12 and reckoned according to the Julian calendar (see Charlesworth [ed.], *Old Testament Pseudepigrapha*, II, p. 162 n. j). 4.14 should be corrected to agree with 4.12 (see also Pesce in *Isaia*, p. 26).

timescale of Dan. 12.12 as a prophecy of the Beloved One's parousia and it assumes that Daniel had spoken about the author's own generation.

Asc. Isa. 4.13 says that those who resist Beliar will be displaced. The author describes this situation in terms of flight from desert to desert.[147] This verse, with its reference to those who 'saw' Jesus, has sometimes been taken as an indication that some of the original Christians were still alive at the time of writing, but this is not its primary meaning. The thought is rather that few of those who had seen Jesus 'would be *left in those days as his servants*', so that the verse is an indication of apostasy rather than of the longevity of the original Christian generation. The verse anticipates the experience of marginalization, for which the author offers no prospect of avoidance, under the belief that it would contrast with the millenarian kingdom which was expected in the imminent future.

An Expected Change in Order

Asc. Isa. 4.14-18 reasserts the nearness of that expected intervention. The *Asc. Isa.* stands in the Christian millenarian tradition which expected Christ to reign with his saints on earth.[148] A new order is anticipated in which the faithful will receive many benefits:

> And after [one thousand] three hundred and thirty-two days the LORD will come with his angels and with the hosts of the saints from the seventh heaven, with the glory of the seventh heaven, and will drag Beliar, and his hosts also, into Gehenna (4.14).

The source for this passage is Paul's eschatological prediction in 2 Thess. 1.7 ('and to grant rest with us to you who are afflicted, when the Lord Jesus is revealed from heaven with his mighty angels in flaming fire'). The author interprets Paul with reference to Dan. 12.12.[149] He states

---

147. Knibb notes that the desert was a traditional place of safety during persecutions; he mentions 1 Kgs 17.2-5 and other literature (in Charlesworth [ed.], *Old Testament Pseudepigrapha*, II, p. 162 n. m). The Gospel stories of John the Baptist and Acts 21.38 connect messianic movements with the desert (see further Kittel, 'ἔρημος', *TDNT*, II, pp. 658-59). I see the desert material in the *Ascension of Isaiah* as the author's way of advocating caution against unnecessary involvement with the Romans which might result in investigation and martyrdom.

148. See my account of Christian millenarianism in Chapter 3.

149. Paul in 1 Thess. 3.13 and 2 Thess. 1.7 used a form of words which was

that Beliar's removal will mean the end of Roman domination. There is perhaps a hint in this passage that the unworthy church leaders will be punished as well (a view which is also supported by the work's uncompromising dualism) so that the punishment will be total in its effects.

According to 4.15 the Beloved One will 'give rest to the pious whom he finds in the body in this world, but *the sun will be ashamed*'.[150] 'Rest' signifies a change from the problems which are described earlier in the Vision. *Asc. Isa.* 4.16 anticipates that those who have died (especially the martyrs) will descend from heaven to enjoy these benefits. This is a striking view of the first resurrection and it depends on the view, which is reflected in Judaism, that martyrs passed to heavenly immortality.[151] The author says that the Lord will 'strengthen those who are found in the body' and 'serve those who have kept watch in this world'. This is an allusion to Lk. 12.37b, from the parable of the Watching Servants, which says of the returning Master: 'He will come and serve them' (a saying for which there is no Matthean parallel).[152] The point of the allusion is that the Lord will serve the saints in this way in the context of their earthly life to which the dead will be

---

derived from Zech. 14.5 (LXX); see R.J. Bauckham, *Jude, 2 Peter* (Waco, TX: Word Books, 1982), pp. 94-101. Our author's use of 2 Thess. 1.7 is confirmed by the language used for his parousia prediction and by his anticipation of 'rest' in the millenarian kingdom. 'Fire' is also a feature of the 'final judgment' in *Asc. Isa.* 4.18. The term 'saints' which is used in *Asc. Isa.* 4.14 also suggests a knowledge of 1 Thess. 3.13.

150. The italicized words, Knibb believes, are a gloss (Charlesworth [ed.], *Old Testament Pseudepigrapha*, II, p. 162 n. p). The verse as it stands alludes to Isa. 24.23 ('The moon will be confounded, and the sun ashamed').

151. The *Ascension of Isaiah* agrees with Revelation 20 in describing two resurrections. The thought of this passage is that the righteous passed to heavenly immortality. There are parallels for this view in *Jub.* 22.27-31; Phil. 1.23; and *Ign. Rom.* 2.2. See the discussion of this issue by G.W.E. Nickelsburg, *Resurrection, Immortality and Eternal Life in Intertestamental Judaism* (HTS 26; Cambridge, MA: Harvard University Press, 1972); and also J.H. Charlesworth, 'The Portrait of the Righteous as an Angel' in G.W.E. Nickelsburg and J.J. Collins (eds.), *Ideal Figures in Ancient Judaism* (Chico, CA: Scholars Press, 1980), pp. 135-51. The author of the *Ascension of Isaiah* developed the Christian millenarian tradition by promising a heavenly immortality after the millenarian kingdom.

152. Bauckham believes that the author knew only *pre*-Lukan tradition, not the Gospel itself (see his article, 'Synoptic Parousia Parables Again', *NTS* 29 (1983), pp. 129-33 [p. 130]).

1. An Introduction to the Ascension of Isaiah

restored. This element of the work's eschatology links the *Ascension of Isaiah* with the New Testament millenarian tradition.

Asc. Isa. 4.17, however, *departs* from the earlier Christian view when it looks forward to an immortal life in the seventh heaven after the earthly reign of the saints. This heavenly state is to be an incorporeal one. *Asc. Isa.* 4.17 states explicitly that the human body is to be left behind in the world, in what represents a revision of the Christian millenarian tradition. This part of the apocalypse anticipates the later Gnostic eschatology but the author significantly retains the millenarian hope which the Gnostics rejected. *Asc. Isa.* 4.18 says that all heavenly and earthly places which have permitted Beliar's dominance will be punished after the heavenly translation of the saints. The implication is that everything will disappear so that the heavenly life will be the only meaningful one. *Asc. Isa.* 4.19-21 finds prophecies about the Beloved One in the whole of the canonical Isaiah. *Asc. Isa.* 4.21 is an early witness for the doctrine of the 'descent to hell'. It says that the Beloved One went to Sheol after his crucifixion and supports this idea from Isa. 52.13–53.12.[153] *Asc. Isa.* 4.21-22 finds further predictions of his activity in the Psalms, Proverbs and minor prophets (including Daniel).[154] The Mosaic writings are significantly excluded from the list as if the author did not regard them as helpful in the same way as the rest of the Hebrew Bible. This was probably because of their use by the Jews.

---

153. This represents important evidence for the interpretation of the Fourth Servant Song in early Christian literature. Isa. 53 is understood here as a prophecy of the descent to Sheol and not in terms of vicarious atonement. M.D. Hooker, *Jesus and the Servant: The Influence of the Servant Concept of Deutero-Isaiah in the New Testament* (London: SPCK, 1959) has an evaluation of the New Testament usage of Isa. 53.

154. This list includes a Jewish apocryphon which is called 'the words of the righteous Joseph'. This has often, but not universally, been identified with the Jewish mystical writing called the *Prayer of Joseph* which is mentioned by Origen in *In Joh.* 2.31. If this is a correct identification, that work doubtless features here because it describes a connection between the angel Israel and the patriarch Jacob which is similar in many respects to the tone of the *Ascension of Isaiah* Christology. This reference confirms that there was a certain fluidity regarding which books might be included among the Writings in the early second century CE.

The Prophet's Martyrdom

Chapter 5 resumes the narrative of Isaiah's martyrdom.[155] The author explains that Beliar was angry with Isaiah and that Manasseh sawed the prophet in half with a wood saw (5.1).[156] Belchira and all the false prophets stand by to deride Isaiah's misfortune (5.2). In 5.3-6 Belchira offers Isaiah an opportunity to save his life if he will recant his visions of the Beloved One.[157] Isaiah scornfully refuses this and spurns the destruction of his flesh (5.9-10).[158] The execution continues in 5.11-12; Isaiah sends his disciples to Tyre and Sidon to remove them from danger (5.13).[159] I see this verse as a warning against voluntary martyrdom, as if the author upheld the importance of martyrdom but wanted to discourage those who deliberately sought it. The martyr meets his death with exemplary courage and speaks with the Holy Spirit until he breathes his last (5.14).[160] The prophet's death is once again assigned to Beliar's influence (5.15-16). This is a significant comment in view of Beliar's connection with the Romans (ch. 4).

Like 4.1-13 this chapter offers evidence that the apocalypse was written under the influence of the events of 112 CE. It tells the story of how a Christian prophet refused to honour pagan demands for worship in a context where Beliar (whom the author says inspired the Romans) is a prominent figure. Isaiah's trial before the representative of Beliar shows the injustice of the punishment which had been imposed on the

---

155. E is our only witness for the whole of this chapter besides GL 3.16-18.

156. The noun that is translated 'wood saw' has implications for determining the original language of the incorporated Isaiah traditions; see Knibb in Charlesworth (ed.), *Old Testament Pseudepigrapha*, II, pp. 146-47 (but I disagree with Knibb about the existence of a written 'Martyrdom of Isaiah').

157. *Asc. Isa.* 5.8 contains a flattering promise: 'I will turn their heart and make Manasseh, and the princes of Judah, and the people, and all Jerusalem worship you'. This echoes the story of the temptation of Jesus in Mt. 4.8-9. Justin Martyr later drew a parallel between the death of Isaiah and Jesus; see *Dial.* 120.5; and Acerbi, *Serra Lignea*, pp. 14-16.

158. The reference to Isaiah 'cursing' his opponents in 5.9 perhaps counters the demand for Christians to 'curse Christ' which is mentioned by Pliny *Ep*. 10.96.

159. The reference to the 'cup' (that is, of suffering) in 5.13 suggests the author's knowledge of Mt. 20.22-23 and/or 26.39.

160. There is a possible parallel with the death of Stephen in Acts 7.55-56. Stephen, was also a Christian martyr who was said to be πλήρης πνεύματος ἁγίου.

Christians by the Romans. The author reminds readers that they must accept the experience of testing if it comes their way, but he hints that they are ill-advised to provoke it unnecessarily. *Asc. Isa.* 5.13 is a veiled instruction to withdraw from public attention if persecution arises. This is partly connected with his desire to preserve the prophetic office in the church, which would not be served by the self-immolation of such prophets as remain. Nevertheless, the description of Isaiah's death recognizes that the prophets might still suffer in this way.

The Second Vision

There is a marked change of tone at the beginning of ch. 6, where 'the Second Vision' begins. The Second Vision is a description of Isaiah's mystical ascension to the seventh heaven which stands in the tradition of Jewish apocalyptic revelation. The mysteries revealed in this part of the apocalypse are soteriological ones. The author explains that the Beloved One has defeated Beliar and that readers can find security through their continued trust in his intervention. This will lead to their own participation in the immortal life of the seventh heaven (8.24-5; 11.35). The author's desire to create a more systematic understanding of the death of Jesus shows how a tradition of Christian doctrine was emerging in the early second century. This was a time when a more reflective understanding of salvation was considered necessary. The revelatory element in chs. 6–11 consists in the disclosure that the Beloved One had destroyed Beliar on the cross. This means that the author's interpretation of the descent and passion is given a prominent position and constitutes the specifically 'revealed' element in chs. 6–11 together with the hope for heavenly immortality.

The second half of the apocalypse is set chronologically earlier than the first half in the 'twentieth' year of Hezekiah's reign (6.1; cf. 1.6).[161] Isaiah has come in from Gilgal to examine and ordain the junior prophets (6.5). Such ordination was evidently an attempt to preserve the obsolescent ministry of the prophets in the church. It can only be presumed that it reflects what was done in the readers' own circle. While Isaiah is speaking, all those in the royal courtroom hear a door

---

161. The Slavonic text and L2 have a shorter text here and throughout ch. 6. Bori in his 'L'estasi del profeta', shows that the longer E text is the more original; see also Acerbi, *L'Ascensione di Isaia*, pp. 233-46, on this problem.

open (in the air above them) and the voice of the Holy Spirit (6.6).[162] The prophet then enters a mystical trance. The *Ascension of Isaiah* briefly describes the techniques which were used to induce heavenly ascension.[163] Isaiah enjoys a cataleptic experience:[164]

> His mind was taken up from him,[165] and he did not see the men who were standing before him. His eyes indeed were open, but his mouth was silent, and the mind in his body was taken up from him.[166] But his breath was [still] in him, for he was seeing a vision (6.10-12).

This narrative has been worked over in the course of transmission, but the evidence that normal functions are suspended is clear to see. *Asc. Isa.* 6.14 says that only the innermost circles of prophets and not the general assembly recognize what has happened. *Asc. Isa.* 6.16-17 restricts knowledge of it to an inner circle in an indication that the contents of the Vision apply to the prophets alone (cf. 3.26-27; 6.14).

Asc. Isa. 6.13 and 7.2-3 state that Isaiah's ascension is assisted by an angel guide.[167] This angel tells him:

> You will see one greater than me, how he will speak kindly and gently with you; and the Father of the one who is greater you will also see, because for this purpose I was sent from the seventh heaven, that I might make all this clear to you (7.7-8, E text).

162. See Rev. 4.1. This reference to the Spirit gives the narrative a distinctively Christian flavour.

163. There are parallels in this description with the Jewish work called *Hekhaloth Rabbati* which is described by I. Gruenwald, *Apocalyptic and Merkabah Mysticism* (Leiden: Brill, 1980), pp. 57-62. In this (later) Jewish writing a rabbi made a heavenly ascension (which is curiously called 'the descent to the *merkabah*') surrounded by his disciples. Mystical ascension had a long pedigree in Judaism before the Christian period. It goes back to the earliest portions of the Enochic literature. One major issue of interpretation, which cannot be resolved with confidence, is how far this literature represents actual mystical praxis rather than, say, imaginative exegesis of the biblical theophanies. David Halperin has drawn attention to the latter as an important element in early rabbinic spirituality in his book, *The Merkabah in Rabbinic Literature* (New Haven: American Oriental Society, 1980).

164. Some of the psychological issues which are raised by this kind of experience are explored by K. Wapnick, 'Mysticism and Schizophrenia', in R. Woods (ed.), *Understanding Mysticism* (London: Athlone Press, 1980), pp. 321-37.

165. GL supports E in this phrase; S and L2 omit it.

166. S and L2 again omit.

167. The angel guide was a familiar feature of the apocalyptic tradition. See for example 2 *En.* 1.4-10 (two 'men' are mentioned), and P. Schäfer, *Rivalität zwischen Engeln und Menschen* (Berlin: de Gruyter, 1975), pp. 10-18.

1. An Introduction to the Ascension of Isaiah

Here, the angel pledges a binitarian vision in the seventh heaven.[168] There is a tension in the work's theology, for when Isaiah enters the seventh heaven in ch. 9 he sees *three* divine beings because the Spirit is included in worship as well (see 9.27-42).[169] The Spirit is a divine being in the *Ascension of Isaiah*, but in practice the interest falls on the Beloved One's achievement so that there is no developed presentation of the Spirit's role in the apocalypse. The author's concern for soteriology explains why this should be so.[170] We should note that the Christology of 7.7-8 has a strong angelomorphic dimension. The Beloved One is said to have a greater glory than the *angelus interpres* (E text) as if his comparison with the angels was not deemed inappropriate in the lost Greek original.[171]

---

168. E must be compared with the other versions in 7.8. L1 supports E in its comment, *Et eminentiorem ipsius majoris videbis*. L2 reads: *Meliorem et dulciorem in hoc enim missus sum, ut notificem tibi omnia haec*. S apparently supports E: *Et majorem majoris* but Bonwetsch notes that the immediate context has suffered corruption (in Charles, *Ascension of Isaiah*, p. 104, ns. 18-20). The GL introduces material which is not found in any of the other versions and it must be regarded as secondary. The difference between these versions in the present state of evidence is that E and L1 (?S) attests a binitarian theology but that this is not so obvious in L2. It is sobering to observe, as Bauckham does, that *all* versions of the *Ascension of Isaiah* may have suffered abbreviation in the course of transmission ('Worship of Jesus', p. 333).

169. Simonetti thinks that there are two conflicting trinitarian theologies in the apocalypse. One of these is 'triangular' and presents the Beloved and Spirit as assistants of God. The second is more hierarchical and approximates to early Christian 'Logos-christology' in which the Spirit is made subordinate to the Beloved One; see Simonetti's article 'Note sulla Cristologia dell' *Ascensione di Isaia*' in Pesce (ed.), *Isaia*, p. 193. I have a review of this problem in Chapter 2. The *Ascension of Isaiah* is an important text for the history of the Trinitarian question in early Christianity. Origen would later understand the two seraphim of Isa. 6 as Christ and the Spirit (*De Princ.* 1.3.4, cf. 4.3.14). On this identification see Daniélou, *Jewish Christianity*, pp. 134-40; Acerbi, *Serra Lignea* pp. 20-32 and G.C. Stead, 'The Origins of the Doctrine of the Trinity, I', *Theology* 77 (1974), pp. 508-17, especially pp. 514-15. The significance of binitarianism in early Christianity is explored by A.F. Segal, *Two Powers in Heaven* (Leiden: Brill, 1978), pp. 205-33; by C.C. Rowland, *The Open Heaven* (London: SPCK, 1982), pp. 94-113; and Hurtado, *One God*, pp. 41-124. The *Ascension of Isaiah* is an early text where *three* divine beings are said to be *worshipped* (9.27-36).

170. This point was recognized by F.C. Burkitt, *Jewish and Christian Apocalypses*, p. 47: 'It is really a piece of "dogmatics", an essay in christology.'

171. See further Chapter 2.

In 7.9-12 Isaiah journeys upwards through the firmament. This is the region where Sammael ('Satan' S, L2, GL 2.9) dwells. The prophet sees a great struggle in the firmament and observes how the angels there envy one another. He is told by his companion that what happens in the firmament also happens on earth. Beliar's arrogance has persisted since creation and will last until the Beloved One appears to destroy him:

> And we went up into the firmament, I and he, and there I saw Sammael and his hosts; and there was a great struggle in it, and the words of Satan, and they were envying one another. And as above, so also on earth, for the likeness of what [is] in the firmament is here on earth. And I said to the angel, 'What is this envying?' And he said to me, 'So it has been ever since this world existed until now, and this struggle [will last] until the one comes whom you are to see, and he will destroy him' (7.9-12).

This passage relates the experience of human conflict to belief in demonic activity. It implies that Beliar influences human situations from his position in the firmament. The meaning of this view is not further explained (but see the description of Beliar in ch. 4, where his incarnation is described). In terms of the Second Vision's soteriology, 7.9-12 sets out the problem which the Beloved One's descent was undertaken to remedy. It explains in cosmological terms the cause of the problems which confronted the author and limits the authority of the oppressors by defining it. The presentation of Beliar as an aerial power who is excluded from the heavens is a vivid demonstration that the disciples of the Beloved One had a superior cosmic patron who shared the divine glory in the seventh heaven.[172] This was a way of creating hope in a situation where the author and his friends were powerless to determine their fate if they remained faithful to the profession of Christianity.

Isaiah enters the first of the seven heavens in 7.13. He sees a throne there which is surrounded by angels (7.14).[173] The angels on the right are said to be more glorious than those [on the left][174] and to offer better praises to God (7.15). I see the work's angelological arrangement

---

172. This understanding of Beliar's role was perhaps suggested by a reading of Ephesians. See further Chapter 4.

173. L2 and S add that an angel sat on the throne—the scene which Isaiah would witness in the higher heavens—but E constitutes the harder reading. Col. 1.16 and *T. Levi* 3.8 use 'throne' absolutely as the name for an angelic being (for which see also the E text of *Asc. Isa.* 7.15, 7.27, 8.8, 11.25, and GL 2.40).

174. The bracketed words are supplied by Knibb from L1, *Et non tales erant angeli ad sinistra(m) quales ad dextra(m)*.

1. An Introduction to the Ascension of Isaiah

as related both to the resurrection passage (3.16-17) and to the seer's vision of the three divine beings in chs. 9 and 11. It reflects the Trinitarian theology which gives the Second Vision its character but it also retains the element of subordination in which the Spirit was regarded as inferior to the Beloved One and the Beloved to the Father (cf. 7.23; 11.32-33). The prophet is told that this angelic worship is directed: 'To the praise of [the One who sits in][175] the seventh heaven, the One who rests in the holy world, and to his Beloved, from where I was sent to you (7.17)'.[176] This binitarian reference makes no provision for the Spirit's reception of worship (but the Spirit *is* included in the worship of God in ch. 9).

Isaiah ascends into the second heaven in 7.18-23 and sees a similar scene, but with an important difference. The central throne is now occupied by an angel who is said to be more glorious than the other angels there.[177] Isaiah falls on his face to worship this angel but is prevented from doing so by his companion (7.21). This angel-guide tells him not to offer worship until he has entered the seventh heaven. The implication of this scene is that the prophet, when he sees a seated being, thinks that he has entered the presence of God himself. The scene itself has a conventional nature[178] and it emphasizes the distance between God, the firmament and the human world on which the soteriology depends. Isaiah finds the same angelic structure in the third, fourth and fifth heavens, except that the angels in each successive heaven have greater splendour than their inferior counterparts. 7.23 is an early Trinitarian reference which calls the Spirit an angel (a frequent designation in the apocalypse) and gives him the status of a psychopomp.[179]

As he journeys upwards Isaiah discovers that the sixth and seventh heavens have an outer atmosphere to pass before entry. Isaiah enters the

---

175. The bracketed words are supplied by Knibb from L1: *Gloriae sedentis septimi caeli*. L2 has *Magnae gloriae Dei, qui est super septimum coelum* (S similar).

176. In E, L1, S, and L2 this is a binitarian reference; GL 2.13, though, is monotheistic (cf. the different versions of 7.7-8).

177. L1 unfortunately finishes mid-way through 7.19 with its reference to *angelos dextros et sinistros et sedes media*.

178. For a list of other passages where this point is made see Bauckham, 'Worship of Jesus'. Revelation 19.10, 22.8-9 make for obvious comparisons. There is interesting material also in the Akhmimic text of *Apoc. Zeph.* 9.12–10.9 where the angel Eremiel refuses to permit worship of himself.

179. This recalls the function of Michael in Jewish literature. See Daniélou, *Jewish Christianity*, p. 128, and cf. *2 En.* 22.6.

atmosphere of the sixth in 8.1 and finds neither central throne nor seated angel there. He is told that this is because this region is directed by God and the 'Chosen One' (8.7). The Beloved One's descent is then predicted (8.9-10). Isaiah enters the sixth heaven itself (8.16-28) and he sings praises with the angels there (8.17). *Asc. Isa.* 8.18 is a Trinitarian reference in which the angels are said to have praised the three divine beings equally (cf. 11.32-33). Isaiah asks to stay permanently in the seventh heaven but he is told that the time of his death has not yet arrived (8.25-28) and that he must return to the earth. The conclusion of the apocalypse, however, promises that he will return there (11.35). That situation is anticipated also by *Asc. Isa.* 4.17. The apocalypse leaves no doubt that heavenly immortality is the final destiny of the righteous. The presence of Enoch and others as transformed humans in the seventh heaven (ch. 9) anticipates this final translation.

In 9.1 Isaiah enters the air of the seventh heaven. The angel chorusmaster of the sixth heaven tries to prevent his further passage, saying: 'How far is he who dwells among aliens to go up?'[180] The prophet is, however, admitted when the Beloved gives him a heavenly garment (9.2). *Asc. Isa.* 9.5 is an important title catena which calls the mediator 'Your LORD, the LORD, the LORD Christ, who is to be called in the world Jesus'.[181] This passage calls the Beloved by the divine title (E probably renders ὁ θεός in the lost Greek original).[182] This cluster distinguishes between titles which the Beloved always enjoyed ('Lord') and others (in this context 'Jesus') which are held appropriate only to the earthly appearance. In the seventh heaven Isaiah sees all the righteous from the time of Adam onwards (9.7-12).[183] These people have been 'stripped of [their] robes of the flesh' and they resemble the angels

---

180. The theme of angelic opposition to humans in rabbinic literature is explored by Schäfer, *Rivalität*, pp. 75-218.

181. S and L2 remove this catena and replace it with a reference to the 'Son of God' (cf. their version of 10.7). E is significantly supported at this point by GL 2.37.

182. This title is rare in the New Testament but it was becoming more frequent in the second century: see for example *Ign. Eph.* 18.2.

183. S and L2 mention only *justos...quosdam*, but GL 2.27 supports E in naming names (including Seth and Jared not mentioned in E). These people are antediluvian heroes and it is likely that the author thinks only of the pre-Flood generation as transformed in this way. These prefigured the post-millenarian destiny of the righteous in the *Ascension of Isaiah* (cf. 4.17).

1. An Introduction to the Ascension of Isaiah 61

there (9.8-9).[184] They stand beside heavenly thrones[185] but they do not wear the crowns which had been reserved for them (9.10).[186] Isaiah is told that they will receive these artefacts once the Beloved One has made his saving journey (9.12, 18). This is an already 'realized' situation from the author's point of view. The Second Vision looks back on the Beloved's descent as a past event and implies by this that the full eschatological benefits had already been provided. This was a way of offering readers assurance about their heavenly destiny, which is made an item of revealed knowledge in the apocalypse. Readers, too, were promised robes, crown and thrones when earthly life was finished, as if the enthronement of Enoch were symbolic of their future experience (9.24-26, cf. 4.17).

Asc. Isa. 9.13-18 contains a further prediction of the descent. It includes the statement that the Beloved will remain on earth for 545 days after the resurrection (9.16).[187] *Asc. Isa.* 9.17 anticipates that many of the righteous will ascend to heaven with him.[188] Isaiah also sees a record of human deeds. These are the heavenly ledgers which are familiar from other apocalyptic texts (9.19-23).[189]

Isaiah finally sees the three divine beings in 9.27-42. According to 9.27 he witnesses 'one standing (there) whose glory surpassed that of all, and his glory was great and wonderful'.[190] This is the Beloved One. All

---

184. This is Christian view and not a Gnostic one; see Daniélou, *Jewish Christianity*, p. 192.

185. Cf. Rev. 3.21 where victorious Christians are promised that they will occupy Christ's throne; and Mt. 19.28; Lk. 22.30.

186. 'Crowns' are a symbolic description of the reward which Christians will enjoy in heaven: cf. Rev. 2.10; 3.11; 4.4; 1 Pet. 5.4; *4 Ezra* 2.43-45; *Herm. Sim.* 8.2.1, 3, 6.

187. The figure of 545 days parallels the Ophite belief, which is recorded by Irenaeus, *Adv. Haer.* 1.3.2, that the risen Christ remained on earth for a period of eighteen months. The *Ascension of Isaiah*, however, makes no allusion to any esoteric teaching imparted during this period (and the phrase is omitted by L2 and S). The date of the *Ascension of Isaiah* suggests that the Gnostics borrowed the figure from a source such as this apocalypse.

188. This strange comment perhaps derives from a strand of tradition similar to Mt. 27.52-53 or perhaps even from that passage itself. I see it as an attempt to deal with the fate of those who had died before the Beloved One's descent.

189. See further Daniélou, *Jewish Christianity*, pp. 200, 202, who discusses other passages.

190. S and L2 have removed any suggestion that the Lord's glory could be described by comparison with the angels. They transfer the words 'whose glory

the righteous, including Adam, Abel and Seth, and the angels, approach him and offer worship (cf. 7.17). Isaiah joins with them (9.28-29). The Beloved is transformed to resemble an angel (9.30)[191] and he is introduced to Isaiah as 'the LORD of all the praises which you have seen' (9.32). In 9.33 Isaiah sees 'another glorious [person] who was like him'.[192] Isaiah's companion identifies him: 'This is the *angel of the Holy Spirit* who has spoken in you and also in the other righteous'.[193]

In 9.35-36 the Spirit receives angelic worship (cf. 8.18). The conclusion of the vision (11.32-33) also seats him on the left of God's throne. For all the ambiguity that surrounds his position (notably the designation 'angel' and the subordinationism of 7.23) the Spirit is made a divine being in the *Ascension of Isaiah*. He stands on the left of the Beloved One (9.36) and is here identified as the inspirer of prophecy

---

surpassed that of all' to the description of Michael which they have introduced in 9.23 (cf. the similar references to Michael in their versions of *Asc. Isa.* 9.29, 42). The E text merits comparison with 7.7-8 which says that the Beloved's glory was greater than that of the *angelus interpres*. Its Christology is again an angelomorphic one.

191. There is a problem of interpretation here. The E text is translated by Knibb: 'And he was transformed and became like an angel' (in Charlesworth [ed.], *Old Testament Pseudepigrapha*, II, p. 171 n. o2). All the E manuscripts have the third person singular. S and L2 however read the first person singular as if the *prophet* were transformed upon seeing the Beloved One. A reference to the Beloved One's transformation is the more difficult reading and it agrees with the information that is supplied in 9.1-5. Isaiah is there said to have donned his heavenly garment upon entry to the seventh heaven; he must therefore be presumed to have no further need of transformation. 9.30 effectively describes the first stage of the Beloved One's descent.

192. S and L2 read *similem eius in omnibus*. M. Simonetti compares this phrase with the ὅμοιός κατὰ πάντα formula of the Council of Sirmium (357 CE) to emphasize its later character: see his book, *La crisi ariana nel IV secolo* (Rome: Institutum Patristicum Augustinianum, 1975), pp. 245, 267, 259; and cf. E. Norelli, 'Sulla pneumatologia dell'*Ascensione di Isaia*', in Pesce (ed.), *Isaia*, p. 260 n. 61. The secondary nature of S and L2 at this point is noticed also by Vaillant, 'Un apocryphe pseudo-bogomile', p. 112. One should not of course conclude from Knibb's translation that the author spoke about the 'persons' of the Trinity in the later technical sense.

193. On the work's understanding of the Spirit see Simonetti, 'Note sulla cristologia', pp. 188-89, 206-207; Norelli, 'Sulla pneumatologia dell'*Ascensione di Isaia*', pp. 211-76, esp. p. 261 on its 'double perspective'; and Daniélou, *Jewish Christianity*, pp. 128-29. The Spirit is characteristically called an angel in the *Ascension of Isaiah* (cf. 3.16-17). This explains why he was not transformed to accord with the angels' form in 9.33.

1. An Introduction to the Ascension of Isaiah

('who has spoken in you and also in the other righteous'; cf. 4.21-22).[194] The *Ascension of Isaiah* is thus an important text for the early doctrine of the Holy Spirit as for other aspects of Christian belief.

Asc. Isa. 9.37-38 allows Isaiah a fleeting glimpse of God:

> I saw the Great Glory while the eyes of my spirit were open, but I could not thereafter see, nor the angel who [was] with me, nor any of the angels whom I had seen worship my LORD.[195]

This passage permits a theophany for the briefest of moments, but it prevents a protracted vision of the deity, which the apocalypse makes the prerogative only of the transformed righteous (9.37-38). The *Ascension of Isaiah* shows a greater reserve in this than the biblical theophanies (and *1 En.* 14).[196] *Asc. Isa.* 9.27-39 resembles 11.32-33 in that the Beloved and Spirit attend the throne of God. Here however they are portrayed as *standing*, evidently in homage to the deity, rather than seated as in the final scene. This reflects the fact that 11.32-33 draws on 1 Pet. 3.22 (which supplied the notion of ascension and heavenly enthronement) and it further shows the character of the *Ascension of Isaiah*'s Trinitarianism, which retains a deeply-set subordinationism.

The work's portrait of the Beloved One has two distinct axes. 9.27-34 allows the Beloved to receive angelic worship (cf. 7.17) and calls him the 'LORD' (cf. 9.5, 10.11 in the E text). Worship of two heavenly powers had distinguished Christianity from other Jewish groups from the very beginning. The *Ascension of Isaiah* is perhaps the earliest text to develop such worship in a Trinitarian direction. According to 9.40, however, the Beloved One himself joins with the angels in worshipping God: 'I saw how my LORD and the angel of the Holy Spirit worshiped and both

---

194. *Asc. Isa.* 9.35-36 was used by the Egyptian heretic Hieracas, who is reported by Epiphanius (*Panarion* 67.3), who reproduces a form of text longer than both E and L2 and S and which combines elements from both. This is a brief glimpse into the complicated textual history which the apocalypse has enjoyed. Epiphanius's citation is discussed by Acerbi, 'L'*Ascensione di Isaia*', in Pesce (ed.), *Isaia*, p. 277, and in his *Serra Lignea*, pp. 42-47.

195. On the place which theophanies occupied in the Jewish mystical understanding see J. Jeremias, *Theophanie: Die Geschichte einer alttestamentlichen Gattung* (Neukirchen–Vluyn: Neukirchener Verlag, 1965); C.C. Rowland, 'Visions of God in Apocalyptic Literature', *JSJ* 10 (1979), pp. 137-54; *idem*, *Open Heaven*, pp. 94-113.

196. Cf. *Apoc. Abr.* 16.3.

together praised the LORD'.[197] This passage shows that, despite his affinity to God, the Beloved One is a subordinate who shares the angels' duty of the heavenly liturgy. This subordinationism is a consistent and distinctive feature of the *Ascension of Isaiah*'s Christology. The apocalypse shows that, despite its author's increased interest in the Beloved One's heavenly position when compared with first-century literature, his theology had not yet moved in the direction of the co-equality which characterized the later christological settlement. This raises important issues of monotheism and Trinitarianism which must be considered in this book.[198]

Chapter 10 describes how God commissions the Beloved One to make his saving journey. Subordinationism is evident here too in the assumption that the Beloved must undertake the mission which was enjoined on him in this way. There are analogies to this in the Jewish angelophanic tradition. *Asc. Isa.* 10.8-16 explains the nature of the Second Vision's soteriology:

> 8 Go out and descend through all the heavens. You shall descend through the firmament and through that world as far as the angel who [is] in Sheol, but you shall not go as far as Perdition.[199] 9 And you shall make your likeness like that of all who [are] in the five heavens, 10 *and you shall take care to make your form like that of the angels of the firmament and also [like that] of the angels who [are] in Sheol*.[200] 11 And none of the angels of that world shall know that you [are] LORD with me of the seven heavens and of their angels. And they shall not know that you [are] with me 12 when[201] with the voice of the heavens I summon you, and their angels and their lights, and when I lift up [my voice] to the sixth heaven, that you may judge and destroy the princes and the angels and the gods of that world, and the world which is ruled by them, 13 for they have denied me and said, 'We alone are, and there is no one besides us'. 14 'And afterwards you shall ascend from the gods of death to your place, and you shall not be transformed in each of the heavens, but in

---

197. S and L2 introduce a reference to Michael at this point: '*Et cum eis Michael et angeli omnes adoraverunt et cantaverunt*'.

198. I shall do this in Chapter 2.

199. The E *Haguel*, meaning 'Perdition', signifies the place of final punishment (see Knibb in Charlesworth [ed.], *Old Testament Pseudepigrapha*, II, p. 173 n. l). This is early evidence for the doctrine of the descent to hell (cf. 9.16-17).

200. The words between asterisks (*) are omitted in S and L2.

201. There are variations between the E manuscripts at this point; see Knibb in Charlesworth (ed.), *Old Testament Pseudepigrapha*, II, p. 173 n. p.

1. *An Introduction to the Ascension of Isaiah* 65

glory you shall ascend and sit at my right hand,[202] 15 and then the princes and the powers of that world will worship you.' 16 This command I heard the Great Glory giving to my LORD.

This passage presents a scenario in which the angels who ruled the world from their position in the firmament (namely Beliar and his cohorts) have denied the Most High God's existence. On the author's level of conflict this was reflected in what were perceived as the arrogant demands of the Roman state. The Beloved One is instructed to 'judge and destroy' these angels through his descent. Although the thought is elliptical, the word 'afterwards' at the beginning of v. 14 leaves little doubt about when this act of judgment takes place. Despite the textual problems in v. 12, the E translation states that the 'judgement and destruction' happened before the ascension 'from the gods of death'. This last phrase is clearly a reference to the resurrection so that the judgment of the angels must be associated with the cross. This view of the crucifixion brings the *Ascension of Isaiah* close to the thought of Col. 2.15, where Paul (or his imitator) says that Jesus disarmed the 'principalities and powers' when he died. I think that the author of the *Ascension of Isaiah* knew this passage and that he developed it when constructing his soteriology.

This interpretation of 10.14 explains the meaning of the enigmatic statement in 3.18 (cf. 9.26) that those who 'believed in his cross' would be saved. The cross is made the moment of the Beloved One's victory over malevolent cosmic powers in the *Ascension of Isaiah*. Belief in the cross means belief that the Beloved One has defeated Beliar in this way (despite the fact that readers' circumstances argue to the contrary). *Asc. Isa.* 3.18 is not primarily an anti-docetic reference but an indication that salvation had been provided. This brings Christology to the forefront of the Second Vision, for it is through the Beloved One's descent that the heavenly hope has been made possible.

The rest of ch. 10 narrates the descent itself. The Beloved One descends through the heavens and disguises his identity as an angel so that the angels in the lower heavens fail to recognize him. He even supplies the correct password to the gatekeepers to conceal his identity (see for example 10.25).[203] This part of the Second Vision distinguishes

---

202. Manuscript B of the Ethiopic text includes a reference to the Beloved One's death and resurrection at this point.

203. The heavenly warders featured in Gnosticism and in Jewish mystical literature; see G. Scholem's account of the dangers attending the unwary mystic in

the angels in the firmament from those in the air, which creates an unsystematic cosmology (10.29-30). This however emphasizes the point that the aerial powers have failed to perceive the hidden descent, which is crucial to the soteriology.

Chapter 11 describes the Beloved One's appearance as Jesus. Here we find the difference between the two branches of the textual tradition which I have noted. The Ethiopic text (E) includes some traditions about Jesus which are similar to the information that is found in 3.13-18. This material, however, is omitted by L2 and S which comment only: '*Et vidi similem filii hominis, et cum hominibus habitare et in mundo. Et non cognoverunt eum.*'[204] The longer, E, version of ch. 11 is the more original; the parent of S and L2 evidently omitted this section because of its docetic tendencies.[205] The longer version in E has affinities with Matthean special material, but it probably derived from a summary which was distinct from the canonical Gospels and which circulated in the oral tradition.

E describes how the virgin Mary (a Davidide) was betrothed to Joseph who was also of David's line.[206] Mary was found pregnant

---

his book, *Major Trends in Jewish Mysticism* (London: Thames & Hudson, 1955), pp. 51-52.

204. Notice the allusion to 1 Cor. 2.8 in the last phrase. Although this is a feature of the later redaction, my belief is that the original author also knew and used this Pauline passage (see below).

205. Docetism is the suggestion that there was something unreal or illusory about the humanity of Jesus. It was a major element in some early Christologies, especially Gnostic ones. See P. Weigandt, 'Doketismus im Urchristentum' (PhD dissertation, University of Heidelberg, 1961), and A. Bakker, 'Christ an Angel? A Study of Early Christian Docetism', *ZNW* 32 (1933), pp. 255-65. The docetism found in the *Ascension of Isaiah* is neither the denial that Christ suffered in the flesh which Ignatius criticized nor the view of Basileides (which is censured by Irenaeus, *Adv. Haer.* 1.24) that Simon of Cyrene (and not Jesus) perished on the cross. It is a naïve form which gives the Beloved One superhuman properties but which insists that he died on the cross. The presence of this kind of docetism in the *Ascension of Isaiah* marks an important difference from Johannine Christology (on which see M. Hengel, *The Johannine Question* [London: SCM Press, 1989], pp. 68-72).

206. Mary's Davidic ancestry is examined by R.E. Brown, *The Birth of the Messiah* (London: Geoffrey Chapman, 1977), pp. 287-88. Other sources support the apocalypse in this, notably the *Prot. Jas* 10.1; *Ign. Eph.* 18.2; and Justin, *Dial.* 45.4. See J. Fischer, 'Der davidische Abkunft der Mutter Jesu: biblische-patristische Untersuchung', *Weidenauerstudien* 4 (1911), pp. 1-115. On Mary in the apocalypse see F. Buck, 'Are the "Ascension of Isaiah" and the "Odes of Solomon" Witnesses

1. An Introduction to the Ascension of Isaiah

before the marriage (11.2-3). The angel of the Spirit appeared to Joseph in a dream and Joseph respected Mary's virginity through continence (11.4-6).[207] After a two-month pregnancy Mary was astonished to see an infant appear. She was found to be a virgin after the delivery (11.7-10).[208] The holy couple were warned to silence by a heavenly voice but the strange circumstances were soon common knowledge in Bethlehem (11.11-13). Some noted the absence of a midwife, in a tradition about Jesus which is not found in any of the Gospels: 'Many said: "She did not give birth; the midwife did not go up [to her] and we did not hear [any] cries of pain"' (11.14a).[209]

The author next states that people failed to recognize the Beloved One's heavenly origins (11.14b). This statement holds ideas in common with Jn 7.25, and I think it possible that the writer knew (a form of) John's Gospel itself.[210] This is particularly so if he has himself interpolated this reference into the traditions which he received. The reason given for this ignorance of the Beloved One's origins is that his descent was 'hidden from all the heavens and all the princes and every god of this world' (11.16).[211] *Asc. Isa.* 11.17 states that the Beloved sucked

---

to an Early Cult of Mary?', in *De primordiis cultu Mariani* (Rome: *Pontificia Academia Mariana Internationalis*, 1970), IV, pp. 371-99. On Joseph, J.M.C Sánchez, 'San José en los libros apocrifos del Nuevo Testamento', *Cahiers de Joséphologie* 19 (1971), pp. 123-49.

207. Some MSS of E have erasures in this section concerning Joseph's refusal to divorce Mary; see Knibb in Charlesworth (ed.), *Old Testament Pseudepigrapha*, II, pp. 174-75 nn. d-o.

208. This is an early affirmation of the *virginitas post partum*. The *Ascension of Isaiah* is apparently its earliest witness; see Brown, *Birth*, p. 518 n. 2; J.N.D. Kelly, *Early Christian Doctrines* (London: A. & C. Black, 5th edn, 1977), p. 492 (he mentions the *Ascension of Isaiah*); J.M. Ford, 'Mary's *Virginitas post Partum* and Jewish Law', *Bib* 54 (1951), pp. 94-101; and J.S. Plumpe, 'Some Little-Known Early Witnesses to Mary's *Virginitas in Partu*', *TS* 9 (1948), pp. 567-77.

209. The absence of a midwife is noticed also by the author of *Acts of Pet.* 24 (c. 175 CE) who evidently knew the *Ascension of Isaiah*. There is a similar statement in *Odes* 19.9 (on the date of which see L. Abramowski, 'Sprache und Abfassungszeit der Oden Salomos', *OrChr* 68 [1984], pp. 80-90).

210. I examine this matter in Chapter 4.

211. *Asc. Isa.* 11.16 is often compared with *Ign. Eph.* 19.1. Charles (*Ascension of Isaiah*, Introduction, p. xxxii), argued that Ignatius knew the apocalypse. This opinion is accepted by Daniélou, *Jewish Christianity*, p. 207. Pesce, however, believes that Ignatius knew only the traditions reported in the apocalypse, not the *Ascension of Isaiah* itself (see his *Isaia*, p. 23 n. 16). This must clearly be so if my

Mary's breast to avoid detection (which implies that the suckling was not done from real need): 'And I saw [that] in Nazareth he sucked the breast like an infant, as was customary, that he might not be recognized'. *Asc. Isa.* 11.18 describes how the adult Jesus worked 'signs and miracles' in the land of Israel and in Jerusalem. *Asc. Isa.* 11.19 presents the betrayal of Jesus as an event which had been inspired by the jealous aerial powers and in which the Jews were ignorant of his identity:

> And after this the adversary envied him and roused the children of Israel, who did not know who he was, against him. And they handed him to the ruler,[212] and crucified him, and he descended to the angel who [is] in Sheol.

There are similarities between this passage and 1 Cor. 2.8, where Paul states that 'the rulers of this age' failed to recognize 'the Lord of Glory'. The date of the *Ascension of Isaiah* makes the author's use of this Pauline text likely. Paul however has no 'hidden descent' tradition in 1 Cor. 2.8, and we must conclude that the author of the *Ascension of Isaiah* himself introduced this broader cosmological framework. *Asc. Isa.* 11.20 mentions the crucifixion and 11.21 the resurrection, after which the Beloved is said to have remained on earth 'many days'.

Asc. Isa. 11.22-33 narrates the Beloved One's ascension back to the seventh heaven. Up to this point the author claims that no one has recognized the Beloved One. In the ascension the Beloved at last reveals who he is. He casts aside his disguise so that his identity is revealed, first of all to the angels. Two views of the ascension are held together at this point in the apocalypse. The first is the notion of the earthly departure of Jesus (*Asc. Isa.* 11.22) which is also found twice in Luke.[213] The second is a mythological reflection on the ascension which is similar to the material incorporated in 1 Pet. 3.22 (*Asc. Isa.* 11.23-33). The evident seam between 11.22 and 11.23 is a good indication that the author was drawing on a source in 11.2-22 (as he did in 3.13-18).

---

date for the apocalypse *after* the death of Ignatius is accepted. It is worth making the point that Ignatius has no christological tradition of the hidden descent through the heavens.

212. That is, Pilate; cf. Mt. 27.2.

213. Lk. 24.50-52; Acts 1.9-11. Early Christian views about the ascension of Jesus are examined by A.F. Segal, 'Heavenly Ascent in Hellenistic Judaism, Early Christianity, and their Environments', *ANRW*, II.23.2, pp. 1333-94. The notion that the Beloved 'sent out the twelve disciples' before ascending reflects a knowledge of Mt. 28.19 so that we find a fusion of Gospel traditions at this point.

1. An Introduction to the Ascension of Isaiah

The ascending mediator is said to have been worshipped by the angels. According to E, 'all the angels of the firmament, and Satan, saw him and worshipped' (11.23). These beings are greatly distressed and they comment further: 'How did our LORD descend upon us, and we did not notice the glory which was upon him, which we [now] see was upon him from the sixth heaven?' (11.24). There is a textual problem at this point. The E text omits the Beloved's passage through the first heaven,[214] but the likelihood is that the lost Greek original did describe how the firmament angels worshipped the Beloved One, which is what E says in its present form. There is corroborating evidence for this view in 10.16, which expects that 'the princes and the powers of that world will worship you' in the ascension back to the seventh heaven. It would be strange if this prediction made by the Most High God were not realized at the end of the apocalypse. We must therefore note the textual problem but also consider its likely resolution. The ascending mediator seats himself at the right hand of God and the Spirit is said to be seated on the left (11.32-33).[215] As in 1 Pet. 3.22, heavenly enthronement is a powerful soteriological symbol in the apocalypse. It provided assurance to readers who were troubled by the prospect of conflict in their lives, and used a tradition of Christology to sustain hope about their heavenly destiny which was conceived analogously with that of the Beloved One.

The Second Vision concludes with Isaiah's dismissal from heaven.[216]

---

214. See Knibb in Charlesworth (ed.), *Old Testament Pseudepigrapha*, II, p. 175.

215. The specific element 'at the right hand' was derived from Ps. 110.1, which was mediated through the author's use of 1 Pet. 3.22. Early Christian use of this Psalm verse is examined by D.M. Hay, *Glory at the Right Hand* (Nashville: Abingdon Press, 1973); by M. Gourgues, *A la Droite de Dieu: Résurrection de Jesus et actualisation du Psaume 110.1 dans le Nouveau Testament* (Paris: Lecoffre, 1978); by C. Markschies, '*"Sessio ad dexteram"*: Bemerkungen zu einem altchristlichen Bekenntnismotiv in der christologischen Diskussion altkirchlichen Theologen', in M. Philonenko (ed.), *Le Trône de Dieu* (WUNT, 69, Tübingen: Mohr, 1993), pp. 252-317; and by M. Hengel, 'Sit at my Right Hand', in his *Studies in Early Christology* (Edinburgh: T. & T. Clark, 1995), pp. 119-225. I suspect that the Spirit's position 'on the left' of the *merkabah* in *Asc. Isa.* 11.33 was developed in extension of this image from Ps. 110.1.

216. L2 adds in 11.34: *quod nec oculus vidit, nec auris audivit, nec in cor hominis ascendit, quanta praeparavit deus omnibus diligentibus se* (S similar). This is an allusion to Isa. 64.4 which Paul had cited in 1 Cor. 2.9. Jerome knew this part of the *Ascension of Isaiah* in the L2 version (see his *Comm. in Is.* 64.4). Jerome's use of the apocalypse is examined by Acerbi, *Serra Lignea*, pp. 32-37, esp. 34-35.

The prophet is told that he must return to the world to live out his natural span. He is however promised a permanent ascension once his earthly days are over (11.34-35). *Asc. Isa.* 11.36-40 explains that Isaiah told the vision to those who surrounded him but that it was not intended for general circulation. The author says that the Vision will be fulfilled in the 'last generation', which he evidently sees as his own. He shares with 1 Cor. 10.11 (and 1QpHab) the belief that he is living in the final days and that he can apply Scripture to the history of his own generation as the eschatological generation. *Asc. Isa.* 11.41-43 looks back to the earlier chapters of the apocalypse and explains that it was on account of these visions and prophecies that Sammael Satan sawed Isaiah in half through the hand of Manasseh (11.41). Hezekiah delivered these oracles to Manasseh in the twenty-sixth year of his reign (11.42). Manasseh did not remember them, but, 'became the servant of Satan and was destroyed' (11.43).[217] The end of the apocalypse reaffirms the demonology that is expressed throughout the *Ascension of Isaiah* and which criticizes the Roman harassment of the Christians in a thinly-veiled way. The conclusion of the *Ascension of Isaiah* insists that the times are near and that everything which has been seen by Isaiah is soon to be fulfilled.

---

217. L2 reads in vv. 41-43: *Cessavit autem loqui et exivit ab Ezechia rege*, and concludes with the words *Explicit visio Isaiae prophetae*. S agrees in thought with the *Cessavit* etc., but in different language. The Slavonic scribe has added *Ipsi autem Deo nostro gloria nunc et semper et in saecula saeculorum. Amen*. MSS C and D of E have a version of L2's postscript (see Knibb in Charlesworth [ed.], *Old Testament Pseudepigrapha*, II, p. 176 n. m2).

Chapter 2

THE CHRISTOLOGY OF THE *ASCENSION OF ISAIAH*

My first research task is to explore the Christology of the *Ascension of Isaiah*. We have seen that the apocalypse comes from the early second century CE and that it includes two visions which describe the activity of the Beloved One. The Beloved One in the *Ascension of Isaiah* is a divine being who receives worship from the angels but who remains subordinate to God (see esp. chs. 9–11). The apocalypse gives special prominence to the theme of his hidden descent, which provides the setting for the description of the life of Jesus (3.13-18; 10.16–11.33). The author places the story of Jesus within a mythological framework in which the mediator's hidden descent and transformation into human likeness are dominant themes.

It has often been questioned whether the New Testament writers (with the exception of the author of John and perhaps the authors of Hebrews and Ephesians) thought about Christ as a pre-existent being associated with Jesus.[1] There is no doubt that this form of belief surfaces in the *Ascension of Isaiah*, which agrees with other second-century sources such as Ignatius and Justin Martyr in assuming a heavenly pre-existence

---

1. Many scholars assume that Phil. 2.5-11 and other passages present the messiah as a pre-existent heavenly being. Those who hold this view include J. Weiss, *Earliest Christianity* (ET New York: Harper & Row, 1959), II, p. 478; E. Käsemann, 'Kritische Analyse von Phil. 2.5-11', in *Exegetische Versuche und Besinnung: Erste Band* (Göttingen: Vandenhoeck & Ruprecht, 1960), pp. 51-95; and E. Lohmeyer, *Kyrios Jesus: Eine Untersuchung zu Phil. 2, 5-11* (Heidelberg: Carl Winter, 1928). This interpretation has been questioned by others who see in Phil. 2 merely a contrast between the human Jesus and Adam as his counterpart. That case has been argued by Dunn in his *Christology*, pp. 114-21. It goes back in essentials to Luther (see also J. Murphy-O'Connor, 'Christological Anthropology in Phil. ii.6-11', *RB* 83 [1976], pp. 25-50). The question of pre-existence has recently been examined by J. Habermann, *Präexistenzaussagen im Neuen Testament* (Frankfurt: Peter Lang, 1990), who finds the idea reflected in Phil. 2.5-11 (pp. 91-157).

for the Beloved One.[2] The apocalypse stands in a tradition of Christology which had yielded 'incarnational' beliefs at least by the time of the Fourth Gospel (c. 100 CE).[3] The *Ascension of Isaiah* develops that tradition through its description of the hidden descent and its use of 'transformation' language, which are the distinctive features of the Christology. It will be argued in this chapter that the author was influenced in this development of the christological tradition by the resources of Jewish angelology.

The origins of Christology have been much researched in recent years and likely sources of influence identified.[4] The Jewish mediatorial tradition has featured strongly in such analysis, and rightly so. The scholarly consensus is that this provided the raw materials for passages such as Jn 1.1-18, Col. 1.15-20, Heb. 1.1-4, and other references where Jesus is described as an exalted heavenly mediator. There is of course a key difference from Judaism in that Jesus is universally presented in the Christian literature as a unique being who transcended all other mediators. Jesus was incorporated by the Christians in the *worship* of God,

2. See for example *Ign. Eph.* 7; Justin, *Dial.* 56.13. On this aspect of Justin's thought see D. Trakatellis, *The Pre-Existence of Christ in Justin Martyr* (Missoula, MT: Scholars Press, 1976), pp. 53-92.

3. By 'incarnational beliefs' in this context I mean John's assertion that the divine Word (or Son of Man) was uniquely connected with the human Jesus. My belief is that the *Ascension of Isaiah* Christology represents a development from the Johannine perspective. I shall argue that case in this chapter of the book. The contribution which was made by angelology to Johannine Christology is examined by J-.A. Bühner, *Der Gesandte und sein Weg im vierten Evangelium* (WUNT, 2; Tübingen: Mohr, 1977), pp. 374-99. Bühner argues that Johannine Christology draws on a fusion of prophetic and angelic categories in which heavenly descent and ascension were important themes. I examine the question of whether the author of the *Ascension of Isaiah* knew the Fourth Gospel below in Chapter 4.

4. Among the major studies I should mention A. Grillmeier, *Christ in Christian Tradition* (ET London: Mowbrays, 2nd edn, 1975); M. Hengel, *The Son of God* (ET London: SCM Press, 1976); R.H. Fuller, *The Foundations of New Testament Christology* (London: Fount Paperbacks, new edn, 1979); F. Hahn, *The Titles of Jesus in Christology: Their History in Early Christianity* (London: Lutterworth Press, 1969); O. Cullmann, *The Christology of the New Testament* (London: SCM Press, 2nd edn, 1963); R.G. Hamerton-Kelly, *Pre-Existence, Wisdom, and the Son of Man: A Study in the Idea of Pre-Existence in the New Testament* (SNTSMS, 21; Cambridge: Cambridge University Press, 1973); Dunn, *Christology*; and Habermann, *Präexistenzaussagen*.

2. The Christology of the Ascension of Isaiah

quite unlike any figure in Judaism.[5] This binitarianism (the worship of two heavenly powers) was the distinctive feature of first-century Christianity. Early Christology was thus a development of the Jewish mediatorial background rather than a simple perpetuation of what was already entertained there.

New Testament Christology has been almost exhaustively sifted to discover its connections with Jewish beliefs about mediators. One nearly despairs of finding something fresh to say in that area. The apocryphal and pseudepigraphal literature, by contrast, has been substantially neglected in this search for the origins of Christology. Such neglect is unfortunate, for a text like the *Ascension of Isaiah* is not much later than the New Testament literature and it has deep roots in Jewish belief which deserve to be uncovered. *All* the available evidence must be examined if we are to make an accurate judgment about the question of christological origins. This is an important concern given the relative paucity of the primary sources, which means that such evidence as we have should not be treated with contempt.

Another issue must be mentioned in this context. This is that, in terms of the Jewish mediatorial background, angelology has received far less attention as a source for Christology than it deserves. Many scholars treat it as a peripheral source, perhaps because of the attempts which were made in the nineteenth century to contrast Christianity as a religion of grace with an apocalyptic Judaism in which God was a distant deity surrounded by a variety of mediators.[6] Martin Werner's overstatement of the case for an 'angel-Christology' in Christian literature did little to revive the popularity of this source in the scholarly imagination.[7] Yet the strand of belief which associates an angel with God or God's throne (the

---

5. The fact that worship addressed to Jesus constituted a new religious phenomenon is noticed by Bauckham, 'Worship of Jesus'; and by Hurtado in his *One God*.

6. Nineteenth-century scholarship readily accepted that angels functioned as mediators in Judaism. This view is expressed by F. Weber, *System der altsynagogen palästinischen Theologie aus Targum, Midrash, und Talmud dargestellt* (Leipzig, 1880), pp. 172-89; and by W. Bousset, *Die Religion des Judentums im Neutestamentlichen Zeitalter* (Berlin: Reuther & Reichard, 1903), pp. 291-313. Two articles by G.F. Moore changed scholarly opinions on this issue: see his 'Christian Writers on Judaism', *HTR* 14 (1921), pp. 197-254; and 'Intermediaries in Jewish Theology', *HTR* 15 (1922), pp. 41-79. The matter is reviewed by E.P. Sanders, *Paul and Palestinian Judaism* (London: SCM Press, 1981), pp. 33-34.

7. In his book *Entstehung*.

merkabah) in the context of an apocalyptic vision was by all accounts an important source for Christology. Christian writers developed this image to present the heavenly Jesus as a unique mediator who shared the divine worship and occupied a position which no Jewish figure had attained. This Christian use of a Jewish apocalyptic tradition deserves exploration to see whether scholarly scepticism about the influence of angelology on Christology is justified. The *Ascension of Isaiah* makes an excellent test case for such a study because it contains substantial evidence for the influence of Jewish angelophanic motifs on its Christology.

These comments serve to introduce what I want to do in this chapter. My aim is to examine how the *Ascension of Isaiah* portrays the Beloved One and to ask whether Jewish angelology can be shown to lie behind that description. I shall argue that angelology was indeed a major source for the author who made the Beloved One a divine being, the companion of God's throne in company with the Holy Spirit (11.32-33), and yet a subordinate who undertook the descent at the divine behest (10.17–11.33) and who even joined with the angels in their worship of God (9.40-42). My belief is that more than one strand of angelology must be considered in this examination of the work's Christology. Both the development of an exalted angel in apocalyptic literature and Jewish descriptions of an angelophany are relevant sources for this investigation, and have left their mark on the apocalypse.

My study is limited to the *Ascension of Isaiah*, but I think that it has implications for other literature. The *Ascension of Isaiah* did not arise in a vacuum, but looks back on almost a century of christological reflection. Part of my task will be to show that angelomorphic ideas were a feature of first-century Christology. This constitutes valuable evidence with which to address the issue of christological origins and to rehabilitate angelology as a source for Christology, as ought to be done. The author of the *Ascension of Isaiah* was not the first Christian writer to use angelology in this way. His was by contrast a development and a making more explicit of ideas which had circulated in the first century. Such ideas endured long after the composition of the apocalypse, so that 'angelomorphic Christology' must be seen as a significant factor in the early Christian world, despite the concern which this suggestion has caused scholars in the past century.

2. The Christology of the Ascension of Isaiah

The Issue in Earlier Scholarship

Scholarship has already debated the sources of the *Ascension of Isaiah*'s Christology at some length. Fifty years ago Martin Werner suggested that the author conceived of Christ and the Spirit analogously to Origen's interpretation of Isaiah 6 as the two seraphim who attended the Father, and thus as angelic beings.[8] Werner was swiftly challenged in this view by Wilhelm Michaelis who argued that the Beloved One (unlike the Spirit) was *distinguished* from the angels in the apocalypse.[9] Michaelis also drew the conclusion that angelology contributed little to other Christology.

This exchange of opinions created a debate in studies of the *Ascension of Isaiah* and indeed in wider scholarship. We must certainly acknowledge that aspects of Werner's case were infelicitous. Werner believed that late Judaism (which he thought was typified by Dan. 7.9-14 and by the *Similitudes of Enoch*) held an 'angel-messianiology' in which the messiah was a high heavenly power who attended God. He argued that this belief was carried over into Christian literature and that Christ in Phil. 2.5-11 is a being who has been *temporarily promoted from the angel world* and who will return to that position once his task has been accomplished. This is not an accurate description of the New Testament Christology, which is characterized throughout by a belief in the uniqueness of Jesus and by the conviction that he had achieved a final and permanent mediation which made other mediators redundant.[10] Werner's overstatement of this argument meant that his whole case tended to be rejected by scholars when in fact his comments about the *Ascension of Isaiah* (and especially its dependence on Isa. 6) have much to commend them.[11] This

---

8.   Werner, *Entstehung*, pp. 327-28.
9.   W. Michaelis, *Zur Engelchristologie im Urchristentum* (Basel: Heinrich Majer, 1942), pp. 79-85.
10. This view is expressed already in Phil. 2.9-11 where the transformed Jesus is held to share the worship of God.
11. A more balanced assessment of the 'Christ as angel' motif is offered by J. Barbel, *Christos Angelos: Die Anschauung von Christus als Bote und Engel in der gelehrten und volkstümlichen Literatur des christlichen Altertums* (Theophaneia, 3; Bonn: Peter Hanstein, 1941). See also L. Stuckenbruck, *Angel Veneration and Christology: A Study in Early Judaism and in the Christology of the Apocalypse of John* (WUNT, 70; Tübingen: Mohr, 1995).

point is often ignored by those who research the historical development of Christology.

Werner's suggestion of an angelic background for the *Ascension of Isaiah*'s Christology was developed by later researchers. Daniélou devoted considerable space to it in his book on Jewish Christianity. He argued that Werner's interpretation was correctly founded, at least so far as the use of Isaiah 6 in the *Ascension of Isaiah* was concerned,[12] and he saw the influence of Michael and Gabriel traditions in the apocalypse.[13] Daniélou did not conclude that the Beloved One was an angel, however. He described a Christian use of angelology in which concepts derived from that source were used to present Christ as a mediator who *transcended* the angels through his affinity to God. This is the approach which I have termed 'angelomorphic Christology' in this book (as opposed to 'angel-Christology' which I take to imply the presentation of Christ quite literally as an angel in Werner's sense).

The Rome Conference (1981) also discussed the interpretation of the work's Christology. Simonetti argued that angelology lay in the background of the Christology but thought that it had been superseded in the moves towards an early 'Logos'-Christology in which the Beloved was regarded as the principal divine power.[14] Simonetti identified two conflicting trinitarian theologies in the apocalypse. He suggested that a hierarchical relationship between God and the Beloved was displacing the 'triangular' view which had been derived from Isaiah 6 and made the Beloved and Spirit subordinates of the Father. This conclusion diverted attention from angelology, which Simonetti tends to regard as a peripheral source in much the same way as did Michaelis.

Pesce accepted Simonetti's thesis about the angelic background of the Christology but denied that this source had been set aside in the apocalypse. Pesce contended that the Beloved One's position in the *Ascension of Isaiah* is similar in this respect to that of the Angel of the Presence in *Jubilees*, Sar Ha-Orim at Qumran and Michael in other Jewish literature.[15] This is as an exalted mediator subordinate only to God. We should no doubt add to this assessment the observation that the Beloved One is *distinguished* from these Jewish mediators because he shares the worship of God. The most recent research on the apocalypse thus

12. *Jewish Christianity*, pp. 134-40.
13. *Jewish Christianity*, pp. 134, 144.
14. In his paper, 'Note sulla cristologia', pp. 185-209.
15. In his *Isaia*, p. 68.

2. *The Christology of the Ascension of Isaiah* 77

accepts the likelihood of an angelic background for its Christology but disputes the significance of this source for the present form of the *Ascension of Isaiah*.

Debate about whether angelology influenced Christology stretches beyond the confines of *Ascension of Isaiah* studies. Many scholars agree with Michaelis that the Christians rejected it as a means of describing Jesus. An article by Talbert in 1975 concluded that the Christians distanced themselves from the 'angel' component in the Jewish mediatorial tradition, despite accepting other elements.[16] Dunn surveyed the evidence for an angelic influence on the New Testament Christology and concluded that this was negligible. He found the source appropriate only for the Johannine presentation of the Holy Spirit.[17] Hengel, too, argues that 'angel-Christology' (in the sense that Christ was an angel, for which Werner contended) was a feature only of fringe groups such as the Elkesaites and not of the New Testament as such.[18] He notes that Paul speaks rather of the messiah as 'equal with God' (Phil. 2.6) and that Hebrews reject a comparison between the Son and the angels on the grounds of his heavenly enthronement (ch. 1).[19]

These scholars focus—rightly, of course—on the distance and difference between Christ and the angels in primitive Christian literature. The New Testament never presents Jesus as an angel, and it universally criticizes any attempt to do so.[20] A formal 'angel-Christology' was found only in sectarian groups such as the Elkesaites, who believed that the Son of God was an angel 96 miles high.[21] It is wrong to impose this belief on the New Testament literature, and I have no intention of doing so here. I want rather to explore the possibility, which is mentioned by Daniélou and taken up by Pesce, that angelology exercised a more subtle influence on the *Ascension of Isaiah*. Accordig to this view, angelomorphic categories were used to present the Beloved One as a

---

16. 'Descending-Ascending Redeemer'.
17. *Christology*, p. 158.
18. *Son*, p. 85.
19. In a letter to me.
20. Heb. 1 polemicizes attempts to see Jesus in angelic terms. It is possible that the hymn in Col. 1.15-20 and other material in that letter was introduced to make the point that Jesus was a unique mediator who rendered all others redundant. The Jewish cultic background to the Colossian controversy is examined by F.O. Francis, 'Humility and Angel Worship in Col. 2.18', in *idem* (ed.), *Conflict at Colossae* (SBS, 4; Missoula, MT: Scholars Press, 1973), pp. 163-95.
21. See below for a description of the Elkesaite Christology.

mediator who transcended the angels and shared the worship of God. This involved a creative reworking of Jewish material in the light of Christian theology which allowed for the possibility of the mediator's unique position and for the worship of two heavenly powers. This is the approach to the *Ascension of Isaiah* which I shall explore in this chapter, and which I believe has implications for the study of other early Christian literature.

An Exegetical Study of the Apocalypse

To argue the case for an angelomorphic Christology in the *Ascension of Isaiah* demands a preliminary exegetical study of the apocalypse. This is in addition to the survey which I presented in Chapter 1 and it focuses specifically on the work's Christology.

One of the conclusions that I reached when researching this book is that the author of the *Ascension of Isaiah* often alludes without acknowledgment to the New Testament literature and that he weaves elements of its thought into his Christology. We find an example of this at the beginning of the apocalypse. The summary of the Beloved One's activity in 1.3-4 (E text) contains the phrase 'his angels, and his authorities, and his powers'. This phrase echoes the sequence of nouns in 1 Pet. 3.22 which describes how, after the resurrection, Jesus Christ entered heaven and was enthroned at the right hand of God with angels, authorities and powers subject to him. The concept of Christ's victory over principalities and powers is a familiar one in the New Testament (see for example Col. 1.16),[22] but of all the comparable references *only* 1 Pet. 3.22 matches the *Ascension of Isaiah* word for word at this point.

This observation might be dismissed as mere coincidence or as use of common tradition until we examine the conclusion of the *Ascension of Isaiah* in 11.23-33. This passage describes how the angels worshipped the Beloved One as he ascended to the throne of God and how they lamented their failure to recognize him in his descent. The first angels to worship him, despite the textual problem in 11.23-24, were the rebellious ones in the firmament. This passage represents the author's

---

22. This theme was studied classically by G.B. Caird, *Principalities and Powers* (Oxford: Clarendon Press, 1956). W.A. Carr argued that the concept of malevolent angels was hostile to Paul's thought (see his book, *Angels and Principalities* [SNTSMS, 42; Cambridge: Cambridge University Press, 1981]), but his thesis has not commanded wide assent.

2. *The Christology of the Ascension of Isaiah* 79

insistence that the aerial powers who had once been insubordinate (10.12-13) had been made to recognize God and the Beloved One as the true cosmic authorities (cf. 10.15-16). The *Ascension of Isaiah* uses this tradition to make the point that all cosmic rivals had been defeated (11.32-33), which has implications on the author's social level. The sequence of thought in *Asc. Isa.* 11.23-33, which involves the offering of worship and by implication angelic surrender, is strikingly similar to 1 Pet. 3.22. This makes it unlikely that the affinity to 1 Pet. 3.22 in *Asc. Isa.* 1.3 is coincidental. I think, on the contrary, that the author of the *Ascension of Isaiah* knew 1 Pet. 3.22 and that he modelled aspects of his Christology on that passage.[23] It suggested the idea of victory over angels which this author developed through his use of the seven-storied cosmology.

We must also mention the influence of 1 Cor. 2.8 and Col. 2.15 on the *Ascension of Isaiah*. The apocalypse gives signs that its author (or his source) knew 1 Cor. 2.8 in 11.19, where it says that the Jews did not know who Jesus was when they delivered him to the 'ruler' (i.e. Pilate). This reading of 1 Cor. 2.8 set Paul's view in a cosmological framework in which the hidden descent assumes prominence. This is presented as the explanation of why the Beloved went unrecognized on earth. The fact that a New Testament idea is being developed justifies the claim that what we find in the *Ascension of Isaiah* is an early form of 'exegesis'.

There are affinities too between *Ascension of Isaiah* 10 and Col. 2.15. *Asc. Isa.* 10.14, on my interpretation (which I explained in Chapter 1), implies that the moment of Beliar's defeat was the Beloved One's death on the cross (despite the fact that the thought is elliptical at this point). This idea is similar to that in Col. 2.15, where Paul states that on the cross God had 'disarmed the principalities and powers and made a public example of them, triumphing over them in him [Christ]'. My conclusion is that the author's meditation on this passage helped to shape the form of his Christology and that once again he wove an existing idea into a new and more complex mythological pattern. The author's tendency to regard the New Testament Christology as authoritative but to set it in a wider framework is a characteristic feature of the *Ascension of Isaiah*. His use of the New Testament literature must be acknowledged in

---

23. This is an early example of the influence which the New Testament literature was coming to exercise on the post-apostolic writers. One should add that the exegetical interests of this author's circle, which are so evident in the apocalypse, were receptive to the study of this literature.

company with his more obvious use of the Hebrew Bible (cf. 4.21-22).

This preliminary observation introduces my exegetical study of the apocalypse. In what follows I shall isolate the evidence to support my contention that Jewish angelology was a source for the author's Christology. The two visionary summaries in ch. 1 show the tenor of the Christology when they anticipate the Beloved One's saving intervention. The first summary (1.3-4) expects the defeat of the 'prince of this world'. The second (1.5), when corrected as by Knibb, describes the Beloved One's descent from heaven and his 'transformation' into human likeness. The beginning of the apocalypse thereby introduces the two themes which are most characteristic of the *Ascension of Isaiah*'s Christology.

The First Vision incorporates a binitarian theology; that is to say, it acknowledges the existence of two heavenly powers. The reference to the Beloved One as 'the Lord' in 4.14 presents him in divine terms, as does the probable use of the ὁ θεὸς title in the lost Greek original of 9.5. This places the apocalypse in line with the theological conviction of first-century Christianity about the worship of Jesus. The distinctive feature of the *Ascension of Isaiah*, which is especially obvious in the Second Vision, is the second-century development of this binitarian perspective in a trinitarian direction with the references to the worship of the three divine beings.[24] In the First Vision, however, the trinitarian perspective is implicit rather than explicit. The author is concerned mainly to describe the saving activity of the Beloved One.

The First Vision thus presents the Beloved One analogously to God. This is evident from the description of the resurrection in 3.16-17. This passage describes how the Beloved One left the tomb on the shoulders of Michael and the angel of the Holy Spirit. Daniélou is right to relate it to the conventions of Jewish *merkabah* mysticism.[25] On this interpretation, 3.16-17 alludes to the deity's seated position to make the Beloved One a divine being who was attended by the highest angels, with the implication that he sat in the place of God. There are important parallels to this in Jewish throne mysticism, not least perhaps in the description of

---

24. Trinitarianism is a feature of some first-century writings (for example Mt. 28.19) but the *worship* of the three divine beings is a significantly new theological statement in the *Ascension of Isaiah*. The first-century evidence is examined by A.W. Wainwright, *The Trinity in the New Testament* (London: SPCK, 1962).

25. *Jewish Christianity*, pp. 254-55. Norelli, in his article 'La resurezzione', argues that the Spirit is a σύζυγος of Christ.

2. The Christology of the Ascension of Isaiah

Moses which is found in the *Exagoge* of Ezekiel the Tragedian (see below). *Asc. Isa.* 3.16-17 is an early account of the resurrection which makes the point that the Beloved One transcended all other heavenly beings except God. The appearance of this passage within the Jesus traditions in the *Ascension of Isaiah*, despite the fact that it has no parallel in the canonical Gospels, raises the possibility that it was derived from the oral tradition and that it thus had a history which predates even the Gospels. If this is so, then the *Ascension of Isaiah* shows that Jewish *merkabah* mysticism was from an early date recognized as a significant source for Christology. This passage should be set beside the synoptic transfiguration narrative and Rev. 1.13-14, both of which draw on Jewish apocalyptic traditions to present the heavenly Christ as a second divine being.

The description of the parousia in 4.12, 14 expects that the Beloved One will discharge the eschatological activity of God. The author follows Paul (in 1 Thess. 3.13 and especially in 2 Thess. 1.7) in applying Zech. 14.5 to the parousia. Paul himself had probably been influenced in this use of the prophetic text by earlier Christian tradition. The *Ascension of Isaiah* follows Paul in giving the mediator the title 'Lord', which derives from the LXX source but which is here applied to a divine being subordinate to the Most High God. The Beloved One's anticipated destruction of Beliar in 4.14-18 is thus presented as a divine act which will be accomplished by God's subordinate.

At the start of the Second Vision, 7.7-8 promises Isaiah a vision of two heavenly powers: 'one greater than me' (the *angelus interpres*) and 'the Father of the one who is greater'.[26] This promise associates the Beloved One with God and distinguishes him from other heavenly beings. It expresses in visionary terms what the pre-Pauline formula in 1 Cor. 8.6 had said about the heavenly Lord in the language of the Jewish Wisdom tradition. The E text of *Asc. Isa.* 7.7-8 makes a comparison at this point between the Beloved One and Isaiah's companion

---

26. God is called the Beloved One's 'Father' in this reference. 'Father' is used in two senses in the *Ascension of Isaiah*. The first is God's fatherhood to the Beloved, apparently in a unique sense. This is found for instance in 10.6 in the words 'the Father of the Lord'. *Asc. Isa.* 8.18, however, uses the phrase 'Primal Father' to describe God's supremacy over the cosmic system. *Asc. Isa.* 7.7-8 uses the term 'Father' in the first sense and this distinguishes the Beloved from the angels. On the use of 'Father' in the *Ascension of Isaiah* see also Simonetti, 'Nota sulla cristologia', pp. 197-99.

angel when the angel describes him as 'one *greater than* me'. This does not mean that the Beloved was an angel (the *Ascension of Isaiah* offers no support for that view) but it does indicate that a comparison with the angels was felt appropriate to describe the Beloved One. Even in S we find the comment *Et majorem me videbis*, although L2 is apparently different.[27] The phrasing of E shows that the lost Greek original had an angelomorphic Christology in which the Beloved One was described as God's most glorious subordinate in a way which presented him analogously with other heavenly beings.

Isaiah enters the first heaven in 7.13-17. He sees an unoccupied throne which is surrounded by angels who offer the heavenly liturgy.[28] Their worship is said to be directed to 'the praise of the [One who sits in] the seventh heaven...and to his Beloved'. This passage stands in a tradition of Christology (cf. Phil. 2.9-11) but once again that tradition is developed, in this case by the offering of worship to the Beloved One *before* his descent from the seventh heaven. The *Ascension of Isaiah* thereby acknowledges that worship of the Beloved must be eternal rather than only post-resurrectional. This represents a step towards the *homoousion* formula which came to dominate later Christology (although of course in many other respects the apocalypse does not share the language of the later christological settlement).

Chapter 8 includes a prediction of the descent. The angel tells Isaiah that he will see the Beloved One descend through all the heavens 'until he resembles your appearance and likeness' (8.10). This again supports the view that the descent involves the heavenly mediator's appearance as a human person, so that the themes of the hidden descent and of transformation into human likeness receive a considerable emphasis.

Chapter 9 contains substantial evidence for the work's Christology. Isaiah is challenged when he tries to enter the seventh heaven (9.1) but admitted when the Beloved One gives him a heavenly garment. The Beloved One is then described by a catena of titles:

> And the one who turned to you, this is your LORD, the LORD, the LORD Christ, who is to be called in the world Jesus, but you cannot hear his name until you have come up from this body (9.5 E, as translated by Knibb).

27. Much depends on unravelling the textual corruption at this point. This issue must await the new edition.

28. L2 and S place an angel on this throne.

2. The Christology of the Ascension of Isaiah

With this we may for convenience compare the other major title cluster in E, that in 10.7 (at the beginning of the Beloved One's commission): 'And I heard the voice of the Most High, the Father of my LORD, as he said to my LORD Christ, who will be called Jesus...' In both references L2 and S offer shorter and significantly different versions of the clusters: *Et praecipiens est filius Dei, et nomen eius non potes audire donec de carne exibis* (9.5, L2); *Et post haec audivi vocem aeterni dicentem domino filio...* (10.7, L2). Only the *dominus* of 10.7 (L2) agrees with E's version of that verse. The L2 text of 9.5 is quite different and it makes 'Son (of God)' a prominent title when this is used only sparingly in E. Although we cannot be certain that E represents a *precise* rendering of the Greek, there is support for its version of the clusters in GL 2.37:[29]

ἤκουσα τῆς φωνῆς τοῦ μεγάλου καὶ ἐπηρμένου θεοῦ καὶ πατρὸς τοῦ κυρίου ἡμῶν Ἰησοῦ Χριστοῦ...λεγούσης τῷ κυρίῳ μου καὶ Χριστῷ, ὃς κληθήσεται Ἰησοῦς ἐν τῷ κόσμῳ τούτῳ.

The GL looks like a conflation of *both* passages from E. The basic framework is provided by 10.7, but the phrase ἐν τῷ κόσμῳ τούτῳ has been introduced from 9.5. This evidence confirms that 'Jesus', 'Lord' and 'Christ' belong in a Greek text of the *Ascension of Isaiah* and that E is essentially a reliable tradent at this point. This casts suspicion on the texts of L2 and S and demonstrates their tendency towards abbreviation (and in this case towards doctrinal correction) on which Bori has also commented.

The reliability of E in 9.5 and 10.7 can be corroborated on internal grounds. A change from the text of E to that of S/L2 is easy to understand given the more precise definition which Christology achieved in the patristic period, and the dominance of the *filius* title there. Emendation in the opposite direction, however, is difficult to support. It would demand explaining why E omitted 'Son' 10.7 when it uses that title in 8.25 and 9.14, and why—notably in 9.5—it should have introduced vagueness and repetition when the original was perfectly clear. By far the better explanation is that E offers the (more) original reading. The title clusters were adapted by the parent of L2 and S because they were thought to represent an imprecise Christology. This

---

29. The significance of GL 2.37 is noted by Norelli, 'Sulla pneumatologica dell'*Ascensione di Isaia*', p. 221 n. 21; and by Knibb in Charlesworth (ed.), *Old Testament Pseudepigrapha*, II, p. 169, n. w.

was one in which the distinction between 'earthly' and 'heavenly' titles which was suggested by the phrase 'called in the world Jesus' supported a view of the incarnation as Christ's temporary manifestation, which (although it was a feature of the original apocalypse) conflicted with the emerging 'two natures' Christology and had docetic tendencies.[30]

Isaiah enters the seventh heaven in 9.6 and sees Adam, Enoch and the other righteous standing beside their heavenly thrones. They have been 'stripped of [their] robes of the flesh' and stand 'in their robes of above...like the angels who stand there in great glory' (9.8-9). Isaiah asks why they have received their robes but have not ascended their thrones or donned their crowns. He is told that this is because the Beloved One has not yet made his saving journey (9.12). 9.13 introduces a further prediction of the descent. The author states that this will happen 'in the last days' and that 'the Lord' will be called 'Christ after he had descended and become like you in form'. This passage states further that after the Lord has descended people will 'think that he is flesh and a man' (9.13). L2 and S have reworked this section to remove the implication that the flesh is merely an appearance. They state only that 'the Son of God...will be like you in form'. Again, however, the E text demonstrates the original author's understanding of the hidden descent and the Beloved One's appearance *in the form* of Jesus which I have held to be characteristic of his Christology.

The author states that the 'god of this world' (i.e. Beliar) will 'stretch out [his hand against the Son]'. He adds that people will set hands on him and hang him on a tree, 'not knowing who he is' (9.14). Here too there are allusions to New Testament literature. The 'god of this world' features in 2 Cor. 4.4, and he makes three appearances under a similar title in John's Gospel.[31] The author derived this title from the New Testament literature. The notion that the Beloved One was crucified in

---

30. 'Two natures' christology added to the statement that Christ was 'truly God and truly human' (*Vere deus, vere homo*—a phrase which was coined by Irenaeus, *Adv. Haer.* 4.6.7) the belief that he was 'one and the same' in both natures. See W. Pannenberg, *Jesus: God and Man* (ET London: SCM Press, 1968), pp. 283-84.

31. Jn 12.31, 14.30 and 16.11. The significance of these references is examined by A.F. Segal, 'Ruler of this World: Attitudes about Mediator Figures and the Importance of Sociology for Self-Definition', in E.P. Sanders (ed.), *Jewish and Christian Self-Definition* (London: SCM Press, 1985), II, pp. 245-68. Once again the *Ascension of Isaiah* represents a development of the first-century view when it identifies the 'king of this world' with the Romans and then by implication with all the human agencies whom the author deemed to be opposed to him.

2. The Christology of the Ascension of Isaiah

ignorance of his identity recalls 1 Cor. 2.8; the laying of hands on Jesus Mt. 26.50; and his death by hanging on a tree Gal. 3.13 (cf. also 1 Pet. 2.24; Acts 5.30; 10.39). This verse thus represents a catena of New Testament allusions.[32] The author further states that the Beloved One's descent will be 'concealed even from the heavens, so that it will not be known who he is' (9.15).[33]

He goes on to say that, when the Lord has plundered the angel of death, he will rise (literally, 'ascend') again on the third day and remain in the world for 545 days (9.16). L2 (similarly S) includes the words 'and he will seize the prince of death, and will plunder him, and will crush all his powers, and will rise on the third day'. The E text offers early evidence for what would later be called the doctrine of the 'descent into hell' in which the departed were freed from their imprisonment there; Daniélou sees the author drawn by a reading of the comprehensive cosmology of Phil. 2.10 to include Sheol within the sphere of the Beloved One's descent and victory.[34] L2 and S have developed this view to indicate that in his descent to hell the Beloved One will destroy the devil. Many of the righteous will ascend with the Lord, says 9.17. These will receive their robes, thrones and crowns when he has ascended into the seventh heaven (9.18). This was of course a realized situation from the author's perspective. Readers were invited to assume that Enoch and the others had ascended their thrones at the moment when the Beloved occupied his, at the conclusion of his appearance as Jesus (see 11.32). This is not just a christological statement but also a demonstration that a heavenly throne awaited them after the millenarian kingdom (cf. 4.17).

In 9.27 Isaiah sees the Beloved One. The Beloved is described in E as 'one standing [there] whose glory surpassed that of all, and his glory was great and wonderful'. All the righteous and angels approach him and worship; Isaiah is said to join with them. The Beloved One is then called 'the Lord of all the praises which you have seen' (9.32). This

---

32. It is possible that these allusions had already been collected in the form of a Florilegium.
33. There is a parallel to this in *Ign. Eph.* 19.1: 'The virginity of Mary and her giving birth eluded the ruler of this age, likewise also the death of the Lord—three mysteries of a cry which were done in the stillness of God' (Schoedel's translation). Ignatius however has no tradition of a hidden descent to match the *Ascension of Isaiah*.
34. *Jewish Christianity*, p. 234. I discuss the descent to hell further in Chapter 4.

passage recalls the language of 7.7-8 and it again represents an angelomorphic Christology. The phrase '[his] glory surpassed that of all' represents a comparison with the angels despite the fact that the title 'Lord' implies the attribute of divinity. The parent of L2 and S modified this view by removing the comparative: *Et conversus vidi dominum in gloria magna*. As in other passages, it is likely that E represents the more original text. The fact that it constitutes the harder reading in 9.27 confirms that it preserves an angelomorphic Christology which stood in the Greek apocalypse.

In this connection we must consider the three references to Michael which L2 and S include in ch. 9. Before he sees the robes and the crowns of the righteous Isaiah asks:

> *Quis est iste praeeminens omnes angelos in gloria sua? Et respondens dixit mihi: Iste est magnus angelus Michael deprecans semper pro humanitate et humilitate* (9.23, L2).

Michael then worships the Beloved One: *Et Michael appropinquans adoravit, et cum eo omnes angeli adoraverunt et cantaverunt* (9.29). Michael also worships God in 9.42: *Et cum eis Michael et angeli omnes adoraverunt et cantaverunt*.[35] E has no such references to Michael in the Second Vision, but 3.16-17 (E) does call Michael 'the chief of the holy angels' in a close approximation to this view. Given the tendency of L2 and S to emend the text elsewhere (for example in 9.5; 10.7), we must suspect that these references to Michael are secondary to the original writing and that they were introduced to remove the angelomorphic basis of its Christology. This was done by placing *Michael* in the position in which the original author had placed the Beloved One. The L2 description of Michael in 9.23 as *praeeminens (omnes) angelos* does this by transferring the property of being the all-surpassing angel from the Beloved One in the E text of 9.27 to a named archangel to remove the possibility that the Beloved One could be construed in that position. This shows the interests of the later redactor, and the fact that textual interference must be suspected further emphasizes the angelomorphic character of the E text.

The textual problem in 9.30 has christological implications. E says that the Beloved was transformed to resemble an angel, but L2 and S read the first person singular at this point to indicate that *Isaiah* was transformed in this way. E here constitutes the harder reading and makes the

---

35. All references are from L2; S is similar.

2. *The Christology of the Ascension of Isaiah*

better sense. Since Isaiah has been transformed on entering the seventh heaven (9.1), he does not need further transformation in 9.30. The thought is that the *Beloved One* changes his appearance to resemble an angel. This is to aid the prophet's vision and it is effectively the first stage in his descent. The fact that the angelic form is *assumed* is an indication that in this author's view the Beloved One ordinarily transcended the angels. The author nevertheless found angelic language helpful to describe his mediation and descent.

The worship of the angel of the Holy Spirit in 9.33-36 further defines the Christology. The Spirit is described as 'another glorious [person] who was like him' (i.e. the Beloved One). 9.33 says that the Spirit 'was not transformed to accord with their form' (the reference is to the angels). This was because he was already (and evidently permanently) in angelic likeness, as 3.16-17 and 7.23 show. Like the Beloved One, the Spirit nevertheless receives worship from the angels. He stands on the Beloved's left (in what represents a subordinate position). Both are portrayed as standing before God, in distinction from the concluding passage (11.32-33) where they sit on heavenly thrones. This is not so much an inconsistency in the theology as a demonstration of their subordination to God, which is emphasized again in 9.40 where both the Beloved One and the angel of the Holy Spirit are made to worship the Great Glory. This subordinationism was inherited from the New Testament (cf. 1 Cor. 15.28; Jn 14.28) and my belief is that it is *developed* in the *Ascension of Isaiah* by the insistence that these divine beings must offer *worship*. Worship was an angelic function.[36] The author ranked the Beloved One and the angel of the Holy Spirit with the angels in this respect because he wanted to retain a form of monotheism in a context where the alternative was to describe three equal but independent divinities. This was a problem which later writers would overcome by the notion of 'consubstantiality'. We thus find in *Ascension of Isaiah* 9 a portrait of the Beloved One as a divine being who transcended the angels but for whom some angelic functions were not felt inappropriate despite the fact of his worship by the angels.

Asc. Isa. 10.7-16 describes the Beloved One's commission by God to descend from the seventh heaven. This passage displays a strong subordinationist interest in terms of the Beloved One's obedient response to his charge. No previous Christian source had commented so explicitly

---

36. For evidence of this angelic function in apocalyptic literature, see for example *1 En.* 61.9-13; *2 En.* 20.3-4; *Apoc. Abr.* 10.9; and *T. Job* 48–50.

on Christ's heavenly commission by God, nor on the hidden descent.[37] The *Ascension of Isaiah* develops the christological tradition in this. The author was influenced in this development by reflection on the angelophany, which was an essentially Jewish concept (see below).

The Beloved One is instructed to descend through all the heavens as far as Sheol (but not to Haguel, the place of perdition), and to disguise his appearance so that he resembles the angels through whom he passes. The commission has it that none of these will recognize that 'you [are] LORD with me of the seven heavens and of their angels' (10.8-11) until the moment of the ascension. 10.7-16 makes no reference to the mediator's appearance as Jesus. However, this is clearly presupposed by the rest of the Vision. The mythological interest has briefly displaced the interest in the human Jesus at this point, but in terms of the wider apocalypse this is essentially a question of perspective. The *Ascension of Isaiah* here briefly anticipates, but without reaching, the Gnostic silence about a real incarnation for the Saviour. In this sense it represents a bridge between primitive Christianity and Gnosticism, and shows one of the ways in which a Christian mediatorial interest was developed in the early second century.

The author says that the Beloved One's identity is to remain hidden until

> with the voice of the heavens I summon you, and their angels and their lights, and when I lift up [my voice] to the sixth heaven, that you may judge and destroy the princes and the angels and the gods of that world, and the world which is ruled by them, for they have denied me and said, 'We alone are, and there is no one besides us' (10.12-13).

Here we find the heart and the meaning of the Second Vision's saving drama. The moment of destruction and judgment is not specified, but I have argued that it is disclosed by the words: 'And *afterwards* you shall ascend from the gods of death to your place...' (10.14). This phrase denotes the resurrection-ascension and indicates that the judgment of Beliar and his associates takes place, in all probability, on the cross (cf. Col. 2.15). The revelatory element in the *Ascension of Isaiah* consists in

---

37. Jn 3.7 and 1 Tim. 1.15 allow for the Son's 'sending into the world', but there is no precise analogy for this report of the commission in first-century literature. It seems likely that this was the author's own creation. I think that it was modelled on a mediator's commission which was a familiar theme of Jewish literature (see below).

2. The Christology of the Ascension of Isaiah

an apocalyptic presentation of the cross as the moment when demonic forces are defeated.

The second half of ch. 10 describes how the Beloved One responds to this instruction. From the fifth heaven and downwards he appears as an angel, and supplies the correct password to the heavenly gatekeepers in order to conceal his identity (10.24). When he passes through the firmament, the angels of the air are too busy to notice him because of their civil warfare (10.29-31). Near the bottom of his descent he appears as Jesus. Here L2 and S have the shorter form of text which omits the traditions about Jesus found in E. I have argued that these stood in the original *Ascension of Isaiah* and that S and L2 represent a redaction of the apocalypse at this point. As in the *Epistula Apostolorum* and the eighth *Sibylline Oracle*, the E text describes how the Beloved One incarnated himself in Mary's womb in what appears to represent speculation about the conception of Jesus.[38]

The Jesus traditions in E have what I have termed a naïvely docetic quality. By this I mean that they give Jesus superhuman properties but that they do not question the reality of his death, as some Gnostic theologians (notably Basileides) would do. This naïve docetism reflects the tension between the humanity of Jesus and the presentation of his life within the scheme that is determined by the Beloved One's hidden descent and transformation into human likeness. The birth of Jesus is said to have taken Mary by surprise after a two-month pregnancy (11.8). There is a further docetic element in 11.17, where it is implied that the infant Jesus took food to escape recognition as a heavenly visitor rather than from physical need. This docetism, which must be distinguished from anything that we find in the New Testament including the Christology of John's Gospel,[39] has its roots in Jewish angelology and

---

38. See my discussion of these texts below. I shall argue that the *Ascension of Isaiah* might be considered as a source for this later literature.

39. E. Käsemann (*The Testament of Jesus* [ET; London: SCM Press, 1966]) used the phrase 'naïve docetism' to describe the Johannine Christology (pp. 26, 66, 70). By this he meant that the Evangelist offered a Christology in which the tensions between the human Jesus and the heavenly mediator had not been fully identified. The *Ascension of Isaiah* makes a useful exegetical foil for John because the Gospel lacks any of the docetic information which is presented by the apocalypse (notably the abnormal pregnancy and the strange view of the suckling). The term 'naïve docetism' is in many ways more appropriate to the thought-world of the *Ascension of Isaiah* than to the Christology of John when this information is considered. The *Ascension of Isaiah* however agrees with Jn 19.34 that Jesus really died on the cross.

specifically in the view, typified by Tob. 12.19, that a heavenly mediator only *appeared* to eat and drink when he was on earth. After the resurrection the Beloved remains on earth 'many days' (11.21), but there is no suggestion that he imparts esoteric teaching during that period (cf. 9.16).

The ascension is described twice in this part of the apocalypse. The first description (11.22) is connected with the commission of the twelve disciples by the Beloved One. This was resourced by the incorporated Gospel traditions. The second description (11.23-33) is more mythological and shows signs of influence by 1 Pet. 3.22. According to 11.23-24 the Beloved One ascends into the firmament where he is worshipped by the angels, since his angelic disguise has been removed. The textual problem in 11.24-25 (E), by which the Beloved moves directly from the firmament to the second heaven, should not be allowed to conceal the probability, which is supported by 10.16 ('and then the princes and the powers of that world will worship you'), that Beliar and his cohorts are the first to offer him worship, as the E text states. This is a sign of their subjection, which contrasts strikingly with their earlier arrogance.

The Beloved One takes his seat at the right hand of God (11.32). This passage contrasts with 9.27-36 where the Beloved and Spirit stand before God. This notion of heavenly ascension and enthronement was derived from first-century Christology and ultimately from the interpretation of Ps. 110.1, which had become a popular proof-text in the New Testament literature.[40] The apocalypse closes with a picture of the three enthroned divinities, which develops the view found in 1 Pet. 3.22 by including the Spirit within this image of enthronement.

This short study has drawn attention to the main features of the *Ascension of Isaiah*'s Christology. It seems that we are dealing with a development of the ideas found in the New Testament literature. This sense of development is evident in the way in which the author alludes to New Testament ideas but weaves them into a broader picture whose framework is determined by his cosmology. The two motifs which characterize the work's Christology are those of the Beloved One's hidden descent and of his transformation into human likeness. These

---

The author's view of the reality of the Beloved One's death was an important reason why the *Ascension of Isaiah* was valued by mainstream Christian writers (see below).

40. On the use of Ps. 110.1 in early Christian literature see the literature which I mentioned in n. 215 in Chapter 1.

2. The Christology of the Ascension of Isaiah

determine what is said about Jesus and about salvation in the *Ascension of Isaiah*. The work's docetism is a consequence of this view.

This assessment of the material gives impetus to the suggestion that Jewish angelology contributed to the the *Ascension of Isaiah*'s Christology. I have already mentioned the analogy between *Asc. Isa.* 11.17 and Tob. 12.19. A substantial analogy with angelology is provided by the high estimation of angels as mediators in Jewish apocalyptic literature and by Jewish descriptions of the angelophany. This material must now be examined in order to isolate those strands of angelology which have the best claims to be considered an influence on the Christology of the *Ascension of Isaiah* in this respect. This chapter will isolate the relevant evidence and show how it impinges on the interpretation of the *Ascension of Isaiah*.

The Jewish Background of Christology

To test this hypothesis we must examine the nature of the material from which Christology was constructed, and then the earliest development of Christology in the first century CE.

Classical material should be considered first. This is sometimes overlooked in the study of Christian origins. Thus J.D.G. Dunn's book *Christology in the Making* tended to ignore the pagan parallels to Christian incarnational claims, particularly the stories about the gods assuming human form, for which he was taken to task by C.R. Holladay.[41] I do not want to ignore such material myself, but my research indicates that a Jewish background exercised a much greater influence on the *Ascension of Isaiah* than a classical one. The pagan parallels seem altogether more remote given our work's affinity to the Jewish apocalyptic tradition.

The relevant classical material can be presented briefly. Ovid tells the story of how Jupiter and Mercury visited Baucis and Philemon disguised as human beings (*Met.* 8.626-721). Something of this understanding may be reflected in Acts 14.12 where Barnabas and Paul are hailed as gods. Vergil's *Fourth Eclogue* describes how a child prodigy was 'sent down from high heaven'. In Horace's *Odes* 1.2 Mercury is again said to

---

41. C.R. Holladay, 'New Testament Christology: A Consideration of Dunn's *Christology in the Making*', *Semeia* 30 (1984), pp. 64-82.

have assumed human form.[42] This diverse material has a superficial similarity to the description of the hidden descent which is a prominent feature of the *Ascension of Isaiah*. Despite this similarity, we must not ignore some important *differences* between the *Ascension of Isaiah* and this pagan mythology. The christological title 'Beloved One' seems deliberately archaic and this, together with many other Semitizing phrases, indicates that the author worked within a Jewish orbit which has no precise pagan parallel. His theology moreover represents a binitarianism in which the Beloved is held to be the subordinate of the Most High God. This represents an implicit sense of distance from pagan polytheism in which a variety of gods were venerated. Distance from pagan ideas is suggested also by the setting of the apocalypse in its situation of conflict with Rome. In ch. 4 the author turns to a distinctively Jewish idea (the angelophany) to describe the Beloved's epiphany rather than to pagan stories about the gods. One should no doubt add the point that the author would hardly have admitted pagan ideas when he was at pains to resist the demands of pagan religion. This suggests that a Jewish background was more significant for the work's Christology even when we acknowledge that the classical parallels must not be dismissed.

Jewish apocalyptic literature presents an extensive body of evidence for belief in heavenly mediators.[43] The 'Jewish mediatorial tradition', as I shall call it, falls into three broad divisions. These are beliefs about Wisdom, beliefs about the transformation of human beings and beliefs about exalted angels.[44] That the Wisdom tradition helped the rise of Christology has been shown by a number of scholars and the case can be regarded as proven.[45] There is also agreement that beliefs about the

42. Further classical material is offered by Talbert in his 'Descending-Ascending Redeemer'.
43. On this issue see Weber, *System*, and Bousset, *Judentums* (but also Moore's criticism in 'Christian Writers' and 'Intermediaries'); Talbert, 'Descending-Ascending Redeemer'; Segal, *Two Powers*, pp. 84-97, 135-46; Rowland, *Open Heaven*, pp. 94-113; *idem*, *Christian Origins* (London: SPCK, 1985), pp. 35-39; Bühner, *Gesandte*, pp. 322-73; J.A. Fossum, *The Name of God and the Angel of the Lord: Samaritan and Jewish Concepts of Intermediation and the Origin of Gnosticism* (WUNT, 36; Tübingen: Mohr, 1985), pp. 192-238, 257-338; S. Kim, *The Origin of Paul's Gospel* (WUNT, 4; Tübingen: Mohr, 1981), pp. 205-223; and Hurtado, *One God*, pp. 17-92.
44. I have followed Hurtado's division of these categories.
45. See for example Hamerton-Kelly, *Pre-Existence*; R.A. Piper, *Wisdom in*

2. The Christology of the Ascension of Isaiah

transformation of exceptional people like Moses and Enoch stand behind some well-known early Christian passages in which Jesus is presented as an exalted mediator (with the difference about Christian theology already noted).[46] It is often said, however, that the Christians turned away from angelology as a source for Christology, as for instance by the scholars whom I reported at the beginning of the chapter. This conclusion, I think, must be questioned when we acknowledge the different facets which angelology assumed in the postbiblical period and when we consider the evidence of a text like the *Ascension of Isaiah*.

Examination of the Jewish mediatorial tradition as a whole shows the wide-ranging nature of the material from which early Christian beliefs about Jesus were constructed. It indicates that any study of christological origins must be broadly based. Before presenting the evidence, I must note that there has been considerable debate concerning what it reveals about Jewish theology. It has been argued both that we find there a widening of the monotheistic concept in the direction of an incipient binitarianism, and that this conclusion is an over-evaluation of the evidence which rather depicts the supreme God attended by a variety of assistants. It is not my purpose to offer a detailed review of this problem in this chapter, for my interest lies in the way in which this material was interpreted by the early Christians. Nevertheless, a brief assessment must be made of the issue since it concerns the question of how far Christian theology represented a *new* form of religious belief when compared with its Jewish parent.

It is true to say that in the portrait of Moses in the *Exagoge* of Ezekiel

---

the *Q Tradition: The Aphoristic Teachings of Jesus* (SNTSMS, 61; Cambridge: Cambridge University Press, 1989); M.J. Suggs, *Wisdom, Christology and Law in Matthew's Gospel* (Cambridge, MA; Harvard University Press, 1970); S.L. Davies, *The Gospel of Thomas and Christian Wisdom* (New York: Seabury, 1983); E.J. Schnabel, *Law and Wisdom from Ben Sira to Paul* (WUNT, 16; Tübingen: Mohr, 1985); Dunn, *Christology*, pp. 163-212; and the collection of essays edited by R.L. Wilken, *Aspects of Wisdom in Judaism and Christianity* (Notre Dame: University of Notre Dame Press, 1975).

46. W.A. Meeks has commented on the way in which Moses is used as a foil for Jesus in the Fourth Gospel in his book *The Prophet King* (NovTSup, 14; Leiden: Brill, 1967), esp. pp. 297-301. The likelihood that 1 Pet. 3.19-22 dialogues with Jewish Enoch traditions is explored by B. Reicke, *The Disobedient Spirits and Christian Baptism* (Lund: Ejnar Munksgaard, 1946) pp. 100-103; and by W.J. Dalton, *Christ's Proclamation to the Spirits: A Study of Peter 3.18–4.6* (Rome: Pontifical Biblical Institute, 1965), pp. 163-76.

the Tragedian and of the angel which is seen by the visionary in Dan. 10.5-6 (both of these texts are described below) we have a figure of exceptional stature. On the other hand, despite his exalted position, this figure is never said to be *worshipped* in Jewish literature.[47] Worship is a reliable guide to religious belief because it shows what powers pass for divine in a particular faith-community. This Jewish attitude to the angel is substantially different from Christian worship of the exalted Jesus. Although I shall return to this problem later in the chapter, I want to state firmly at the beginning that the worship of Jesus *distinguished* Christian theology from Jewish theology. Angels were never worshipped in Judaism. The worship of Jesus was a new religious development introduced by early Christianity. This distinction is pertinent for the assessment of the question of whether there was an 'incipient binitarianism' in pre-Christian literature. Although some Jewish texts allow mediators to occupy the throne of God, and even to be called by the divine title, these mediators are never said to be worshipped in company with God in the extant literature. This difference from Judaism must be duly acknowledged when evaluating the birth of Christology. If 'binitarianism' is taken to mean the *worship* of two heavenly powers, then pre-Christian Judaism was not binitarian. If, however, our interest turns to the exceptional position which some mediators attained in Jewish apocalyptic literature, then we do find a pattern that is analogous to early Christology but without the offering of worship. This is an issue to which we shall return throughout this chapter.

Wisdom and Word Traditions

The first and best-known expression of the Jewish mediatorial tradition is its Wisdom or Logos strand. This strand exercised a (by now) well-documented effect on Christology.[48] It enjoyed a considerable history

---

47. Both Bauckham ('Worship of Jesus') and Hurtado (*One God*) have made this point.

48. On Jewish Wisdom speculation see H.J. Hermisson, *Studien zur israelitischen Spruchweisheit* (Neukirchen–Vluyn: Neukirchener Verlag, 1968); M. Küchler, *Frühjüdische Weisheitstraditionen: zum Fortgang weisheitlichen Denkens im Bereich des frühjüdischen Jahweglaubens* (Göttingen: Vandenhoeck & Ruprecht, 1979); B. Lang, *Frau Weisheit: Deutung einer biblischen Gestalt* (Düsseldorf: Patmos Verlag, 1978); D. Morgan, *Wisdom in Old Testament Traditions* (Oxford: Basil Blackwell, 1981); L.G. Perdue, *Wisdom and Cult* (Missoula, MT: Scholars Press, 1977); H.H. Schmid, *Wesen und Geschichte der Weisheit* (Berlin: Topelmann,

2. The Christology of the Ascension of Isaiah

before the rise of Christianity. The book of Job reveals a view of divine Wisdom which is much less comprehensive than in later writers. For Job Wisdom was an undefinable entity whose origins and operations could not be discerned by human enquiry. It might be spoken of only in negative terms (28.12-19). Its origins were hidden from humanity (28.21) and bound up with the fear of the Lord (28.28). Wisdom is here neither the heavenly being nor the creative agent which it is in later Jewish literature. As von Rad observes, it is defined rather in terms of the natural order of things,[49] the results of which could be seen while the governing principles remained hidden.

We find a different view of Wisdom in the book of Proverbs. Prov. 8.22 (along with Prov. 3.19) became a valuable proof-text for Christian writers since it discusses the question of Wisdom's origins.[50] Prov. 8.22 says that God created Wisdom as the beginning of his work. This passage enshrines a form of primordial speculation which displays significant differences from the Genesis creation account. Proverbs says that Wisdom was there before the beginning of the earth (8.23-29): she assisted God in his work of creation, perhaps even taking the role of confidante (8.29). It is not accidental that Wisdom should here be presented as a female figure, *Hokhmah*, a feminine aspect which is preserved in the LXX translation *Sophia*. The gender of the noun offers a clue to the origin of these beliefs about Wisdom. Norman Whybray observes that behind the passage stands a dialogue with the Mesopotamian love goddess Ishtar–Astarte.[51] Other scholars compare Israelite Wisdom with the cult of Isis in Egypt.[52] As with many cases of religious assimilation, it seems that the Jewish author was presenting an indigenous figure in the terms suggested by a rival religion. The desired characteristics, when they were applied to a native figure, allowed the

---

1966); G. von Rad, *Wisdom in Israel* (ET London: SCM Press, 1972); and U. Wilckens, *Weisheit und Torah* (Tübingen: Mohr, 1959).

49. *Wisdom*, p. 148.

50. On the interpretation of Prov. 8.22 in postbiblical Judaism see M. Hengel, *Judaism and Hellenism* (2 vols.; ET London: SCM Press, 1974), I, pp. 153-56, 162-63.

51. *Wisdom in Proverbs* (London: SCM Press, 1965), pp. 87-92.

52. See W.L. Knox, 'The Divine Wisdom', *JTS* 38 (1937), pp. 230-37; *idem, St Paul and the Church of the Gentiles* (Cambridge: Cambridge University Press, 1939), ch. 3; A.J. Festugière, 'A Propos des arétalogies d'Isis', *HTR* 42 (1949), pp. 209-34; and B.L. Mack, *Logos und Sophia: Untersuchungen zur Weisheitstheologie im hellenistischen Judentum* (Göttingen: Vandenhoeck & Ruprecht, 1983), pp. 38-42.

author to deny the influence of the source theology. Wisdom thus achieved almost a personified status in this text through the influence of a foreign goddess.

An emerging feature of Proverbs is the way in which it associates Wisdom with the expressed will of God. Chapter 1 describes how she cried out in the streets, mocked the simple ones and contrasted them with those who sought the fear of the Lord (1.20-33).[53] Prov. 8.32-36 says that those who found Wisdom obtained favour from the Lord but that others who hated her preferred death. Perhaps this view was due to the belief that Wisdom had been there in the very beginning (8.22). Her accessibility meant that people could acquire something which had always been God's creative purpose. The result of this was that in later literature Wisdom came to be associated with what Judaism regarded as the ultimate expression of the divine purpose—the Torah or Jewish Law.[54]

This tendency to attribute personified traits to Wisdom is exemplified by the Wisdom of Solomon. Wis. 7.22 presents Sophia as the 'breath of the power of God, and a pure emanation of the glory of the Almighty'. According to Wis. 9.4 she was the companion of God's throne. Sirach developed the portrait of Wisdom too. Sirach 24 is almost a parable of the giving of the Law in which Wisdom, who is portrayed as a member of the divine Council (24.2), is instructed to make her dwelling in Jacob and Israel (24.8). Her identification with the Torah is made explicit in Sir. 24.23. This passage probably influenced the Johannine Prologue, but the Fourth Evangelist goes beyond what is said here when he describes the taking on of human *flesh* by the Logos (Jn 1.14).[55] Bar. 4.1 also associates Wisdom with the Torah and claims that she was 'the book of the commandments of God'. There is a further development of this theme in *1 Enoch* 42, which describes how Wisdom descended to

53. See the discussion of this passage by W. McKane, *Proverbs* (London: SCM Press, 1970), pp. 272-77.
54. Schnabel has a discussion of the relevant passages (*Law and Wisdom*; pp. 93-165 on the intertestamental writings and pp. 166-226 on the Qumran literature).
55. The Prologue's debt to the Jewish Wisdom tradition is often mentioned as a topic in research. See for example P. Borgen, 'Logos was the True Light: Contributions to the Interpretation of the Prologue of John', *NovT* 14 (1972), pp. 115-30; and E.J. Epp, 'Wisdom, Torah, Word: The Johannine Prologue and the Purpose of the Fourth Gospel', in G.F. Hawthorne (ed.), *Current Issues in Biblical and Patristic Interpretation: Studies in Honour of M.C. Tenney* (Grand Rapids: Eerdmans, 1975), pp. 128-46.

2. The Christology of the Ascension of Isaiah

earth but found no welcome there and so returned to her place among the angels. As in Wis. 9.4, Wisdom is here portrayed in personified terms as a heavenly being analogous to the angels. *1 Enoch* 42 might perhaps be described as a parable of how people in Israel refused to obey the Law.

The problem of interpretation which I mentioned earlier is pertinent here. Wisdom in Jewish literature has been understood both as a personification of the will or the mind of God and as an independent deity analogous to God.[56] It is impossible to review this issue without detailed exegesis of the literature and examination of scholarly opinions, neither of which I can do with justice. I do however want to observe that the issue for us boils down to whether or not the Christians inherited a portrait of Wisdom—or of any other mediator—which was already 'binitarian' in outlook. The ancient writers who are mentioned in this summary offer a 'high' evaluation of Wisdom by making her God's assistant, even his co-worker in creation; but nothing in the literature indicates that she was *included in the cult* as Jesus was in early Christianity. It is impossible to extract a binitarianism in the sense of the worship of two heavenly powers from this literature. It never occurred to these writers that Wisdom should be worshipped in this way. There was no Jewish 'Wisdom cult' to match the cultic devotion addressed to the various deities of the surrounding nations. As a personification of the divine will, especially when identified with the Torah, Wisdom was the means of access to God, so that her mediation could be celebrated in the most monotheistic of contexts. But she herself was neither venerated nor presented as a divine figure. Early Christian use of Wisdom imagery was thus a development rather than a straight perpetuation of Jewish ideas about Wisdom.

Not even in Philo did Wisdom or the Logos acquire a formal independence from God.[57] Philo uses the term 'Logos' more than 1400

---

56. This debate is summarized by Dunn in his *Christology*, pp.168-76, where he notes four major interpretations of the issue. These are: (1) Wisdom as an independent deity, as in other religions; (2) Wisdom as a hypostasis, a quasi-personification of certain attributes proper to God, occupying an intermediate position between personalities and abstract beings; (3) Wisdom as a personification of divine attributes; and (4) Wisdom as the personification of cosmic order.

57. Studies of Philo's thought about Wisdom and the Logos include E.R. Goodenough, *An Introduction to Philo Judaeus* (Oxford: Basil Blackwell, 1962), pp. 100-10, 141-44; and H.A. Wolfson, *Philo: Foundations of Religious Philosophy in*

times in his writings. As a Jewish writer his subject matter was the exegesis of the Old Testament with its angelophanies and its understanding of God as an enthroned deity. Philo's biblical reflection was undertaken in the light of more than one philosophical tradition. Platonism supplied the distinction between the visible and the true or 'ideal' world of which this tangible world was but a copy (*Op. Mund.* 36; *Ebr.* 132; *Rer. Div. Her.* 280). From Stoicism Philo derived the concept of the immanent Logos which permeated the world, the so-called λόγος σπερματικός (*Rer. Div. Her.* 119; cf. *Op. Mund.* 143; *Leg. All.* 1.46). He reshaped this view by insisting that God transcended the Logos and therefore could not be understood by human thought (*Somn.* 1.66).

Philo's remodelling of Stoicism makes it unwise to place too much emphasis on the status of the Logos as an independent being in his writings. In one vein *Conf. Ling.* 146 portrays the Logos as an archangel and as the leader of the heavenly host; *Quaest. in Gen.* 2.62 even calls him the 'second God', while *Quaest. in Exod.* 2.13 identifies him with the angel who led the Israelites through the wilderness. In *Fug.* 101-102, too, Philo takes up Plato's image of the Charioteer to distinguish between God as the passenger and the Logos as the driver who held the reins.

This strand however must be counterbalanced by observing that 'Logos' for Philo also means 'speech' or 'reason'. There are numerous passages which demonstrate this alternative meaning. Where *Migr. Abr.* 70–85 and *Abr.* 83 separate the Stoic ideas of the λόγος ἐνδιάθετος and the λόγος προφορικός (unexpressed and uttered thought), *Sacr.* 80–83, *Ebr.* 157 and *Somn.* 1.102-14 hold the two together in a way which suggests, in the words of one commentator, that for Philo the Logos means primarily 'the formulation and expression of thought in speech'.[58]

This wide-ranging nature of the material defines the terms in which Philo speaks about the Logos and his relation to God. Far from being a separate being, as the archangel analogy might suggest, *Op. Mund.* 20 presents the Logos as the mind of God which had been discernible in the creation of the universe (a view which is similar in some respects to Prov. 8.22) and as 'the idea of ideas' (*Migr. Abr.* 103; *Quaest in Exod.* 2.24). Philo concludes from his exegesis of Gen. 28.11 that the Logos was the 'place' of which God had spoken (*Somn.* 1.65-67). This is

Judaism, Christianity and Islam (Cambridge, MA: Harvard University Press, 1947), I, pp. 226-89.

58. Goodenough, *Introduction*, p. 103.

tantamount to the assertion that the Logos was the visible or perceivable aspect of a God who remained incomprehensible to the human mind (*Leg. All.* 1.36-37; *Poster. C.* 15, 168-69; *Quaest. in Exod.* 2.67). On other occasions Philo said that the Logos was that which could be seen of God (*Somn.* 1.239; *Ebr.* 44; *Praem. Poen.* 45; *Qaest. in Exod.* 2.67); he thought that the Logos could only be perceived through the intellect (*Gig.* 60-61; *Congr.* 79), and that it drew one from the corporeal towards the incorporeal (*Sacr.* 8).

This analysis confirms that it would be wrong to suggest that for Philo, as for any other Jewish writer, the Logos was an independent being in the same sense that Justin Martyr would later call Christ 'Logos' and 'Angel'—as a second divinity with separate (though subordinate) existence from the Father (see Justin, *Dial.* 56.13; 61; 128). For Philo, the Logos was the mind of God as it came to expression. It was distinct from God inasmuch as it was the will of God in personified form; but part of God because God was the creator and, as in all Jewish theology before Gnosticism, reigned unchallenged in heaven.[59] The notion of a 'second God' (*Quaest. in Gen.* 2.62) did not imply any binitarianism or worship of the Logos: merely a devolution of divine authority which allowed this being who was part of God to act so that God himself was not compromised by anthropomorphism (as Philo's Platonic heritage demanded that he should not be). Philo's Logos teaching, in this respect at least, falls within the mainstream Jewish understanding in which God was the unrivalled deity and a particular agent his deputy.

Transformed Patriarchs

A second expression of the Jewish mediatorial tradition is the connection which is made between an exceptional human being and an exalted heavenly mediator in a variety of postbiblical literature. Already in the Bible we find hints that significant people came to an uncertain or mysterious end. These include Enoch, who 'was not, for God took him' (Gen. 5.24, AV); Moses, whose grave was known only to God (Deut.

---

59. Recent scholarship on Gnosticism has exposed its debt to Judaism. See, for instance, the essay by B.A. Pearson, 'The Problem of "Jewish Gnostic" Literature', in C.W. Hedrick and R. Hodgson (eds.), *Nag Hammadi, Gnosticism and Early Christianity* (Peabody: Hendrickson, 1985), pp. 15-35. Pearson has a later collection of essays which repay study in this connection: *Gnosticism, Judaism, and Egyptian Christianity* (Minneapolis: Fortress Press, 1990).

34.6); and Elijah, who spectacularly ascended to heaven on the chariot and horses (2 Kgs 2.11-12). Postbiblical writers developed a cycle of tradition around such figures. They presented Moses, Enoch and other people as exalted heavenly beings who occupied a position analogous to Wisdom in the literature just considered.

Enoch exercised a fascination for later writers through the obscurity and suggestiveness of Gen. 5.24.[60] The book of *Jubilees* says that Enoch was the first to learn 'knowledge and wisdom' (4.17) and that he was told everything on earth.[61] *Jub.* 4.17-26 and *2 En.* 10.1-7 make Enoch a heavenly scribe who wrote down the revealed mysteries. *1 Enoch* 12–14 (which ranks among the earliest apocalyptic literature) makes Enoch a mediator between God and the Fallen Watchers and grants him a vision of the throne of God:

> And I observed and saw...a lofty throne—its appearance was like crystal and its wheels like the shining sun; and [I heard?] the voice of the cherubim; and from beneath the throne were issuing streams of flaming fire... He who is great in glory sat on it, and his raiment was brighter than the sun and whiter than any snow. And no angel could enter, and at the appearance of the face of him no creature of flesh could look... And the Lord called me with his own mouth and said to me, Come hither, Enoch, to my holy word. And he lifted me up and brought me near the door (*1 En.* 14.18-25, abridged).

This passage is older than the book of Daniel. It stands in a mystical tradition which had its origins in the biblical theophanies. Where previously the throne of God had appeared to prophets on earth—Micaiah ben Imlah (1 Kgs 22.19), Isaiah (6.1-4), and Ezekiel (1.26-27) all saw the theophany—in this postbiblical text a human being ascends to heaven and enters the divine presence within the second of two splendid palaces. This vision of the *merkabah* is set before either of Enoch's tours through the heavens. It is thereby made the first and most important item of revealed knowledge which is presented in the apocalypse.

Chapters 36–71 form a separate section in *1 Enoch* which is generally

---

60. See further Odeberg, ''Ενώχ' in *TDNT*, II, pp. 556-60; D.S. Russell, *The Method and Message of Jewish Apocalyptic* (London: SCM Press, 1964), pp. 110-13; E.E. Urbach, *The Sages: Their Concepts and Beliefs* (Jerusalem: Magnes Press, 1975), I, pp. 198-201; and J.C. VanderKam, *Enoch and the Growth of an Apocalyptic Tradition* (Washington: Catholic Biblical Association of America, 1984).

61. See also *T. Abr.* (B recension) 11.3, and *Targ. Ps.-J.* to Gen. 5.24 for a similar understanding of Enoch's role.

2. *The Christology of the Ascension of Isaiah*

called the *Similitudes of Enoch*. Doubts have been expressed, both about the relation of ch. 71 to the rest of the *Similitudes*, and about the place of this material in the wider Enoch apocalypse.[62] The *Similitudes* are made up from more than one source and they have enjoyed a complex literary history. They describe the activity of a mediator who is called in the two respective sources the Son of Man and the Elect One.[63] The 'Son of Man' title represents an interpretation of the night-time vision in Dan. 7.9-14 (see below) in which the man-like figure of that passage is identified as an independent heavenly being in his own right; Moule calls attention to the definite article in his name in the *Similitudes* as an indication that the Danielic passage is being exegeted.[64] This Son of Man/Elect One is said to be the messiah (*1 En.* 48.10; 51.4) and he is installed on the *merkabah* (*1 En.* 45.3; 51.3; 55.4; 61.8; 62.2-6; 70.27) as the heavenly judge. Hurtado draws attention to the connections between this view of the enthroned figure and the Jewish royal ideology which is found in passages such as Ps. 45.6 and Sir. 47.11.[65] The significance of the *Similitudes* for the study of early Christian theology is that they reveal a form of belief, roughly contemporary with the period of Christian origins, in which a mediator distinct from God occupies his throne. The title 'Lord of Spirits' which is used in the *Similitudes* suggests that God was seen as a transcendent deity who was no longer confined to his throne (cf. *1 En.* 62.14 in this context), as if the mediator's exalted position was related to the author's reluctance to portray God in the same anthropomorphic terms as the biblical theophanies. The deity's unrivalled transcendence is never questioned in the *Similitudes*, however; nor is the mediator at any point offered worship.

The concluding chapter of the *Similitudes* (ch. 71) introduces a twist into this story of the Son of Man. Enoch is there identified as the mediator of his own vision:

---

62. On this matter see Rowland, *Open Heaven*, p. 184, and the works which he cites (n. 56).
63. The fusion of sources is examined by J. Theisohn, *Der auserwählte Richter* (Göttingen: Vandenhoecht & Ruprecht, 1975); see also E. Sjøberg, *Der Menschensohn in dem Äthiopischen Henochbuch* (Lund: Gleerup, 1946), esp. pp. 61-82.
64. C.F.D. Moule, *The Origin of Christology* (Cambridge: Cambridge University Press, 1977), p. 15.
65. *One God*, p. 54.

And that angel came to me and greeted me with his voice, and said to me, *You are the Son of Man* who was born to righteousness, and righteousness remains over you, and the righteousness of the Head of Days will not leave you' (*1 En.* 71.14).[66]

R.H. Charles removed this reading in his translation, but the meaning of the Ethiopic is accurately rendered by Knibb. The *Similitudes* close by making *Enoch* the divine vizier who occupies the throne of God and who judges the nations on behalf of God. This view has certain similarities with what the Christians believed about Jesus, not least with the 'Son of Man' passages in the Gospels.[67] Yet it remains true to say that Enoch is identified with an exalted angel and that he is not made a second God. He is no more said to be worshipped than is the mediator with whom he is identified.

The charge has sometimes been levelled that the *Similitudes* in their present form depend on Christian influence and that the portrait of Enoch was created either by Christians or perhaps by Jews who were concerned to resist what the Christians were saying about Jesus.[68] Considerable problems arise when viewing the *Similitudes* as a Christian text. For one thing, 'Son of Man' is a title which has only marginal importance outside the Gospels (Acts 7.56 and the book of Revelation contain the only other examples); and 'Elect One' is used much less frequently in the New Testament than 'Christ',[69] which is almost a surname for Jesus. Moreover, Christians believed that the risen Jesus had his *own* throne in heaven (this idea was anticipated in the *Testament of Abraham*[70]). The notion that Jesus occupied God's throne is supported only by Rev. 5.6 and even there the exegesis is disputed.[71] One might be

---

66. Translation by M.A. Knibb in H.F.D. Sparks (ed.), *The Apocryphal Old Testament* (Oxford: Clarendon Press, 1984), p. 256.

67. For example Mt. 13.41 where the Son of Man sends out *his own* angels to carry out the judgment.

68. A post-Christian date is assigned to the *Similitudes* by J.T. Milik, *Ten Years of Discovery in the Wilderness of Judaea* (ET London: SCM Press, 1959), pp. 33-34. See also J.C. Hindley, 'Towards a Date for the Similitudes of Enoch', *NTS* 14 (1968), pp. 551-65; and M.A. Knibb, 'The Date of the Parables of Enoch', *NTS* 25 (1978–79), pp. 345-59.

69. 'Elect One' is a peculiarity, in fact, of the Lukan Gospel (9.35; 23.35) in the New Testament literature. It occurs also in a variant of Jn 1.34 but this reading is generally rejected by scholars.

70. See below on the *Testament of Abraham*.

71. Rev. 5.6 has been held to support both the Lamb's position on the throne

2. *The Christology of the Ascension of Isaiah*

inclined to say that the Son of Man's position on the *merkabah* in the *Similitudes of Enoch* marks a *difference* from Christian speculation rather than a point of contact given the different status of the figures concerned. Finally, it seems unlikely that a Christian author would have given prominence to Enoch and made no reference to Jesus when the whole basis of Christianity was the conviction that Jesus (and he alone) had mediated between God and humanity. The *Similitudes* more obviously represent a Jewish apocalyptic interest which ran parallel to the rise of Christianity but which was not extensively influenced by it.

The Enochic tradition continued long beyond the first century CE. In recent years considerable attention has been devoted to the early *Hekhalot* text called variously *Sefer Hekhalot*, *Hebrew Enoch* and *3 Enoch*.[72] This text is a compilation, or perhaps a summary, of Jewish mystical traditions which preserves echoes of earlier ideas about Enoch. *3 Enoch* is later than the New Testament (fifth century CE) and it does not for that reason illustrate the rise of Christology, but it does show the culmination of certain tendencies which are evident in the earlier Enochic literature and which had had a considerable history by the time that *3 Enoch* was written. The first part of the work (chs. 1–12) describes Enoch's ascension to heaven and his transformation into the throne-angel Metatron (cf. *1 En.* 71.14). This is prefaced by a description of Rabbi Yishma'el's heavenly ascension.[73] Yishma'el is said to have ascended through the six heavens until he encountered angelic opposition from Qefziel on trying to enter the seventh heaven (cf. *Asc. Isa.* 9.1). The text tells how Metatron prevented the rabbi from being thrown down from heaven (cf. *Asc. Isa.* 9.1 again) and how he conducted him safely into the seventh heaven where, despite further angelic opposition, the rabbi saw the *merkabah* and its holy occupant.

---

and his position between the throne and the 24 elders. The second exegesis is preferred by G.B. Caird, *A Commentary on the Revelation of St John the Divine* (London: A. & C. Black, 1966), pp. 75-76.

72. See H. Odeberg, *III Enoch or the Hebrew Book of Enoch* (Cambridge: Cambridge University Press, 1928). This text is discussed also by P. Alexander, in Charlesworth (ed.), *Old Testament Pseudepigrapha*, I, pp. 223-53; Gruenwald, *Apocalyptic*, pp. 191-208; Rowland, *Open Heaven*, pp. 334-40; and Segal, *Two Powers*, pp. 60 n. 2, 61 n. 4, 67 n. 24, 197.

73. Gruenwald sees this preface as a literary device which defines the setting of the work as a rewriting of the Enochic saga in terms of the *merkabah* tradition; *Apocalyptic*, pp. 192-94.

For our purposes the interest of *3 Enoch* lies in the exalted position which is accorded Metatron in the work. His name, argues Saul Lieberman,[74] was derived from the Greek *Synthronos* which means someone who stands beside the throne of a king or deity. Enoch-Metatron is called 'the Prince of the Divine Presence' (12.1) and even 'the Lesser Yahweh' and 'Youth' (12.5) in this text. The author next relates a story about Rabbi Elisha ben Abuyah (the notorious heretic who was often called 'Rabbi Aher'). He describes how Aher ascended to heaven and saw Enoch-Metatron on a throne. This prompted him to remark, 'There are two powers in heaven!' (16.3). To guard against this impression, Metatron was punished with sixty lashes of fire and dethroned (16.5). This story was a familiar one in Judaism and it is found also in *b. Ḥag.* 15a.[75] The version in *3 Enoch* offers a confused account of the story by seating Metatron at the gate of the seventh palace in ch. 10 but then in ch. 16 in a more exalted position, 'sitting on a throne like a king with all the ministering angels standing by me as my servants and all the princes of the kingdoms adorned with crowns surrounding me'. This confusion probably shows the stages of development through which the material has passed. The portrait of the enthroned Metatron, however, calls to mind the biblical theophanies, in which the seated position was the prerogative of God.

It is difficult to resist the conclusion that Metatron, like Enoch in the *Similitudes*, functions as the divine vicegerent in *3 Enoch*. The title 'Lesser Yahweh' suggests that he does. Gruenwald shows how Enoch-Metatron became the target of criticism in rabbinic literature, evidently because his ascension and heavenly mediation could be construed as prefiguring that of Jesus.[76] There is, however, a clear difference between *3 Enoch* and Christian beliefs. Enoch ascended to heaven and became an angel; Jesus was made a divine being and included in the cult. Gruenwald mentions the possibility that this portrait of Enoch was created to *deny* the similarities between Judaism and Christianity by making Metatron an angel and not a god.[77] Enoch-Metatron's dethronement should thus perhaps be construed as a reaction against earlier

74. In the Appendix to Gruenwald, *Apocalyptic*, pp. 235-41.
75. On the different forms of the story see Rowland, *Open Heaven*, pp. 334-38, who concludes that the account in *3 En.* 16 is later than that found in *b. Ḥag.* 15a. The Talmudic version describes Metatron's punishment but omits other details.
76. *Apocalyptic*, pp. 200-201.
77. *Apocalyptic*, p. 201.

2. The Christology of the Ascension of Isaiah

apocalyptic views, including both Christian theology and the material found in the *Similitudes*, which protected God from a subordinate who might be perceived as a rival. It also quite graphically made the point that Enoch could *not* be perceived as the 'Lesser Yahweh' by those who wished to remain orthodox within Judaism.

Moses, too, was presented as an exalted heavenly being.[78] All Jews of the period looked to the Sinai theophany as the moment when God had entered into covenant relationship with their nation. According to the book of Exodus Moses, Aaron and the elders ascended the mountain and they 'saw the God of Israel' (Exod. 24.10). This stimulated the mystical imagination concerning what had happened to Moses, as did the uncertainty which surrounded his burial (see Deut. 34.6). His position as the Jewish Lawgiver meant that in company with Abraham Moses became a legendary figure in the nation's history. Given this pedigree it would be surprising had the events of his life not been made the subject of reflection; and indeed they were. The Sinai theophany clearly fascinated later writers.[79] The second-century BCE Alexandrian poet called Ezekiel the Tragedian (not to be confused with the canonical Ezekiel) understood it to involve Moses' heavenly ascension and his installation on the throne of God, which he describes in his work called the *Exagoge*:

> On Sinai's peak I saw what seemed a throne
> so great in size it touched the clouds of heaven.
> Upon it sat a man of noble mien,
> becrowned, and with a scepter in one hand

---

78. See Meeks, *Prophet King, passim*; J. Jeremias, "Μωυσῆς', in *TDNT*, IV, pp. 848-73; E.R. Goodenough, *By Light, Light: The Mystic Gospel of Hellenistic Judaism* (New Haven: Yale University Press, 1935), pp. 199-234; E. Schillebeeckx, *Christ: The Christian Experience in the Modern World* (London: SCM Press, 1980), pp. 309-321; and P. Borgen, 'God's Agent in the Fourth Gospel', in J. Neusner (ed.), *Religions in Antiquity: Essays in Memory of Erwin Ramsdell Goodenough* (Leiden: Brill, 1968), pp. 137-48.

79. It also inspired Christian mystical exegesis. See, for instance, the interpretation of Gregory of Nyssa in his *Vita Moysis* and of Gregory Nazianzen in his *Second Theological Oration*. The impact of this tradition of Christian theology is examined by V. Lossky, *The Mystical Theology of the Eastern Church* (Cambridge: James Clarke, 1973). Some early Christian writers denied that Moses saw God at all; see Jn 3.13, 6.46 and *Asc. Isa.* 3.8-10. This first- and second-century material must be seen in the context of Christian self-definition against Judaism early in the Common Era.

> while with the other he did beckon me.
> I made approach and stood before the throne.
> He handed o'er the sceptre and he bade
> me mount the throne, and gave to me the crown;
> then he himself withdrew from off the throne.
> I gazed upon the whole earth round about;
> things under it, and high above the skies.
> Then at my feet a multitude of stars
> fell down, and I their number reckoned up.
> They passed by me like armed ranks of men.
> Then I in terror wakened from the dream (ll. 68-82).[80]

This poem makes God vacate his throne for Moses so that the mediator begins to exercise judgment in heaven, apparently on God's behalf. The striking nature of this assertion, together with the fact that the text is found only in fragmentary form, has led to its being given more than one interpretation by scholars. Meeks argues that it falls into just the sort of category which we have been considering, that of the translation of a human being to exalted status in heaven. Van der Horst even argues that it signifies Moses' 'deification'. Jacobson, however, maintains that it is *set against* this kind of understanding and that Ezekiel was offering an anti-mystical perspective which dialogued with the emerging mediatorial tradition in Judaism. Holladay thinks that the background of the story is classical mythology, and specifically stories about the relationship between Zeus and Apollo in which Moses is presented in the familiar Hellenistic guise of 'the seer'.[81]

Hurtado, however, is surely right to insist that the Jewish tradition that Moses had witnessed a theophany on Sinai cannot easily be dismissed from one's mind when reading the *Exagoge*.[82] He notes Meeks's identification of two major beliefs about Moses in pre-Christian literature.

---

80. Translation by R.G. Robertson, in Charlesworth (ed.), *Old Testament Pseudepigrapha*, II, pp. 811-12. The text is found in Eusebius, *Praep. Evang.* 9.28-9; Clement, *Strom.* 1.23.155; and Ps.-Eustathius, *Comm. in Hex.* (see Migne, *PG* 18.729).

81. Meeks, *Prophet King*, pp. 148-49; P. van der Horst, 'Moses' Throne-Vision in Ezekiel the Dramatist', *JJS* 34 (1983), pp. 21-29; H. Jacobson, 'Mysticism and Apocalyptic in Ezekiel's *Exagoge*', *Illinois Classical Studies* 6 (1981), pp. 272-93; C.R. Holladay, 'The Portrait of Moses in Ezekiel the Tragedian', in G.W. Macrae (ed.), *SBL 1976 Seminar Papers* (Missoula, MT: Scholar's Press, 1976), pp. 447-52.

82. *One God*, p. 58.

2. The Christology of the Ascension of Isaiah

These are Moses as prophet and king.[83] This is precisely the combination of ideas that is found in the *Exagoge*, where the view of Moses as prophet or visionary has been merged with a regal function symbolized by his possession of the sceptre which allows Moses to function evidently as the divine vicegerent. I take the poem in this sense. Moses' position on the *merkabah* is probably related, as in the *Similitudes of Enoch*, to the desire to circumvent an anthropomorphic theology. This led to a transformed and visible person being installed in the place of God as the deity was made more transcendent and not allowed to be perceived through mystical experience.

This transformation of Moses seems not to have compromised monotheism to any final degree. There is no suggestion that Moses was offered worship: the fact that stars fell at his feet cannot be equated with human veneration. Moses is depicted merely as a vice-gerent who discharged functions on behalf of the transcendent deity. For this reason I find problems with van der Horst's suggestion that Moses is 'deified' in this passage. It is true to say that Moses occupies the place of God and that he discharges certain divine functions (such as ruling the stars). Yet he is never called divine nor offered worship. This reserve determines the nature of the portrait and means that the issue is less straightforward than van der Horst assumes. Moses is not in fact a god but a divine chief agent. Ezekiel the Tragedian's poem is however remarkable for its early date. It was written before the book of Daniel, and anticipates a view which is found in later apocalyptic texts and which directly influenced Christian beliefs about Jesus.

The view of Moses as an exalted figure is found also in Sir. 45.2, 'He made him equal in glory to the holy ones' (Greek text; the Hebrew is defective but it possibly designated Moses as *'elohim*—a title which was attributed to Melchizedek by the Qumran community).[84] The context of this reference suggests that the earthly Moses is meant rather than a transformed counterpart beyond the grave. Although the occasion which prompted the analogy is not specified, Sirach probably alludes to the Sinai theophany and to the interpretation of that event which is found in Ezekiel the Tragedian. We know from *Jub.* 1.27 that Sinai was perceived as a numinous occasion when the Angel of the Presence wrote down the Law for Moses. The *Testament of Moses* (11.16) also

---

83. Meeks, in his book *Prophet King*.
84. This textual defect is noticed by Hurtado, *One God*, p. 56. See below on the Qumran literature.

presents the human Lawgiver as endowed with unrivalled understanding. This view seems to have been a common one in postbiblical Judaism.

Speculation about Moses as the divine vizier reached its zenith with Philo. According to the *Vita Mosis*, on Sinai Moses came closer to perfect communion with God than any human being before or since:

> For as God thought Moses worthy to share in the portion he had reserved for himself, he committed to Moses the entire cosmos as a possession fit for God's heir, Wherefore each of the elements was made subject to Moses...[85]

Moses for Philo was a mystagogue and the ideal philosopher; *Rer. Div. Her.* 205 calls him an archangel and the eldest Logos.[86] *Vit. Mos.* 1.156, 158 attributes the divine title to him and *Sacr.* 8, in exegesis of Exod. 7.1, even states that God appointed Moses as God. Holladay cogently argues that this last passage should not be taken to imply a formal binitarianism:[87] *Det. Pot. Ins.* 161-62, in another discussion of Exod. 7.1, swiftly adds the rejoinder that Moses did not become God in reality. Philo's language is striking nonetheless. Meeks identifies the need to counter claims by pagan kings to divinity as the reason for the presentation of Moses in this way.[88]

There are thus similarities between what Philo says about Moses and his view of the Logos. Both Moses and the Logos could be construed in the position of divine chief agent, and even given the divine title, but without the suggestion that this entitled them to worship. In this, Philo was not the creator of his own understanding but drew on an apocalyptic tradition which we have seen to go back at least to Ezekiel the Tragedian in the second century BCE. He stands within a wider understanding which allowed a significant figure to rise to prominence in heaven within a monotheistic context.

The Qumran community thought of Melchizedek as a divine vizier. An interpretation of Psalm 82 ranked him above the gods:[89]

---

85. *Vit. Mos.* 1.155-6. Translation from the LCL series.
86. See also *Agr.* 51; *Somn.* 1.215.
87. C.R. Holladay, *Theios Aner in Hellenistic Judaism* (SBLDS, 40; Missoula, MT: Scholars Press, 1977), pp. 136-41.
88. 'Moses as God and King', in Neusner (ed.), *Religions in Antiquity*, pp. 324-77.
89. On this text see A.S. van der Woude and M. de Jonge, 'Melchizedek and the New Testament', *NTS* 12 (1965–66), pp. 301-306; M. Delcor, 'Melchizedek from Genesis to the Qumran Texts and the Epistle to the Hebrews', *JSJ* 2 (1971),

2. *The Christology of the Ascension of Isaiah*

[And h]e will, by his strength, judge the holy ones of God, executing judgement as it is written concerning him in the Songs of David, who said, ELOHIM *has taken his place in the divine council; in the midst of the gods he holds judgment.* And it was concerning him that he said, [Let the assembly of the peoples] *return to the height above them*; EL [God] *will judge the peoples*...And Melchizedek will avenge the vengeance of the judgements of God (11QMelch).[90]

This passage takes the 'Elohim' and 'El' of the Massoretic text, not as God himself but as Melchizedek, a subordinate who presided over the heavenly council. Melchizedek was addressed by a divine title (within the context of biblical exegesis), he enjoyed the seated position reserved for God in the theophanies and exercised the main divine function of judgment. The 'gods' in this passage are perhaps polytheistic divinities who have been downgraded to become angels and are thus regarded as subordinates of the true God. The possibility that Melchizedek is portrayed in quasi-divine terms has been questioned by Carmignac, but a substantial consensus of scholars accepts it as a plausible interpretation. We should remember that Sir. 45.2 identified Moses as *'elohim* if the Hebrew text can be reconstructed to yield that noun. Philo, too, called Moses 'god' on the basis of Exod. 7.1. Within this wider context the designation of Melchizedek as the divine vice-gerent would not be out of place. Melchizedek is no more said to be worshipped than the other figures we have considered. He is rather made a vizier who discharges judgment on behalf of the transcendent deity.

A major question to address in respect of 11QMelch is whether or not this Melchizedek is to be identified with the Melchizedek who makes a brief appearance in Gen. 14.18-24.[91] This picture of the heavenly mediator is not obviously suggested by that passage unless the fact that the biblical Melchizedek blessed the father of the Jewish nation was taken as

pp. 115-35; J.A. Emerton, 'Melchizedek and the Gods: Fresh Evidence for the Jewish Background of John 10.34-36', *JTS* 17 (1966), pp. 399-401; J.A. Fitzmyer, 'Further Light on Melchizedek from Qumran Cave 11', *JBL* 86 (1967), pp. 25-41; M.P. Miller, 'The Function of Isaiah 61.1-2 in 11Q Melchizedek', *JBL* 88 (1969), pp. 467-69; and F.L. Horton, *The Melchizedek Tradition* (SNTSMS, 30; Cambridge: Cambridge University Press, 1976), pp. 64-82. J. Carmignac, 'Le Document de Qumran sur Melkisédeq', *RevQ* 7 (1970), pp. 343-78, disputes the identification of Elohim with Melchizedek in this passage.

90. Translation by G. Vermes, *The Dead Sea Scrolls in English* (Harmondsworth: Penguin Books, 1975), p. 267.

91. See further Horton, *Melchizedek*, pp. 167-70.

evidence that he had supernatural properties. On the other hand, the name is an unusual one and it would be strange to find two unrelated Melchizedeks in Jewish tradition. Whatever the resolution of this problem, 11QMelch presents the mediator in the place of God and as exercising judgment for him. Hurtado interestingly compares Melchizedek in 11QMelch with the figure of Michael in the book of Daniel who is the heavenly patron of the righteous Israelites (Dan. 12.1).[92]

The *Testament of Abraham* presents Abel as an enthroned mediator who exercized sovereignty over the nations:[93]

> And between the two gates there stood a terrifying throne, with the appearance of terrifying crystal, flashing like fire. And upon it sat a wondrous man, bright as the sun, like unto a son of God...The Commander-in-chief said... 'This is the son of Adam, the first-formed, who is called Abel, whom Cain the wicked killed. And he sits here to judge the entire creation, examining both righteous and sinners' (*T. Abr.* [Recension A] 12.4-5, 13.2-3, the last reference abridged).[94]

This passage evidently draws on *1 En.* 14.10, 17 in the two nouns 'crystal' and 'fire'. This means that it offers an interpretation of the Jewish theophanic tradition in which the *merkabah* (or a throne resembling it) was occupied by a heavenly being who was distinct from God. The possibility that Abel has his *own* throne in this passage should not be ignored. In this respect the text provides an interesting analogy with what *Asc. Isa.* 11.32 (and other Christian texts) say about the Beloved One, and it may perhaps indicate that possession of a throne was attributed to heavenly mediators in Judaism before the rise of Christianity. That Abel should have been chosen for this position reflects the desire to find vindication for his death which is recorded in Gen. 4.4-5.

---

92. *One God*, p. 79.
93. The *Testament of Abraham* is a Jewish work from the early Common Era. See F.H. Borsch, *The Son of Man in Myth and History* (London: SCM Press, 1967), p. 170; *idem*, *The Christian and Gnostic Son of Man* (SBT, 14; London: SCM Press, 1970), p. 117; and A.B. Kolenkow, 'The Angelology of the Testament of Abraham', in G.W.E. Nickelsburg (ed.), *Studies on the Testament of Abraham* (SBLSCS; Missoula, MT: Scholars Press, 1976), pp. 153-62. On the Cain and Abel story in Jewish and Christian exegesis see K.G. Kuhn, "Ἀβελ', in *TDNT*, I, pp. 6-8; and V. Aptowitzer, *Kain und Abel in der Agada, den Apokryphen, der hellenist., christlich. und muhammed. Literatur* (Kohut Memorial Foundation, 1922).
94. Translation from Charlesworth (ed.), *Old Testament Pseudepigrapha*, I, pp. 889-90.

2. The Christology of the Ascension of Isaiah

Many of the works which have been mentioned so far do not allow for a 'pre-existence' of the figure concerned. One text, however, does describe a mediator's descent and his connection with a human being in such terms. The *Prayer of Joseph*, which is preserved by Origen in his *Commentary on John* (2.31) describes the angel Israel's prominence in the heavenly world:[95] 'I [am] Israel, the archangel of the power of the Lord and the chief captain among the sons of God...the first minister before the face of God'.[96] The author of this Jewish apocryphon agrees with Philo in making Israel the principal heavenly power; the phrase 'chief captain' holds terminology in common also with *Joseph and Asenath* 14 (which is cited below). This tends to suggest that such descriptions had a traditional nature despite the fact that the figure in question and what is said about them varied from text to text. The *Prayer of Joseph* goes on to say that the angel Israel had appeared on earth as the patriarch Jacob. This alludes to Jacob's change of name which is recorded in Gen. 32.28:[97]

> And when I was coming up from Syrian Mesopotamia, Uriel, the angel of God, came forth and said that I [Jacob–Israel] had descended to earth and I had tabernacled among men and that I had been called by the name of Jacob.

This sentence makes Uriel remind Jacob, who was oblivious of his heavenly origins, who he was: Israel the angel prince, whom the author identified with the Jewish patriarch in a context where descent from heaven is specifically mentioned.[98] Like the later *3 Enoch*, the purpose

---

95. The date of this apocryphon is not certain but it is possibly mentioned by *Asc. Isa.* 4.22 ('the words of Joseph the Just'). That would place it no later than the first century CE. There is an introduction and translation to the textual fragment by J.Z. Smith, in Charlesworth (ed.), *Old Testament Pseudepigrapha*, II, pp. 699-714; see also Smith's article, 'The Prayer of Joseph', in Neusner (ed.), *Religions in Antiquity*, pp. 253-94. The writing was preserved by Origen in the context of his presentation of John the Baptist as an incarnate angel.

96. Translation from Charlesworth (ed.), *Old Testament Pseudepigrapha*, II, p. 713.

97. Perhaps this view of the Jewish nation as a heavenly body is the ancestor of the strange comment in *Asc. Isa.* 3.15 that the 'angel of the church' descended from heaven.

98. Notice the absence of any 'docetic' style of reference in this text qualifying the humanity of Jacob. There is nothing to match the description of the birth and suckling of Jesus which is found in the *Ascension of Isaiah* (although we must

of the *Prayer of Joseph* may have been to counter Christian claims about Jesus by insisting that others besides he were closely connected with God. It is interesting to observe that God's assistant should explicitly be said to be an angel and not a divine being in this text. This strengthens the case for supposing that apocalyptic Judaism knew no tradition of a second divine being who received worship.

Exalted Angels

The third expression of the Jewish mediatorial tradition was the development of an exalted angel, which is found in apocalyptic literature from the second century BCE. A number of texts set such a figure above the heavenly host in subjection to God and attribute to him a variety of functions. There is diversity in the sources both about this angel's appearance and about his activity, but the significance of this strand is left in no doubt by the literature which describes it. Like the other branches of the tradition, the development of the exalted angel offered an important resource to the Christians as they formulated their beliefs about Jesus.

The origins of this third strand lie deep in the Hebrew Bible. The passages which are sometimes called the 'Pentateuchal angelophanies' do not adequately distinguish between the 'Angel of the Lord' and Yahweh himself. This allows the messenger to be presented in terms that are analogous to God.[99] Gen. 16.7-14 demonstrates this sense of confusion. The narrator describes in this passage how the Angel of the Lord appeared to Hagar in the wilderness. At the conclusion of the story we read the comment: 'She called the name of the LORD (יהוה) who was speaking to her El-Roi, for she said, "Have I indeed seen God and still live after that vision?"' (Gen. 16.13). This implies that Yahweh was present in the apparition even though it is specifically described as an angelophany.[100] It would be wrong to claim that the angel is a divine

---

remember that the text is fragmentary, and so we cannot say what was in the portion which has been lost).

99. The 'Pentateuchal angelophanies' are Gen. 16.7-14; 18.1-15; 31.11-13; 32.24-30; Exod. 3.1-6; Josh. 5.13-15; and Judg. 2.1. Their meaning and interpretation are discussed by F. Stier, *Gott und sein Engel im Alten Testament* (Münster: Aschendorff, 1934).

100. G. von Rad explains this story as the redressing of an earlier Canaanite theophany (see his *Old Testament Theology* [2 vols.; ET London: SCM Press, 1961]), I, pp. 285-89).

2. *The Christology of the Ascension of Isaiah* 113

'hypostasis' in this passage, still less a divine being in his own right.[101] He functions simply as God's mouthpiece, as the transcendent deity speaks directly through his messenger.[102] Yet there *is* an ambiguity in the text, one which was noticed by the earliest commentators, who reworked the material to remove it. In a discussion of Genesis 18— where Abraham's third visitor is called 'the Lord' (Gen. 18.17)— *B. Meṣ* 86b, *Gen. R.* 50.2, and the Jerusalem Targum to Gen. 18.2 all identify the visitor as Michael and not as Yahweh.[103] This guards against the anthropomorphic difficulties presented by the theophany. Philo, however, interpreted these Pentateuchal angelophanies as appearances of the Logos, and John the Evangelist and Justin Martyr referred them to Christ who was thereby held to have been active in Old Testament times.[104] This ambiguous distinction between God and the angel formed a major way in which Christians were able to 'prove' the activity of the pre-existent Christ from the Hebrew Bible and to hold him distinct from God as their tradition of worship demanded.

Postbiblical Judaism greatly emphasized the importance of the angels and their activity.[105] Two passages from Daniel show this process of development in the mother of apocalypses. The night-time vision in Dan. 7.9-14 describes how a man-like being was presented before the Ancient of Days and invested with universal authority:

> Thrones were set in place and one ancient in years took his seat, his robe was white as snow and the hair of his head like cleanest wool...I was still watching in visions of the night and I saw one like a man coming with the clouds of heaven; he approached the Ancient in Years and was presented to him. Sovereignty and kingly power were given to him, so that all people and nations of every language should serve him; his sovereignty was to be an everlasting sovereignty which should not pass away, and his kingly power such as should never be impaired (Dan. 7.9, 13-14, NEB).

This passage has long vexed commentators.[106] Some have seen the

---

101. The importation of language from later christological discussion, although it is often done, is inherently confusing and it is therefore best avoided.
102. Thus Dunn notes in his *Christology*, p. 158: 'The "Angel of Yahweh" is simply a way of speaking about Yahweh himself'.
103. This information is derived from Ginzberg, *Legends*, I, pp. 240-45; V, pp. 234-38.
104. See above on Philo; and Jn 8.58; Justin, *Dial.* 61, 128.
105. For an account of postbiblical angelology see Russell, *Method*, pp. 240-44 and the literature which is cited there.
106. See M.D. Hooker, *The Son of Man in Mark* (London: SPCK, 1967), pp.

man-like figure as a symbol in the prophet's dream. This view holds that he functions as the representative of the people of the saints of the Most High who are said to inherit the kingdom in 7.27. Other scholars however identify the man-like figure as a real heavenly being who was presented at that moment before God and invested with universal authority by the deity.[107] This exegetical issue is impossible to resolve without detailed discussion which I cannot attempt. Nevertheless, it is worth briefly mentioning Emerton's suggestion that the background to the passage is the relationship between El and Baal in Ugaritic mythology.[108] El was the senior God; Baal became his subordinate.[109] This raises the possibility that polytheistic notions somehow survived in Judaism and that they surfaced at this time of national emergency; but we have no precise knowledge of how they were preserved over such a long period, nor why they should appear in this form during the Antiochian crisis.

The earliest interpreters of Daniel 7 understood the passage as a vision of two heavenly beings. As we have seen, *1 Enoch* 46 makes Daniel's man-like figure an independent being:

> At that place, I saw the One to whom belongs the time before time. And his head was white like wool, and there was with him another being, whose face was like that of a human being. His countenance was full of grace like that of one among the holy angels. And I asked the one—from among the angels—who was going with me, and who had revealed to me all the secrets regarding the One who was born of human beings, 'Who is this, and from whence is he going as a prototype of the Before-Time?'. And he answered me and said to me, 'This is the Son of Man, to whom belongs righteousness and with whom righteousness dwells'. (*1 En.* 46.1-3a).

11-32; Borsch, *Son of Man*, pp. 137-45; A. Ferch, *Daniel 7* (Berrien Springs: Andrews University Press, 1979); and C.C. Caragounis, *Son of Man* (WUNT, 38; Tübingen: Mohr, 1986), pp. 61-80.

107. For the first interpretation see Moule, *Origin*, pp. 11-22; and R. Leivestad, 'Exit the Apocalyptic Son of Man', *NTS* 18 (1971–72), pp. 243-67. For the second, see S. Mowinckel, *He That Cometh* (Oxford: Basil Blackwell, 1956), pp. 346-450; and H.E. Tödt, *The Son of Man in the Synoptic Tradition* (London: SCM Press, 1965), pp. 22-31.

108. J.A. Emerton, 'The Origin of the Son of Man Imagery', *JTS* 9 (1958), pp. 225-42.

109. There is further material in M. Pope, *El in the Ugaritic Texts* (VTSup, 2; Leiden: Brill, 1955).

2. The Christology of the Ascension of Isaiah

Daniel's imprecise 'one like a son of man' is here identified as a specific figure, '*the* Son of Man' in an interpretation which (despite attempts to prove otherwise) was not obviously influenced by Christian ideas.[110] The independence of the second figure in Daniel 7 is maintained also in *4 Ezra* 13, which was written not long after the fall of Jerusalem. This text presents the messiah as a superhuman being who came up from the sea:

> As I watched, the wind brought a figure like that of a man out of the depths, and he flew with the clouds of heaven. Wherever he turned his face, everything he looked at trembled, and wherever the sound of his voice reached, everyone who heard it melted as wax at the touch of fire (*4 Ezra* 13.3-4, REB).[111]

The Gospels also assume that the Son of Man (as the expected eschatological figure) would act independently as the judge:

> ἀποστελεῖ ὁ υἱὸς τοῦ ἀνθρώπου τοὺς ἀγγέλους αὐτοῦ, καὶ συλλέξουσιν ἐκ τῆς βασιλείας αὐτοῦ πάντα τὰ σκάνδαλα καὶ τοὺς ποιοῦντας τὴν ἀνομίαν (Mt. 13.41).

Here the Son of Man (the title, as in the *Similitudes*, has the definite article) is presented as an independent mediator who sends out 'his own' angels. He is even presented as the owner of the kingdom.

Although they do not determine the original meaning of Daniel 7, these early interpretations of the passage all understand the 'one like a son of man' as an independent figure of outstanding authority. Daniel 7 was given a messianic interpretation in rabbinic Judaism, but it seems doubtful that this meaning belonged to the original text.[112] The importance of the passage lies in the seer's claim to have seen an exalted angel who was presented before God in the heavenly court and invested with the divine prerogative of sovereignty. As in Ezekiel the Tragedian, whose *Exagoge* probably predates Daniel, this should be seen as a development of the theophanic tradition in which a second figure acquired God's function of judgment, but still within a monotheistic context, as God himself became more transcendent.

---

110. The significance of this identification is recognized by Moule, *Origin*, p. 15; see further P.M. Casey, 'The Use of the Term "Son of Man" in the Similitudes of Enoch', *JSJ* 7 (1976), pp. 11-29.

111. The messianism of *4 Ezra* is complex. There is a valuable article on it by M.E. Stone: 'The Concept of the Messiah in 4 Ezra', in Neusner (ed.), *Religions in Antiquity*, pp. 295-312.

112. *B. Ḥag.* 14a.

Another passage from Daniel develops the theophanic tradition. The angelophany which is recorded in Dan. 10.5-6 narrates an angel's appearance in language which drew on Ezek. 1.26-27 and other passages from that prophet:[113]

> On the twenty-fourth day of the first month, I found myself on the bank of the great river, that is the Tigris; I looked up and saw a man clothed in linen with a belt of gold from Ophir round his waist. His body gleamed like topaz, his face shone like lightning, his eyes flamed like torches, his arms and feet sparkled like a disc of bronze; and when he spoke his voice sounded like the voice of a multitude (Dan. 10.4-6).[114]

Several passages from Ezekiel contributed to this description:

> In the fire was the semblance of four living creatures in human form. Each had four faces and each four wings; their legs were straight, and their hooves were like the hooves of a calf, glittering like a disc of bronze (Ezek. 1.6-7).

> The appearance of the creatures was as if fire from burning coals or torches were darting to and from among them; the fire was radiant, and out of the fire came lightning (Ezek. 1.13).

> I heard, too, the noise of their wings; when they moved it was like the noise of a great torrent or of a cloud-burst, like the noise of a crowd or an armed camp (Ezek. 1.24).

> Above the vault over their heads there appeared, as it were, a sapphire in the shape of a throne, and high above all, upon the throne, a form in human likeness. I saw what might have been brass glowing like fire in a furnace from the waist upwards; and from the waist downwards I saw what looked like fire with encircling radiance (Ezek. 1.26-27).

> Then I saw six men approaching from the road that leads to the upper northern gate, each carrying a battle-axe, one man among them dressed in linen with pen and ink at his waist (Ezek. 9.2).

> [The prophet's address to the king of Tyre, a description of Primal Man] 'You were in an Eden, a garden of God, adorned with gems of every kind: sardin and chrysolite and jade, topaz, cornelian and green jasper, lapis lazuli, purple garnet and green felspar. Your jingling beads were of gold' (Ezek. 28.13).

Ezekiel 1 describes a theophany in which God appears in human form

---

113. See C.C. Rowland, 'A Man Clothed in Linen: Daniel 10.5-6 and Jewish Angelology', *JSNT* 24 (1985), pp. 99-110; and *Open Heaven*, pp. 98-99.
114. All passages in this section are cited from the NEB.

2. The Christology of the Ascension of Isaiah

seated on his throne-chariot. This passage became an important source for later Jewish literature.[115] Ezekiel's theophany and its accoutrements supplied the reference to the bronze, torches, lightning, noise and the notion of the angel's human appearance which are found in Daniel 10. Later passages from Ezekiel—notably those concerning the Linen-Clothed Man and Primal Man, both of them extraordinary beings—contributed the linen dress, topaz and gold to that passage. Dan. 10.5-6 thus drew on a variety of material in which the portrayal of an angel as an exceptional figure who was visually connected with the deity was the dominant feature.

We should ask, with R.H. Charles,[116] whether this angel's appearance (which resembled God's) does not suggest that he enjoyed an exceptional or even a unique position in the heavenly court. This angel seems analogous to the man-like figure of Daniel 7 and perhaps also to Michael in Daniel 12. He is a divine chief agent like the other figures considered in this chapter. As with the others there is no suggestion that this angel received worship despite his visual affinity to God. For this reason it would be wrong in my opinion to call Daniel 10 a 'binitarian' text.

It has been argued that this sharing of divine characteristics goes back to theophanic developments which are found as early as the book of Ezekiel. Christopher Rowland notices a tension between the two theophanies which are recorded by that prophet. Ezekiel's call-theophany (1.26-27, cited above) describes God in anthropomorphic terms as a figure seated on his throne-chariot.[117] Ezekiel 8 however offers a different view:

---

115. On the significance of Ezekiel's call-theophany for Jewish theology see O. Procksch, 'Die Berfungsvision Hezekiels', *BZAW* 34 (1920), pp. 148-49; H.R. Balz, *Methodische Probleme der neutestamentliche Christologie* (Neukirchen–Vluyn: Neukircherner Verlag, 1967), p. 80; J. Maier, *Vom Kultus zu Gnosis* (Salzburg: Otto Müller, 1964), p. 118; M. Black, 'The Throne-Theophany Prophetic Commission and the Son of Man', in R.G. Hamerton-Kelly and R. Scroggs (eds.), *Jews, Greeks, and Christians: Religious Culture in Late Antiquity* (Leiden: Brill, 1976), pp. 57-73; W. Zimmerli, *Ezechiel* (2 vols.; Neukirchen–Vluyn: Neukirchener Verlag, 1969), I, pp. 1-85; and C.C. Rowland, 'Visions of God in Apocalyptic Literature', *JSJ* 10 (1979), pp. 137-54.

116. *A Critical and Exegetical Commentary on the Book of Daniel* (Oxford: Oxford University Press, 1929), p. 257: 'The being here referred to is not only a supernatural being, but one holding a pre-eminent dignity amongst such beings.'

117. *Open Heaven*, pp. 95-97.

> On the fifth day of the sixth month in the sixth year, I was sitting at home and the elders of Judah were with me. Suddenly the hand of the Lord God came upon me, and I saw what looked like a man. He seemed to be all fire from the waist down and to shine and glitter like brass from the waist up (Ezek. 8.1-2, NEB).

Although the form of God is similar to that which appeared in ch. 1, in ch. 8 the heavenly figure appears without any reference to the throne-chariot. Rowland thinks that this development has a great significance for the history of Jewish theology. He believes that it attests 'the separation of the form of God from the divine throne-chariot to act as quasi-angelic mediator'.[118] This assessment offers a view of Ezekiel's theology in which the deity was not exclusively tied to his throne and in which the form of God could act almost as an angelic being in heaven.

It must be said in response to this suggestion that Rowland's exegesis depends on an argument from silence. Rowland argues from the premise that, because Ezekiel 8 does not mention the throne of God, the divine form must have become distinguished from it. This is not the only possible reading of the text, nor is it necessarily the most plausible one. In later visions of God (for example in *1 En.* 14) the throne itself becomes the subject of mystical interest, so that it *remained* an important element in the theophanic tradition. Rowland's view would be a striking development for which there is not much other evidence in Ezekiel. It should be noted, but the ambiguity of the evidence must be acknowledged as well. On the other hand, if the author of Daniel had *read* Ezekiel in this way and assumed that the human form of God was a separable entity, this would explain how aspects of the theophany came to be associated with an angel in Daniel 10. Even so, as I said, we should beware of assuming that Daniel 10 formally attests a binitarian theology. What we find there is yet another way of describing the divine chief agent, one which uses visual rather than enthronement categories to form a description of the subordinate figure. This angel, as Charles recognized, was an exceptional being, but he was no more entitled to worship than any other of the mediators described in Jewish literature despite his visual similarity to Ezekiel's deity.

Daniel's angelology exercised a substantial influence on later apocalyptic writers. The description of the Exalted Christ in Rev. 1.13-14 is modelled strikingly on the *two* Danielic passages just mentioned:

---

118. *Open Heaven*, p. 97. For a different view see Hurtado, *One God*, pp. 86-87. Hurtado thinks that there was no sharing of divinity as such with the angel.

2. The Christology of the Ascension of Isaiah

ἐν μέσῳ τῶν λυχνιῶν *ὅμοιον υἱὸν ἀνθρώπου*,[119] ἐνδεδυμένον ποδήρη καὶ περιεζωσμένον πρὸς τοῖς μαστοῖς ζώνην χρυσᾶν·ἡ δε κεφαλὴ αὐτοῦ *καὶ αἱ τρίχες λευκαὶ ὡς ἔριον λευκόν, ὡς χιών*,[120] καὶ οἱ ὀφθαλμοὶ αὐτοῦ ὡς φλὸξ πυρός, καὶ οἱ πόδες αὐτοῦ ὅμοιοι χαλκολιβάνῳ ὡς ἐν καμίνῳ πεπυρωμένης, καὶ ἡ φωνὴ αὐτοῦ ὡς φωνὴ ὑδάτων πολλῶν.

The debt which this passage owes to Daniel 10 includes the reference to the angel's girdle, his eyes, his feet and his voice. From Daniel 7 derives the reference to the man-like figure and to the white hair.[121] The author of Revelation offers a Christianized version of the Jewish angel tradition in which the heavenly Christ was made a divine being who received worship. The *Apocalypse of Abraham* and *Joseph and Asenath* also drew on Daniel 10 in their angelological imagery:

> [The seer's response to an angelophany] And I stood up and saw him who had taken my right hand and set me on my feet. The appearance of his body was like sapphire, and the aspect of his face was like chrysolite, *and the hair of his head like snow.*[122] And a kidaris [was] on his head, its look like that of a rainbow, and the clothing of his garments [was] purple; and a golden staff [was] in his right hand (*Apoc. Abr.* 11.3)[123]

> [Asenath's response to an angelophany] And the man called her a second time and said, 'Asenath, Asenath'. And she said, 'Behold [here] I [am], LORD. Who are you, tell me.' And the man said, 'I am the chief of the house of the Lord and commander of the whole host of the Most High. Rise and stand on your feet, and I will tell you what I have to say.' And Asenath raised her head and saw, and [behold] there was a man in every respect similar to Joseph, by the robe and the crown and the royal staff, except that his face was like lightning, and his eyes like sunshine, and the hairs of his head like a flame of fire of a burning torch, and his hands and feet like iron shining forth from a fire, and sparks shot forth from his

---

119. From Dan. 7.13.
120. From Dan. 7.9.
121. See C.C. Rowland, 'The Vision of the Risen Christ in Rev. i.13ff.: The Debt of an Early Christology to an Aspect of Jewish Angelology', *JTS* 31 (1980), pp. 1-11; T. Holtz, *Die Christologie der Apokalypse des Johannes* (Berlin: Akademie Verlag, 1962), pp. 116-28; and G. Kretschmar, *Studien zur frühchristlichen Trinitätstheologie* (BHT, 21; Tübingen: Mohr, 1956), p. 222.
122. Again from Dan. 7.9.
123. Translation by R. Rubinkiewicz in Charlesworth (ed.), *Old Testament Pseudepigrapha*, I, pp. 681-705. See also J.H. Charlesworth, *The Pseudepigrapha and Modern Research* (Missoula, MT: Scholars Press, 2nd edn with Supplement, 1981), pp. 68-69 for further discussion and bibliography.

hands and feet. And Asenath saw [it] and fell on her face at his feet on the ground (*Jos. Asen.* 14.9).[124]

The dependence of these passages on Daniel 10 is easy to discern. The chrysolite, topaz and gold of Jaoel's staff in the *Apocalypse of Abraham* derive from that passage, as do the angel's face and eyes, legs and feet in *Joseph and Asenath*. Jaoel in the *Apocalypse of Abraham* is further said to be indwelt by the ineffable name of God and to exercise a leading role among the angels (10.9).[125] *Joseph and Asenath* and Revelation further include a detail which is not found in Daniel 10 when they allude to the angel's 'white hair'. This feature derives in all probability from the description of the Ancient of Days which is found in Dan. 7.9-10.[126] Rowland plausibly argues that the source for this element in the two descriptions may have been the LXX reading of Dan. 7.13, which differs from Theodotion's text at that point to assert that the man-like figure came *as* the Ancient of Days.[127] These unrelated texts indicate that the significance of Daniel's angelology was recognized in the early Common Era and that its use of theophanic traditions was developed in a way which emphasized the exalted status of the angel who mediated revelation.

This conclusion is a significant one for the study of christological origins. Rev. 1.13-14 used Daniel's angelology to present the heavenly Christ as a figure who received worship with God (chs. 4 and 5) but in a context where the Jewish origins of the Christophany are plain to see. This Christian vision retains the idea of the mediator's visual similarity to God and shares this feature with the Jewish apocalypses. The Christology of Rev. 1.13-14 thereby has a marked angelomorphic basis. It is the *worship* addressed to the Christian mediator which marks a difference

---

124. Translation by C. Burchard in Charlesworth (ed.), *Old Testament Pseudepigrapha*, II, pp. 187-88. *Joseph and Asenath* is a Jewish romance which was written around the turn of the eras. For an introduction to this text see Burchard in Charlesworth (ed.), *Old Testament Pseudepigrapha*, II, pp. 177-247, and Charlesworth, *Pseudepigrapha and Modern Research*, pp. 137-40. The debt which both passages owe to Dan. 10.5-6 is discussed by Rowland, 'Man Clothed in Linen'.

125. This description of Jaoel has attracted considerable attention. Rowland argues that Jaoel was the companion of God's throne like Wisdom in Jewish literature (*Open Heaven*, p. 103). Fossum makes a connection with later Gnostic views and maintains that he is 'a personification of the divine name' (*Name of God*, p. 318; cf. Segal, *Two Powers*, p. 196). But Hurtado voices cautions about the extent to which Jaoel embodies divine attributes (*One God*, pp. 87-90).

126. This point is made by Rowland, 'Man Clothed in Linen', p. 333.

127. *Open Heaven*, p. 98.

2. *The Christology of the Ascension of Isaiah*

from the Jewish literature and reveals the distinctive religious interest of the early Christians. This difference from the Jewish apocalypses shows quite plainly the distinction between Jewish and Christian theology. The Jewish texts never include the second figure in worship; the New Testament Apocalypse always presents the heavenly Christ in this way. This comaprison illustrates the way in which the Christians modified the Jewish mediatorial tradition through the development of their belief in the divinity of Jesus.

The Interpretation of this Material

I have indicated in the course of this discussion that, although the Jewish mediatorial tradition has been identified as an important source for Christology, there has not always been agreement about this. The issue turns on whether or not Judaism before the rise of Christianity ever regarded any mediator as divine and thus whether the inclusion of Jesus within the cult was a new development (what Hurtado calls 'a mutation') in Jewish religious thought.

As an example of this debate we might cite the opinion of scholars such as Weber and Bousset who concluded that Wisdom and Logos in Jewish apocalyptic literature were divine 'hypostases' in the sense of heavenly agents who enjoyed independent existence from God.[128] Two articles by George Foot Moore in the 1920s criticized this view, not least because Bousset and others tended to devalue Judaism when compared with Christianity as a religion in which the deity was made remote and inaccessible.[129] This debate opened up again during the Second World War when Martin Werner produced his thesis about the existence of an early Christian 'angel-Christology', which resulted in the swift (but less detailed) reply of Wilhelm Michaelis.[130] Werner's arguments that angels were venerated in Judaism and that the Jews believed that the messiah would return to the angel world when his task was complete both failed to commend themselves to scholarship. We have seen that neither view is correct. They tended most unfortunately to obscure the more helpful aspects of Werner's book. As a result, there arose the general assumption that Michaelis had been right in his criticism of Werner and that angelology contributed little of significance to the development of Christology.

---

128. See Weber, *System*; Bousset, *Judentums*.
129. 'Christian Writers', 'Intermediaries'.
130. See *Engelchristologie*.

In this tradition stands Dunn, who dismisses the influence of angelology on Christology in a mere ten pages.

This debate about the significance of Jewish mediators has continued in scholarship after the publication of Dunn's *Christology* in 1980. The position that Judaism before the rise of Christianity was binitarian in outlook has been supported by J.-A. Fossum in his study of the origins of the Gnostic Demiurge. Fossum believes that the exalted angel in Judaism shared 'the divine nature' or 'the divine mode of being'; he thinks that the angel Jaoel in the *Apocalypse of Abraham* is a 'personification of the divine name'.[131] Fossum, however, is strongly criticized for this view by Hurtado, who observes that the worship of Jesus was a new religious phenomenon, giving Christianity a binitarian theology which Judaism had not previously contemplated.[132]

Although I accept that this material offers a high view of the mediator's position, I also feel that Hurtado is right to look for *differences* as well as for points of contact between Jewish and Christian theology. Christianity swiftly distinguished itself from Judaism through its cultic veneration of Jesus. The early and consistent worship of Jesus in early Christianity makes for a contrast rather than a parallel with Jewish apocalyptic literature. This difference must be acknowledged before we can begin to affirm the similarities which exist between the two strands of belief. The overwhelming conclusion which emerges from this approach to the material is that the early Christians drew on Jewish mediatorial ideas but that they used them in a different way which was guided by their belief in the divinity of Jesus and their offering of worship to him.

Philo's evidence is significant for this conclusion. Where ben Sirach possibly called Moses *Elohim*—the title which was applied to Melchizedek at Qumran—only Philo called a mediator 'the second God'. Philo was quick to explain that this statement must not be taken literally, and he never said that the Logos should be worshipped. Philo's understanding contrasts in this respect with that of Justin Martyr, who knew Philo's work but adapted his language to present Christ as 'another God and Lord subject to the Maker of all things' (*Dial.* 56.13) to yield a binitarian theology.[133] Justin's Christ was 'another God': a divine being who was called 'angel' among other titles (*Dial.* 61, 128). The origins of

---

131. Fossum, *Name of God*, pp. 307-21.
132. *One God*, pp. 85-90.
133. Justin's probable knowledge of Philo (among other sources) is examined by Trakatellis, *Pre-Existence*, pp. 61-68.

2. The Christology of the Ascension of Isaiah

this belief lie in New Testament Christianity. Not even in the heights of pre-Christian Alexandrianism do we find the belief that the Logos was a second deity or that he was entitled to worship. This conclusion about Philo confirms the evaluation I have placed on the other Jewish evidence considered. The various figures surveyed in the literature function as viziers or vice-gerents who discharge action on behalf of the transcendent God. Yet they never finally compromise the divine authority or represent a binitarian mutation. Hurtado's phrase 'divine chief agent' well expresses their exalted position and retains the sense of distance from God which the material suggests.

Despite my caution, the evidence indicates that all the conditions which were necessary for the Christian reformulation of monotheism had already been created in the Jewish apocalyptic literature which is examined here. Once the *worship* of Jesus is recognized as a new religious development, it can be seen that belief in such ideas as Wisdom who accompanied God, a human being who was exalted to supreme status in heaven and an angel who appeared in the place of God, anticipated what the Christians came to believe. A religion which installed a chief agent in close proximity to God, even a strongly monotheistic religion, ran the risk of producing binitarian or even polytheistic offshoots once the gap between the mediator and God itself became the subject of speculative interest.[134] The evidence suggests that the Jewish mediatorial tradition was modified in several ways in the early Common Era. Christian theology is merely one example. Within a Jewish context certain rabbis speculated about an angel mediator in a way which others thought unhelpful.[135] Gnosticism, too, developed the mediator's position by introducing the divine rival called the Demiurge who was alleged to have created the human world in rebellion against greater powers.[136] Gnosticism can now only in part be seen as a Christian deviation. Texts like the *Apocalypse of Adam* and the *Apocryphon of John* look back directly to Judaism and indicate that Gnostic demiurgical notions developed polemically from *Jewish* beliefs. These different examples show how the Jewish mediatorial tradition was modified once the notion of 'absolutely only one' divinity was weakened by the attention accorded to his subordinate.

---

134. See further Rowland, *Open Heaven*, pp. 110-11.
135. See the evidence for this collected by Segal in his *Two Powers*, esp. pp. 109-134.
136. See further below.

Descent and Ascent as Themes within the Tradition

One further strand of belief demands our attention. An important aspect of the *Ascension of Isaiah* is its description of the hidden descent, which is combined with the theme of the Beloved One's transformation into human likeness. These two themes determine the presentation of the human Jesus in the apocalypse.

The demonstration that the hidden descent has a background in Jewish angelology strengthens the case for supposing that this source influenced the Christology of the *Ascension of Isaiah*. I shall now briefly mention the Jewish evidence for the descent of heavenly mediators. Heavenly descent (and ascension) were attributed to Wisdom and angels in Jewish literature. Sirach 24 describes how Wisdom 'tabernacled' in Israel in response to the divine command. Her descent to earth is not described in this passage, but the author seems to presuppose such a view and indicates that the earthly appearance was undertaken in response to the divine command. The later *1 Enoch* 42 develops Sirach's view to create a parable of Wisdom's hostile reception in Israel. This parable includes a description of Wisdom's descent from heaven, her rejection on earth and subsequent return to heaven. Here we find a pattern of movement analogous to the Christology of the *Ascension of Isaiah*, but without the suggestion that the mediator appeared as a human person.

Descent and ascent were features of the angelological tradition too. The book of Tobit has often been neglected in the search for Jewish parallels to Christian 'incarnational' beliefs.[137] Tobit develops the theme of an angelophany in some detail and offers some striking parallels to ideas which are found in the *Ascension of Isaiah*. Tob. 3.16-17 describes how the angel Raphael was sent by God to accomplish a double act of healing. Chapter 5 finds him on earth in human form. This disguise is sustained throughout the drama until Raphael reveals his identity in ch. 12. As soon as he has done this the angel returns to heaven (Tob. 12.15-20). Tobit 12 includes the statement that the mediator merely *appeared* to eat and drink (12.19), which I believe has parallels with early Christian docetism. Tobit is far from the only text to describe an angelophany in this way. Other texts which do so include the *Prayer of Joseph*, which we have considered already, and the *Testament of Abraham*, which calls

---

137. Tobit's significance for New Testament Christology is recognized by Segal in his article, 'Heavenly Ascent', p. 1372.

2. The Christology of the Ascension of Isaiah

the angel Michael 'a most handsome soldier' (2.4) in the context of his earthly appearance. The idea has foundations in the Pentateuchal angelophanies where either God or his angel are said to appear in human likeness (see for example Gen. 18; Judg. 13). This wider material shows that Tobit's understanding is not unique in Jewish tradition. It testifies to a popular belief which we might not unreasonably suppose to have enjoyed an extensive circulation in the early Common Era. This material suggests that the case for specifying an angelological influence on the *Ascension of Isaiah* might have more than one aspect.

The Impact of this Material on First-Century Christology

Many New Testament passages bear a striking resemblance to this Jewish material: much more so than to the pagan parallels which I have already mentioned. Thus for instance the author of 1 Peter describes how Jesus journeyed from earth to heaven. He states that the angels submitted to Jesus before he sat down beside the throne of God (3.22).[138] This passage calls to mind Jewish stories about Moses, particularly the early speculation of Ezekiel the Tragedian; and about Enoch, who like Moses occupied a heavenly throne in Jewish tradition. Hebrews too describes how the Son ascended into the heavenly sanctuary to make his act of atonement (4.14; 10.19-20).[139] In Paul we find the description of Christ in terms which were suggested by Jewish beliefs about divine Wisdom. Paul says that Christ was the agent of creation (1 Cor. 8.6) and the very image of the invisible God (Col. 1.15).[140] The Wisdom tradition helped to create the portrait of Jesus as the eschatological bearer of Wisdom which is found in Mt. 11.28-30.[141] It further influenced the author of the Logos poem which stands behind the Johannine Prologue, who developed the thought of Sirach 24 by describing how the Word of God appeared in Israel as a human person (rather than as the Torah).[142]

---

138. See Dalton, *Christ's Proclamation*, pp. 163-201. Dalton notes that Christ is portrayed as a new Enoch in this passage.

139. This strand of Hebrews' thought is examined by O. Hofius, *Der Vorhang vor dem thron Gottes: Eine exegetische-religionsgeschichtliche Untersuchung zu Hebräerbrief 6,19f. und 10,19f.* (WUNT, 14; Tübingen: Mohr, 1972).

140. On this aspect of Pauline Christology see B.A. Pearson, 'Hellenistic–Jewish Wisdom Speculation and Paul', in Wilken (ed.), *Aspects of Wisdom*, pp. 43-66.

141. This is noticed by Suggs, *Wisdom*, pp. 79-83.

142. For a recent review of ths debate see M. Scott, *Sophia and the Johannine Jesus* (JSNTSup, 71; Sheffield: JSOT Press, 1992).

This correspondence makes it desirable to pursue the relationship between Jewish and Christian mediatorial beliefs as a means of understanding the context in which Christian theology emerged. In doing this, as I said, we must take account of the fact that Christians modified Jewish views and that they did not perpetuate an existing binitarianism. One of the mistakes of the History of Religions school was to assume that the relationship between Christianity and Judaism was a matter of 'parallels' alone. This is an oversimplification of the issue. Religious assimilation often leads to the reworking of existing material in a polemical context which produces a *new* form of belief through which the influence of the source religion is negated. This is particularly true when the religion which is making the change finds itself overpowered or threatened by its parent, as is often the case with sectarian movements.

Sectarianism, broadly speaking, was the position in which the first Christians found themselves over against mainstream Judaism. Christianity modified the Jewish mediatorial tradition from the outset by including Jesus in the cult.[143] There was no precise analogy for this in pre-Christian Judaism. Jesus was held to be the 'one mediator' between God and humanity according to 1 Tim. 2.5 (cf. Heb. 9.15; 12.24). For the first time in Judaism a single mediator was held to transcend all others. The fact that Jesus was seen in the position of the divine vice-gerent meant that Moses and Enoch were displaced and that they became the subject of polemic in some Christian literature (for example Jn 3.13; 6.46; 1 Pet. 3.19, 22).[144] The book of Acts and many other New Testament documents show the hostility which this Christian devotional praxis provoked from the Jews; not least because the proclamation of a crucified messiah was anathema on biblical authority.[145]

Christianity thus represented a religious innovation which built on Jewish images about the divine chief agent but which asserted the divinity of Jesus in a way which had both theological and eschatological consequences. Christology, or beliefs about Jesus viewed as the messiah, became a matter of importance for that reason. It was *the* factor which

---

143. See the elucidation of this point by Bauckham, 'Worship of Jesus'; and by Hurtado, *One God*.

144. I discuss this matter further in Chapter 4.

145. Crucifixion as a manner of death infringed the Deuteronomistic prohibition against exhibiting the corpses of those who had met their death by stoning. Paul makes this point in Gal. 3.13. The biblical authority is provided by Deut. 21.23.

2. *The Christology of the Ascension of Isaiah*

distinguished Christians from Jews. Christology itself underwent a process of development as the first century progressed. We must examine that development to understand what the christological tradition learned from Jewish mediatorial speculation, and then to place the *Ascension of Isaiah* in its rightful position in that tradition.

The Worship of Jesus in the New Testament Literature

The earliest Christology advocated the belief that Jesus, the state criminal who had been executed by the Romans, shared the divine nature in heaven.[146] This view is expressed in the Hymn which Paul incorporated when he wrote to the Philippian Christians: 'He became obedient unto death, even death on a cross. Therefore God has highly exalted him and bestowed on him the name which is above every name' (Phil. 2.8-9). This Hymn made Jesus' exaltation a consequence of his shameful death. He now bore the name κύριος, the Septuagintal name of God himself (but not yet θεός at this early period).[147] The apotheosis of Jesus is presented by the author of Acts as having been the theme of the first ever Christian sermon. Peter is reported as telling the crowd at Pentecost:

> This Jesus...you crucified and killed by the hands of lawless men...But God raised him up, having loosed the pangs of death, because it was not possible for him to be held by it...Being therefore exalted at the right hand of God...God has made him both Lord and Christ, this Jesus whom you crucified (Acts 2.23-24, 33, 36).

Resurrection was followed by exaltation in this report: Jesus is called Lord as well as Christ, which implies the attribute of divinity (cf. 1 Cor. 8.6). His position 'at the right hand' of God distinguishes him from all other mediators. This phrase alludes to Ps. 110.1. It picks up Jewish royal ideology and gives it a cosmic significance by making the messiah the

---

146. See further Hengel, *Son*, pp. 1-2.
147. Zech. 14.5 is an example of the kind of Hebrew text which was used to resource early Christian belief in the 'lordship' of Jesus (see 1 Thess. 3.13; 2 Thess. 1.7). Isa. 45 also stands behind Phil. 2.5-11 which I have partially cited here. In this latter case we meet the interesting phenomenon of a Hebrew text which was written to exclude other deities being used to support a binitarian theology. Hengel comments on this development in Phil. 2.5-11 that the 'name above every name' is 'the tetragram YHWH, for which κύριος was already being substituted in the reading of the LXX: God gave his unspeakable name to his subordinate' (*Studies in Early Christology*, pp. 155-56; see also pp. 379-83 of the same volume).

heavenly companion of God who shared his title and glory.[148] The transformed Jesus was thus believed to be no ordinary mediator but a divine being who was entitled to worship and who had been installed at the right hand in the position of divine vicegerent.

The belief that Jesus was divine arose within a short period of his death. Jesus had been crucified by the Romans as a messianic pretender.[149] The conclusion of all four Gospels with the story of the empty tomb, together with Paul's visionary experience of the heavenly Christ (Gal. 1.15-16; 1 Cor. 15.8), presents belief in the resurrection of Jesus as the major factor in this rethinking of attitudes. Paul told the Corinthian Christians that if Christ had not risen from the dead then their faith was in vain (1 Cor. 15.17). He assumes the resurrection and makes it the key to his argument in this chapter (as he does in several of his letters).

This is not the place to engage in discussion of what the concept of 'resurrection' meant in early Christian literature.[150] Suffice it to say that Paul never mentions the empty tomb and that the original ending of Mark (16.8) makes the women keep silent about their discovery of the tomb. This does not encourage the conclusion that the empty tomb by itself was the cause of resurrection belief. The New Testament evidence indicates by contrast that it was visionary experience of the heavenly Jesus which prompted this belief in the disciples.[151] They came to the conviction that Jesus had been transformed through the shame of his death into a unique mediator who shared the divine glory and worship. The resources for this view were provided by the Jewish mediatorial tradition.

---

148. See the discussion of Markschies, '"*Sessio ad dexteram*"', and Hengel in his *Studies in Early Christology*, pp. 119-225.

149. This point is commonly accepted by scholars. See the discussion of it by E.P. Sanders, *Jesus and Judaism* (London: SCM Press, 1985), pp. 294-318.

150. The issues of interpretation which surround the New Testament evidence for the resurrection are surveyed in two recent books. See P. Avis (ed.), *The Resurrection of Jesus* (London: Darton, Longman & Todd, 1993); and S. Barton and G.N. Stanton (eds.), *Resurrection: Essays in Honour of Leslie Houlden* (London: SPCK, 1994).

151. The Pauline evidence is decisive on this issue. Both 1 Cor. 15.8 and Gal. 1.15-16 imply that Paul's 'conversion' was prompted by a mystical vision of the heavenly Jesus. The resurrection appearances which are described in the Gospels can similarly be explained as apocalyptic or mystical visions. See the stimulating essay on this subject by M.D. Goulder, 'Did Jesus of Nazareth Rise from the Dead?', in Barton and Stanton (eds.), *Resurrection*, pp. 58-68.

2. *The Christology of the Ascension of Isaiah* 129

Within that Jewish background we must examine the promotion of certain human beings to exalted status in the apocalyptic literature. Like Enoch in *1 Enoch* 71, Moses in Ezekiel the Tragedian and Abel in the *Testament of Abraham*, Jesus was held to rank above the angels and to stand in the position of divine vicegerent (with the cultic difference noted). It is not too much to claim that this Christology would have been *inconceivable* without the prior resources of the Jewish strand which provided the means for describing Jesus' transformation into a heavenly being. This was in spite of his recent and ignominious death and the fact that Judaism had reserved this position for exceptional figures from the distant past.

The novel feature of Christian theology was the inclusion of Jesus in the cult. Paul explains this new aspect of belief when he includes what appears to be a credal or liturgical saying in his first letter to the Corinthians:

> For us, there is one God, the Father,
> from whom are all things and through whom we exist
> and one Lord Jesus Christ,
> through whom are all things and through whom we exist (1 Cor. 8.6).

The formula begins with words based on the Shema, the Jewish daily prayer, which declares that 'there is one God'.[152] Paul's form of words shows that the thought of the Shema has been fundamentally recast. Monotheism is here counterbalanced by belief in a heavenly 'Lord'. Paul is careful to avoid saying that there are two *Gods*. Jewish monotheism may have been modified, but it had by no means been set aside. The suggestion that there were two θεοὶ would have been unthinkable in a Jewish ambience.[153] The meaning of Jesus' 'lordship' in this statement is defined by the conviction that he was God's agent *through whom* the creation had been effected, as distinct from God the creator. This distinction echoes themes which stemmed from the Jewish Wisdom tradition, particularly the strand in Prov. 3.19 and 8.22 (cf. Wis. 8.4-6 and Philo, *Det. Pot. Ins.* 54) where Wisdom is called the Lord's co-worker who operated at the beginning of things. Jesus was thereby

---

152. For the Jewish background see Hurtado, *One God*, pp. 97-98; G.H. Giblin, 'Three Monotheistic Texts in Paul', *CBQ* 37 (1975), pp. 527-47; and R.A. Horsley, 'The Background of the Confessional Formula in 1 Cor. 8.6', *ZNW* 69 (1978), pp. 130-34.

153. The distinction between the two terms is briefly examined by D.E.H. Whiteley, *The Theology of St Paul* (Oxford: Basil Blackwell, 1964), p. 104.

identified with creative divine Wisdom in a context in which he was called 'Lord' and made an independent divine being.

The Use of Psalm 110.1 in Early Christianity

The Christians developed their beliefs about the exaltation of Jesus by positing his enthronement at the right hand of God. This view was derived originally from reflection on Ps. 110.1 (LXX).[154] Psalm 110 was addressed in the Hebrew Bible to the Jewish monarch.[155] Verse 1 falls into two parts. The first half is an instruction from 'the Lord' to 'my Lord' to sit at his right hand. The second half says that this situation would pertain until his enemies had been subdued. 'The Lord' in this context is clearly God himself. 'My Lord' in the original Psalm was the Jewish king. In the Christian interpretation of the Psalm the title is referred to Christ, whose divinity is established on the basis of the LXX text.

According to the Gospels the earliest Christian use of Ps. 110.1 was on the lips of Jesus himself. Mk 12.35-37 and parr. record a saying of Jesus in the Temple which appears to deny Davidic sonship to the messiah.[156] Jesus is made to argue, on the basis of Ps. 110.1, that the messiah was not David's son but his Lord. Given that early Christianity universally presented Jesus as a Davidide (see Mt. 1.1; Lk. 2.4; Rom. 1.3), it seems unlikely that this pericope was created by the early church. Despite its problems, it probably records something which Jesus himself said. This impression is strengthened by the observation that Ps. 110.1 is used in this context in a *different* sense from other New Testament usage. Jesus is made to pick up the opening line of the verse—the reference to the messiah as David's Lord—but not the later phrases which refer to the king's enthronement at the right hand of God. Perhaps later Christian usage was suggested by the recollection that Jesus himself had

---

154. The influence of Ps. 110 on New Testament Christology is examined in the literature which I mentioned in Chapter 1. Markschies, '"*Sessio ad dexteram*"', and Hengel, *Studies in Early Christology*, are the two most significant recent contributions.

155. It is generally taken as a pre-exilic royal Psalm. See Hay, *Glory*, p. 19; and A. Weiser, *The Psalms* (London: SCM Press, 1962), p. 693.

156. See further C.E.B. Cranfield, *Mark* (Cambridge: Cambridge University Press, 1959), p. 382.

2. *The Christology of the Ascension of Isaiah* 131

cited the passage, albeit in a different way.[157] If this is so, there was an early process of interpretation in which the reference acquired a new significance in the light of the beliefs about Jesus which emerged after his resurrection.

The earliest New Testament use of Ps. 110.1 does not dwell on the concept of heavenly enthronement, either. In 1 Cor. 15.24-25 Paul states that Christ would destroy every rule, authority and power, and reign until his enemies had been placed beneath his feet. This passage uses the second half of the verse—but not the first—to describe the messiah's final victory at the eschaton. It might be argued that the concept of 'reigning' *presupposes* belief in enthronement (for that is how a king is perceived); but the silence of 1 Cor. 15.24-25 on this matter is significant even if enthronement can be inferred from the passage.

The earliest documented use of Ps. 110.1 (LXX) to support belief in Christ's heavenly enthronement is Rom. 8.34 (55–56 CE).[158] Paul there makes belief in Christ's enthronement a consequence of his resurrection and connects it with the theme of his intercession for Christian believers. Enthronement beliefs undergird Col. 3.1, Eph. 1.20, 1 Pet. 3.22 and a considerable number of references in Acts, by which time (c. 80–90 CE) the idea had become almost a commonplace of Christology. One ought perhaps to observe that there was an inevitability about this development given what the Jewish mediatorial tradition had said about the enthronement of Moses and other heavenly figures. Belief in the enthronement of Jesus was related to this complex of ideas but it was set within the new religious and theological context created by early Christianity. The specific use of Ps. 110.1 to support this idea was due to the conviction that Jesus was the messiah and to the belief that as messiah he was a heavenly being. Ps. 110.1 was applied to a heavenly rather than to an earthly monarch through the influence of Christian theology.

Christian use of Ps. 110.1 (LXX) to support Jesus' heavenly enthronement was thus a feature of early but not, in fact, the earliest christological reflection, to judge by the evidence that we have. It is found only in literature later than Romans. In 1 Corinthians 15 Paul used Ps. 110.1 to describe Christ's *earthly* rule. Subsequent New Testament usage describes Jesus' heavenly position in more detail once the belief in his exaltation

157. This is the suggestion of C.H. Dodd, *According to the Scriptures* (London: Nisbet & Co., 1952), p. 110.
158. Hengel notes that the wording of the citation of Ps. 110.1 in Rom. 8.34 is inexact (in his *Studies in Early Christology*, p. 141).

had become established. This sharper definition was probably a response to the continuing delay of the parousia which had created the need for reassurance about the truth of Christian eschatology in view of the timescale which Christianity had originally envisaged (see Mk 9.1; cf. 2 Pet. 3.4). There is an important parallel for the belief in the enthronement of Jesus in the portrait of Abel as a seated figure which is found in the *Testament of Abraham*. Since Jesus was believed to be divine, it must have seemed natural that he should have his *own* throne in heaven by analogy with the theophany. His position on the *merkabah* itself, which some scholars think is suggested by Rev. 5.6 and which is paralleled by the *Similitudes of Enoch* and by Ezekiel the Tragedian, did not command wide assent in Christian theology.[159] This development of the concept of heavenly enthronement in first-century Christianity prepared the way for the notion of the *three* enthroned divinities which is found for the first time in the *Ascension of Isaiah*.

Among the clearest expressions of such 'enthronement Christology' in the New Testament is 1 Pet. 3.22. This is the verse which, as I have shown, was used by the author of the *Ascension of Isaiah*. Its author combined belief in Christ's enthronement with a mythological description of his ascension to heaven and the submission of the angel world which made Christ an unparalleled mediator. The passage draws extensively on the Jewish mediatorial tradition. Its reference to angelic surrender probably owes something to the traditions about Enoch which are found in the early chapters of *1 Enoch*, which describe the fall and punishment of the Watchers (who make their first appearance in Jewish literature in Gen. 6).[160] These traditions about the insubordination of the angels are presented in Christianized form in 1 Pet. 3.22, which asserts that these angels *submitted* to Jesus and thereby makes Jesus a superior mediator to Enoch (who merely passed on the divine message in the story told by *1 Enoch*). The superiority of Jesus is further emphasized in 1 Peter 3 by the account of his heavenly enthronement, a position which Enoch acquired in the *Similitudes of Enoch* but not in the earlier portions of *1 Enoch* where the Watchers' story is narrated. Even when 1 Peter 3 is compared with the *Similitudes*, we must speak about a difference in the status of the two figures in the relevant literature. Jesus in the Christian vision is made a divine being but Enoch is (merely) the divine chief

---

159. See above on the exegesis of Rev. 5.6.
160. See Reicke, *Disobedient Spirits*, and Dalton, *Christ's Proclamation*. I discuss this matter in Chapter 4.

2. The Christology of the Ascension of Isaiah

agent. This difference is illustrated by the fact of angelic submission in the Christian text. The *Ascension of Isaiah* further expanded this idea of Christ's heavenly journey by combining it with the theme of the hidden descent and of the enthronement of the Holy Spirit to yield an early trinitarian vision (see *Asc. Isa.* 10.17–11.33).

Visionary Experience in Christian Literature

We find the influence of the Jewish mediatorial tradition in a number of early Christian visions of Christ. Visionary experience attended the birth of Christianity. Joseph and Zechariah received angelic visitations, and Jesus himself reportedly saw a vision of the Spirit at his baptism.[161] The earliest record of Christian visionary experience is Paul's account of his so-called 'conversion' in Gal. 1.16. This passage was written some years after the event and displays significant differences from the later descriptions of the event found in the book of Acts.[162] Where Acts describes a vision of Jesus who appeared in a vision and spoke to Paul, Paul's own account says that God revealed his Son 'in me'. This implies an interior experience which deserves to be compared with Paul's language of justification and use of the term 'in Christ' and which suggests the apostle's awareness of a mystical relationship with Jesus as the core of his personal religion. 1 Cor. 15.8 also suggests that Paul's conversion was effected by a vision of the heavenly Jesus. This confirms the importance of visionary revelation for this prolific New Testament writer.

Both the longer ending of Mark (16.12) and Luke 24 were influenced by Jewish angelology in their descriptions of the resurrected Jesus. Mk 16.12 says that the risen Jesus appeared to two disciples 'in another form'. The Lukan account of the journey to Emmaus (ch. 24) has what appears to be a more elaborate description of this incident. It describes how the risen Jesus appeared to the two disciples and how they failed to recognize him. One must presume that this was because his risen body was visibly different from its crucified counterpart. The fact that the risen Jesus could adapt his form in this way implies that the disciples witnessed the appearance of a *heavenly* visitor (and not a resuscitated

---

161. On the apocalyptic significance of the baptism of Jesus see F. Lentzen-Deis, *Die Taufe Jesu nach den Synoptikern* (Frankfurter Theologische Studien, 4; Frankfurt: Josef Knecht, 1970), pp. 99-127.

162. See the discussion of this matter by H.D. Betz, *Galatians* (Philadelphia: Fortress Press, 1979), pp. 64-75.

human being). There is a precedent for this in the book of Tobit where Raphael assumes a human form that masks his heavenly nature. This is the implication too of the summary of the story in Mk 16.12.

At two points we can glimpse the way in which the Christians perceived the appearance of their heavenly Lord. The vision of the exalted Christ in Rev. 1.13-14 uses imagery derived from Dan. 10.5-6 to present Christ as a heavenly mediator in terms which recall the theophany. We have seen that behind Dan. 10.5-6 stands the influence of Ezek. 1.26-27 and other passages from that work.[163] Rev. 1.13-14 transfers the same divine attributes to a subordinate divine being which Daniel had assigned to the angel (and which other apocalypses continued to assign to an angel). This represents an interesting development of Jewish tradition. Ezekiel had described the theophany. Daniel used this theophany to form his angelophany. The author of Revelation in turn used Daniel's angelophany to describe the appearance of a second divine being, which drew out the theophanic significance of Daniel's angelophany and which represents a direct link back to Ezekiel. The Jewish theophanic tradition was clearly an important source for this early Christian vision of Christ.

There is a further description of the heavenly Jesus in the transfiguration narrative which is recorded in all three Synoptic Gospels.[164] The three passages describe how Jesus' clothes became dazzling white. Behind this incident probably stands the influence of *1 Enoch* 14. Rowland observes that no less than five words are held in common with the Greek text of *1 En.* 14.20-21.[165] These are the sun, the face, the colour white, the snow and the clothing. This evidence indicates that the transfiguration narrative drew on the Jewish theophanic tradition to present Jesus as a divine being. The transfiguration is perhaps the clearest

---

163. See Rowland, 'The Vision of the Risen Christ'.

164. See Mt. 17.1-7; Mk 9.2-8; Lk. 9.28-36. The transfiguration narrative is examined by A.M. Ramsey, *The Glory of God and the Transfiguration of Christ* (London: Longmans, Green, 1945); A. Riesenfeld, *Jésus transfiguré: L'arrière-plan du récit évangelique de la transfiguration de Nôtre-Seigneur* (ASNU, 16; Copenhagen: Munksgaard, 1947); B.D. Chilton, 'The Transfiguration: Dominical Assurance and Apostolic Vision', *NTS* 27 (1981), pp. 115-24; B.E. Reid, *The Transfiguration: A Source- and Redaction-Critical Study of Luke 9.28-36* (Paris: Gabalda, 1993); and A.A. Trites, *The Transfiguration of Christ: A Hinge of Holy History* (Hantsport: Lancelot Press, 1994).

165. *Open Heaven*, p. 367. Rowland notes that 'snow' is found only in some manuscripts and that the Greek word for 'clothing' is different in the two strands of literature.

2. The Christology of the Ascension of Isaiah

declaration of the divinity of Jesus in the Gospels. The passage gains its effect from the use of imagery which Jewish tradition had applied to the theophany. It makes the point that Jesus was a *second divine being* who related uniquely to God in a way which Judaism had not anticipated. This vision of the heavenly Jesus was read back into the story of his life, perhaps in anticipation of his return from heaven, under the conviction that the earthly Jesus was the identifiable counterpart of the heavenly Lord.

The Emergence of a 'Pre-Existence' Christology in the New Testament

At some point in the first century the Christians began to speak about Jesus as the incarnation (or earthly appearance) of a heavenly mediator. It has been disputed when this development took place. The Pauline correspondence has been studiously examined in this context. Opinions have been advanced both for and against the proposition that Paul thought that Christ was a pre-existent being who became identified with Jesus. The evidence, it must be said, is ambiguous.[166] It is exemplified by the difficulty of deciding whether the ἐν μορφῇ θεοῦ ὑπάρχων of Phil. 2.6 describes the life of a heavenly being or merely that of the human Jesus when compared with Adam as his predecessor. The meaning of the 'sending' terminology in Gal. 4.4 and Rom. 8.3, and the reference to the 'riches' of Jesus in 2 Cor. 8.9, have provoked a similar uncertainty.

This matter is too complicated to permit a superficial analysis, as the extensive secondary literature on the subject shows.[167] I shall not review it in detail here. I do however want to observe that, despite what can be said in favour of the 'pre-existence' interpretation of Phil. 2.6-11 (an exegesis with which I have some sympathy), nothing in the Pauline literature offers an explicit view of the *hidden* descent to match the evidence of the *Ascension of Isaiah*. The notion that the messiah disguised his identity when he descended through the heavens was a second-century Christian belief and not a first-century one. 1 Cor. 2.8 is no exception to this statement because it describes how the *crucified* Jesus escaped his

---

166. The debate up to the early 1980s is summarized in the revised edition of R.P. Martin's *Carmen Christi* (Grand Rapids: Eerdmans, 2nd edn, 1983). The most recent treatment is that of Habermann in *Präexistenzaussagen*.

167. This literature has been extensively reviewed by Habermann, *Präexistenzaussagen*.

tormentors' understanding. Rom. 10.6-8 does mention an attempt to bring Christ down (from heaven), but only I think in a hypothetical sense. There is no tradition of hiddenness in Eph. 4.8-9, which mentions the descent from heaven. If Paul did allude to the messiah's heavenly pre-existence in Philippians 2, it is evident from a comparison with the *Ascension of Isaiah* that much has to be *inferred* from that passage about the messiah's connection with Jesus and is not made explicit there. This does not exclude the possibility of a 'pre-existence' interpretation of that passage, but it does show some of the difficulties which attend its exegesis. The idea of pre-existence, if it is expressed in Philippians 2, is found there only in a naïve form. The question of whether Paul taught an 'incarnational' Christology should thus perhaps be judged an 'open' one on the evidence of the texts themselves.

There are strong hints that Christology was developing in the direction of a heavenly pre-existence in Hebrews, Ephesians and John, all of which were written after the fall of Jerusalem (70 CE). Hebrews opens with the assertion that God had communicated eschatologically through his Son. The assertion which is made in this context that God had made the world through the Son reflects Christian use of Jewish Wisdom speculation; but something more than primordial speculation is offered in this passage.[168] Heb. 1.6 asserts that God had brought his first-born Son into the οἰκουμένη.[169] Later in the letter the author describes how Jesus 'partook' of human flesh and blood (2.14).[170] This hints that his life was preceded by the mediation at creation of which 1.2 speaks. These passages seem to represent an extension of the view which had been adopted by Col. 1.15-20, where Christ was identified with the creative Wisdom of God. Hebrews makes the point that the Son had mediated at creation but also that he had become identified with Jesus at a specific moment of history. This point is not elaborated in any detail; but it is difficult to escape the conclusion that Hebrews offers at least embryonic

---

168. See H. Hegermann, *Die Vorstellung vom Schöpfungsmittler im hellenistischen Judentum und Urchristentum* (TU, 82; Berlin: Akademie Verlag, 1961), pp. 110-23, 133-37.

169. The exegesis of Heb. 1.6 has been disputed, but there are reasonable grounds for taking it as a reference to the incarnation. The different interpretations which have been proposed for this passage are surveyed by H. Attridge, *Hebrews* (Philadelphia: Fortress Press, 1989), pp. 55-56.

170. See the discussion of Attridge, *Hebrews*, pp. 79-82.

2. The Christology of the Ascension of Isaiah

evidence for the Son's pre-existence in heaven before the ministry of Jesus.

Ephesians also contains a passage which implies that Christ as a heavenly being descended from heaven (4.8-9); but nothing is said in this context to indicate how the author thought that this descent was related to the person of Jesus. The context of this assertion is an elaboration of the reference to God's ascension which is found in Ps. 68.18 and which the author understood as a reference to the ascension of Christ. He gives his view that this ascension had been preceded by a descent and that Christ in this sense had descended into the 'lower parts of the earth'. The meaning of the last phrase has been disputed.[171] Some have seen it as a reference to the 'descent to hell', but that idea is by no means prominent in the New Testament literature.[172] Others have taken it, with greater plausibility, as a reference to Christ's descent from heaven to earth and thus as an 'incarnational' reference.[173] Even if this second interpretation is adopted, again, much has to be inferred from the passage about the incarnation and is not made explicit there. The wider context of belief nevertheless tends to support the conclusion that an 'incarnational' Christology was emerging around the time that Ephesians was written (c. 80–90 CE).

The formula incorporated in 1 Tim. 3.16, which says that Christ was 'manifested in the flesh', implies the view that a heavenly being *appeared* as a human person.[174] The wider context of the letter makes it

---

171. See the summary of A.T. Lincoln, *Ephesians* (Dallas: Word Books, 1990), pp. 244-47.

172. See my Chapter 4 on this subject.

173. Those who hold this view include E. Percy, *Die Probleme der Kolosser- und Epheserbriefe* (Lund: Gleerup, 1946), pp. 273-74; and H. Schlier, *Christus und die Kirche im Epheserbrief* (Tübingen: Mohr, 1930), pp. 192-93.

174. This hymn (for such it is) has been examined most recently by Hengel, *Studies in Early Christology*, pp. 285-87. Hengel thinks that the Pastorals are late documents (c. 110 CE or even later) and that 1 Tim. 3.16 has no original relation to its context. In Chapter 4 I shall argue that the author of the *Ascension of Isaiah* was aware of this hymnic summary, which he must have derived from the same liturgical source as the author of the Pastorals. Previous studies of 1 Tim. 3.16 include E. Norden, *Agnostos Theos* (repr.; Darmstadt: Wissenschaftliche Buchgesellschaft, 1956), pp. 254-63; R. Deichgräber, *Gotteshymnus und Christushymnus in der frühen Christenheit* (SUNT, 5; Göttingen: Vandenhoeck & Ruprecht, 1967), pp. 133-37; W. Stenger, 'Der Christushymnus in 1 Tim. 3,16: Aufbau-Christologie-Sitz im Leben', *TTZ* 78 (1969), pp. 33-48; and J. Murphy-O'Connor, 'Redactional

clear that Christ's entry into the world featured in its author's thought (1.15). This brings the Christology of 1 Tim. 3.16 close to the more explicit pattern of Christology which is found in the *Ascension of Isaiah* (although considerable differences still remain between the two). Once again a full explanation of what 'manifestation in the flesh' involved in terms of how the mediator related to Jesus has to be inferred from the context and is not explained there. The fact that we are dealing with hymnic language indicates that liturgical thought in the later first century was beginning to permit the suggestion that Christ had appeared as Jesus. This marks a definite development from the earliest form of Christology which had begun from a consideration of the transformation of the human Jesus into a divine being.

Explicit formulation of incarnational belief is found in the Logos poem which John the Evangelist incorporated (perhaps with modifications) in the Prologue to his Gospel (Jn 1.1-14).[175] This poem begins with a description of Jesus in terms that are familiar from the Wisdom tradition. It opens with a reference to the Word who had always been with God and who had assisted the work of creation. Verses 14-18, however, introduce a dimension which Judaism had never anticipated. John explains that the divine Word *became flesh* at a particular historical moment (1.14). This signifies the Evangelist's belief that a person (and not a book) had fully revealed the Father (1.17-18). John's Christology, although it is profound, is a simple one. It asserts that the divine presence had become associated with a particular human individual. Such incarnationalism finds only an inexact parallel in the Jewish Wisdom tradition. There are greater parallels in Jewish angelology, as Bühner has shown.[176] These parallels are found especially in the Gospel's use of the terms 'descent' and 'ascent' in the context of the humanity of Jesus. Jn 3.13 in this respect states that the Son of Man had descended from heaven; 6.62 alludes to his future ascension to heaven. I leave to one side here the question of whether the body of the Gospel offers a *different* form of Christology from that which is expressed in the Prologue. The point at issue is that John is willing to consider the possibility that a divine being

---

Angels in 1 Tim. 3.16', *RB* 91 (1984), pp. 178-81. This last article is criticized by Hengel, *Studies in Early Christology*.

175. The pre-Johannine status of the Prologue is acknowledged by, among other scholars, Dunn in his *Christology*, p. 239.

176. Bühner, *Gesandte*, pp. 341-73.

2. *The Christology of the Ascension of Isaiah*

became associated with Jesus. This is the context in which he mentions the possibility of a future heavenly ascension (6.62).

By the end of the first century, then, and probably before it, Christianity had begun to think about Jesus as a human person who was connected with a pre-existent heavenly mediator. The language of heavenly descent and ascent had been introduced, albeit obliquely, into the christological tradition. My brief study has shown how the Jewish mediatorial tradition resourced first-century Christology at its different stages of development. We may briefly summarize that influence here. The earliest Christology celebrated the apotheosis of Jesus. As the first century progressed, the Christians developed this assertion in different ways: first by the language of heavenly enthronement and of Christ's visual similarity to God, and then by the myth of the mediator's descent from heaven. Although the precise moment when the notion of 'incarnationalism' was introduced is disputed (and it would be wrong to assume that Christology developed according to a strict historical sequence), there is no doubt that it had been articulated by the time of the Fourth Gospel (c. 100 CE). This was the tradition of Christology which the author of the *Ascension of Isaiah* inherited and which he made the subject of further development early in the second century.

The Angelomorphic Christology of the Ascension of Isaiah

An appropriate next step is to explore the contrast which I believe to exist between the *Ascension of Isaiah* and the Johannine Christology. The two texts are separated from each other by perhaps twenty years (this is the period between 100 and 120 CE). They also represent different literary genres: John is a Gospel and the *Ascension of Isaiah* an apocalypse. My belief is that the difference between them is not just one of genre but also of Christology.

The apocalyptic outlook of the *Ascension of Isaiah* permits a greater interest in the mediator's activity than is found in the Gospel. John's presentation is that of the human Jesus: Jesus is held to be the Son who had revealed God (Jn 6.46). The descent of the Son of Man, which is mentioned in 3.13, supports this understanding because it signifies a connection between Jesus and the heavenly mediator. What John means by his frequent references to the 'sending' of the Son in the Gospel is never fully explained.[177] Perhaps this was because it lay beyond the

---

177. For example Jn 3.17; 4.34; 5.23 and other references. The Jewish

Evangelist's purpose to comment on events which took place in the heavenly world. John does accept the possibility that Jesus' mission had a heavenly origin (see 3.14; 17.4-5). But the Evangelist has no version of the hidden descent to match the Christology of the *Ascension of Isaiah*. Neither does he allow what is said about the Son of Man's descent to provide the *structure* for the portrait of Jesus in the same way that the *Ascension of Isaiah* relates the hidden descent to the incorporated Jesus traditions. Nor does John offer any vision of the heavenly world.[178] These are areas where the *Ascension of Isaiah* makes a fresh contribution to the christological tradition. The two ideas which distinguish the apocalypse from earlier literature are the hidden descent and the Beloved One's transformation into human likeness. They represent a more 'developed' and systematic mythology than we find even in the Fourth Gospel.

The naïve docetism of *Ascension of Isaiah* 11.2-22 also conflicts with the Johannine perspective. The Fourth Evangelist was accused of a 'naïvely docetic' Christology by Käsemann, but it is important to observe that the mediatorial strand in his Gospel does not substantially 'reduce' the humanity of Jesus within it.[179] John omits precisely those elements which give the *Ascension of Isaiah* its docetic character. These are the abnormal pregnancy and the suggestion that Jesus did not really need suckling (ch. 11). It is the *use* of a mediatorial Christology in the two texts that represents the difference between them. The description of the Son of Man in the Fourth Gospel does not detract from the humanity of Jesus as happens with the description of the Beloved One's hidden descent in the *Ascension of Isaiah*. Despite this, the author of the *Ascension of Isaiah* agrees with John (and indeed with Ignatius) in insisting upon the reality of the death of Jesus (cf. Jn 19.34), and he mentions the conception and birth which the Gospel overlooks. This observation helps to set the different varieties of early Christian docetism in perspective. Not even the *Ascension of Isaiah*, which is more obviously docetic than John, questions the reality of the passion in the

---

background to this terminology is explored by Borgen in his essay, 'God's Agent in the Fourth Gospel'.

178. Jn 3.13 is set against such a view. Jn 6.46 gives as the reason for this the fact that the Son had seen the Father, so that no further revelation was needed in view of the revelation which had been accomplished by Jesus.

179. Käsemann in his *Testament*. This approach has been questioned by Hengel, *Johannine Question*, pp. 68-72.

2. *The Christology of the Ascension of Isaiah* 141

way that was done by Basileides and in a different way by Cerinthus.[180] In this book I have taken the view that the term 'naïve docetism' is more appropriate to the Christology of the *Ascension of Isaiah* than to John. John lacks any convincing evidence for docetism, and the adjective 'naïve' which I have applied to the *Ascension of Isaiah* acknowledges the fact that the apocalypse accepts the reality of the death of Jesus. his distinguishes its Christology from 'full-blown' docetism. I thus tend to see the docetic aspect of the *Ascension of Isaiah* in the same terms in which Käsemann saw the Johannine christology.

This view of the matter upholds Hengel's caution about the use of the adjective 'docetic' to describe the Johannine Christology. The term 'docetism' must be used with reference, not just to the fact that a particular Christology has a mediatorial element, but to the *extent to which* that mediatorial element is allowed to determine the presentation of the humanity of Jesus. We might construct a 'docetic trajectory' in early Christian literature which ranges from the Christology of Mark, through the introduction of the mediatorial idea in John, and thence through the *Ascension of Isaiah* to the full-blown docetism of Basileides. The crucial stage in this trajectory lies between John and the *Ascension of Isaiah* and *not* between Mark and John. It is in the willingness to attribute to Jesus abnormal human properties (which is found in the *Ascension of Isaiah*) and then to question the reality of his death (found in Basileides) that naïve and then developed docetism is found.

My research thus yields the conclusion that the *Ascension of Isaiah* represents a development of the christological tradition in the early second century. This development can be seen on a number of fronts. Descent and ascent are described more explicitly there than in first-century literature (including John). This is due in no small measure to the inclusion of the seven-storied cosmology against the general trend of primitive Christian literature. This device draws attention to the heavenly world as the sphere of decisive action in the spirit of Jewish apocalyptic

---

180. According to Basileides, Jesus exchanged forms with Simon of Cyrene on the way to the cross so that the Saviour evaded the crucifixion (see Irenaeus, *Adv. Haer.* 1.24). A different form of belief was expounded by Cerinthus, who taught that Christ was a heavenly mediator who descended on Jesus at his baptism and who returned to heaven before the crucifixion (see Irenaeus, *Adv. Haer.* 1.26). There is however no reason to think that Cerinthus was a *docetist* as such. I discuss this matter further in my book *The Ascension of Isaiah* (GAP, 2; Sheffield: Sheffield Academic Press, 1995), pp. 85-86.

revelation. The traditions about Jesus and the mythological descent are formally separate elements in the *Ascension of Isaiah* (cf. the restriction which is placed on 'Jesus' by 9.5 and 10.7); the author's description of the mediator's transformation into human likeness provides the bridge between the historical and the mythological material. The emerging trinitarian perspective which appears in the *Ascension of Isaiah* insists that *three* divine beings are *worshipped* by the angels. Moreover, the christological titles are used in a different way in the apocalypse from the New Testament literature, and they support the view that Jesus was the temporary appearance of the Beloved One.[181] These substantial differences between the *Ascension of Isaiah* and first-century literature deserve exploration in this chapter.

My argument is that the author's development of the christological tradition was aided by his knowledge of Jewish mediatorial ideas. At the start of the Second Vision Isaiah is promised a vision of two heavenly beings. One of these is said to be greater than the *angelus interpres*. The other is called his Father (7.7-8). This passage in the E text makes a formal comparison between the Beloved One and the angels.[182] The use of language demands careful interpretation but it does indicate that angelomorphic Christology—by which I mean the use of analogies with the angels despite the attribution of divinity to the Beloved One—is an important feature of the *Ascension of Isaiah*. This quantitative distinction between the Beloved One and the angel is remarkable for the fact that it does not exclude a connection with the angel world as would be done by later literature.

A similar conclusion about the Christology emerges from 9.27. The E text states that the Beloved One's glory surpassed that of all the angels in the seventh heaven. This also represents a comparison with the angels and involves a rather ambiguous distinction from them. The parent of L2 and S felt a problem in this passage. It transferred the *praeeminens omnes angelos* which E applies to the Beloved One in 9.27 to the interpolated description of Michael in 9.23. The E text thereby indicates that the Beloved One was seen before his descent in a position analogous to that of the Jewish exalted angel despite the fact that he received the worship of the angels. This view runs parallel to the Gospel

---

181. On this matter see further Simonetti 'Note sulla cristologia', pp. 197-202, and my own discussion below.

182. It is possible that S supports E at this point, but its text at this point is unfortunately marred by corruption.

2. *The Christology of the Ascension of Isaiah* 143

transfiguration story and to Rev. 1.13-14 where angelomorphic language is used to support the presentation of the heavenly Christ as a divine being.[183] The impression gained from *Asc. of Isa.* 9.27 is that the Beloved One is an exceptional being with greater glory than the angels. The E text leaves open the question of how precisely he is to be regarded in respect of the angels through its use of angelomorphic language. Post-Arian Christology would address this question by the imposition of an unbridgeable gulf between the two parties.

These two passages develop the first-century Christology in several respects. That the Beloved One should be worshipped by the angels agrees with the first-century understanding in which the exalted Jesus was universally called 'the Lord' (see for example Phil. 2.9-11). The author however extends this view so that the Beloved was worshipped *before* his descent (7.17; 9.27-34). This was the logical development of the belief that he had always been 'Lord with God' (10.11) which is a feature of the work's theology. I see the cosmology, with the trinitarian implications suggested by its arrangement, as in part an attempt to emphasize the *eternal* authority of the three divine beings through the suggestion that the cosmic structure reflects their permanent authority.[184] The *Ascension of Isaiah* thereby adds to the creational views of Col. 1.15-20 and Jn 1.1-2 the notion that the Beloved One was *worshipped* before his earthly manifestation. This should be compared with the use of 'the Lord' in 9.5 which, if it translates ὁ θεὸς in the lost original, goes beyond the anarthous θεὸς of Jn 1.1 to make the point that the Beloved One was a second divine being, which explains why worship should be offered in this way. The author has taken substantial steps towards the creation of a Christian cosmology which had merely been implicit in a passage such as Eph. 1.6 (and of which Rev. 4–5 shows an earlier stage of development).

The trinitarian view which is a feature of *Asc. Isa.* 9.27-42 (and which 7.23 adds to 7.7-8) also has an angelomorphic dimension. The portrait of the three divine beings has emerged from the belief that God was attended by the Beloved One as by a subordinate. We can see this origin in 7.7-8 and 7.17, which more closely mirror first-century Christology. The notion of the Spirit's divinity was emerging in first-century Christianity (see for example Mt. 28.19) but the *Ascension of Isaiah* is

---

183. This point is made by Rowland, 'The Vision of the Risen Christ'.
184. On the work's cosmology see further Bietenhard, *Himmlische Welt*, pp. 215-21.

an early text to include the three divine beings in worship.[185] The author was perhaps aided in his view by Mt. 28.19 but he was probably also influenced by a Christian understanding of Isaiah 6, as Werner and Daniélou have suggested.[186] In this case 1 Pet. 3.22 may have been an important linking text in the presentation of the Spirit as an enthroned divinity (11.32-33) given the fact that it enthrones Christ on the right hand of God's throne. Our author's meditation on it could easily have led to the belief that the Spirit must be enthroned on the left as a matter of consistency, which was then supported by a reading of Isaiah 6. The subordinationism which is inherent in the pneumatology is a necessary accompaniment of the subordination that exists within the Christology. This was related to the beliefs of the Jewish mediatorial tradition which insisted that God reigned supreme.

Behind this understanding ultimately stands the Jewish view that a divine chief agent could rise to prominence in heaven. It is necessary to observe in this connection that, despite what I have said about the work's trinitarianism, the bulk of the Second Vision (as indeed of the First) is a vision of *two* divine actors, in which the Spirit plays a merely subsidiary role. The bulk of the material has a direct parallel in Jewish visions of God and a subordinate, and represents a more explicit use of this material than such relatively brief first-century echoes as the transfiguration narrative and Rev. 1.13-14. The author of the *Ascension of Isaiah* clearly knew this Jewish strand. He used it to construct his narrative of salvation which was based on the premise that the Beloved One was the subordinate of the Most High God. It is a marked feature of the *Ascension of Isaiah* that the Beloved One's subordination is often emphasized, in what appears to be an attempt to deny that there were two (or three) *co-equal* powers in the seventh heaven.

The author further develops first-century Christology by insisting that the Beloved One and Spirit must worship God (9.40). Not even Philo had said this about the Logos. One ought to reflect for a moment on why the author should have permitted a statement like 9.40. The answer seems to lie in the observation that, given his more substantial portrait of the Beloved One's divinity when compared with earlier literature, he wished to avoid the suggestion that there were three independent Gods

---

185. The significance of Mt. 28.19 is examined by J. Schaberg, *The Father, the Son and the Holy Spirit: The Triadic Phrase in Matthew 28.19b* (SBLDS, 61; Chico: Scholars Press, 1982).

186. See Werner, *Entstehung*; Daniélou, *Jewish Christianity*.

2. *The Christology of the Ascension of Isaiah* 145

in heaven. Perhaps he was even reacting against demiurgical notions which were beginning to yield early forms of Gnostic theology.[187] His work certainly offers no support for that when it deliberately excludes Beliar from the heavens. I see 9.40 as an attempt to preserve a form of monotheism in which the Most High God was given precedence over the two lesser divinities.[188] This had the effect of reinforcing the subordination which is evident in the *Ascension of Isaiah*'s Christology and pneumatology, and which had been a central feature of the Jewish mediatorial tradition beforehand.

Angelomorphic influence is evident in the First Vision as well. The early chapters of the apocalypse describe the activity of a subordinate who discharged activity on behalf of the transcendent deity. There is a visual demonstration of the Beloved One's subordination in the resurrection passage (3.16-17).[189] This passage sets the Beloved One in the seated position which had been reserved for God in the biblical theophanies. That recalls what was said about Moses in Ezekiel the Tragedian's *Exagoge* and about Abel in the *Testament of Abraham*, but in a Christian reinterpretation where the Beloved One is the recipient of worship as well as an enthroned heavenly being. The subordinationism of the Jewish mediatorial strand is significantly retained in this Christian vision of the resurrected Jesus because it is understood that the Beloved One was *not* the Most High God. *Asc. of Isa.* 3.16-17 shows how Jewish *merkabah* traditions helped the development of early Christology.

The Christology of the *Ascension of Isaiah* can thus be presented in terms of the author's development of the earlier christological tradition in which Jewish mediatorial ideas continued to exercise an influence as that tradition was developed. *Asc. Isa.* 9.40 in particular shows how the subordinationist implications of the Jewish mediatorial tradition were retained and even emphasized despite the fact that the Beloved One received the angels' worship. The author's use of Jewish material is not surprising given its contribution to first-century Christology and his own interest in apocalyptic ideas. The fact that the Beloved One was worshipped as divine was not perceived as a barrier to the use of mediatorial language in this way.

---

187. Fossum has a discussion of the issues which surround this point in his *Name of God*, pp. 213-20.
188. See further below.
189. See further Norelli, 'Sulla pneumatologia dell' *Ascensione di Isaiah*', and Verheyden, 'L'Ascension d'Isaïe'.

The Hidden Descent and Jewish Angelology

The most distinctive feature of the *Ascension of Isaiah*'s Christology is its view of the Beloved One's hidden descent. The demonstration that this, too, has an angelic background strengthens the case for detecting an angelological influence on the Christology.

Once again we must speak of the author's development of New Testament Christology. The notion that a heavenly mediator was connected with Jesus is found in first-century literature (notably in Jn 3.13, and cf. 1 Tim. 3.16 and Eph. 4.8-9), but the *Ascension of Isaiah* introduces a more explicit understanding which is related to the cosmology and describes the heavenly commission and hidden descent of a divine emissary. The result of this is that a theory is offered about how the mediator came to be related to the human Jesus which is lacking in most first-century literature.

The model which best explains the hidden descent in the *Ascension of Isaiah* is provided by the angelophany. The Jewish angelophanic tradition is exemplified (but by no means exhausted) by the book of Tobit. It matters more for this assessment to show that the angelophany contributed to the *Ascension of Isaiah*'s Christology than to argue the different (but I think still quite reasonable) case that the author of the apocalypse knew Tobit itself.[190] Tobit describes how the angel Raphael was sent to earth to accomplish two acts of healing. The angel's commission by God in the heavenly court is described explicitly (Tob. 3.16-17). His appearance on earth as a human being forms the heart of the drama. The angel's descent is not described but the beginning of ch. 5 finds him on earth in human guise. This evidently presupposes that he had transformed himself into human likeness. His appearance as an ordinary Israelite convinces Tobias, who hires him as a travelling-companion. This ruse is sustained until the dénouement in ch. 12 when (and only when) the truth about his heavenly identity is revealed. Towards the end of the story the angel says to the others:

> That day when you got up from your dinner without hesitation to go and bury the corpse, I was sent to test you; and again God sent me to cure

---

190. Tobit was used extensively by the early Fathers. The walls of the Roman catacombs—the secret burial place of the Christians—were decorated with scenes from Tobit. This confirms its popularity as inspirational material. There is no doubt that Tobit was a well-known text in early Christian circles.

2. *The Christology of the Ascension of Isaiah*

both you and Sarah your daughter-in-law at the same time. I am Raphael, one of the seven angels who stand in attendance on the Lord and enter his glorious presence (12.13-15).[191]

This produces the alarmed reaction which is common in angelophanies:[192] 'Both of them were deeply shaken and prostrated themselves with fear' (12.16). The angel then explains that he has not been bound by human needs: 'Take note that I ate no food; what appeared to you was a vision. And now, praise the Lord, give thanks to God here on earth; I am ascending to him who sent me' (12.19-20a). After saying this he disappears. The angelophany is concluded once the angel's task is complete, as if he can remain on earth no longer once his identity has become known.

Several points of correspondence suggest that an angelophany of this kind resourced the narrative of the hidden descent in the *Ascension of Isaiah*. Tob. 3.16-17 describes the mediator's commission as a heavenly event. The *Ascension of Isaiah* also links the ministry of Jesus with God's commission of a heavenly mediator (ch. 10); the apocalypse describes the Beloved One's commission explicitly. The author says that it has resulted in the mediator's descent to earth (ch. 11), just as Raphael had been sent from heaven. The *Ascension of Isaiah* has a more elaborate cosmology than Tobit, which the author introduced for his own purposes against the tenor of other Christian literature, but the commission of a heavenly mediator is a common theme in both texts. This correspondence must not be ignored.

In both texts the commission is said to result in the mediator's appearance as a human being. Heavenly commission had been predicated of divine Wisdom by Sirach 24, but Tobit's angelophany provides a more exact parallel for the *Ascension of Isaiah* because it describes the mediator's appearance as a *human person*. Language about the Beloved One's 'transformation' into human likeness is a prominent feature of our apocalypse (see for example 3.13). This had not been used in Tobit, but Tobit does state that Raphael appeared as a human being, so that the understanding seems to be a similar one. The picture drawn by the Christian text, which is determined by the cosmology, is once again more sophisticated. The author describes successive transformations for

---

191. On the seven archangels in Jewish theology see G. Dix, 'The Seven Archangels and the Seven Spirits', *JTS* 28 (1927), pp. 233-50. The translation of Tobit is cited from the NEB.

192. Cf. for example Dan. 10.7-9.

the Beloved One, of which his transformation into the form of Jesus is the last in the series. Nevertheless, he agrees with Tobit in the assumption that the Beloved One's *heavenly* identity had been concealed by the assumption of a human identity. The traditions about Jesus have been inserted into the mythological framework to support this belief.

The *Ascension of Isaiah* further agrees with Tobit in making the ascension the moment when the mediator's identity is revealed (*Asc. Isa.* 11.23-33).[193] The author states that it is in the Beloved One's ascension to heaven, after the victory of the cross, that the angels recognize him as 'our Lord'. This passage presupposes that the concealment of his heavenly identity had been successful. Raphael's self-revelation and his ascension to heaven are almost simultaneous events in Tobit (the term 'ascending' is used in Tob. 12.20). This provides a further parallel with the *Ascension of Isaiah*. There is a difference between the texts in that the *Ascension of Isaiah* describes the Beloved One's self-revelation *after* he has left the earth whereas Tobit makes it Raphael's final action before his departure. However, this comparison does no more than suggest that again the author of the *Ascension of Isaiah* has adapted the angelophanic tradition to suit his purposes and that Tobit perhaps preserves the original form of the tradition.

Finally, the docetic element in *Asc. Isa.* 11.2-22 (E) should be compared with Raphael's statement about himself in Tob. 12.19. *Asc. Isa.* 11.17 states that the Beloved sucked Mary's breast 'like an infant, as was customary, that he might not be recognized'. This implies that the suckling was undertaken to conceal the mediator's heavenly identity, as if it were an act of accommodation. Tob. 12.19 states that people had had a *vision* of Raphael eating and drinking, which is intended to deny that the angel needed human food. The suggestion in both texts is that there was more to the mediator's human identity than met the eye, and that human functions had been assumed to protect the secret of the heavenly identity. Tob. 12.19 is a significant passage for the development of early Christian docetism, and illustrates the source from which such beliefs emerged.

These parallels with Tobit have a cumulative effect which makes them difficult to ignore. My conclusion is that, under the influence of the existing christological tradition (which had already employed angelological motifs), the author of the *Ascension of Isaiah* turned to Jewish

---

193. On Tobit as a source for early Christian thought about the ascension of Jesus, see Segal, 'Heavenly Ascent', p. 1372.

2. *The Christology of the Ascension of Isaiah*

angelology to resource his account of the Beloved One's descent. It is not necessary to insist that he knew Tobit specifically because the Jewish evidence for an angelophany is wider than that text.[194] The *Prayer of Joseph* confirms that angelophanic ideas were circulating in the early Common Era. If the *Ascension of Isaiah* alludes to the *Prayer of Joseph* in 4.22, that would confirm the importance of angelophanic categories in our author's thought. We do not know exactly how angelophanic ideas were transmitted to the author of the *Ascension of Isaiah*, but we can have a measure of confidence in claiming that he was influenced by them. The probability is that they pervaded the atmosphere of popular religious belief and that this is why they presented themselves to the christological tradition.

This conclusion brings me back to the question with which I began this chapter. We can now say more clearly what influences helped the author to construct the details of his Christology. The notion of the Beloved One's heavenly mediation drew on a Jewish visionary strand which linked an exalted mediator with God. There seems to be a correspondence in this with the development of an exalted angel in apocalyptic literature in terms of the seer's vision of God and a subordinate figure. This strand had been used by earlier Christian authors such as the Evangelists and the author of Rev. 1.1-4. The author of the *Ascension of Isaiah* used this Jewish strand in a context where the Beloved One was made a divine being who received worship. He developed the christological tradition through the insistence that the Beloved was worshipped *before* his descent, so that his mediation was a permanent one. He counterbalanced the tritheistic implications of this assertion by the marked subordinationism of 9.40. To this understanding he added the notion of the hidden descent and the Beloved's transformation into human likeness which gives the Christology its distinctive form and to which the Jesus traditions were also added. This represents the adaptation of a Jewish angelophanic tradition, as we have seen from the comparison with Tobit. Two strands of angelology were thus employed as the motif of the descent was fused together with the portrait of the Beloved One's heavenly mediation to yield the portrait of the divine subordinate who had been commissioned by God to destroy the work of Beliar.

One of the uncertain issues in my research has been the question of how far the author was himself an innovator and the extent to which he

---

194. See my presentation of the evidence above.

drew on ideas that were current at the time. We lack the evidence to answer this question with confidence. Nevertheless, the author's undoubted ingenuity as a scriptural exegete, combined with the absence of a 'hidden descent' motif in Ignatius, suggests that he himself may have been responsible if not for the creation then at least for the assembly of these ideas in their present form. His apocalypse allows us to see the christological tradition at an important stage of development. This author addressed a situation in which the need was felt for a more detailed understanding of what Jesus had achieved, including the question of his relation with God in heaven, than had been provided by first-century literature. This resulted in the development of the christological tradition as shown by the apocalypse. The author of the *Ascension of Isaiah* is a much-neglected precursor of Justin Martyr and one of the earliest Christians to make Christology the subject of detailed reflection in its own right. His work is remarkable for its use of Jewish traditions.

The upshot of my research is that I broadly agree with Daniélou and Pesce about the work's debt to angelology,[195] but I think it necessary to modify Pesce's conclusions advanced in his 1981 paper. First of all, the evidence for a Jewish mediatorial background is more extensive than Pesce allowed. We must take account of a variety of texts which present a mediator in the context of an apocalyptic vision with God. We must also allow for the substantial difference between Jewish and Christian literature signified by the worship of Jesus which was a new religious development in Christianity. Moreover, the Jewish angelological influence on the Christology has more than one aspect. Both the hidden descent and the description of the Beloved One's mediation were influenced by ideas of this kind. This conclusion confirms the importance of the Jewish mediatorial tradition and especially of its angelological strand for the Christology of the *Ascension of Isaiah*.

Monotheism, Binitarianism and Trinitarianism in the Apocalypse

My study has raised the question of what theological understanding emerges from the *Ascension of Isaiah*. This question must be addressed on several levels. At the heart of this author's view, God reigns unchallenged in the seventh heaven. This is evident from the fact that Beliar is confined to the firmament (7.9-12), and also from the

---

195. See Daniélou, *Jewish Christianity*; Pesce (ed.), *Isaia*.

2. *The Christology of the Ascension of Isaiah* 151

observation that the Beloved One and the Spirit as subordinate divinities must worship God (9.40). Clearly, the author was sensitive to the need not to present them (still less Beliar) as divine rivals. The title 'Lord' (which is used in 4.14 and elsewhere) recalls the theology of 1 Cor. 8.6 where Paul had been careful not to say that there were two Gods. The Beloved One *is* called God in the E text of 9.5, but this is done in the context of Isaiah's vision of the seventh heaven, in which the Beloved One's subordination to God is also a prominent theme. I see 9.40 as the author's deliberate attempt to balance his interest in the Beloved One's (and the Spirit's) mediation by the assertion of the pre-eminence of God over the two other divine beings. We thus find a theology in which notions of co-equality are absent by design.

The concept of monotheism which this suggests is what we should again call a 'mutation' in respect of earlier Jewish theology. It is impossible to deny that the apocalypse advocates the worship of three divine beings. However, this is done in a context in which the pre-eminence of the Most High God over his subordinates is assured. The author, in company with other Christians, retained links with the Jewish profession of belief in the one God and his apocalypse in this respect stands at an important 'mid-way' stage in Christian theology. It shares with sources such as John and Ignatius the willingness to call the Beloved One 'God'.[196] It has not however reached the stage of attempting to overcome the logical problems posed by belief in three divinities, which led to the later credal assertion that the 'one God' subsisted in 'three persons'. This belonged to a period beyond the second century. Subordinationism reappears in Justin Martyr, who worked after the author of the *Ascension of Isaiah*.[197]

It is also impossible to ignore the early evidence which the *Ascension of Isaiah* offers for the inclusion of the Spirit in worship (9.35-36). The origins of belief in the Spirit's divinity are complex.[198] I have argued that his position at the left hand of God in *Asc. Isa.* 11.33 may have been suggested by a reading of Isaiah 6 and perhaps of 1 Pet. 3.22 to yield the notion of the two enthroned subordinates. At some stage scriptural exegesis might have passed over into mysticism in this community's religious praxis, so that exegesis and visionary experience

---

196. For example Jn 20.28; *Ign. Eph.* 18.2.
197. See below on this aspect of Justin's thought.
198. On this subject see further C.F.D. Moule, *The Holy Spirit* (London: Mowbrays, 1978), pp. 22-51.

together perhaps fuelled this emerging belief. The Spirit's enthroned position is described analogously with the Beloved One's in the *Ascension of Isaiah*. The belief that the Spirit had inspired Scripture (4.21-22) and that he inspired contemporary prophecy (3.26-27), not least the prophecy which was produced by the author's circle, would have reinforced the conviction that he was a divine being, which had its roots in first-century Christianity.[199] The *Ascension of Isaiah* offers early evidence for Christian worship of the three divine beings, but as we have seen the Spirit plays little part in the Second Vision's drama of salvation.

Simonetti detects more than one trinitarian strand in the *Ascension of Isaiah*. He thinks that a hierarchical view (see for example 7.23) was displacing the earlier triangular view which is represented by ch. 9. He argues that the author was moving away from an angelomorphic influence to an early form of Logos Christology in which the Spirit was made subordinate to the Beloved One.[200] It is true that 7.23 and the binitarian references (e.g. 7.7-8, 17) suggest the author's awareness of a hierarchy of divine beings, but this does not mean that angelology has been superseded in the apocalypse, as Simonetti claims. 'Logos' and 'angel' overlapped as mediatorial titles in the early Common Era. Philo had described the Logos in archangelic terms (*Conf. Ling.* 146) and Justin Martyr would later call Christ 'angel', 'Word' and 'second God' in the same breath (*Dial.* 61, 128). Angelomorphic Christology was a feature of many later Christian writers, as I shall go on to discuss. None of them found it contradictory to present Christ as a divine being and to do this in angelomorphic language. In the specific case of the *Ascension of Isaiah* we must note that the author introduced the theme of the hidden descent which he modelled on the angelophany, so that to this extent at least we must speak of the lingering influence of Jewish angelology in the apocalypse.

Nor are the trinitarian views found in the *Ascension of Isaiah* necessarily incompatible with each other (despite the fact that the trinitarianism is not 'consistent' when viewed by later standards). The Spirit's position 'on the left' of the Beloved One in 9.35-36 and 11.33 implies a hierarchical view which is exacerbated by the Spirit's consistent portrayal as an angel. The theme of the Spirit's subordination to the Beloved One runs throughout the apocalypse. The trinitarianism of the *Ascension of Isaiah* is thus fluid, and determined by hierarchical

---

199. These roots can be discerned, for example, in Mt. 28.19.
200. 'Note sulla cristologia', p. 193.

2. The Christology of the Ascension of Isaiah

considerations. The Spirit's apparent superiority to Michael in 3.16-17 provides an interesting example of how the author understood his place in the heavenly world which would benefit from further commentary.[201]

We do well to ask what is meant by the concluding vision of the three enthroned divinities in *Asc. Isa.* 11.32-33. The conclusion is inescapable that the author conceives of three independent divinities of whom the Most High God is the most important. It was this notion of 'separateness' which caused problems for later theologians. They were confronted by the Arian suggestion that the Son, if he were an independent being and subordinate to the Father, must also be *different* from the Father.[202] This is not at all what the author of the *Ascension of Isaiah* meant to suggest. He used Jewish apocalyptic language to emphasize the divinity of the Beloved One and the Spirit in distinction from the angels of the seventh heaven. It was only when angelomorphic Christology was held to imply 'existence in a different substance' from the Father that such language began to cause a problem. This problem, however, was one which troubled theologians in the fourth century, and it must not be read back into Christian literature of the early second century.

The Christological Titles in the Apocalypse

A consequence of the author's development of earlier Christology is the fact that the christological titles are used in a different sense in the *Ascension of Isaiah* than in the New Testament literature. Generally speaking, they support the author's view that Jesus was the earthly appearance of the Beloved One. A short study shows the main differences from first-century literature.

The difference between the two branches of the textual tradition is significant in this context. L2 and S, which Bori showed to derive from a patristic redaction of the apocalypse, reduce E's two major clusters (9.5; 10.7) to the 'Son (of God)' title which prevailed when that redaction was made. They also introduce some material about Michael in ch. 9 which was absent from the original apocalypse. We saw that E's version of the title clusters in both cases constitutes the harder reading.

---

201. Some lines of discussion in this respect are laid down by Verheyden in his 'L'Ascension d'Isaïe', pp. 272-74.

202. On the nature of Arian theology, and especially the question of its Jewish background, see R. Lorenz, *Arius Ioudaizans?* (Göttingen: Vandenhoeck & Ruprecht, 1980), pp. 141-63.

In both it supports the view of the descent as the mediator's temporary appearance. The notion that certain titles were appropriate only to the incarnation was a feature of the original apocalypse.

'Son' occurs only infrequently in the E text (as opposed to L2 and S). The original author preferred 'Beloved One', which he used with a frequency much greater than that of other Christian literature. 'Beloved One' (ὁ ἀγαπητός) occurs in other versions besides E (3.13 Gk; 3.13 L1 *dilectissimi*; GL 1.2) and it cannot be regarded as an addition by the Ethiopic translator.[203] Armitage Robinson identified 'Beloved One' as a title for the messiah in pre-Christian Judaism:

> Both Matthew and Luke regarded ὁ ἀγαπητός as a separate title, and not as an epithet of υἱός. And it is interesting to note that the old Syriac version emphasized this distinction by rendering 'My Son and Beloved'. In Eph. i.9[204] St Paul uses ἐν τῷ ἠγαπημένῳ as equivalent to ἐν τῷ Χριστῷ in a context where he is designedly using terms derived from Jewish sources. Certain passages of the LXX were explained by Christian interpreters as Messianic (Psalm xliv [xlv] tit.; Zech. xii.10). Lastly, we have several passages in early Christian writings in which ὁ ἠγαπημένος is used as a title of Christ, e.g. Barn. iii.6, iv. 3, 8.[205]

The evidence of Ps. 44.1 (LXX) is decisive on this issue. Its superscription (ᾠδὴ ὑπὲρ τοῦ ἀγαπητου) uses 'Beloved One' in the absolute in a context where the subject is the Jewish king. This confirms that the title was used messianically in pre-Christian Judaism. Christian usage of the title is shown by Eph. 1.5-6:

> προορίσας ἡμᾶς εἰς υἱοθεσίαν διὰ **Ἰησοῦ Χριστοῦ** εἰς αὐτόν, κατὰ τὴν εὐδοκίαν τοῦ θελήματος αὐτοῦ, εἰς ἔπαινον δόξης τῆς χάριτος αὐτοῦ ἧς ἐχαρίτωσεν ἡμᾶς **ἐν τῷ ἠγαπημένῳ**.

The fact that ἠγαπημένος is used here in apposition to Χριστός implies that the titles are synonymous. Both have a messianic sense. There seems to be no significant difference in meaning between ἠγαπημένος and ἀγαπητός; Eph. 1.6 uses a variant of the title found in the *Ascension of*

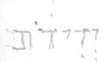

---

203. Epiphanius, *Pan.* 67.3, also uses the title in a citation of *Asc. Isa.* 9.35-36.
204. The correct reference is in fact Eph. 1.6, which is cited below. Charles reproduced this mistake from the original.
205. J.A. Robinson, 'Ascension of Isaiah', in J.H. Hastings (ed.), *A Dictionary of the Bible* (Edinburgh: T. & T. Clark, 1900), II, pp. 499-501. I have cited Robinson from Charles, *Ascension of Isaiah*, pp. 3-4. *T. Benj.* 11.2 should be added to the list of Jewish sources which use this title.

2. *The Christology of the Ascension of Isaiah* 155

Isaiah in the same messianic sense.[206] That 'Beloved One' is used in a messianic sense in the *Ascension of Isaiah* is confirmed by internal evidence as well.[207] The author uses 'Christ' in apposition to 'Beloved One' in 8.18 (E) and Χριστὸς is found in GL 2.37.[208] This places the status of the Beloved One as the messiah in the *Ascension of Isaiah* beyond doubt, although of course the distinctive feature of the apocalypse is the way in which the 'Beloved One' title is used, which involves the notion of this messiah's heavenly mediation, his hidden descent and transformation into human likeness.

The question of why the author used 'Beloved One' was discussed at the 1981 Conference. Simonetti argued that he avoided 'Son' because he thought it contained inappropriate notions of physical generation, and that he substituted 'Beloved One' to circumvent these.[209] 'Son' certainly refers only to the human Jesus in the *Ascension of Isaiah* (8.25; 9.14).[210] According to 8.25 (E) the Beloved 'is to be called in the world the Son!' *Asc. Isa.* 9.14 anticipates that 'the god of that world' would 'stretch out [his hand against the Son]'.[211] This agrees with the restriction of meaning which is placed on 'Jesus' by 9.5 (cf. 10.7; GL 2.37) and on 'Christ' by 9.13. 'Son' and 'Jesus' are evidently used only in connection with the earthly manifestation in the *Ascension of Isaiah*. This is a distinctive feature of the author's usage.

206. I cite as the authority for this statement BAGD, pp. 4-5 (the entry 1d, ἠγαπημένος) and 6 (under ἀγαπητός). These scholars provide evidence that both words were used for people deeply loved, especially by God.

207. A conclusion which is accepted by Simonetti, 'Note sulla cristologia', p. 201.

208. See the E text of 4.13 (although this is corrupt), 9.5, 13, 17, and 10.7. *Asc. Isa.* 9.13 seems to suggest that 'Christ' was a title appropriate only to the earthly manifestation, but 10.7 uses it in apposition to 'LORD' to describe the mediator when in heaven.

209. 'Note sulla cristologia', pp. 201-202.

210. 'Son' is used also in *Asc. Isa.* 4.21, which is a citation of Isa. 52.13 (LXX), but there it must reflect the Greek παῖς rather than υἱός. The reference should be noted for the sake of completeness.

211. Charles believed that 8.25 was an interpolation by the E scribe: see his *Ascension of Isaiah*, p. 58. The phrase, is, however, included by Knibb in Charlesworth (ed.), *Old Testament Pseudepigrapha*, II, p. 169, without adverse comment. There are textual problems also in 9.14 where E reads 'by the hand of his son'. This is rightly corrected by Knibb on the basis of L2. Whether 8.25 is an interpolation is perhaps less likely than Charles supposed. The title makes good sense in its context and, even if it is excised from 8.25, it certainly belongs in 9.14.

This restricted usage of 'Son' indicates that the meaning of 'Beloved One' is given by the mediator's heavenly position. 'Beloved One' designates a mediator who stands in close relation with God. The title reflects the Jewish view that a subordinate could discharge authority but also the Christian worship of Jesus as divine. The title conveys an implicit subordinationism as well as this assertion of uniqueness and divinity. Its frequent use perhaps has a polemical edge. The author may have wanted to distance himself from Judaism or to comment on the allegiance of pious Christians to their Saviour in view of the impending persecution. The title clearly distinguishes the Beloved One from other heavenly beings in the seventh heaven (cf. the 'Chosen One' title in *Asc. Isa.* 8.7), including the angel of the Holy Spirit.

An issue raised at the Rome Conference was the extent to which 'Beloved One' was intended to recall the heavenly address to Jesus at the baptism.[212] It seems unlikely that it recalls this event at all. The title describes a permanent heavenly mediation and not a single earthly moment. Mk 1.11 (σὺ εἶ ὁ υἱός μου ὁ ἀγαπητός, ἐν σοὶ εὐδόκησα...) shows that 'Son' and 'Beloved' were connected in early Christian tradition; but, as Pesce observes,[213] the baptism is never mentioned in the apocalypse, not even in 3.13-18 and 11.2-22 where it might have been included. Any reference to the transfiguration (where the heavenly address also occurs; see Mk 9.7) is similarly absent. The author's lack of interest in the baptism and the transfiguration probably displays his reluctance to restrict the demonstration of the mediator's glory to significant moments in the ministry of Jesus because he believed that the Beloved One was permanently divine despite the concealment of his divinity. There are parallels in this with the Johannine silence about these events, which was apparently for a similar reason.[214]

The restriction that is placed on the name 'Jesus' (9.5; 10.7) is thus determinative for the Christology of the original apocalypse. 'Jesus' is the human form which the Beloved One adopts when he descends from the seventh heaven. The author resists a psilanthropic Christology, but his text leaves some unresolved tensions between the status of the

---

212. See the discussion between Simonetti and Pesce in Pesce (ed.), *Isaia*, pp. 205-206.

213. In his *Isaia*, p. 205.

214. If, as I shall argue in Chapter 4, the author of the *Ascension of Isaiah* knew (part of) John, he might have been aware that the baptism and transfiguration were omitted in this member of the Gospel tradition.

2. *The Christology of the Ascension of Isaiah*

human person and of the heavenly mediator which are exemplified by the naïve docetism.

Other Evidence of Angelomorphic Christology in Christian Literature

Angelomorphic Christology is not a peculiarity of the *Ascension of Isaiah* but is found also in other texts, many of which are later than the apocalypse. The presentation of this wider evidence sets my study of the *Ascension of Isaiah* in perspective. In this next part of the chapter I shall examine three different kinds of material to show the hold which angelomorphic Christology continued to exercise on the Christian imagination. First of all, I shall examine writers who are generally considered to be 'orthodox' in their outlook (to use what I acknowledge is an anachronism). Then I shall examine two different kinds of sectarians: the sectarian Jewish Christians and the Gnostics of the second century and beyond. This wide-ranging review will show that angelomorphic Christology was not confined to fringe groups, as might perhaps be supposed, but that it influenced mainstream writers such as Irenaeus and Tertullian and their successors. This observation will then allow me to reflect on the place which the *Ascension of Isaiah* occupies in second-century Christianity. A particular feature of my research will be the identification of differences between the *Ascension of Isaiah* and the two different kinds of sectarians, which emphasizes the favourable light in which the apocalypse was seen by later mainstream writers.

I shall first consider what I have called 'orthodox' literature. By this I means 'texts which were produced by people who did not feel the need to distinguish themselves and who were not distinguished by others from the Great Church'. Angelomorphic Christology was an important feature of such writers. The shepherd of Hermas describes the Son of God in angelomorphic terms.[215] Hermas has puzzled commentators because he uses the term 'angel' in more than one sense. Revelation is said to be communicated to the seer by a shepherd who is sometimes called an angel (see for example *Sim.* 10.3.1; but some manuscripts have 'shepherd' at this point). This shepherd begins by saying that he has been sent by a 'venerable angel' (*Vis.* 5.2). When that second angel is

---

215. I acknowledge the use which I made of Barbel's *Christos Angelos* in preparing this section. On the angelomorphic Christology of Hermas see H. Moxnes, 'God and his Angel in the Shepherd of Hermas', *ST* 28 (1974), pp. 49-56.

mentioned again, under the title 'Most holy angel' (*Man.* 5.1.7), he is said to perform justification. This, as Daniélou notes,[216] is a divine function which the New Testament associates with the death of Jesus (see for example Rom. 4.25). The angel in question is almost certainly the Son of God. The fact that he is called an angel does not disguise the fact that he exercises divine functions.

This impression about the angel's identity is strengthened by the *Eighth Similitude* of Hermas which describes how a 'glorious and very tall' Angel of the Lord distributed willow branches (8.1.1-2). This idea seems to have been based on early Christian penitential practice. The angel judges between righteous and ungodly. He crowns those whom he judges worthy and admits them to 'the tower' (which represents the church). These too are divine functions, as if the angel is the Christian Saviour.

In this light we should examine the collocation of nouns 'holy angel' and 'Lord' which occurs in *Herm. Sim.* 5.4.4. It seems likely (but it is not completely certain) that the two are identified and that the angel is the Lord (Jesus). *Sim.* 9.12.7-8 moreover reworks the notion of the seven Angels of the Face to present the Son of God as a 'glorious and mighty man' who was attended by six other 'men', as if he were the angel chief and the others his subordinates.

An angelomorphic Christology then in all probability extended to the Roman church by the late first or early second century CE. It must have spread there from the eastern Mediterranean. Hermas's willingness to call the Son 'an angel' shows the more restricted nature of the *Ascension of Isaiah*'s Christology; the author of the apocalypse states that the Beloved *transformed* himself into angelic form (9.30) but never advocates the view that he actually was an angel. Even in Hermas, despite the use of the 'angel' title, it is clear that the Son transcends the angels through his divine nature and functions. The divinity of the Son is a major feature of all angelomorphic Christology, as I have argued already. This is why it must be distinguished from 'angel-Christology' of the kind for which Werner contended.

The willingness to call Christ 'angel' is a feature also of Justin Martyr. Justin identified Christ with the 'Angel of the Lord' who appears in the Pentateuch.[217] The pre-existence of Christ is a major element in Justin's

---

216. *Jewish Christianity*, pp. 119-21.
217. See Trakatellis, *Pre-Existence*, pp. 53-92 for a discussion of this strand of Justin's thought.

2. *The Christology of the Ascension of Isaiah* 159

arguments against Trypho. It is mentioned in two groups of passages in the *Dialogue* (chs. 56–62 and 125–29) and referred to elsewhere (see *1 Apol.* 62–63; *Dial.* 37–38; 75–86 and 113–14). Justin refers the appearances to Abraham, Jacob, Moses and Joshua and the theophanies in Exod. 23.20-21 and Ps. 98.6-8 to the pre-existent Christ in this way.

The basis of Justin's argument emerges from *Dial.* 56.11. This is that Scripture speaks about the existence of a God next (ἕτερος) to the universal creator. In his discussion of the Mamre theophany (Gen. 18) Justin states that this other God was subject to the Maker of all things and that he was called an angel because he announced the divine message. In his discussion of Genesis 28 (*Dial.* 58) Justin repeats that this God was called both Angel and Lord. *Dialogue* 61 predicates many names for Christ, including 'Angel'. This designation appears again in *Dialogue* 128.

We must not ignore the fact that such sustained reflection on the biblical theophanies goes beyond the brief New Testament allusions to those passages (for example Jn 8.58; 1 Cor. 10.4). Justin's exegesis has points in common with Philo who understood the relevant passages as appearances of the Logos. Like the author of the *Ascension of Isaiah*, Justin offers no evidence for a formal co-equality between the two divine beings. On the contrary: his abiding presupposition is the absolute transcendence of the Father over the Son (see esp. *Dial.* 60.2). Christ is thereby held subordinate to the high God (*Dial.* 60.5) and 'begotten by the Father's will' (*Dial.* 61.1). It is this merely relative view of the Son's transcendence which allows Justin to say that the second God appeared and even that he conversed in the manner suggested by the Pentateuch. That is the rationale of Justin's angelomorphic Christology.

We find a development of Justin's exegesis in Irenaeus. In this case it is set against the Gnostic declaration that the world was the work of an inferior creator.[218] Irenaeus follows Justin in making Christ the agent of the Pentateuchal angelophanies, but he significantly never uses the term 'angel' to describe him. Barbel thinks that this is because of the use which was made of angelophanic motifs by the Gnostics.[219] Nevertheless it is clear that Irenaeus knows a Christology of this kind. *Adv. Haer.* 3.6.1 follows Justin in using Gen. 19.24 ('The Lord rained upon Sodom

---

218. See further J. Lawson, *The Biblical Theology of St Irenaeus* (London: Epworth Press, 1948), for an introduction to Irenaeus's theology. I discuss the main ideas of Gnosticism below.

219. *Christos Angelos*, p. 63.

160   *Disciples of the Beloved One*

and Gomorrah fire and brimstone from the Lord out of heaven') to assert that the Son was a divine being analogous to the Father and that he was attested as such by the Holy Spirit. Ps. 110.1 is used in this passage to support the idea of the Son's permanent mediation, in a development from the ascensional understanding of that passage which we noticed in the *Ascension of Isaiah*. *Adv. Haer.* 3.6.2 shows that the 'descent-ascent' pattern had become established in Christology by the later second century when it says that the descent was undertaken 'for the salvation of men'.

In at least one passage in Irenaeus we find evidence that the *Ascension of Isaiah* probably featured among the sources for his Christology. In a passage from the *Demonstratio* (10), which is now extant only in Armenian, Irenaeus apparently says that the Word and the Spirit were called cherubim and seraphim. The translation of this passage is disputed, but I have followed the reading of Smith which is accepted also by Daniélou.[220] The similarity to the *Ascension of Isaiah* at this point is striking: Irenaeus gives the names of particular classes of angels to Christ and to the Spirit who are presented as angelic beings. There is a strong possibility that Irenaeus knew the *Ascension of Isaiah*, and this is supported by other evidence which I shall mention in a moment. In this case we should have to say that Irenaeus viewed the apocalypse with favour and that he *distinguished* its view of the Beloved One from the different varieties of christological heresy which he criticizes in *Adv. Haer.* 3.11.2-3.[221] This must be regarded as important evidence for the

220. J.P. Smith, *Proof of the Apostolic Preaching* (London: Longmans, Green, 1952), p. 54; Daniélou, *Jewish Christianity*, p. 138. See also E. Lanne, 'Chérubim et Séraphim', *RSR* 43 (1955), p. 530. Smith's translation reads: 'This God, then, is glorified by His Word, who is His Son for ever, and by the Holy Spirit, who is the Wisdom of the Father of all. And their Powers (those of the Word and of Wisdom), which are called Cherubim and Seraphim, with unfailing voice glorify God, and the entire establishment of heaven gives glory to God, the Father of all.'

221. *Adv. Haer.* 3.11.2-3 is an important passage for discussion of the *Ascension of Isaiah*. In a review of the different varieties of heresy which he deems undesirable Irenaeus offers the following summary: 'For if anyone carefully examines the systems of them all, he will find that the Word of God is brought in by all of them as not having become incarnate and impassible, as is also the Christ from above. Others consider Him to have been manifested as a transfigured man; but they maintain Him to have been neither born nor to have become incarnate; whilst others [hold] that He did not assume a human form at all, but that, as a dove, He did descend upon that Jesus who was born from Mary' (Anti-Nicene Christian Library translation [ed. A. Robertson and J. Donaldson; repr.; Edinburgh: T. & T. Clark,

2. The Christology of the Ascension of Isaiah

'mainstream' acceptance and use of the *Ascension of Isaiah* in the later second century CE. A favourable attitude towards the *Ascension of Isaiah* was a feature of several writers in the patristic period. This will prove to be an important observation when we compare the apocalypse with Jewish Christian and Gnostic material.

Tertullian similarly understood the Pentateuchal angelophanies as appearances of the Logos.[222] He thought that they signified the permanent relationship between the Father and the Son (see for example *Adv. Prax.* 14). The permanence of this relationship determined the way in which Tertullian believed that angelomorphic language could be applied to the Son as the Father's close associate. *De Carne Christi* 14 is a crucial passage for understanding Tertullian's thinking on this issue. There he takes the reference to the 'Angel of the Great Council' in the LXX text of Isa. 9.6 to make the point that Christ discharged an angel's ministry but that he did not share the angels' nature. Tertullian distinguishes Christ in this respect from Michael and Gabriel, in a refinement of angelomorphic Christology which proved to be important for later writers.

This distinction was invaluable when Tertullian came to write against Marcion. Tertullian claims (*Adv. Marc.* 3.27) that those attributes which Marcion had despised in God were precisely the human qualities which the Son had assumed in the incarnation and which depended on the lowering of his condition beneath that of the angels. This meant that they did not belong to his original nature. Tertullian cites the theophany in Genesis 18 to demonstrate that Christ had assumed real flesh in the incarnation. Given that God was able to supply flesh to the accompanying angels, he argues that it is easier to suppose that God provided Christ with a real body than with the docetic qualities which Marcion had assumed he possessed (*Adv. Marc.* 3.9-10).

The Roman presbyter Novatian (c. 200–258 CE) also interpreted the Pentateuchal angelophanies as appearances of Christ. In his exegesis of the Tower of Babel story (Gen. 11) Novatian said that Christ was the

---

1989], I, p. 427). The notion of Jesus as a transfigured human which is mentioned here approximates to the form of the *Ascension of Isaiah*'s Christology, but Irenaeus adds the qualification about the unreality of the birth which is controverted by the apocalypse. The fact that the *Ascension of Isaiah* insists on the Beloved's real participation in the birth and death of Jesus accounts for the text's later acceptance in mainstream circles.

222. See Barbel, *Christos Angelos*, pp. 70-79.

angel who had descended to confound human speech (*De Trin.* 17). An angelomorphic Christology pervades all of his writings. Novatian even called Christ *angelorum omnium princeps* (*De Trin.* 12), which calls to mind texts such as the *Prayer of Joseph* and Philo, *Conf. Ling.* 146, and Christian writings such as the Pseudo-Clementine literature (see below). Novatian identified Christ as the angel who had appeared to Hagar in Genesis 16; and he evidently knew Tertullian's view of Christ as the Angel of Great Counsel whom he called 'both Angel and God' (*De Trin.* 18).

Angelomorphic Christology featured even in Alexandrian Christianity, for all its allegorizing tendencies. Clement identified Christ as the man who had wrestled with Jacob and as the angel of Exod. 23.20 (*Paidagogos* 1.7). He calls the Logos an angel and refers in the same passage to the 'mystical angel Jesus'. Origen identified the Logos as the third angel of Genesis 18 (*In Gen. Hom.* 4) and as the commander of the heavenly host who is mentioned in Josh. 5.14 (*In libr. Jes. Nav. Com.* 6.2). We should bear in mind that it was Origen who preserved the *Prayer of Joseph* (*In Joh.* 2.31), in which Jacob's identification with the angel Israel is the major theme. This shows that he was willing to contemplate the possibility that an angel could incarnate himself as a human being, which he mentions in his discussion of John the Baptist.

Origen evidently knew the trinitarian explanation which is placed on Isaiah's vision by the *Ascension of Isaiah*.[223] His discussion of Isaiah 6 in *De Princ.* 1.3.4 (cf. 4.3.14; *Hom. Is.* 1.2; 4.1) interpreted the two seraphim of that passage as Christ and the Spirit, a view which was strongly criticized by Jerome (*Comm. in Is.* 3.6.2). Origen claimed to have derived this exegesis from a Hebrew, who in this context must have been a Jewish Christian. His use of the Isaiah passage shares with the *Ascension of Isaiah* the tendency to see Christ and the Spirit in angelomorphic terms. It is by no means improbable that Origen knew the apocalypse given that it was used also in Egypt by Hieracas.[224]

This study reveals a number of similarities between the *Ascension of Isaiah* and later literature, but also one important difference. Much of the later material is preoccupied with exegesis of the Pentateuchal angelophanies. Justin Martyr developed this theme; its foundations lay in first-century Christianity (and before that in Philo). Any reference to the

223. Origen's knowledge of the *Ascension of Isaiah* is examined by Acerbi, *Serra Lignea*, pp. 20-32. See also Daniélou, *Jewish Christianity*, pp. 134-40.
224. Hieracas's use of the apocalypse is mentioned by Epiphanius, *Pan.* 67.3.

Pentateuchal angel is absent from the *Ascension of Isaiah*. It is perhaps rash to conclude that the author did not *know* this tradition of exegesis (surely he did given that he knew 1 Corinthians and John). The omission more probably reflects the fact that, according to *Asc. Isa.* 4.21-22, he regarded only the second and third divisions of the Hebrew Bible as helpful prophecies of the Beloved One. His reserved or even hostile attitude towards Moses was responsible for his selection of material; the Pentateuchal angelophanies might even have helped his argument had he included them. It was only in the *middle* of the second century with Justin Martyr that the identification of Christ with the Pentateuchal angel became an established and well-documented feature of the christological tradition. The angelomorphic Christology of the *Ascension of Isaiah* by contrast drew more directly on the Jewish exalted angel strand and on the angelophany. Despite this difference, the *Ascension of Isaiah* shares with Hermas and Justin the conviction that the use of angelomorphic language confirmed rather than denied the fact of the Beloved One's divinity.

The Hidden Descent in Patristic Literature

A particular area in which the *Ascension of Isaiah* develops first-century Christology, and in which it was itself a resource for subsequent development, is the hidden descent motif.

The hidden descent became an important feature in later writers who used Jewish-Christian symbolism. Irenaeus says in *Demonstratio* 84: 'But because the Word came down invisible to creatures, He was not known to them in his descent.' This passage so closely resembles the Christology of the apocalypse that we must agree with Daniélou that the *Ascension of Isaiah* served as its source.[225] Irenaeus is thus a marker for the earliest documented use of the *Ascension of Isaiah*, which may be assigned to the later second century.

Another early tradent of the hidden descent tradition was the author of the *Epistula Apostolorum*, who worked in the middle of the second century CE (and probably in Egypt).[226] *Ep. Ap.* 13–14 describes how

---

225. *Jewish Christianity*, p. 207.
226. On this text see C. Schmidt, *Gespräche Jesu mit seinen Jüngern nach der Auferstehung* (TU, 43, Berlin: Hinrichs, 1919); A. Ehrhardt, 'Judaeo-Christians in Egypt', in F.L. Cross (ed.), *Studia Evangelica* (TU, 68; Berlin: Akademie Verlag,

Christ passed through the heavens, clothed with the Wisdom of the Father, and how he resembled the angels and archangels as he journeyed down from heaven. He proceeded from there to the Orders, Powers and Dominations. Four of the archangels followed Christ to the fifth firmament since he resembled one of them, but he told them to return to the Father. This evidence matches the statement of *Asc. Isa.* 10 that it was only in the fifth heaven and downwards that the Beloved One changed his form. The *Epistula Apostolorum* explains the incarnation by making Christ appear to Mary disguised as the archangel Gabriel:

> At that time, I appeared in the form of the archangel Gabriel to [the virgin] Mary, and spoke with her, and her heart received me; she believed, and laughed: and I, the Word, went into her and became flesh; and I myself was servant for myself, and in the form of an image of an angel.[227]

Here we find the element of willing deception which occurs also in the *Ascension of Isaiah* This is combined with a speculative exegesis of the Matthean infancy narrative which identifies Christ with Gabriel.

The Eighth *Sibylline Oracle* is also indebted to this fusion of ideas:

> In the last times [the Word] came upon earth, and having abased himself, he arose a new light from the womb of the Virgin Mary...First of all he showed himself as Gabriel in pure and mighty form; then, as an archangel, he spoke these words to the young maiden: Receive God in your spotless womb, O Virgin (*Sib. Or.* 8.456-61).[228]

Here too the Word appears as Gabriel. This results in the incarnation. Although the imagery is different again from that of the *Ascension of Isaiah*, the notion that the descent was undertaken in angelic form stems from a common background. The *Ascension of Isaiah* represents an early form of this tradition; the *Epistula Apostolorum* and *Sibylline Oracles* 8 are later elaborations of it. The identification of Christ with Gabriel is the principal development after the *Ascension of Isaiah*. It is not impossible that these two later authors knew the apocalypse.[229] On this view the notion that Christ resembled an angel might have been responsible for his subsequent identification with Gabriel.

1964), III, pp. 360-82; and M. Hornschüh, *Studien zur Epistula Apostolorum* (Berlin: de Gruyter, 1965).

227. Translation from E. Hennecke (ed.), *New Testament Apocrypha*, I, p. 199.
228. Translation from Daniélou, *Jewish Christianity*, p. 131.
229. Early use of the *Ascension of Isaiah* is explored by Acerbi, *Serra Lignea*, pp. 13-67.

2. The Christology of the Ascension of Isaiah

The tradition of the hidden descent persisted in Christian literature until at least the fourth century, when it surfaced in the Greek text called the *Physiologos*:

> So our Saviour, the spiritual lion sent by the eternal Father, hid the signs of His spiritual being, that is His divinity. With the Angels He became an Angel, with the Thrones a Throne, with the Powers a Power, with men a man during his descent. For he descended into the womb of Mary, to save the race of human souls that had strayed. Consequently, they did not recognize Him in his descent from on high, and they said: 'Who is this King of Glory?' Then the Holy Spirit answered: 'The Lord of Hosts, He is the King of Glory.'[230]

There are some obvious differences between this passage and the *Ascension of Isaiah*. The lion analogy, the sending of the archangels back to God, the notion of salvation for straying human souls (which, however, has parallels in Gnosticism), and the use of Psalm 24 to explain the mediator's identity have no parallel in our apocalypse. Yet the angelomorphic basis of the *Physiologos*'s Christology is clear to see, and its understanding of the hidden descent similar to what is found in the *Ascension of Isaiah*. The *Physiologos* agrees with the *Ascension of Isaiah* that the angelic appearance was an accommodation and in referring this disguise to salvific purposes. It may be that the *Ascension of Isaiah* helped to promote this form of belief even when we concede that the *Physiologos* has also used other sources.

A word of explanation is needed about Irenaeus's use of the *Ascension of Isaiah* Despite his abhorrence of the different forms of Gnosticism, including its Redeemer mythology, Irenaeus was happy to cite an account of the descent similar to that found in the apocalypse in which the Word proved invisible to the creatures. This indicates that the cause of offence to him in Gnosticism was not the descent as such, nor probably even the notion of deliberate concealment, but the use which the Gnostics made of these ideas to support their esoteric teaching with its dualistic anthropology and errant Christology. The ethical rigorism of the *Ascension of Isaiah*, its millenarian eschatology and refusal to countenance full-blown docetism were all important reasons for its favourable reception in later Christianity. That the author made the Beloved pass

---

230. The translation is reproduced from Daniélou, *Jewish Christianity*, p. 207. On this text see also E. Peterson, 'Die Spiritualität des griechischen Physiologos', *BZ* 47 (1954), pp. 70ff.

through Mary's womb and genuinely die on the cross were crucial factors in promoting this high evaluation of the apocalypse.

Jewish-Christian Christology

Now we pass to the two other groups that I mentioned. Angelomorphic Christology was a special feature of some of the Jewish-Christian sectarian groups. I leave to one side on this occasion the question of whether these groups actually existed as separate bodies in the second century. Patristic reports about them are often confused (see below), and it may be that the fathers dealt with what they saw as a problem by presenting these people as discrete groups when this was not the case. I do not want to discuss that problem now. I do however want to pursue the question of the 'orthodox' status of the *Ascension of Isaiah* by noticing its distance from the reported beliefs of these Jewish-Christian groups. Such an examination confirms the point that its Christology cannot be dismissed as the product of a merely peripheral or sectarian interest but that it deserves comparison with the thought of mainstream Christian writers.

Research into sectarian Jewish Christianity has yielded two basic insights about it. First of all, it is generally agreed that H.J. Schoeps did scholarship a disservice when he equated Jewish Christianity with Ebionism to the exclusion of other documented groups.[231] Secondly, the study which was made by Klijn and Reininck of patristic reports about these groups shows that many of the fathers did not have access to first-hand information about them and consequently that they do not offer a well-informed account of what these sectarians really believed.[232] This means that all research in this area must proceed with caution since we cannot assume that the primary sources are accurate and unbiased.

What the fathers say about Cerinthus is a case in point.[233] Klijn and Reininck show that Cerinthus was charged with a variety of offensive doctrines, including millenarianism, because he was the best-known

---

231. H.J. Schoeps, *Theologie und Geschichte des Judenchristentums* (Tübingen: Mohr, 1949). Schoeps was anticipated in this view by Epiphanius.
232. A.F.J. Klijn and G.J. Reininck, *Patristic Evidence for Jewish-Christian Sects* (NovTSup, 36; Leiden: Brill, 1973).
233. The primary source is Irenaeus, *Adv. Haer.* 1.26. For an evaluation see Klijn and Reininck, *Patristic Evidence*, pp. 3-19; and G. Bardy, 'Cérinthe', *RB* 30 (1921), pp. 344-73.

2. The Christology of the Ascension of Isaiah

agitator in Asia. This is a significant insight when we come to examine his Christology. Irenaeus (*Adv. Haer.* 1.26) records Cerinthus as having taught that Christ descended on Jesus in the form of a dove after the baptism and that he left him again before the crucifixion. The context of this report is Irenaeus's own repudiation of Gnosticism. This leads him to convey the impression that Cerinthus was a typical 'Gnostic'. Irenaeus also says that John wrote his Gospel against Cerinthus and other heretics who denied that God had created the world (*Adv. Haer.* 3.2.1). Klijn and Reininck conclude that in fact Irenaeus knew only the tradition, which can be traced back to Polycarp, that John had met Cerinthus in the Ephesian bath-house and that he had pointed him out as the 'enemy of truth' (*Adv. Haer.* 3.3.4). This casts doubt on the reliability of the report in *Adv. Haer.* 1.26, especially on the Gnostic slur but also perhaps on the attribution of this form of Christology to Cerinthus himself. It is possible that this belief came conveniently to be associated with Cerinthus and that its real perpetrator remains unknown.

This is not to say that the evidence is insignificant or that Irenaeus simply made up his report. He is likely to be reporting an authentic form of belief even if Cerinthus was not its original exponent. For our purposes, it is important to note that this form of Christology displays an important difference from the *Ascension of Isaiah*. Cerinthus allegedly denied that Christ participated in the birth and the death of Jesus (although he accepted that *Jesus* really died). As we have seen, the author of the *Ascension of Isaiah* insists that the *Beloved One* experienced both events. This is an area in which he would have agreed with Ignatius and with Irenaeus against all the varieties of developed docetism. The fact that the *Ascension of Isaiah* contains traces of docetism was mitigated in the eyes of Irenaeus and others by its author's view of the passion (and the incarnation), which were wholeheartedly 'orthodox'. If *Adv. Haer.* 1.26 does represent an authentic sectarian view, whose Christology was intended to mark a difference from Great Church belief, then we must rank the *Ascension of Isaiah* with the theological mainstream and not with the sectarians for the reason specified.

The Elkesaites also reportedly held a Christology which had angelic overtones.[234] This is an interesting observation since behind their movement Klijn and Reininck discern a book of revelation (the so-called book of Elkesai) which 'contained little of importance for the study of

---

234. See Klijn and Reininck, *Patristic Evidence*, pp. 54-67; and W. Brandt, *Elkesai* (Leipzig, 1912).

168   *Disciples of the Beloved One*

Jewish Christianity'.[235] They argue that the basis of Elkesaism was an apocalyptic-syncretistic missionary movement, primarily of *Jewish* origin, which came to birth during the Roman invasion of Parthia and which only subsequently came into contact with Christianity. Elkesaism thus gives us valuable information about Jewish views of angelic mediation but not necessarily about mainstream Christology. Epiphanius, who had evidently had access to the Elkesaite book, cites several passages from it. He reports the Elkesaites as teaching that Christ was an angel of enormous proportions accompanied by the Holy Spirit who was a female angel (*Panarion* 19.4.1-2). This agrees with Hippolytus's report about Alcibiades, whom he says was inspired by Elkesaite beliefs (*Haer.* 9.13.2-3). These reports indicate that the Elkesaites (and their interpreters) stood on the *fringe* of Christianity and that they presented the Saviour, quite literally, as an angel. This is the position which I have called an 'angel-Christology' in this book. Yet Klijn and Reininck argue that Elkesaite beliefs were Jewish in character and only superficially Christianized. The female nature of the Spirit reflects Jewish ideas about Wisdom and the portrait of Christ is roughly the equivalent of the exalted angel in apocalyptic literature. Elkesaism cannot be taken as evidence for what mainstream Christians believed, which was characterized by an *angelomorphic* rather than an *angel*-Christology. The *Ascension of Isaiah* is no exception to this rule. Its author never makes the Beloved One an angel, except by the adoption of a disguise, and his insistence on the Beloved's worship by the angels is a notable feature of the apocalypse. Comparison with the Elkesaites illustrates the difference between these two forms of 'angel-based' Christology. It is to be doubted whether an angel-Christology, which implies the absence of divinity, was ever held by mainstream Christians at all.

Irenaeus says that the *Ebionites* differed from Cerinthus in their view that the world was created by God (*Adv. Haer.* 1.26) but that they did not hold the same christological view (*non similiter*) as Cerinthus and Carpocrates.[236] This reference has caused problems of interpretation. Some scholars omit the *non*, after Hippolytus, who used Irenaeus, but Klijn and Reininck argue that it should be retained.[237] This would explain Irenaeus's later comment that the Ebionites could not be saved because they did not believe that God had become human (*Adv. Haer.* 4.33.4;

235. *Patristic Evidence*, pp. 66-67.
236. See further *Patristic Evidence*, pp. 19-43.
237. *Patristic Evidence*, p. 20.

2. The Christology of the Ascension of Isaiah

5.1.3). He records them as having taught that Jesus was the son of Joseph and Mary (*Adv. Haer.* 3.21.1). This means that they held a psilanthropic Christology which made Jesus merely a man: the *non similiter* implies that according to their teaching Christ did not descend on Jesus.

This form of belief is confirmed by Tertullian (*De Carne Christi*), who reads back rejection of Ebionism into the New Testament period. Tertullian identifies Ebion as a particular individual and states that his doctrine was similar to that of Valentinus and Marcion (*De praescr. haeret.* 33.3-5, 11). Tertullian adds that it would have been convenient for the Ebionites had Jesus been an angel for then Ebion could have called him a prophet on the basis of Zech. 1.14 (*De Carne Christi* 14). Tertullian does not claim that Ebion *said* that Jesus was an angel, as Werner thought: merely that such a belief would have been convenient for him. Origen describes two groups of Ebionites who were divided by their attitude to the virgin birth (*Contra Cels.* 5.61, 65; see also his *Comm. in Matth.* 16.12). An explanation of this is offered by Epiphanius, who describes a *development* in Ebionite belief and says that Ebion originally thought that Jesus was the son of Joseph (*Pan.* 30.2.2) but that he later revised this opinion under the influence of Elkesai (*Pan.* 30.3.1). Epiphanius himself describes three Ebionite Christologies (*Pan.* 30.3.5-6) and claims that some thought that Adam was Christ, but that others said that Christ was a spirit, the first creation, and the Lord of the angels (see also *Pan.* 30.14.2; 30.16.3; cf. 30.18.5). *Pan.* 30.16.4 says additionally that Jesus was created as one of the archangels and that he reigned over creation. This again comes close to an 'angel-Christology' like that reportedly held by the Elkesaites.

Patristic reports about Ebionism are thus very confused. This makes it difficult to decide exactly what the Ebionites believed. The psilanthropic Christology that is attributed to them, however, together with their scepticism about the virgin birth and their (possible) understanding of Christ as an angel, are all absent from the *Ascension of Isaiah*. This further distinguishes the apocalypse from the Jewish Christianity which was judged 'unorthodox' by mainstream writers, and it confirms my suggestion of a distance between its Christology and the views which the fathers attributed to Cerinthus and to the Elkesaites.

I am wary of drawing definite conclusions in this area given the difficult nature of the evidence, which leaves open a number of questions. My study does however confirm that, despite the obviously 'Jewish' nature of the *Ascension of Isaiah* and its conceptual imagery, its

170 *Disciples of the Beloved One*

Christology cannot easily be identified with the beliefs which the church fathers attributed in a hostile way to certain Jewish-Christian groups. This is a further and a valuable indication of the way in which the text was perceived in antiquity which must be set beside the other evidence presented in this chapter. It seems that those groups whose members were known to be *Jewish Christians* and thus sectarians entertained a variety of christological beliefs which differed markedly from those of mainstream Christian writers in the second century. The *Ascension of Isaiah* must significantly be ranked with the latter in terms of its Christology.

The Ascension of Isaiah and Gnosticism

The *Ascension of Isaiah* also stands its distance from the belief system of Gnosticism. Gnosticism is the name given to a complex of religious ideas which flourished from about the middle of the second century CE, and which were characterized by a pessimistic view of this world as the creation of an inferior divinity ('the Demiurge') and by the conviction that human souls must be liberated through the revelation of knowledge to discover their true heavenly home.[238] Gnosticism is known from the cache of literature that was discovered at Nag Hammadi in 1945, but the teachings of the Gnostics had been known for longer than this through the critical reports of the church fathers. Gnosticism has enjoyed a revival of scholarly interest in the last twenty years. This has been fuelled by the discovery that it reflected the experience of alienation in the social world of late antiquity, rather than simply the 'acute Hellenization of

---

238. There are a number of introductions to Gnosticism. Some of the most important are K. Rudolph, *Gnosis* (ET Edinburgh: T. & T. Clark, 1983); U. Bianchi, *Le origini dello Gnosticismo* (Leiden: Brill, 1967); R. McL. Wilson, *The Gnostic Problem* (London: Mowbrays, 1958); *idem*, *Gnosis and the New Testament* (Oxford: Basil Blackwell, 1968); E. Yamauchi, *Pre-Christian Gnosticism* (London: Tyndale Press, rev. edn, 1983); A.H.B. Logan and A.J.M. Wedderburn, *The New Testament and Gnosis* (Edinburgh: T. & T. Clark, 1983); and R.M. Grant, *Gnosticism and Early Christianity* (New York: Columbia University Press, 1959). Translations of Gnostic literature include J.M. Robinson (ed.), *The Nag Hammadi Library in English* (Leiden: Brill, 1977); and W. Foerster (ed.), *Gnosis* (2 vols.; Oxford: Clarendon Press, 1972–74).

2. *The Christology of the Ascension of Isaiah*

Christianity'; and that it originated in a form of Jewish sectarianism which was only partially influenced by Christian ideas.[239]

To speak about Gnosticism in connection with the *Ascension of Isaiah* demands an important methodological qualification. This is that the earliest Gnostic literature cannot be dated before c. 150 CE but that the *Ascension of Isaiah* was written probably a generation earlier (my provisional date is c. 120 CE). This means that the two strands of literature cannot simply be equated with each other. This point is reinforced by the observation that there are some significant points of differences between the *Ascension of Isaiah* and Gnosticism which confirm that it is right to distinguish the two strands of literature and which make it problematic for scholarship to present the *Ascension of Isaiah* as a 'Gnostic' apocalypse, as has sometimes been done in the past.

These differences from Gnosticism are crucial to the interpretation of the *Ascension of Isaiah*. A significant example is the use of the descent myth in the two strands of literature. The hidden descent is the major feature of the *Ascension of Isaiah*. There is on the face of it a similar view in the Gnostic literature.[240] Simon Magus taught that the Saviour changed his appearance and that he made himself like the Powers, Principalities and Angels (see Irenaeus, *Adv. Haer.* 1.23.3). This Christology has affinities with both the *Ascension of Isaiah* and the *Epistula Apostolorum* where Christ is said to have assumed an angel's form. A similar report about the Gnostics is found in Epiphanius (*Pan.* 21.2.4), who states that in their understanding the Saviour changed his appearance in each heaven, as he does in the *Ascension of Isaiah*. We have no way of telling whether these beliefs really went back to Simon Magus. It may be that, like Cerinthus, Simon was seen as an obvious polemical target by the church fathers because of his personal prominence. Nevertheless, it does seem unlikely that the fathers would simply have invented this information. The report probably does preserve a brand of mediatorial speculation which was found in some Gnostic circles even if the attribution to Simon is more questionable.

This suspicion of authenticity is confirmed by the evidence of the *Pistis Sophia*. This text explains that Christ took the form of Gabriel in order not to be recognized by the Archons (7.12), which calls to mind the *Epistula Apostolorum* and the Eighth *Sibylline Oracle*. The Ophites

---

239. On this last point see Pearson, 'The Problem of "Jewish Gnostic" Literature'.
240. See the discussion of Rudolph, *Gnosis*, pp. 113-71, on this aspect of Gnosticism.

also had a similar understanding of the descent. They claimed that Christ had descended through the seven heavens by assuming the likeness of their sons (see Irenaeus, *Adv. Haer.* 1.30.12); Irenaeus adds to this report their view that 'many of the disciples of Jesus were not aware of the descent of Christ upon him' (1.30.13). Origen (*Contra Cels.* 6.30-31) reports an Ophite text which explained how the Saviour descended through the seven planetary spheres and gave the correct password to the warders. The *Naasene Hymn*, which is preserved by Hippolytus (*Refutatio Omnium Haeresium* 5.10), furthermore makes Christ declare that he would descend through all the aeons 'bearing the seal'.

Yet we must note that Gnosticism used the myth of the Redeemer's descent in a completely different way from the author of the *Ascension of Isaiah*. This is evident from a comparison between our apocalypse and the *Apocryphon of John*. The latter initially mentions the idea that the Saviour could change form at will (2.1.1). This is followed by an extensive cosmogonic section which includes the statement that the world had not been created in the way that Moses had said (2.1.22), and the identification of the jealous Demiurge with the Jewish God (2.1.24). The Redeemer's descent is then described, but not in much detail (2.1.30-31). Any suggestion that the Redeemer transformed himself into human form is absent, as indeed is any version of the Jesus traditions which are found in *Asc. Isa.* 3.13-18 and 11.2-22. The *Apocryphon of John* merely describes how the Saviour entered 'the prison of the body' and called people to a form of heavenly-mindedness which involved their vacation of the present world. There is no reference to the Saviour's death in the *Apocryphon of John*, and thus no attempt to place a meaning on that event to match *Asc. Isa.* 10.14. It seems that the author's interest in the Redeemer's descent has displaced any interest in the humanity of Jesus in the *Apocryphon of John*. We must agree with Schotroff that the text offers no realistic understanding of the incarnation. This confirms that the soteriology of the two different works is fundamentally different. The *Apocryphon of John* takes little interest in Jesus as Jesus and it calls people to *post-mortem* repatriation with the heavenly world. The *Ascension of Isaiah* by contrast takes a more optimistic view of the present creation and its author insists that the blessings of the seventh heaven will be enjoyed only after the millenarian kingdom (4.17).

This difference between the texts is further illustrated by the attitude towards the creation of the world which they enshrine. Cosmogony is an essential element in the *Apocryphon of John*. It provides the grounds for

2. *The Christology of the Ascension of Isaiah* 173

the soteriology which asserts that souls had been imprisoned in human bodies as a result of a fall which had happened in the pre-mundane world. This 'fall' concerned the activity of the jealous Demiurge Yaltabaoth who had created the world as an act of rebellion against higher powers. Such information explained to readers of the *Apocryphon* why revelation was needed. *Gnosis*, for its author, consisted in the provision of knowledge about the catastrophe and it informed the Gnostic initiate about the means of repatriation with the heavenly world after death. Salvation was determined by the individual's response to the revelation of knowledge about the human condition, in which neither incarnation nor atonement as such were central concepts.

This is a very different thought-world from that of the *Ascension of Isaiah*, which takes no real interest in cosmogony. The apocalypse says that the firmament angels had been rebellious *since* the creation (7.9-12), not that their rebellion was the cause of the creation, and it offers no speculation about the creation itself.[241] This failure to establish a mythological cosmogony has implications for the work's soteriology. The *Ascension of Isaiah* was not written to explain the worthlessness of human life but to make human life more tolerable under the experience of marginalization and persecution.[242] The projected relation between earth and heaven is quite different in the two strands of literature. The *Ascension of Isaiah* dimly articulates the heavenly hope (4.17; chs. 9–11) and indicates that this will be secured only after the millenarian kingdom (4.17). Gnostics of every persuasion would have abhorred this millenarian eschatology, and especially the resurrectional promise of 4.16. The Second Vision of the *Ascension of Isaiah* presupposes the thought of the First, and we must presume that the promise of Isaiah's *post-mortem* ascension (11.35) would not eliminate the possibility of the form of resurrection described by 4.16. Gnosticism would effectively sever the thought of *Asc. Isa.* 4.17 from the millenarianism of 4.14-16.

---

241. There is an interesting difference in this from a first-century passage such as Col. 1.15-20 where the event of creation is referred to the mediation of Christ. The *Ascension of Isaiah* adopts what might be called an 'agnostic' or 'neutral' position on this issue. In retrospect it is possible to see this as a *step towards* Gnosticism which created the possibility that creation could later be presented as the work of an *inferior* being. My point here is that this distinctive Gnostic assertion has not yet been reached in the *Ascension of Isaiah*.

242. See my Chapter 3 for a description of the work's social setting.

The soteriology of the *Ascension of Isaiah* has another difference from Gnosticism in that it works from the premise that Beliar was excluded from the heavens. This understanding represents the author's demonstration that God had no rival. That was part of the task of reminding readers that their patron reigned supreme, which bore on their awkward situation with the Romans. It represents a substantial difference from Gnosticism which asserted that rebellion had taken place among the aeons themselves. In the *Ascension of Isaiah*, by contrast with the *Apocyphon of John*, evil is *excluded* from the heavens and confined to the firmament and the human world. The apocalyptic perspective of the work discloses the inviolability of the heavens and offers no explicit support for the notion of a pre-mundane fall which resulted in the creation.

We can further illustrate this difference between the *Ascension of Isaiah* and Gnosticism by observing how the *Apocryphon of John*, in company with the two related tractates *Hypostasis of the Archons* and *On the Origin of the World*, reworks a motif that is prominent in the *Ascension of Isaiah*. The Gnostic texts assign to the Demiurge the words from Isaiah 45 which are attributed to Beliar in *Asc. Isa.* 4.6 (cf. 10.13): 'I alone am, and there is none besides me'. This is done in a context in which the Demiurge is identified with the Jewish God. This marks an obvious development from the *Ascension of Isaiah*, where the words are spoken by Beliar and where Beliar is radically distinguished from the true God, as his position in the firmament shows.

This development allows us to construct a trajectory of how the words from Isaiah 45 were used in the early Common Era. Isa. 45.18 is one of the great Old Testament declarations of monotheism. The original passage allowed Yahweh to assert his authority in the face of any possible rival. First-century Christianity used this passage initially to establish belief in the divinity of Jesus (see Phil. 2.9-11). This represented a widening of the strict monotheism of the original prophecy in a binitarian direction. It is interesting to observe how such a strongly monotheistic passage was used to support an alternative form of belief in early Christianity. The *Ascension of Isaiah* picks up this first-century usage, which had created the possibility that the words could apply to a heavenly being distinct from God, and applies the passage with heavy irony to Beliar as to an aerial power who had wrongly magnified his own position and whom the Beloved One brought to heel. The author did this to make the point that the Romans were acting blasphemously

2. *The Christology of the Ascension of Isaiah*

when they imposed demands for worship on the Christians. The fact that Beliar is defeated by the Beloved One in the salvation narrative of the *Ascension of Isaiah* confirms the truth of the original prophecy that the true God brooked no rival.

The Gnostic literature represents a further development of the passage from Isaiah 45. It returns the words to Yahweh as the speaker but parodies Jewish theology by placing Yahweh in the position in which the author of the *Ascension of Isaiah* had presented Beliar. Yahweh was distinguished in the Gnostic literature from the supreme God and made a power who had acted in rebellion against his superiors. This in effect denied the value of Jewish religion by criticizing its theology, which was an important concern for some Gnostic writers. The presence of this tradition in more than one Gnostic text shows the importance which it exercised there, which amounts to a traditional history.

This trajectory permits a suggestion about how the Gnostic use of Isaiah 45 developed. The Gnostic usage is best understood by positing a 'middle stage' like that represented by the *Ascension of Isaiah*, which applied Isa. 45.18 to a heavenly being distinct from God but did not yet criticize the Jewish deity as the Gnostics would do. Gnosticism can then be seen as developing this understanding by identifying the insubordinate figure with the Jewish God. If the *Ascension of Isaiah* was used by Gnostic writers before Hieracas, the apocalypse may itself have been an important source for the development of this view. We do not know for sure that the *Ascension of Isaiah* was used in this way, but the hypothesis does have something to commend it. It would explain the development of a Gnostic motif which is otherwise difficult to explain on the basis of the first-century evidence alone. The suggestion of some such 'middle stage' seems to be a necessary explanation of the Gnostic material. The *Ascension of Isaiah* in any event has a significant role to play in the discussion of Gnostic origins, not least in its demonstration of a *Christian* interest in the heavenly world which was constructed in an atmosphere of social isolation.

There is a distance, then, between the *Ascension of Isaiah* and Gnosticism in terms of its view of the Beloved One's mission. As with my comparison between the *Ascension of Isaiah* and Jewish Christianity, this difference suggests that the apocalypse is more appropriately linked with mainstream Christian texts than with those produced by sectarian groups. The differences between the *Ascension of Isaiah* and Gnostic

176   *Disciples of the Beloved One*

literature confound the presentation of the *Ascension of Isaiah* as a 'Gnostic' apocalypse.

Is the Ascension of Isaiah a Gnostic Apocalypse?

In the last part of this chapter, I shall refute the suggestion that the *Ascension of Isaiah* is a Gnostic apocalypse and that it can usefully be exegeted with reference to the Nag Hammadi literature. This view was expressed most recently in an article which was published by Andrew Helmbold in 1972.[243] Helmbold identified 13 points of similarity between the apocalypse and Gnosticism which he listed under three main headings ('Methodology of Revelation', 'The Chief Actors', 'The Action'). He claimed that this evidence indicated that the *Ascension of Isaiah* came from what he calls a 'Christian-Gnostic' circle and that the Second Vision was written c. 150 CE.

I shall first of all note Helmbold's 13 projected points of similarity between the *Ascension of Isaiah* and Gnosticism. These are:

1. The dialogue style of revelation
2. Revelation by means of a vision
3. The timing of the resurrection appearances
4. The doctrine of God as unnameable and unfathomable
5. The trinitarian passages
6. Sammael as God's adversary
7. The words 'I alone am God'
8. Visionary ascension to heaven
9. The heavenly warders
10. The passwords used in the heavenly journey
11. The incorporeal resurrection state
12. The motif of the Saviour's descent
13. The battle of Sammael's angels.

I want to show that, in every case, these alleged points of contact with Gnosticism are capable of a wider and different explanation, which I think controverts Helmbold's conclusion that the *Ascension of Isaiah* is a 'Christian-*Gnostic*' text.

---

243. Helmbold, 'Gnostic Elements'. Previous studies of this issue include F. Langen, *Das Judenthum im Palästina* (Freiburg, 1866), pp. 157-67; and W.J. Deane in *Pseudepigrapha* (Edinburgh, 1891), pp. 236-75.

2. *The Christology of the Ascension of Isaiah* 177

I start by observing that Helmbold adopts an approach to the *Ascension of Isaiah* which the most recent scholarship has rejected on literary-critical grounds. In the wake of the Rome Conference it is difficult now to accept that chs. 6–11 were written in isolation from the material in 3.13–4.22.[244] The separation of chs. 6–11 from the rest of the *Ascension of Isaiah* is a peculiarity of the lost parent of L2 and S and not a feature of the original apocalypse. This means that any theory about the origin of chs. 6–11 must take into account its close affinities with the earlier material, where a 'Gnosticizing' influence is much less obvious. Allied to this is the problem of dating. The *Ascension of Isaiah* is unlikely to be as late as 150 CE, the date of the earliest Gnostic literature, and it may have been written as much as thirty years before this. These introductory arguments weaken Helmbold's case even before we turn to points of individual detail.

Both the dialogue style and the device of the vision as the means of revelation (Helmbold's first two points) are found in Daniel and in many subsequent texts.[245] They are not the exclusive prerogative of Gnosticism but a commonplace of the apocalyptic tradition. The fact that they occur in the *Ascension of Isaiah* and in Gnosticism simply shows how pervasive that tradition had become. It does not offer conclusive proof that the *Ascension of Isaiah* is a Gnostic apocalypse.

The origins of the belief that Christ spent a significant period on earth following the resurrection (point 3) are admittedly obscure. The *Ascension of Isaiah* does not however allude to any esoteric information which was imparted by the Beloved One during this period. That is precisely what the Ophites (and other Gnostics) understood the extended resurrection appearances as disclosing. The revelatory element in the *Ascension of Isaiah* consists rather of an apocalyptic understanding of the cross in which the Beloved One's victory over Beliar is made the grounds of security. Teaching about heavenly immortality occurs only in the context of the millenarian hope in the *Ascension of Isaiah*; and matters of dating suggest that the Ophites could have borrowed this figure from the *Ascension of Isaiah* but not the other way round.[246] The absence of any

---

244. See my Chapter 1.
245. See the discussion of these two motifs with reference to the apocalyptic literature in J.J. Collins (ed.), *Apocalypse: Morphology of a Genre* (*Semeia* 14 1979).
246. The Ophites may also have borrowed from the *Ascension of Isaiah* the

esoteric teaching *by the Saviour* in the *Ascension of Isaiah* distinguishes the apocalypse from Gnosticism.

The *Ascension of Isaiah* presents God as transcendent (point 4). This reflects the influence of the Jewish mystical tradition rather than of Gnostic theology. The *Apocalypse of Abraham* (16.3) is similarly unwilling to allow the seer a vision of God; *Asc. Isa.* 9.37-38 repeats a convention which was found in apocalyptic circles. It marks a development in this from the biblical theophanies and from *1 Enoch* 14. The trappings of God's heavenly court in the *Ascension of Isaiah* are in any event linked much more firmly to the Jewish mystical tradition than to the aeonic emanations of the Gnostic cosmology.

The trinitarian understandings of the *Ascension of Isaiah* and of Gnosticism (Helmbold's point 5) are quite different. Both the *Trimorphic Protennoia* and the *Apocryphon of John* introduce a female divinity into the triad. There is nothing like this in the *Ascension of Isaiah*. It seems that these Gnostic writers were deliberately reacting against 'orthodox' Christian views.[247] The *Ascension of Isaiah*'s Trinitarianism has more in common with the New Testament literature (for example Mt. 28.19) than with Gnosticism. It reveals a view which was still in process of development rather than sufficiently well known to be challenged as the Gnostics did. The subordination and angelic designation of the Spirit, and not the Spirit's presentation as a female divinity, are the distinctive features of the *Ascension of Isaiah*'s pneumatology.

'Sammael' as the name for God's adversary (point 6) can be paralleled from non-Gnostic Jewish literature.[248] This title is by no means exclusively Gnostic and has its origins in Jewish apocalyptic literature. The claim to be the unique God, which is founded on Isa. 45.18, has a wider history in Jewish sectarianism. Segal shows that a cluster of passages including this one featured in the rabbinic defence against the 'Two Powers' controversy from about the end of the first century CE.[249]

---

belief (which is recorded by Irenaeus, *Adv. Haer.* 1.30.13) that many were not aware of the descent of Christ upon Jesus.

247. There is a study of this aspect of Gnostic Trinitarianism by E. Pagels, *The Gnostic Gospels* (London: Weidenfeld & Nicolson, 1979), pp. 48-69. An interesting parallel is the Montanist assertion that 'Christ appeared to me in the likeness of a woman'. The Montanist evidence is mentioned by Epiphanius, *Adv. Haeres.* 49.1.

248. For example Sir. 25.24; *3 Bar.* 4.8. See the list of passages compiled by Ginzberg, *Legends*, VII (index volume), pp. 414-15.

249. *Two Powers*, p. 89: 'We can conclude that Deuteronomy 32:39 became a

2. *The Christology of the Ascension of Isaiah* 179

Ascension through the seven (or more) heavens to the presence of God (point 8) is a familiar Jewish apocalyptic motif.[250] It cannot be held Gnostic either in origin or in character. The warders who guarded the heavens in the *Ascension of Isaiah* and Gnosticism (point 9) represent a development in Jewish angelology. They feature in the later *merkabah* tradition.[251] The likely background to this view is the notion of the other 'gods' in Psalm 82, which is worked up in the *Ascension of Isaiah* to accommodate the seven-storied cosmology. It is the presence of an individual *merkabah* in the heavens, and not the heavenly warders stationed between the heavens, which gives the cosmology of the *Ascension of Isaiah* its distinctive character. The secret passwords (point 10) reflect a Jewish mystical interest in magical incantations rather than a narrowly Gnostic preoccupation.[252]

Belief in the incorporeal resurrection state (point 11) looks back to Daniel 12. The idea is found in a variety of Jewish texts before the rise of Gnosticism.[253] The assertion that the resurrection state would be incorporeal is qualified in the *Ascension of Isaiah* by the fact that it is expected after the millenarian kingdom (4.17) in which even the resurrected would share (4.16). This expectation of the millenarian kingdom links the apocalypse with the New Testament literature and distinguishes it from Gnosticism.

Particular attention should be paid to the motif of the Saviour's descent in the *Ascension of Isaiah* (point 12). I have identified the background for this view in Jewish angelology. Angelology had been known in Jewish circles for centuries. It provides a more plausible source for the *Ascension of Isaiah* than a Gnostic mythological tradition which cannot be shown to have existed before 150 CE, especially when we consider that the descent motif is used in *different* ways in the *Ascension of Isaiah* and in Gnosticism and that the two usages cannot easily be harmonized with each other.

---

favourite scripture—like Exodus 20, Dt. 6.4, Isaiah 44–47—to defeat heretical notions of the godhead.'

250. It was studied classically by W. Bousset, *Der Himmelsreise der Seele* (repr.; Darmstadt: Wissenschaftliche Buchgesellschaft, 1971).

251. See Gruenwald, *Apocalyptic*, pp. 106-107.

252. See for instance the *Prayer of Jacob*, which is translated in Charlesworth (ed.), *Old Testament Pseudepigrapha*, II, pp. 720-23. This text comes from the first or second century CE and represents a brief but significant example of Jewish magical incantations.

253. See the discussion of this idea in Nickelsburg, *Resurrection*, pp. 11-27.

Finally, it is necessary to correct Helmbold in the last of his 13 points. Helmbold states that *Asc. Isa.* 7.9-12 describes the battle of Sammael's forces with those of God. In fact the text makes it clear that this was civil warfare in the firmament ('they were envying one another', 7.9). This means that there are only indirect parallels with Revelation 12 in which Michael casts Satan down from heaven. Beliar is *excluded* from the heavens in the *Ascension of Isaiah*. He has no contact with angels in the heavens whatsoever. This idea is fundamental to the work's soteriology.

In every case, I have able to show that Helmbold's evidence has a wider basis and that it is susceptible to a different and a better explanation. This is that the affinities of the *Ascension of Isaiah* are more obviously with apocalyptic literature (including in many cases with pre-Christian material) than with Gnostic literature. The work's apocalyptic roots are obvious and its differences from Gnosticism significant. This makes it difficult if not impossible to present the *Ascension of Isaiah* as a Gnostic apocalypse in the full sense. The evidence by contrast tends to set it in a position mid-way between New Testament Christianity and Gnosticism. The apocalypse shows the emerging Christian interest in cosmology which Gnosticism further developed, but it stands its distance from key Gnostic ideas about cosmogony and salvation. In this the *Ascension of Isaiah* represents an early assembly of the materials which would be used in a different way in Gnosticism. The apocalypse represents a bridge between the New Testament and Gnosticism whose significance would benefit from further exploration. My concern here is to emphasize that it must be distinguished from both strands of thought, and that this is an indicator of the text's socio-religious position.

The Ascension of Isaiah and Gnostic Origins

Some further differences between the *Ascension of Isaiah* and Gnosticism were mentioned by Bianchi at the Rome Conference.[254] One of these was the interpretation of Isaiah's martyrdom.[255] The *Ascension of Isaiah* offers a 'physical' understanding of this event and presents

---

254. U. Bianchi, 'L'*Ascensione di Isaia:* Tematiche soteriologiche di descensus/ascensus', in Pesce (ed.), *Isaia*, pp. 155-83. Bianchi also notes some themes held *in common* with Gnosticism (p. 161).

255. Bianchi, 'L'*Ascensione di Isaia*', pp. 176-78.

2. *The Christology of the Ascension of Isaiah* 181

Isaiah's death as the destruction of his flesh (5.10).[256] The prophet's demise is described in the *Testimony of Truth* in a very different way:

> [...like Isaiah, who was sawed with a saw, (and)] he became two. [So also the Son of Man divides] us by [the word of the] cross. It [divides the day from] the night and [the light from the] darkness and the incorruptible [from] incorruptibility, and it [divides] the males from the females. But [Isaiah] is the type of the body. The saw is the word of the Son of Man which separates us from the error of the angels.[257]

This Gnostic text uses Isaiah's martyrdom to describe the soul's liberation into the heavenly world. This is quite distinct from the view of self-sacrifice for principle's sake that is found in the *Ascension of Isaiah* Bianchi also noticed differences in cosmogony and Christology between the *Ascension of Isaiah* and Gnostic literature which confirm the sense of distance that I have drawn between the two strands of literature in this chapter.

These differences from Gnosticism, particularly in the related areas of cosmogony and soteriology, make it unlikely (as does the matter of dating) that the author of the *Ascension of Isaiah* drew on a form of the Gnostic Redeemer myth. The similarities between the apocalypse and Gnosticism nevertheless help to explain some of the social and ideological changes in the second century which conspired to produce developed Gnosticism. Already in the *Ascension of Isaiah* we find the belief that God had a rival, albeit one who was excluded from the heavens. This was the basic theological conviction which Gnosticism developed, with or without a myth of the Saviour's descent, when it spoke about aeonic rebellion. The *Ascension of Isaiah* also states that heavenly immortality was reserved for those who held to revealed knowledge (9.24-26). This is similar in some respects to the Gnostic soteriology in which the heavenly world was reserved for those who had been enlightened about their lost condition in the world. The 'apocalyptic' or esoteric nature of the *Ascension of Isaiah* suggests that it was

---

256. For this view in Judaism see T. Baumeister, *Die Anfänge der Theologie des Martyriums* (MBT, 45; Münster: Aschendorff, 1980) pp. 60-62 (on Isaiah); and cf. R. Doran's article 'The Martyr: A Synoptic View of the Mother and Her Seven Sons', in J.J. Collins and G.W. Nickelsburg (eds.), *Ideal Figures in Ancient Judaism* (Chico, CA: Scholars Press), pp. 189-221.

257. *Testim. Truth* 9.3.40-41; translation from Robinson, *Nag Hammadi Library*, pp. 409-10. The date of this text is uncertain but it was not written much before the third century CE, and it may be later than this.

designed for a restricted readership, evidently those who saw themselves as 'the elect'. This is a further point of correspondence with Gnosticism. The criticism of the church authorities in 3.21-31 and the world-negating ideology which runs through the apocalypse equally anticipate Gnostic discontent with mainstream bishops, towards whom much of their criticism was directed.[258]

Study of Gnostic origins continues to yield the conclusion that this matter must be examined as much from the perspective of social history as from that of the history of ideas. I have shown that the *Ascension of Isaiah* displays something of the intellectual origins of Gnosticism in terms of its ideas. The apocalypse also shows some of the social convictions which surfaced in Gnostic conventicles when it sets out to bolster the feelings of an isolated group who felt threatened in their world. Perhaps the feelings about marginalization expressed in the *Ascension of Isaiah* were exacerbated during the second century as mainstream repression of fringe groups such as prophets and mystics became more widespread. This might explain why cosmology came to be a key feature of Gnosticism, as it is of the *Ascension of Isaiah*, and why the Gnostics evidently developed the cosmological understanding represented by the apocalypse. Revealed information about cosmology might have been used as an antidote to the lack of control which stemmed from a belief in a universe populated by more powerful gods and daemons and their supporters. The significance of the *Ascension of Isaiah* for the study of Gnostic origins thus lies as much in its social as in its intellectual position. It sets ideas which were drawn from first-century Christianity in a broader cosmological framework but without achieving either the intellectual synthesis or the position outside the church of the Gnostics. This matter could most profitably be made the subject of further research, not least perhaps in terms of Pétrement's suggestion that the *Ascension of Isaiah* had a Simonian provenance.[259]

Summary and Conclusions

In this chapter I have argued that the *Ascension of Isaiah* stands at a crucial point in the formation of Christian doctrine. It was written in the

258. See further Pagels, *Gnostic Gospels*, pp. 28-47.
259. S. Pétrement, *A Separate God: The Christian Origins of Gnosticism* (ET London: Darton, Longman & Todd, 1991), pp. 324-28: 'It may have been written by a Simonian around the time of Menander' (p. 326).

2. The Christology of the Ascension of Isaiah 183

first third of the second century CE. This was a time when the original Christian generation had died and when the entire basis of Christianity was under review, not least concerning the question of eschatology. The author of the apocalypse knew some of the New Testament literature and wove its thought into a more complex mythological pattern. The result of this is that the *Ascension of Isaiah* demonstrates an early dogmatic interest which balances its support for an imminent and millenarian eschatology. The nature of the achievement of Jesus is made a topic for more detailed reflection than is found in the first-century literature. Such reflection is presented as an item of revealed knowledge which permits disclosure of the heavenly mysteries, including the mystery of the structure of the universe.

My interest in this chapter has been with what stands behind the *Ascension of Isaiah*'s Christology. This has led me to an examination of the Jewish mediatorial tradition and how such material was developed in the context of first-century Christianity. I showed that the Christians set Christ in the position of a unique mediator who received worship and that they thereby created a binitarian theology in contradistinction from Judaism. Despite this, they retained elements that were derived from all three branches of the Jewish mediatorial tradition. This is evident in a number of passages in the New Testament and in other Christian writings. My argument has been that the angelological branch of the mediatorial tradition exercised a particular influence on the Christology of the *Ascension of Isaiah*. Angelology when reinterpreted in the light of Christian theology allowed the author to present the Beloved One as a divine being who was subordinate to God and received the worship of the angels. It also fuelled the description of the hidden descent which in turn became an important theme for later writers.

My study draws attention to the significance of Jewish angelology as a source for Christology. This topic must be considered in future research, given the evidence for 'angelomorphic Christology' in the ancient sources, and the scepticism of some scholars about the importance of this stream of influence on that literature. I want to repeat in conclusion that 'angelomorphic Christology' denotes the portrayal of Christ in terms which were derived from angelology, but not the assertion that Christ was an angel. *All* early Christian writers who used angelology in this way before the Arian controversy did so in a context in which belief in Christ's divinity was unchallenged. Angelomorphic Christology was a way of asserting Christ's affinity to God and not an attempt to assert his creaturely status by ranking him with the angels.

My study has shown that the *Ascension of Isaiah* stands at an important crossroads in the christological tradition. It looks back to the New Testament literature, whose Christology it generally makes more precise and explicit. It also anticipates the more detailed reflection of Irenaeus and Justin Martyr, particularly that part of their writing which is founded on exegesis of earlier literature. The use of language about the hidden descent and the mediator's transformation into human likeness must be acknowledged as the distinctive features of the *Ascension of Isaiah*. This is a significant development in view of the later Nicene assertion that the Son of God 'came down from heaven' for the purposes of salvation. This idea is implicit in the New Testament, and especially in John; but it receives a greater emphasis in the apocalypse, which sets the Jesus traditions in the mythological context of the hidden descent. The importance of a work like the *Ascension of Isaiah* in the move towards the later Nicene position ought not to be neglected. Its early date is a significant factor in this assessment.

The study has further identified the position which the *Ascension of Isaiah* occupies as a bridge between the New Testament and the Gnostic literature. Gnostic origins are complex and must not be over-simplified. Despite this, and even given that scholars have become interested in the *Jewish* roots of Gnosticism, it does seem that Christian elements had their part to play in the development of the synthetic religion. The *Ascension of Isaiah* might explain the attraction which some forms of Christianity exercised for the Gnostics. The apocalypse attests a form of religion in which a growing sense of isolation had permitted the development of a mediatorial interest in which the Saviour's descent was made the remedy for the problems of a hostile environment. The combination of the author's isolated position and his use of the hidden descent motif may have been a fertile one in the minds of later readers. Repression of fringe groups by the church authorities no doubt became exacerbated as Christianity recognized the need to forge out a permanent position in the world, which it did by defining its boundaries and excluding outsiders. The evidence for Christianity in the early second century is not copious. We must carefully examine such evidence as we have from that period. When this is done, the significance of the *Ascension of Isaiah* can hardly

2. The Christology of the Ascension of Isaiah   185

be underestimated. It must feature both in further study of the problem of Gnostic origins and of the other areas which are mentioned in this book.

Chapter 3

THE SETTING OF THE *ASCENSION OF ISAIAH*

Another line of enquiry which must be explored by exegetes is to ask what setting yielded the *Ascension of Isaiah*. The apocalypse offers a number of clues about its origins. The First Vision expresses the hope that the Beloved's imminent appearance will introduce a transformed state from which hostile forces will be removed (4.14-18). The Second Vision explains that Beliar's power has *already* been destroyed on the cross (ch. 10). This material was written to meet a particular situation in the early second century, in which, as is evident from the apocalypse, Beliar was a powerful force. I have suggested that this situation is illuminated by the correspondence between Pliny and Trajan and that the *Ascension of Isaiah* was written to counter repressive activity by the Romans.

Previous studies of the work's setting have concentrated on the prophetic status of the author's circle and the nature of their disputes with other Christians. Much work has been done in both areas over the last fifteen years. The impetus for it sprang from the 1981 conference. Pesce argued there that the *Ascension of Isaiah* came from a 'school' of prophets who interpreted the prophetic writings with reference to Christ and engaged in haggadic retelling of Old Testament narrative which they presented in Christianized form.[1] Pesce thought that the apocalypse was connected with a wandering prophetic circle who organized themselves along the lines of a dynasty and increasingly mistrusted the leaders of the church.[2] Two papers by Bori, one presented at the conference and the other published beforehand, examined the nature of prophetic

---

1. *Isaia*, pp. 46, 55.
2. *Isaia*, pp. 53-55. He summarizes his view on p. 55: 'L'opera suppone necessariamente il lavorio di una scuola profetica teologico-esegetica che legga gli scritti profetici biblici, li interpreti cristologicamente, raccolga tradizioni haggadiche giudaiche e cristiane e specialmente tradizioni profetiche cristiane.'

3. The Setting of the Ascension of Isaiah

experience in the *Ascension of Isaiah*.[3] His 1980 article concluded that the authors of the apocalypse stood within a tradition of ecstatic prophecy either of present experience or recent memory. This showed no trace of the reserve towards the identification of prophecy with ecstasy which was characteristic of the anti-Montanist reaction in the church.[4] Bori's 1981 paper noted the author's sense of distance from the apostolic age (*Asc. Isa.* 3.21) and his lack of awareness of possessing a '*new* prophecy' which was the distinctive feature of the Montanist movement. He concluded from this evidence that the apocalypse was written before the Montanist controversy and he argued (wrongly, in my opinion) for an Asian provenance.[5]

Another member of the Italian research team, Acerbi, saw two sources behind our present text. These are chs. 1–5, with the exception of 3.13b–4.1 which he believed was interpolated into an existing source, and chs. 6–11 apart from 11.41-43.[6] Acerbi noted that 3.21-31 describes internal divisions in the church concerning the abandonment of prophecy.[7] He thinks that 6.13, which insists that Isaiah's angel companion had come from the seventh heaven, constitutes polemic against attempts by others to portray chs. 6–11 as 'false prophecy', as the author turned the tables on his opponents.[8] The overall impression, in which Acerbi follows Bori, is that the apocalypse came from a circle who practised prophecy. This practice was increasingly held suspect by other Christians. That dispute about the status of prophecy stands at the heart of the apocalypse.[9]

In an article which was published in 1991 Robert Hall engaged in source criticism to discern the social setting of the *Ascension of Isaiah*.[10] Hall saw 6.1-17 and 3.13-31 as redactional passages which came from the final author and revealed his views about prophecy. Hall thought that ch. 4 came from an interpolated 'emperor worship source'. He identified the setting of the apocalypse in the author's dispute with fellow Christian prophets about the meaning of the Beloved One's descent and

---

3. 'L'estasi del profeta', and 'L'esperienza profetica nell'*Ascensione di Isaia*', in Pesce (ed.), *Isaia*, pp. 133-54.
4. 'L'estasi del profeta', p. 387. Bori thinks that the parent of S and L2 was made after the Montanist controversy.
5. The last point in 'L'esperienza profetica', p. 144.
6. *L'Ascensione di Isaia*, p. 261.
7. *L'Ascensione di Isaia*, pp. 223-33.
8. *L'Ascensione di Isaia*, pp. 243-44.
9. *L'Ascensione di Isaia*, pp. 243, 246.
10. 'The Ascension of Isaiah'.

ascension. For Hall ch. 6 represents the author's ideal picture of the circle, which was a prophetic school that gathered periodically from different communities to gain instruction and ordination from the senior prophets.[11] This circle saw itself as an outpost of heaven and its members thought that they joined with the angels in their worship of God. They also made heavenly trips to see the deity.[12] The author's rhetorical purpose was to win an audience for his belief in the Beloved One's descent and ascent and to persuade a recalcitrant church that this doctrine was vital. Isaiah was made the patron for this view because he had led a prophetic school, had seen God and was persecuted by rival prophets.[13] Hall thought that the author of the *Ascension of Isaiah* was perhaps a junior member of the community[14] and that the work itself came from circles that were opposed by Ignatius in the early second century.[15]

It is certain that these scholars have opened up new vistas of interpretation on the *Ascension of Isaiah*. Their work connects the text with others that describe the phenomenon of itinerant prophecy, notably passages in the Gospels and the *Didache*; and locates it within a particular context in second-century Christianity. This was a time when the prophets were becoming obsolete in the church.

On the other hand, it must be doubted whether this recent work exhausts the light which can be shed on the work's *Sitz im Leben*. It has all but ignored the anti-Jewish polemic in the First Vision and the hostility towards Rome that is found in 4.1-13. The Second Vision has also been under-explored in terms of its setting (perhaps because it lacks concrete historical allusions like those in the First Vision). All these areas would benefit from further research. They have much to contribute to the emerging portrait of the author and his circle. What is needed now is a renewed discussion of the work's setting and purpose which takes account of *all* the likely sources of opposition to the author and which relates the *Ascension of Isaiah* to the wider social and religious history of the period.

This chapter sets out to provide such a discussion document. I shall try to identify the author's causes of concern and to analyse the response

11. 'The Ascension of Isaiah', p. 291.
12. 'The Ascension of Isaiah', pp. 293-94.
13. 'The Ascension of Isaiah', p. 298.
14. 'The Ascension of Isaiah', p. 294.
15. 'The Ascension of Isaiah', p. 305.

3. The Setting of the Ascension of Isaiah 189

which he made to the difficulties of his situation. I shall examine in the course of my discussion his attitude to the Jews, to the church leaders and the Roman administration. In my assessment I shall comment on the decline of prophecy and on the imposition of the sacrifice test as significant factors for the people who wrote the apocalypse. This will include consideration of the question of whether chs. 6–11 offer a substantially different eschatology from that which is found in the first half of the *Ascension of Isaiah*. I shall conclude that the apocalypse was written to defuse the tensions of the situation of conflict, notably with Rome, by offering an alternative perspective which made that situation more bearable.

A word of caution is needed before embarking on this project. There is a perennial danger of confusing what the author says about his situation with what was actually true there. This caveat relates to several features of the apocalypse. First of all, the text enshrines a dualism which has both cosmological and ethical implications. It divides human beings into two camps: supporters of the Beloved One and followers of Beliar. This criticism of the majority is made from a particular perspective and it does not represent an unbiased assessment of Christianity in the early second century (any more than Ignatius can be regarded as a disinterested historian). The author's dualism with its social implications created this picture and not the other way round. The apocalypse *is* however a significant text once this bias is acknowledged.

Caution is also needed when interpreting the work's narrative portions. These must not be taken to be an allegory of the author's situation. Because the writer includes a passage which eulogizes poverty does not mean that he was poor: nor should this person's penchant for the agrarian life lead to the conclusion that he was one of the underclass of Syrian society. The fact that he could write an apocalypse presupposes an education and greater intellectual resources than those of the ordinary day-labourer. Again, however, what he says about life in the desert (2.7-11; 4.13) is likely to reveal *something* of his beliefs even if the language has a mainly rhetorical force. My contention is that the real life-setting must be distilled from the narrative and must not be confused with it.

Thirdly, the author's use of mythology about Nero (ch. 4) does not imply that the apocalypse was countering the spread of rumours that *Nero himself* was returning. The myth of Nero's return is mentioned in other literature (notably the *Sibylline Oracles*). It would be naïve to interpret *Ascension of Isaiah* 4 without reference to that wider material.

Such a comparison shows that the image of Nero provoked a well-established terror in the Jewish and Christian imagination and that Nero was regarded a symbol for Jewish antipathy to Rome in different kinds of literature. It is in this symbolic rather than in an actual sense that the Nero mythology is used in the *Ascension of Isaiah*. This point needs to be seen as crucial to interpretation.

The Author's Opponents

I shall begin this assessment by considering the question of whom the author regarded as his opponents. I use the term 'opponents' in a loose sense in this context. The evidence indicates that the author was not so much distancing specific groups—although in practice he did that—as erecting barriers between his prophetic circle and *all* other people who were not of his persuasion. It seems that he was conscious of occupying an isolated position in the world and that he dealt with this problem through his construction of the cosmological gulf between Beliar and the Beloved One, which has a social as well as a religious function in the apocalypse. Part of this social function was to demonstrate that all who disagreed with his circle had been deceived by Beliar and that his friends alone were the genuine disciples of the Beloved One who had knowledge of the true God. This was intended to reassure readers who felt pressured on a number of fronts.

Opposition from the Jews

Previous research has all but ignored the anti-Jewish stance of the *Ascension of Isaiah*. The record must be corrected in this area. Relations with the Jews had become a long-standing source of conflict for the Christians by the second century CE. The *Ascension of Isaiah* draws on a history of conflict between the two religions.[16] There is evidence for its author's critical attitude to Judaism in at least four places in the apocalypse. *Asc. Isa.* 3.8-10 speaks harshly about Moses and states that he had denied that God could be seen in a mystical vision. The author by contrast accepted the validity of Isaiah's mystical insight and took it to signify that the prophet had witnessed a binitarian vision. In 3.6-10 the charges which Belchira laid against Isaiah allege that the prophet had

---

16. See J.G. Gager, *The Origins of Anti-Semitism* (Oxford: Oxford University Press, 1985), Parts 2 and 3 for discussion of this evidence. This book unfortunately ignores the evidence of the *Ascension of Isaiah*.

3. *The Setting of the Ascension of Isaiah*

predicted the destruction of Jerusalem (3.6, 10). This charge would have had a particular significance in Christian literature after 70 CE. It made the point that the destruction of Jerusalem accorded with the divine will. Next, 4.21-22—unthinkably for a Jew—fails to mention the Torah in the list of inspired writings. The author mentions only the Prophets and Writings as witnesses for the Beloved One in what is evidently a repudiation of Mosaic authority. Finally, 3.13 and 11.19 insist that the Jews were responsible for the rejection of Jesus. This had become an established theme in Christian literature: 11.19 picks up the hint of 1 Cor. 2.8 that those who crucified Jesus were ignorant of his identity, and develops it with reference to the hidden descent. The fact that this polemic has a traditional history does not obscure the strong force which it exercises in the apocalypse.

We must explore these passages in greater detail in order to understand the nature of the author's relations with Judaism. *Asc. Isa.* 3.8-10 makes Belchira allege that Isaiah had claimed to see more than Moses by saying that he had seen the Lord (this is an allusion to Isa. 6) and had lived to tell the tale. Moses had ordained that 'no man shall see my face and live' (Exod. 33.20b):

> And Isaiah himself has said, 'I see more than Moses the prophet.' Moses said, 'There is no man who can see the LORD and live.' But Isaiah has said, 'I have seen the LORD, and behold I am alive. Know, therefore, O king, that they [are] false prophets' (3.8-10a).

A passage in the Talmud (*b. Yeb.* 49b) shows knowledge of the same exegetical dispute (between Exod. 33 and Isa. 6) at a later period:

> Raba said: He brought him to trial and then slew him. He said to him: Your teacher Moses said: '*For men shall not see Me and live*' and you said, '*I saw the Lord sitting on a throne, high and lifted up.*'[17]

Like the *Ascension of Isaiah* the Talmudist mentions Isaiah's mysticism among the reasons for the prophet's death. He relies on Moses' authority to confound Isaiah for this practice. The Talmudist returns to this theme a few lines later:

> [Do not] the contradictions between the Scriptural texts, however, still remain?—'*I saw the Lord*' [is to be understood] in accordance with what was taught: All the prophets looked into a dim glass, but Moses looked through a clear glass.

17. Translation from I. Epstein (ed.), *The Babylonian Talmud* (London: Soncino, 1936).

Here he gives his view that Moses was right to say that the deity could not be seen. The second half of the passage implies that the prophets merely *imagined* they had seen God in the relevant literature. Moses' authority is affirmed and the mystical prowess of the prophets is sharply qualified in this way.

Using the Talmud to interpret early Christian literature is problematic because of its date, but the correspondence between *b. Yeb.* 49b and *Asc. Isa.* 3.8-10 is impossible to ignore. The *Ascension of Isaiah* shows that the dissonance between Isaiah 6 and Exodus 33 had been recognized in the early second century. The focus of this dispute in the apocalypse, where it evidently features as a well-known scriptural comparison, suggests that its origins were earlier than this, probably in the earliest years of the Jamnian Academy. If we can assume that the Talmud accurately represents an earlier *crux exegeticum*, the *Ascension of Isaiah* seems to be *reacting* against the conventional understanding of the texts in question. Comparison between the sources shows that the Jewish and the Christian branches of the exegetical tradition differ markedly about the interpretation of Isaiah's mysticism. The Talmud asserts that Isaiah only *thought* that he had seen God and that Moses was right to say that God could not be seen. The *Ascension of Isaiah* insists that Isaiah really saw God and gives his vision a Christian interpretation which insists that the Beloved One had appeared in Old Testament times. The concomitant of this is that Moses' insight is sharply criticized. *Asc. Isa.* 3.8-10 effectively pours scorn on the statement, which is here attributed to Moses, that God could not be seen by human beings.

The implausibility of supposing that *Asc. Isa.* 3.8-10 comes from a written 'Martyrdom of Isaiah' suggests that it enshrines the author's own attitude to Judaism. His adaptation of an existing scriptural comparison shows how far he had moved from rabbinic views. Unthinkably for a rabbi, he implies that Moses was wrong and that Isaiah, who was (merely) a prophet, had spoken the truth when he claimed to see God. This scriptural comparison has some additional features. The assertion that Isaiah had seen God is followed in the *Ascension of Isaiah* by the First Vision, with its Christian orientation. This implies that the point in dispute was the status of Christian claims about the Beloved One which the Jews had repudiated.[18] This is signified especially by the fact that the appeal to

18. There is an earlier version of this dispute in Jn 3.13 which denies that *anyone* had ascended into heaven. This passage seems to be set against a view of Moses like that found in Ezekiel the Tragedian's *Exagoge*. J.L. Martyn presents a

3. *The Setting of the Ascension of Isaiah* 193

Moses is assigned to Belchira, who is called both a false prophet and a Samaritan (3.1). The denigration of the exegete calls the value of the exegesis into question. The impression which *Asc. Isa.* 3.8-10 offers is that those who used Exod. 33.20b to deny the validity of Christian theology were 'false prophets'. This criticism seems especially directed against Judaism although of course it could be used against *anyone* who denied the interpretation which the author placed on Isaiah's mysticism (including, I think, fellow Christians). The author ironically preserves the Jewish assertion that Moses had *not* seen God to support his view that Christianity represented a higher revelation than Judaism.

This interpretation of *Asc. Isa.* 3.8-10, which sees the passage as hostile to Moses, gains support from a consideration of 4.21-22. This passage presents a list of writings from the Hebrew Bible which 'the angel of the Spirit' is held to have inspired. The author cites the Prophets and the Writings in this connection but he significantly fails to mention the Torah. The implication of this omission seems to be that the second and third divisions of the Hebrew Bible were found more helpful as prophecies of the Beloved One than the Torah to which of course Judaism attached the greatest importance. The Torah is not in fact cited with approval anywhere in the *Ascension of Isaiah*. Although my argument is from silence (and I recognize that this method has limitations) I can find no evidence to indicate that the author of the apocalypse saw Moses in a positive light. When it is set beside 3.8-10, 4.21-22 offers further evidence of a growing distance from Judaism on the author's part. This probably reflects the prominence of Torah exegesis in the early rabbinic period, to which the author responded by denying the Jewish basis of authority and by promoting the status of the Prophets and the Writings to compensate for his attitude to the Torah. He thus retained a sympathy for the Hebrew Bible but offered a different evaluation of its contents from rabbinic Judaism.

The *Ascension of Isaiah* is not exceptional among Christian literature in its criticism of Judaism, but it does seem to offer a harsher perspective than other texts in its implicit denial that the Torah contained valid revelation. *Ign. Smyrn.* 5.1 and *Barnabas* 1–2 help to establish this point. Ignatius states that neither the prophets nor the Law of Moses had convinced the docetists of their error. Ignatius assumes that the Torah, in

---

polemical situation between Johannine Christianity and the synagogue as a factor behind the Fourth Gospel: see his *History and Theology in the Fourth Gospel* (New York: Harper & Row, 1968).

company with the rest of the Hebrew Bible, was a suitable source for confounding the heretics. Barnabas, who is notoriously anti-Jewish in his outlook, asserts that Jewish customs had prefigured Christian beliefs and practices. That Barnabas not infrequently *cites* the Torah to prove this point again presupposes that Moses was a significant author. Paul, John and Matthew also regarded Moses as an inspired writer.[19] This evidence contrasts strikingly with the implication of *Asc. Isa.* 4.21-22, which excludes Moses from the list of inspired writings, and with *Asc. Isa.* 3.8-10, which implies that Moses had less insight than Isaiah.

We must turn to the Gnostic literature to find a similar attitude to Moses. Several passages in the *Apocryphon of John* redraft the Genesis creation story to state that Moses had been wrong in what he said. An example of this is II.1.22.21-24:

> And I said to the Savior, 'What is the forgetfulness?' And he said, 'It was not the way Moses wrote [and] you heard. For he said in his first book, "He put him to sleep" [Gen 2.21], but [it was] in his perception. For also he said through the prophet, "I will make their hearts heavy that they may pay attention and may not see"' [Isa. 6.10].[20]

This intriguing passage rejects the literal meaning of Gen. 2.21, that God had put Adam to sleep when he created Eve, and substitutes the Gnostic view that Adam's *perception* had been blighted on that occasion. The author's view is that this forgetfulness had made Adam ignorant of his lost heavenly origins. The statement represents a reinterpretation of the Genesis story which was determined by the work's mythological cosmogony (which has parallels in other Gnostic literature).[21] This willingness to criticize Moses is shared with the *Ascension of Isaiah*. Both texts reject the authority of people (clearly Jews) who appealed to Moses by claiming that the Jewish Lawgiver had been wrong, or at least mistaken, in what he said. Both do so in a context in which heavenly revelation has assumed great importance as a norm of authority. This belief in contemporary revelation vindicates the rejection of Moses. The two texts present this as of greater religious authority than the Jewish tradition of exegesis. Both writers thereby distance themselves from Judaism, as if this were a source which had once influenced them but whose limitations their new religious position had exposed.

19. See for example Gal. 3.8; Jn 3.14; Mt. 19.3-9.
20. Translation by F. Wisse in Robinson (ed.), *Nag Hammadi Library*, p. 117.
21. See Chapter 2 for an account of Gnostic cosmology.

3. *The Setting of the Ascension of Isaiah* 195

Gnosticism combined this repudiation of Moses with the view that he had been inspired by an inferior deity—the God of the Jews. This understanding is not found in the *Ascension of Isaiah*, which as we have seen displays significant differences from Gnosticism. I have argued that the *Ascension of Isaiah* is to be understood as a bridge between the New Testament and Gnosticism and not as a Gnostic apocalypse. The different attitude towards Moses in the two texts is an example of this. The critical attitude which is found in the *Ascension of Isaiah* was exacerbated in Gnosticism by the more explicit statement that Moses had been *wrong* in what he said. This Gnostic perspective must not be projected on to the apocalypse despite the fact that it is anticipated there.

We must now consider the material in the *Ascension of Isaiah* that predicts the destruction of Jerusalem. Evidence for this view is found in the first and the third of Belchira's charges against Isaiah, that he had prophesied against Jerusalem (3.6) and compared the city to Sodom (3.10). Lampe notes that, of the two destructions of Jerusalem, it was the second in 135 CE to which Christian writers more often appealed in their polemic against Judaism.[22] Yet the inclusion of the fall of 70 CE within the divine plan is by no means lacking as a theme in earlier Christian literature. Lk. 21.20 mentions the city's fall in its version of the Synoptic eschatological discourse and it is possible that Mt. 22.15 does so as well. *Barn.* 16.4 certainly comments on the Temple's destruction in this way. The date of the *Ascension of Isaiah* is not completely certain but we may say with confidence that the apocalypse looks back on the destruction of Jerusalem in 70 CE. The author implies that what had happened to the city had been permitted by God. He takes the view that Isaiah had been right in his prophecies, including the prophecy of the fall of Jerusalem, and that the disciples of Moses (the Jews) had been confounded by this disaster. The *Ascension of Isaiah* must be added to that list of sources which presents the destruction of Jerusalem as divinely willed in this way.

Ascension of Isaiah 3.13 and 11.19 both emphasize the Jewish responsibility for the death of Jesus. 3.13 mentions the 'torments with which the children of Israel must torment him'; 11.19 states that 'the adversary' roused 'the children of Israel', who did not know who he was, against him and that they handed him to 'the ruler' (i.e. Pilate). The view that the Jews were responsible for the death of Jesus is found in the New Testament in passages as diverse as 1 Thess. 2.14-16; Mt. 27.25;

---

22. Lampe, 'AD 70 in Christian Reflection'.

and Jn 19.1-16.[23] The first of these passages, which comes from Paul's early career, mentions 'the Jews' in an unqualified sense as those who 'killed both the Lord Jesus and the prophets'. Mt. 27.25 makes 'all the people' (again, the term is a universal one) exclaim that the blood of Jesus would be on them and on their children. John 19 presents the Jews (unqualified still) as Jesus' opponents in the lawsuit before Pilate. These passages show the fierceness of the primitive Christian polemic, which turned the responsibility for the messiah's passion on the Jewish nation as a whole. The *Ascension of Isaiah* thus stands within a firmly-established Christian tradition in 3.13 and 11.19.

The traditional nature of this polemic must not be allowed to obscure the possibility that the author of the *Ascension of Isaiah* had himself been in conflict with Jews, especially in the area of scriptural exegesis, to which the apocalypse attaches great weight. This would provide a natural context for the criticism of Moses which is found in *Asc. Isa.* 3.8-10 and 4.21-22. The dispute in 3.8-10 reveals a knowledge of Jewish scribal activity. It probably represents a reply to those who used Exod. 33.20b to deny the possibility of mystical revelation. The charge that the Jews had rejected the messiah is repeated by Justin Martyr (see for example *Dial.* 95) and it would have been a natural one in a polemical context earlier in the second century. The *Ascension of Isaiah* must be considered as a precursor of the later dispute between Justin and Trypho in which christological interpretation of the Hebrew Bible played a major role.

Hostility towards Judaism thus lay in the background of the problems which the author of the *Ascension of Isaiah* experienced. Anti-Jewish polemic is not found in the historical review, nor do the Jews feature in the *Ascension of Isaiah* as named opponents like the church leaders and the Romans. This observation suggests that opposition from Judaism did not form part of the immediate crisis to which the apocalypse was addressed. It must however be noticed for the sake of a complete presentation, and it may have been a significant tension. The author's willingness to deny religious insight to Moses bespeaks a considerable hostility which was based perhaps on his experience of conflict with Jewish teachers. This attitude must be evaluated within the context of his perceptible tendency to denigrate *all* other influences and groups which were not of his own persuasion.

---

23. See Gager, *Anti-Semitism*, pp. 134-59.

3. *The Setting of the Ascension of Isaiah*

Opposition from the Church Leaders
From information that lies outside the historical review we turn to what the author says about his own situation in 3.21–4.22. *Asc. Isa.* 3.21-31 indicates that a further and more immediate source of tension was provided by opposition from fellow Christians, and specifically from the church leaders.

Asc. Isa. 3.21-31 is an important passage for historians of early Christianity. It records a difference of opinion in the early second century about the role of prophets in the church.[24] The author was himself a prophet. We can surmise this from the way that his apocalypse upholds the prophets (see for example 2.7-11) and maintains that they alone preserved the Christian tradition in the post-apostolic period (3.21, 26-27). The author addressed a situation in which, he claimed, true prophets were found 'one here and there in different places' (3.27), and in which he thought that the Holy Spirit had been 'withdrawn from many' (3.26). He names as the reason for this decline of prophecy the behaviour of the church leaders, whom he presents under a variety of dishonourable titles: people who loved office when they lacked wisdom (3.23); 'wicked elders and shepherds' (3.24); unholy shepherds (3.24); slanderers and vainglorious people (3.26); and people who were full of hatred and jealousy (3.29-30). He states that this behaviour had led them to 'make ineffective the prophecy of the prophets who were before me' and to 'make ineffective' Isaiah's own visions in order that 'they may speak what bursts out of their heart' (3.31). This last passage uses the first person form as if to indicate that the author himself had experienced opposition in this way, even if this statement does not progress beyond the level of an allusion.

Prophecy had been the mainstay of first-century Christianity, as the author notes with some bitterness in 3.21. By the time he wrote the prophets had become marginalized figures (3.26-27; cf. 2.7-11; 4.16; ch.

24. On the role of prophets in early Christianity see G. Friedrich, 'Prophets in the Early Church', in *TDNT*, VI, pp. 859-61; M.E. Boring, 'Prophecy (Early Christian)', in D.N. Freedman *et al.* (ed.), *The Anchor Bible Dictionary* (New York: Doubleday, 1992), V, pp. 495-502; D.E. Aune, *Prophecy in Early Christianity and the Mediterranean World* (Grand Rapids: Eerdmanns, 1983); D. Hill, *New Testament Prophecy* (London: Marshall, Morgan & Scott, 1979); and U. Müller, *Prophetie und Predigt im Neuen Testament* (Gütersloh: Gerd Mohn, 1975). R. Horsley distinguishes three types of prophecy: exegetical, oracular and millennial. See his article, 'Popular Prophetic Movements at the Time of Jesus, their Principal Features and Social Origins', *JSNT* 26 (1986), pp. 3-27.

6), and 3.31 indicates an open and powerful opposition to them from the leaders. This situation reveals what was first and foremost a dispute about authority. This dispute centred on the question of whether the prophets or the institutional leaders should hold authority in the church. The kind of prophecy disputed in this way had an ecstatic or mystical dimension which involved the direct experience of revelation like that recorded in *Ascension of Isaiah* 6–11 (and in the First Vision too). It was neither simply prognostication, nor merely scriptural exegesis nor even what Paul had called 'a word of knowledge' (1 Cor. 12.8). It represented a combination of these and embodied the conviction of authority which stemmed from the practice of ecstasy, as we can surmise from ch. 6. We are probably to suppose that this belief in continuing revelation lent authority to the author's view of history which he expresses in the First Vision, in which the church leaders are denigrated.

It is important to define the status of 'the early Christian prophet' more closely to explain why this conflict with the leaders arose. The definition which was proposed by M.E. Boring twenty years ago is relevant for this study. Boring defines a 'prophet' as 'an immediately inspired spokesman for the (or a) deity of a particular community, who receives revelations which he is impelled to deliver to the community'.[25] The significant part of this definition for our purposes is the phrase 'immediately inspired spokesman'. What gave this circle the status of 'prophets' was not just the manner in which they received revelation, which probably had more than one aspect, but the *conviction of authority* which stemmed from inspiration. Their self-understanding was as a group of prophets through whom the Holy Spirit spoke directly (3.26-28) and who therefore believed that they had a right to be heard. This was the activity which 3.31 says was being opposed in the church at the time.

We must also ask why this understanding of prophecy was beginning to cause offence in the second-century church. The answer seems to be that it made claims to authority which ran parallel and indeed counter to the claims of church leaders like Ignatius who were trying to focus authority in a ministerial tradition that was distinct from the prophets. This was the threefold order of ministry (twofold in first-century literature like Phil. 1.1 and the *Didache*) which Ignatius claimed stood 'in the

---

25.   'What are we Looking For? Towards a Definition of the Term "Christian Prophet"', in G. Macrae (ed.), *SBL 1973 Seminar Papers* (Missoula, MT: Scholars Press), II, p. 147.

3. The Setting of the Ascension of Isaiah 199

purpose of Jesus Christ' (*Ign. Eph.* 3.2). The emergence of this ministerial tradition had evidently had the effect of marginalizing other claimants to authority. This is an area in which the *Ascension of Isaiah* offers important but neglected evidence for the historical development of Christianity.

We can discover the background to this marginalization by studying earlier and contemporary literature. The first days of the church were marked by an outburst of Spirit-filled activity, according to the book of Acts. This outburst had happened from Pentecost onwards (Acts 2). Passages such as Gal. 4.6 confirm that Spirit-possession was regarded as the hallmark of every Christian believer. 1 Cor. 14.5 insists that every Christian could (and should) prophesy. According to 1 Cor. 12.28 'the prophets' were second only to the apostles in terms of their authority over the Christian body.

Deutero-Pauline literature already reveals a modification of this picture. Eph. 2.20 states that the prophets, like the apostles, were the foundation-stones on which subsequent building had taken place, as if their activity belonged in the past when that letter was written (c. 80–90 CE). This picture is corroborated by 2 Pet. 1.19-21 (late first or early second century CE) which voices suspicion towards contemporary prophets (2.1-3) and equates the 'prophecy of Scripture' with the Hebrew Bible. The exercise of prophecy by all believers was a feature of the first, heady days of Christianity. Its influence was already on the wane in the period documented by the later New Testament literature, although of course we should beware of supposing that this happened according to a precise sequence.

The Pastorals are difficult to date but they come perhaps from c. 110 CE which makes them rough contemporaries of Ignatius. The Pastorals uphold the value of the ministerial offices (1 Tim. 3.1-13; Tit. 1.5-9) and attempt to read back the practice of ministerial ordination to Paul (see 1 Tim. 4.14). They also make the voice of the Spirit uphold the position of the ordained ministers (1 Tim. 1.18; 4.14). This finds an echo in the writings of Ignatius, as will be seen below. The emphasis in these three texts is on the dominance of the institutional offices. Nothing is said there to validate the authority of the prophets as a separate class of people.

The evanescence of prophecy is documented further by non-canonical sources. Hermas fails to rank the prophets with the apostles and the bishops (in the Roman church) even though he was aware of continuing prophetic activity (see *Man.* 11.5.8). The Syrian text called the *Didache*

(c. 70–110 CE) makes for an important comparison with the *Ascension of Isaiah*.[26] The *Didache* incorporates a manual of church order in chs. 7–15 which is similar in some respects to the Qumran Manual of Discipline. This part of the *Didache* takes a considerable interest in prophecy. According to *Did.* 10.7 the prophets can give thanks in a free form but other Christians must follow a set form of prayer which is based around the Paternoster. *Did.* 11.7 forbids readers to reprove any prophet who spoke by the Spirit and states that this was an unforgivable sin. Chapter 13 explains that every true prophet deserves his support (13.1) as does the true teacher (13.2). These people are to be distinguished from the false prophets, rules for whose discernment are supplied by ch. 11. These rules involve examination of the prophets' message and their behaviour: those who stay too long or asked for money betray their colours as false prophets. The first-fruits of the produce are reserved for the prophets on the grounds that prophets are the Christian High Priests (13.3). Only in the absence of prophets is such food given to the poor (13.4). This command respects the prophetic office but it also recognizes that not every church has a prophet—otherwise the qualification is meaningless.[27] *Didache* 15 briefly discusses the role of bishops and deacons in the church. The author says that these officials must be respected and he adds that they 'fulfil the ministry of the prophets' in Christian communities. For this reason they are not to be slighted. This passage reveals that the prophets possessed great power, despite the fact that their numbers were decreasing, and that the leaders had yet to gain full support in the churches for which the *Didache* was written. It nevertheless also shows the emergence of a new kind of authority, that of the ministerial offices, as the prophets became fewer in numbers.

The letters of Ignatius, which were written about 110 CE, shed more light on this issue. They reveal the desire of a monarchical bishop to focus authority in his own person, probably because of rival claimants to authority and perhaps because false teaching had become a problem.[28]

---

26. For a history of research into the *Didache* see C.N. Jefford, *The Sayings of Jesus in the Teaching of the Twelve Apostles* (Leiden: Brill, 1989), pp. 1-21. Its date remains uncertain but the parameters which are mentioned here are commonly accepted. It matters less for my argument to fix the date of the *Didache* precisely than to observe that the status of the prophets in that text is different from that in the *Ascension of Isaiah*. We must presume that the situation described in the *Didache* had emerged over a period of time.

27. Friedrich's point, 'Prophets in the Early Church', p. 859.

28. P.N. Harrison argues that Ignatius had lost control of the church in Antioch

3. *The Setting of the Ascension of Isaiah*

Ignatius has little to say about church prophets but he was aware of continuing prophetic activity.[29] He himself had a prophetic gift and used it to support his own view of authority in the church. *Phld.* 7.2 has the form of a prophetic utterance in which Ignatius exclaims, 'Do nothing without the bishop'. This theme is echoed in many of his letters.[30] This oracle, which claims to represent the voice of the Spirit, says that the bishop's authority must be respected at all times. This is a striking claim to authority given that the speaker is the bishop himself. Ignatius used his prophetic gift to bolster his own position against rivals (including no doubt those who claimed to be prophets), to whom he denied the right to speak in the divine name.

This wider literature helps to explain certain features of the *Ascension of Isaiah*. The letters of Ignatius show that Antiochene Christianity was dominated by party factions in the early second century. This is suggested about the Syrian church also by *Asc. Isa.* 3.21-31 with its portrait of the 'wicked shepherds and elders' who jockeyed among themselves for position. Ignatius provides a plausible context in which to interpret *Asc. Isa.* 3.21-31 when he insists on unity with the bishop as the only valid expression of the divine will. *Asc. Isa.* 3.23 (the statement that unworthy people loved office) gives the other side of the picture, which comes from the prophets' point of view. The prophets who found themselves repressed criticized the personal ambition of the leaders and observed (it must be said not incorrectly) that the demise of prophetic authority was against the tenor of apostolic Christianity (3.21). The comment about the Holy Spirit being 'withdrawn' from many (3.26) in a context in which the church leaders are criticized is a significant one in view of Ignatius's claim that the bishop and the other ministers embodied the presence of God. This is the author's way of denying authority to those who currently exercised it. It is in this context that the rite of prophetic ordination (6.4) must be evaluated. This ran parallel to the

through the appearance of a rival party (see his *Polycarp's Two Epistles to the Philippians* [Cambridge: Cambridge University Press, 1936]). W.R. Schoedel, (*Ignatius of Antioch* [Philadelphia: Fortress Press, 1985], p. 11 n. 62) mentions the possibility that the Antiochene split had theological dimensions given the fact that Ignatius's arguments against docetism in his letters to the different churches seem ready prepared.

29. 'The prophets' for him are characteristically the Old Testament prophets; see for instance *Ign. Magn.* 8.2; *Phld.* 5.2.

30. See also *Ign. Smyrn.* 8.1; *Eph.* 6.1; *Trall.* 2.2; *Pol.* 7.1; and cf. Schoedel, *Ignatius*, pp. 10-11.

ordination ritual of the institutional leaders and it evidently represented an attempt to keep the obsolescent office of the prophets alive in the church by the performance of a similar ceremony.

Already in Eph. 2.20 universal prophecy was regarded as a thing of the past. My belief is that the *Didache* represents a transitional stage between the first and second century CE. Its readers needed reminding not to despise the authority of the bishops and deacons on the grounds that they 'exercised the ministry of the prophets' in the church. This comment legitimates the shift from charismatic to institutional authority as it were before the eyes of the reader. It confirms that institutional leadership was emerging at the time of writing but it also reveals that people were suspicious of it and had to be told that the leaders discharged the same function (which was clearly that of authority) as the prophets. This is connected with the author's acknowledgment that not every church possessed a prophet. In the absence of a prophet, the bishops and deacons came into their own. What happened in a church which had *both* prophets and institutional leaders is a question which the *Didache* leaves unresolved. One can only suppose that as prophets became less numerous there was an increase in the numbers of bishops and deacons and in the prestige which they enjoyed. The *Didache* gives no explicit indication that it expected the prophets to pass from the scene, but the implicit acknowledgment of their decline in numbers is a significant one.

The significance of the *Didache* for this study lies in the observation that it attests almost exactly the opposite situation from that which is revealed in the *Ascension of Isaiah*. The *Didache* presents the prophets as dominant figures and the leaders almost struggling for position. The *Ascension of Isaiah* by contrast presents the leaders as dominant and the prophets as fighting to keep their position and even being treated with contempt by the leaders (3.31). This implies that the situation which was anticipated and legitimated by *Didache* 15 was being realized in the experience of those who wrote the *Ascension of Isaiah*. The leaders *were* now discharging the authority which the prophets had exercised. This reflected the small numbers of the prophets and it worked against the interests of such prophets as remained. The *Ascension of Isaiah* was written by a group of prophets, perhaps a small group (cf. 2.7-11), who had seen their authority eroded and who found themselves without power in their dealings with the church leaders (3.31).

3. *The Setting of the Ascension of Isaiah* 203

Robert Hall thinks that the author of the *Ascension of Isaiah* was an opponent of Ignatius. He identifies doctrinal reasons for this assumption, notably the (naïve) docetism that is so evident in the apocalypse.[31] I agree with this view but think that it needs partial correction. Ignatius was indeed aware of docetism but the heresy which he challenged was not the form of docetism that is found in the *Ascension of Isaiah*. *Ign. Trall*. 10.1 criticizes those who claimed that Jesus had suffered in appearance alone. This criticism is implicit also in *Smyrn*. 2.1-2 which insists that Jesus was truly born of a virgin and that he really died on the cross. Ignatius had evidently encountered a form of docetism which questioned the reality of the birth and death of Jesus, especially the latter. This is a matter on which the author of the *Ascension of Isaiah* would have *agreed* with Ignatius whatever the other differences between them. The conclusion is inescapable that it was a disagreement about *authority* and not about doctrine which loomed large in this author's dispute with the church leaders. At the heart of this dispute lay the status of prophecy in the second-century church.

This evidence which the *Ascension of Isaiah* provides for the evanescence of prophecy does much to explain the self-conviction of the Montanists that they possessed a '*new* prophecy', a conviction which was attributed to them some fifty years later by Tertullian. Montanism was a visionary and revivalist movement. It reasserted the original Christian tendency towards Spirit-possession. The evidence for the decline of prophecy in the early second century provides an explanation of why the Montanists should have thought that prophecy could be rediscovered towards the end of the century. It is doubtless an oversimplification to suggest that prophecy really did die out after the writing of the *Ascension of Isaiah* and that it was fortuitously revived by the Montanists. We are dealing here with perceptions rather than with facts, as I said at the beginning of the chapter. Nevertheless, these perceptions are based on actual experience of church life in the two halves of the century and the evidence for this must not be ignored. The *Ascension of Isaiah* quite credibly represents a link between the *Didache* and Montanism. The apocalypse illustrates the nature of the situation which caused people to think that prophecy had to be rediscovered in the later second century. With the demise of Montanism the church dealt its contemporary prophets a death blow and the situation which had been anticipated by the *Didache* and by the *Ascension of Isaiah* reached its

---

31. 'The Ascension of Isaiah', p. 305.

final stage. 'The prophets' were subsequently understood as 'the Old Testament prophets' and not as contemporary figures. The *Ascension of Isaiah* thus supplies crucial evidence for the history of the demise of prophecy in early Christianity.[32]

A brief word is in order about the suggested status of the author as a wandering prophet. There was a tradition of wandering prophecy in first-century Christianity, but this should not be exaggerated on the basis of relatively slender evidence.[33] Jesus himself was a peripatetic, as were some of his disciples, notably those who used the 'Q' collection of sayings (for example Mt. 8.20). The *Didache* shows that wandering prophecy was a significant phenomenon towards the end of the first century when it lays down rules for hospitality to visitors in ch. 11 (and notes with regret the fact that hospitality was sometimes abused). On the other hand 1 Corinthians 12–14 indicates that prophets also remained within the context of a particular church. Due allowance must be made for the presence of these 'settled' figures alongside the wandering charismatics.[34]

Our author has been seen as a wandering prophet because of what is said about the isolation of Isaiah's community in 2.7-11, 3.26-27 and ch. 6. I think that this interpretation runs the risk of confusing what the author says about prophetic isolationism with his actual circumstances, which are difficult if not impossible to discern from the text. 2.7-11 (and 5.13) may have had the different purpose of warning against the temptation towards bravado in the face of Roman investigation, as if the experience of marginalization was anticipated in the future rather than necessarily a feature of the present. The *Ascension of Isaiah* does not reveal much about how readers as prophets functioned as members of churches at the time. They *may* have gathered periodically from scattered Christian communities, as Hall believes; but whether the reference to their isolated existence in 2.7-11 and 3.26-27 indicates that they wandered from town to town is perhaps less clear. I accept that the notion of a prophetic convention which is found in ch. 6 is more suggestive of that. I have concentrated here on the work's evidence for the demise of prophecy in second-century Christianity and I am happy to leave the

32. Its evidence for this subject is however ignored by Friedrich in 'Prophets in the Early Church'; and by Hill, *Prophecy*, pp. 186-92.
33. See Boring's comments about this issue in 'Prophecy'.
34. I have a more detailed examination of this matter in my *Ascension of Isaiah*, pp. 34-38.

3. The Setting of the Ascension of Isaiah

'wandering' issue an open question. Doubtless others will want to discuss it further.

As with the material that is critical of Judaism, this section of the *Ascension of Isaiah* must be seen in due proportion. We can judge from the position of 3.21-31 in the historical review that poor relations with the church leaders (as with the Jews) did not form the *immediate* crisis to which the apocalypse was addressed. They formed a background issue which is mentioned as subsidiary to the specific crisis with the Romans and which impinged upon it given the author's belief that most Christians would tend towards apostasy (4.9). Once again this problem may have been a significant one. 3.21-31 does much to explain the author's sense of distance from others which is exemplified by the seven-storied cosmology. It must have been very painful for him to be marginalized in this way, especially by members of his own religion. This sense of pain did much to fuel the hope for the eschatological climax which he believed that the problem of Roman investigation had made imminent (4.14-18).

Opposition from the Romans

The problem of opposition from the Romans is set at the end of the historical review (4.1-13). This indicates that it was the most immediate and serious of the problems which the author thought that he faced.[35] The *Ascension of Isaiah* was written to deal with the new phase of relations between the Christians and the Romans which emerged in the second century. I have suggested that the setting of the apocalypse is illumined by the correspondence between Pliny and Trajan which deals with the issue of persecution.

In contrast to 3.21-31, which represents the author's own account of post-apostolic Christianity, the material in 4.1-13 has an extensive prehistory in earlier literature.[36] Speculation about Nero's return was a familiar element in pagan and Jewish texts which were written after the emperor's death in 68 CE. Rumours swiftly began to circulate that he had not died but was in hiding in the East. More than one impostor appeared, according to the classical sources.[37] This helped to maintain an

---

35. The reference to the 'vision of Babylon' in 4.19 is significant too. 'Babylon' was a cipher for Rome in Jewish and Christian literature (see for example Rev. 18.2).
36. See Collins, *Sibylline Oracles*, pp. 80-85.
37. See the evidence for this which I noted in Chapter 1.

aura of mystery around the person of Nero. Such material yielded the myth of Nero's posthumous return, a version of which is found in ch. 4 of the *Ascension of Isaiah*. Mythology about Nero persisted well into the second century, as we know from the *Sibylline Oracles*. The depth of feeling which it generated at that time is illustrated by two passages in the Fifth *Sibylline Oracle*, which come from the reign of Hadrian:[38]

> But the one who obtained the land of the Persians will fight,
> and killing every man he will destroy all life
> so that a one-third portion will remain for wretched mortals.
> He himself will rush in with a light bound from the West,
> besieging the entire land, laying it all waste (*Sib. Or.* 5.101-104);

> He will flee from Babylon, a terrible and shameless prince
> whom all mortals and noble men despise.
> For he destroyed many men and laid hands on the womb.
> He sinned against spouses, and was sprung from abominable people (*Sib. Or.* 5.144-46).

Both passages present Nero as a person of superhuman ability but immoral tendencies. This material illustrates the presentation of Nero as a destructive influence which is found in the *Ascension of Isaiah*, and shows the terror which Nero exercised on the Jewish imagination. The Third *Sibylline Oracle* equally makes for a comparison with the *Ascension of Isaiah* because it identifies Nero with Beliar as does our apocalypse. *Sib. Or.* 3.63-74 (which was inserted into the text some time after 70 CE) stands close to the thought of *Ascension of Isaiah* 4:

> Then Beliar will come from the *Sebastenoi*,
> and he will raise up the height of mountains, he will raise up the sea,
> the great fiery sun and shining moon,
> for men. But they will not be effective in him.
> But he will, indeed, also lead men astray, and he will lead astray
> many faithful, chosen Hebrews, and also other lawless men
> who have not yet listened to the word of God.
> But whenever the threats of the great God draws nigh
> and a burning power comes through the sea to land
> it will also burn Beliar and all overbearing men,
> as many as put their faith in him.

This passage identifies Nero with Beliar and expects that he will cause a general apostasy. Portents involving sun and moon are mentioned; the author anticipates that Beliar will be destroyed with fire by God.

38. The Hadrianic date is noticed by Hengel, 'Messianische Hoffnung'.

3. *The Setting of the Ascension of Isaiah* 207

This contact with the *Sibylline Oracles* confirms that *Asc. Isa.* 4.1-13 has roots in Jewish eschatology. It is difficult to comment on the relation between our apocalypse and the Third *Sibylline Oracle*, but the texts probably represent a use of common material. The fact that they display *differences* as well as similarities (for example the burning power from the sea in *Sib. Or.* 3; the sacrifice test in the *Ascension of Isaiah*) makes this conclusion likely. Comparison with the Third *Sibylline Oracle* lets us see where the author of the *Ascension of Isaiah* has made his own interpretation of the tradition. This was in the area of cosmological dualism: especially in the notion of Beliar's descent from the firmament, through which he set his own difficulties, in the context of a grand cosmic drama. The author derived the notion of Beliar's descent from the New Testament writings (see Lk. 10.18; Rev. 12.7-9). He used it as a way of limiting the demon's influence, which becomes clear from a reading of the whole apocalypse, for the Second Vision presents Beliar's descent as the last grasp at power by an adversary who had been shown to be defeated in the heavens. This was a way of denying the authority of the Romans.

It would be wrong to conclude from this material that the author feared that *Nero himself* would return from the grave to recreate the tyranny which he had achieved in the latter part of his reign. The Nero material is used as a symbol of hostility to Rome, as it is in the *Sibylline Oracles*. In the case of the *Ascension of Isaiah* this was because Rome had begun to punish the Christians after 112 CE in a manner that recalled the persecution of 64 CE, when numbers of Christians had last perished (cf. *Asc. Isa.* 4.3).[39] My suggestion about the setting of the *Ascension of Isaiah* is that the author feared that this situation would be repeated in Syria and that persecution was impending.

Behind this specific fear stands a history of Jewish discontent with the fact of Roman rule. A citation from Rabbi Gamaliel (early Common Era) shows that Jewish criticism of Rome had a broad base: 'The empire gnaws at our substance through four things: its tolls, its bath buildings, its theatres, and its taxes in kind.'[40] Gamaliel reflects the anger of a subject people who were required to pay taxes and other dues to a foreign overlord. The end of Trajan's reign (around the time that the

---

39. On the lack of convincing evidence for a Domitianic persecution see my *Ascension of Isaiah*, pp. 40-41, and below.
40. This saying is cited by H. Fuchs, *Der geistige Widerstand gegen Rom in der antiken Welt* (Berlin: de Gruyter, 1938), p. 70.

Ascension of Isaiah was written) was marked by a series of Jewish uprisings throughout the empire which were based on feelings such as these. It is unlikely that Syria and Palestine would have been exempt from this expression of protest.[41] Rebellion against Rome flared up again when Hadrian proscribed circumcision immediately before the Second Revolt.

Roman economic exploitation is a major theme of the *Sibylline Oracles* which, although for the most part written in Egypt, express an anger that was by no means confined to that region. *Sib. Or.* 3.350-55 hopes for a reversal in relations between Rome and Asia in which Rome would repay three times the tribute that it had extracted from its subjects, and twenty times the number of Roman peasants would become serfs in Asia (cf. also *Sib. Or.* 4.145-48). *Sib. Or.* 5.416-17 expects that a heavenly saviour will appear to reverse the balance of power and to return wealth to those from whom it had been plundered. The Eighth *Sibylline Oracle* is harsh in its criticism of Roman exploitation. It censures 'the famous lawless kingdom of the Italians' and complains that Rome would 'expand the toils of the men of the earth' (*Sib. Or.* 8.9-11); Hadrian is especially remembered as an unjust tribute-collector in *Sib. Or.* 8.54-55.

Considerable resentment in Syria stemmed from the taxation system which operated there.[42] Appian (second century CE) observed that because of their rebellions the poll tax imposed on Jews was higher than that on landed property. Syrians (and Cilicians) were subjected to an annual 1 per cent property tax (*Syr.* 8.50). There was also a poll tax: Ulpian says that this was set on men and women from teenage years to 65.[43] Vespasian later introduced the *fiscus Judaicus*, a poll tax of two denarii annually, which took the place of the Jerusalem Temple tax after 70 CE (see Josephus, *War*, 7.6.218). This tax was unpopular, and made more so by Domitian who imposed it on those who tried to leave the

---

41. This is E.M. Smallwood's conclusion, *The Jews under Roman Rule* (Leiden: Brill, 1976), p. 426.

42. See F.M. Heichelheim, 'Roman Syria', in T. Frank (ed.), *An Economic Survey of Ancient Rome* (5 vols. and index; Baltimore: Johns Hopkins University Press, 1933–40), IV, pp. 231-45.

43. The source for this information is *Dig.* 50.15.3; see G.M. Harper, 'Village Administration in the Roman Province of Syria', *Yale Classical Studies* 1 (1928), pp. 156-57.

3. The Setting of the Ascension of Isaiah

Jewish community.[44] It was, however, rescinded by Trajan who also exempted the Christians from payment.

In addition to the taxes there were the customs duties. These were disliked, as we know from the Gospels, Talmud and Midrashim. Customs fraud was apparently rife[45] although the offence was punishable by death.[46] Special taxes were raised at times of emergency. Dio Cassius says that this was done by Hadrian. He also mentions an occasional tax called the *aurum coronarium*[47] which, together with other ad hoc taxes, made heavy demands on Jewish communities. This evidence illustrates the truth of Gamaliel's comment about the burden of taxation that weighed on Jewish pockets. The author of the *Ascension of Isaiah*, as a member of a subject people, would have shared such feelings of resentment in addition to the specific feelings of insecurity which he experienced as a pious Christian who expected persecution.

I have argued in this book that the correspondence between Pliny and Trajan illuminates the setting of the *Ascension of Isaiah*. Pliny's letter to Trajan (*Ep*. 10.96) explains that he had come across Christians in his province and had introduced the sacrifice test to determine their loyalty to the state. Trajan's response, that Pliny had acted correctly but that Christians were not to be made the targets of anonymous denunciation (see Pliny, *Ep*. 10.97), evidently determined the attitude of Roman officials in other parts of the empire. We can surmise this from the *Martyrdom of Polycarp*, which was written in the mid second century, in which elements that are mentioned by Pliny significantly recur.[48]

This development in relations between the Christians and the Romans is reflected in several passages in the *Ascension of Isaiah*. The reference to Beliar's claim 'I am the LORD' (4.6) suggests that a demand for religious worship was involved in the situation which the apocalypse addressed. This reflects Pliny's demand for homage before pagan images. The demand for worship is suggested also by 4.8 where the words 'This is the LORD' are repeated in a passage which also anticipates the acquiescence of apostate Christians (4.9). The description of

---

44. See Smallwood, *The Jews*, pp. 376-85.
45. See *m. Kel*. 17.6-7; *m. Kil*. 9.2, and *b. B. Bat*. 127b.
46. *B. Sanh*. 44b.
47. Dio Cass. 69.12.
48. Polycarp was invited to say 'Caesar is Lord', to offer sacrifice, and later to curse Christ. He refused to do this and was put to death. The evidence suggests that the authorities were initially reluctant to do this.

Nero-Beliar 'setting up his image before him in every city' (4.11) recalls the Bithynian situation and alludes to the imperial statue which Pliny says featured prominently in the sacrifice test. Chapter 5 describes Isaiah's death as an act of religious integrity. The prophet is presented as an ideal Christian who refuses to worship lesser deities and accepts martyrdom as the consequence of this action. This is an indication that martyrdom was seen as a possible outcome for the author's situation, even if the *Ascension of Isaiah* does not encourage its readers deliberately to seek it.

The *Ascension of Isaiah* provides neglected evidence of the Christian response to this situation of conflict with the Romans. 5.13 states that Isaiah instructed his disciples to go to Tyre and Sidon with the rejoinder that for him alone God had mixed the cup. This looks like a warning to readers not to bring themselves to Roman attention unnecessarily; my belief is that the material about prophetic isolation (2.7-11 and 4.13) also finds its meaning in this context. I have suggested that the author was warning against the desire for voluntary martyrdom in the light of the death of Ignatius who had greeted his end with lurid anticipation (see *Ign. Rom.* 4.1). The implication of 5.13, when considered with 2.7-11 and 4.13, is that readers were to withdraw if the situation of persecution arose (although the author *does* commend martyrdom if this became inevitable). Perhaps this was because, in a situation in which the prophets were declining, it seemed important to preserve their numbers, which the author held to be bound up with the fundamental preservation of Christianity (see 3.21).

It will be helpful to set this situation of conflict between the Christians and the Romans in its wider historical context. It would be wrong to speak of any full-scale *persecution* of Christians in the first two centuries, 64 CE apart; but there were indeed some unfortunate incidents which for the most part reveal Roman misunderstanding of the new religion. The 'Neronian Persecution' (64 CE) should be classed as a formal persecution. Tacitus says that Nero fastened on the Christians as a way of diverting responsibility for the fire in Rome which took place in that year. He reports that the emperor 'inflicted the most exquisite tortures on a class hated for their abominations, called Christians by the populace' (*Annals*, 15.44.2-8; cf. *Asc. Isa.* 4.3). Theirs he calls a 'deadly superstition'; he adds that the Christians were punished for their 'hatred of the human race', but that the severity of their punishment brought pity even from an unsympathetic populace.

3. *The Setting of the Ascension of Isaiah*

Claudius's expulsion of the Jews from Rome in 49 CE had brought the Christians to imperial attention before this pogrom. Suetonius says that the expulsion resulted from disturbances made 'at the instigation of Chrestus' (*Claud.* 25.4). One plausible explanation of this statement is that it describes a dispute between Jews and the followers of Jesus (Christ) in the Roman capital. Christians may have been expelled on this occasion as well as Jews, but the fact that they are not mentioned by name suggests that the Christians had not yet been recognized as distinct from the Jews in Rome. This was not the case fifteen years later when the Christians were sufficiently well known to be held in popular disrepute and scapegoated for the fire of Rome.

The problem of whether there was a 'persecution' of Christians at the end of Domitian's reign (c. 98 CE) is a moot one. Smallwood deduces from the fact that Pliny's letter to Trajan mentions Christians who had given up their faith twenty years previously that some action must have taken place at that time.[49] The evidence for a Domitianic *persecution*, however, is scanty. Recent research suggests that the common belief that Domitian proclaimed *himself* 'lord and god' rests on a misinterpretation of passages in Martial, who used such epithets to gain entrance into Domitian's circle. The formula thus represents evidence for sycophancy on the part of subordinates but not necessarily for imperial megalomania.[50] Collins's study of the book of Revelation agrees that there was no Domitianic persecution. She thinks that the apocalypse arose from the need to overcome 'cognitive dissonance' which was caused by a variety of social tensions. It did this by presenting the Christian redeemer as supreme in heaven.[51] The silence of the *Ascension of Isaiah* about a Domitianic persecution is perhaps to be regarded as a significant one, for the author would surely have mentioned it as an outstanding recent event had such a persecution taken place.

The evidence for Roman persecution of the Christians in the first three centuries has been examined by G. de Ste Croix, who comes to the conclusion that such official repression as there was (which was typified by notorious but isolated incidents) was undertaken primarily as the result of negative public opinion which was caused by the belief that the Christians refused to honour the gods.[52] This belief created the fear that

---

49. Smallwood, *The Jews*, p. 381.
50. See Thompson, *Book of Revelation*, pp. 104-109.
51. Collins, *Crisis and Catharsis*, pp. 69-73.
52. 'Why were the Early Christians Persecuted?', *Past and Present* 2b (1963),

the gods might be alienated and social well-being threatened. The Decian Persecution in the third century CE is an example of this popular suspicion. It stemmed from the belief that the restoration of the state cults was essential for national prosperity. De Ste Croix sees the martyrdoms of Ignatius and Polycarp as local actions against the Christians, who were misunderstood, as Tacitus and Pliny show, but not as systematic repressions which, as we have seen, were proscribed in Trajan's reply to Pliny and later proscribed by Hadrian.

This evidence sets the situation which prompted the *Ascension of Isaiah* in a broader perspective. The fact that the author looks back to 64 CE (some fifty years earlier) tends to confirm that there was no Domitianic persecution and so that persecution was a new feature of the readers' experience. It is difficult to accept that ch. 5 is unresourced by actual experience of martyrdom. The death of Ignatius would have been a recent event for the author (and perhaps there were other unknown martyrdoms too). In a situation in which persecution was believed imminent, the author wrote an apocalypse which warned readers of the dangers of accepting Beliar's demand for worship. The text disclosed Beliar's true position as an insubordinate demon (7.9-12) and it emphasized the benefits of continued trust in the Beloved One (4.14-18; 8.24). It thereby encouraged readers to persevere in their faith but without pretending that the future would be easy.

The situation to which the *Ascension of Isaiah* was addressed was thus one characterized by profound social alienation, which the new situation with the Romans brought to a head. Perhaps the most significant feature of the apocalypse is the way in which the author erects defensive barriers against *all* other groups who were not of his persuasion. The evidence indicates that he was conscious of belonging to a marginalized group. He expected his own marginalization within the Christian body to increase if persecution came, because the majority of Christians might acquiesce in the sacrifice test (4.9), whereas his circle as religious pietists would be bound to suffer. The emergence of the new situation of conflict with the Romans exacerbated his feelings of isolation for that reason. This is perhaps why the Romans are presented in the apocalypse as the final eschatological opponents whose hostility presaged the parousia. The *Ascension of Isaiah* was prompted by the specific fear of persecution from the Romans which brought a variety of feelings of isolation and conflict to a head.

pp. 6-38. See also the other literature on this subject cited in Chapter 1 n. 85.

The Author's Millenarian Response

We must now consider the response which the author made to this social tension. The two Visions represent different ways of dealing with the crisis. It will be helpful to consider them separately for this reason. My method is not however intended to revive any of the older literary-critical theories about the apocalypse which were heavily criticized at the 1981 conference.

The First Vision is dominated by the belief that the Beloved One will return from heaven (the event which is called the parousia in scholarly literature) to introduce an earthly kingdom which will be characterized by 'rest' for 'the saints' (4.15) and by the removal of Beliar to Gehenna (4.14). This kingdom will precede the acquisition of immortal life in the seventh heaven (4.17) which this author regards as the final eschatological goal (cf. 8.27; 9.6-18; 11.34-35). Following the translation of the righteous to the seventh heaven, there will be a full-scale destruction in which those elements which had supported Beliar will be punished (4.18). The eschatology of this part of the apocalypse is thus a forward-looking one in which the hope for supernatural intervention and change is paramount.

This response attests what has often been called a 'millenarian' eschatology. 'Millenarianism' is an understanding of salvation which emphasizes the present order as the sphere of forthcoming redemption.[53] Millenarianism was an important feature of early Christian literature. The New Testament writers, who were followed in this by Christians in the second and third centuries, believed that Jesus would return from heaven to establish an earthly kingdom. The *Ascension of Isaiah* offers an *adapted* version of the Christian millenarian hope when it expects both an earthly kingdom (4.14-16) and also a heavenly immortality for the pious (4.17).

The Christian millenarian hope was in part an extension of Jewish temporal messianism with its hope for the transformation of the present life. Yet Christian eschatology introduced some distinctive features from its outset. These included the belief that the messiah had *already* come in

---

53. See below for a discussion of the primary literature. There are valuable studies of early Christian millenarianism by H. Bietenhard, 'The Millennial Hope in the Early Church', *SJT* 6 (1953), pp. 12-30; Daniélou, *Jewish Christianity*, pp. 377-404; and J.M. Ford, 'Millennium', in Freedman *et al.* (eds.), *Anchor Bible Dictionary*, IV, pp. 832-34.

the person of Jesus and that the eschatological climax was in consequence inaugurated rather than entirely of the future. Millenarianism enjoyed considerable support from the earliest days of Christianity up to the time of Augustine in the fifth century. Augustine decided, after his exchange of letters with Tyconius, that the millennial period described by Rev. 20.4 must designate the time of the church. He subsequently criticized any interpretation of the book of Revelation, including its prominent 'this-worldly' eschatology, in literal categories.

Early Christian millenarianism is susceptible to a number of different interpretations but we must begin with the historical question. It is necessary to ask how the eschatology of the *Ascension of Isaiah* coheres with what other Jews and Christians believed in order to determine its place in the development of Christianity in the second century.

Jewish Eschatology
Millenarianism of a kind was a feature of Jewish eschatology before the Christian period. Old Testament scholars often identify three main sources for Israelite future hopes. These are the patriarchal promise traditions, the Zion–David tradition, and traditions about the Sinai covenant.[54] These three elements have in common the fact that they anticipate the promise of blessing within the existing order. In the prophetic literature we can identify a number of passages which incorporate descriptions of future prosperity. Amos 9.13, Isa. 11.6-9 and 30.26 (cf. also 65.25) are examples of these. Amos 9.13 is a later addition to the text which anticipates that the mountains will drip with wine and the hills wave with corn. Isa. 11.6-9 describes how the wolf will lie down with the kid and how the calf and the young lion will grow up together. A little child will lead them, as if hostility in the animal world is expected to be a thing of the past. Isa. 30.26 states that the moon will shine like the sun and that the sun will shine seven times more brightly than normal. Isa. 65.25 repeats the prophecy of Isaiah 11 as if to insist that it is still relevant in the post-exilic period. This material is merely a representative example of the wider biblical evidence which could be adduced to demonstrate the hope for the transformation of the natural order.

---

54. For a survey of these themes see D.E. Gowan, *Eschatology in the Old Testament* (Philadelphia: Fortress Press, 1986).

3. *The Setting of the Ascension of Isaiah* 215

It is difficult to trace a single and consistent theme in biblical eschatology. We should rather identify a complex of ideas which are repeated in a number of texts. These ideas include the hope for the re-gathering of the twelve tribes, the special place of Jerusalem in the future world, the centrality of the (renewed) Temple and the hope that the Gentiles would be made subservient to the Jews.[55] Messianism as the hope for a specific earthly ruler is a feature of some but not of all the Old Testament literature.[56] Several passages predict a glorious eschatological future for Israel without a messiah.[57] The complex of eschatological ideas that existed in the early Common Era was preoccupied with hopes for the 'restoration' of Israel under the belief that the biblical promises still remained to be fulfilled (see below). Broader eschatological ideas feature in the tradition besides hopes about the messiah. These are all 'this-worldly' conceptions.

The emergence of an 'apocalyptic' or 'transcendent' eschatology in the post-exilic period created the belief, certainly by the time of Daniel (164 BCE) and probably before, that a heavenly patron's activity could have decisive consequences for the well-being of the faithful in Israel. In Daniel's night-time vision (ch. 7) the man-like figure's presentation at the heavenly court symbolizes the fact that universal dominion will be given to 'the people of the saints of the Most High' and that 'all dominions would serve and obey them' (7.27). The concluding chapters of Daniel (chs. 10–12) enshrine the belief that Michael will arise at the end of time, after the downfall of Antiochus Epiphanes, and deliver the faithful at a time of trouble (12.1). Many of the dead will rise, says the author, some to everlasting life and others to contempt (12.2). The author also says that the righteous will then shine like stars in the firmament (12.3), in what seems to be a variation on the ancient theme of astral immortality. Behind this form of eschatology stands the hope for vindication which has merged with the hope that Israel would become a great world-power, able to dominate the nations which oppressed it. The conclusion of the work hints that the worthy among the people will find a new form of life altogether.[58]

---

55. There is a convenient summary of the relevant texts in Sanders, *Jesus*, pp. 77-119.
56. It makes its first appearance in Hos. 3.5.
57. For example Amos 9.13-15 mentioned already.
58. See further Collins, *Apocalyptic Vision*, pp. 191-218.

The Enochic literature contains important evidence for millenarianism. From around the time of the Maccabaean uprising, indeed probably from before it,[59] we have the *Apocalypse of Weeks* in *1 Enoch* 93. This passage interprets the seven days of creation as seven weeks of years in which different events had taken place. The Enochic author states that an apostate generation will arise in the seventh week (93.9) and that this will be followed by the election of 'the elect ones of righteousness from the eternal plant of righteousness'. *2 En.* 33.1-2, in the J (or longer) recension of the text, states that the history of the world will last for 7,000 years and that the eighth millennium will mark the end of it; *2 En.* 32.2 (where the text is unfortunately corrupt) apparently makes the seventh day a day of rest. This view stands close to the millenarianism of Barnabas, who held the eighth day to be the beginning of a new world (see below).

We find a more explicit picture of the future in two Jewish apocalypses which were written after the destruction of Jerusalem: *4 Ezra* and *Syriac Baruch*, or *2 Baruch* (c. 100 CE). The eschatology of *4 Ezra* is confused but, in brief, the hope is voiced there that the temporary messianic kingdom will be followed by resurrection, judgment and appropriate reward and punishment (7.28-36). The messiah in this apocalypse is said to be a human figure who dies (7.29). It may be that this was because he was not believed to be the complete answer to the problems which Ezra voiced.[60] In the notion of the temporary messianic kingdom, which was to be followed by resurrection and judgment, we find an approximate parallel (in which it must be said that some have discerned Christian influence) for the eschatology of *Asc. Isa.* 4.14-18; but *4 Ezra* has no tradition of a divinized and heavenly messiah, which is the distinctive feature of the Christian apocalypse.

According to *2 Baruch* 29–30 the messianic age will be characterized by a prodigious fecundity of nature. This is expressed in the images of the earth which yielded its produce ten-thousandfold and of the vine which produced vast amounts of grapes (29.5). This symbolism, which was derived from Amos 9.13, also passed into Christian millenarianism, as we know from the reported teaching of Papias of Hierapolis (see

---

59. The origin of this material is examined by Hengel, *Judaism and Hellenism*, I, vol. 1, pp. 188-89; II, pp. 117 n. 459. He concludes that it was written before the Jewish freedom fight.

60. This is the view of Stone, 'The Concept of the Messiah in 4 Ezra', pp. 295-312.

3. *The Setting of the Ascension of Isaiah*

below). *2 Baruch* states that the dead will rise (30.1-3) and that the wicked will suffer torment (30.4-5). Chapter 39 expects the messianic kingdom to emerge after four other kingdoms. The Anointed One will then convict the last ruler of his wicked deeds on Mount Zion (40.1) and kill him to protect the people. This messiah's dominion will last until 'the world of corruption has ended' (40.3). Later in *2 Baruch* the Anointed One is expected to allow some nations to survive but to destroy others (see 70.9; 72.2).

The *Psalms of Solomon*, which is a Pharisaic text from the first century BCE, anticipates a regrouping of the tribes of Israel by the messiah (17.26-34) after the destruction of 'unrighteous rulers and Gentiles' (17.22), who in this context are clearly the Romans. Jerusalem will then be purged and restored to its pristine condition (17.30). *Sib. Or.* 5.414-30 also anticipates the appearance of a 'blessed man from the expanses of heaven' who will return wealth to the good and who will magnify Jerusalem after he has destroyed foreign cities. Both texts present the future in terms of national restoration and of Israel's world dominion, although it would be wrong to suggest that this is an understanding of eschatology that is universally shared by Jewish literature of the period.

Sanders has shown that the complex of ideas which he calls 'restoration eschatology' was a significant feature of Jewish future hope in the postbiblical period.[61] Several passages anticipate the rebuilding of the Temple (Tob. 14.5; *1 En.* 90.28-29; *T. Benj.* 9.2; and esp. 11QTemple 29.9-10). The hope for the restoration of the twelve tribes was a constituent element of this eschatology (see 2 Macc. 2.18; *Pss. Sol.* 11; *T. Mos.* 3.4; 1QM 2.7; Rev. 21.12 and *t. Sanh.* 13.10). Material about the Gentiles is found there as well.[62] Some texts anticipate that the Gentiles will be destroyed (*1 En.* 91.9; 1QM 12.10). Others suggest that the Gentiles will be added to Israel and saved (Tob. 14.16-17; *1 En.* 90.30-33). All of these passages presuppose a change within the existing order by which present experience will be decisively modified.

There is millenarian speculation of a kind in rabbinic sources too, at least if by this is meant discussion about how long the messianic age will last. *b. Pes.* 68a says that the righteous are destined to resurrect the dead. The Talmudist takes Isa. 30.26 ('the light of the sun shall be sevenfold, as the light of the seven days') to designate the days of the messiah, which are distinguished in this context from the life of the

---

61. *Jesus*, pp. 77-119.
62. See Sanders, *Jesus*, pp. 212-21.

world to come. *b. Šab.* 6a cites a saying of R. Hiyya (which is repeated in *b. Sanh.* 99a) that the prophets had prophesied only for the messianic age but that 'eye had not seen' the mysteries of the world to come, so that the two ages are formally distinguished. *Sanh.* 97a also discusses the messianic age and it records a dispute about how long the world would last which is based around a variety of calculations (including the figure of 6,000 years which became important in Christian circles as a description of the *pre*-millennial period).

A special feature of Jewish eschatology was the way in which martyrdom was expected to yield a form of heavenly immortality.[63] In Dan. 12.2-3 we met the idea that the righteous would 'shine like the stars of heaven' after the selective resurrection in what I suggested was a form of belief in astral immortality. *4 Macc.* 7.3 (cf. 9.22; 14.5-6) attests belief in immediate immortality for martyrs. *Jub.* 23.27-31 also presumes an immediate assumption of the human spirit at death. Some Jewish circles extended this idea beyond martyrological reflection. At Qumran, there existed the promise of 'eternal joy in life without end' (1Q S4.7). This idea surfaces in the Fourth Gospel too (e.g. in Jn 3.3b). Paul thought that death would mean that he would be 'with Christ' (Phil. 1.23). Ignatius too believed that death would yield a form of heavenly immortality. *Eph.* 9.1 uses the phrase 'carried up to the heights by the crane of Jesus Christ'. *Rom.* 2.2 says briefly: 'that I may rise to meet him'. This evidence shows that belief in heavenly immortality was a feature of some Jewish and Christian circles in the early Common Era. This is a tradition which is shared by the *Ascension of Isaiah* as 4.16 shows (although our apocalypse significantly combines it with the hope for the millenarian kingdom). The impression gained from this material is that beliefs about resurrection and immortality were far from systematic at the time, but that the hope for heavenly immortality was an important element of the eschatological tradition and that it could be interpreted in a number of different ways.

Millenarianism of a broad kind is thus an important feature both of the Hebrew Bible and of later Jewish eschatological reflection. Klausner helpfully distinguishes between 'messianic expectation', by which he means the hope for a transformed future which would involve perfection for Israel and for the human race, and 'belief in the messiah', in which a *particular redeemer* (generally a human one) was expected to bring

---

63. See Nickelsburg, *Resurrection*, pp. 11-42, for a description of this strand.

redemption to Israel and thus to humankind.[64] There was no single, consistent Jewish messianic teaching before (or even during) the Christian period. This point must be made firmly. There was, however, a complex of ideas which occur in too many texts to be regarded as incidental. These include hopes for the restoration of the tribes, the recreation of the Temple and the eschatological subordination of the Gentiles. Such material reveals the tendency among Jewish people of the period to think about the future in 'this-worldly' terms and to hope for their own sovereignty. This was the broad eschatological ambience from which Jesus' and the early Christians' hopes about the kingdom of God emerged. It was by no means inaccurate that later Christian critics of millenarianism (such as Jerome) should criticize its supporters for thinking 'in a Jewish way'. Jewish messianism, as Klausner puts it, made no attempt to 'do away with the earthly ground which is under its feet'.[65] We should add that the earliest Christians continued to walk there.

Jesus' Preaching of the Kingdom of God
A consensus of scholarship accepts that millenarianism was the mainstay of primitive Christian eschatology. Norman Cohn identified the origins of Christian millenarian hopes in Jewish eschatology with its belief in imminent divine retribution and in the vindication of the righteous.[66] He isolated Mt. 16.28, the book of Revelation and second-century Montanism as evidence for the continuation of these hopes in Judaism's messianic sect. Sheldon R. Isenberg drew attention to Jesus' role as a millenarian 'prophet' and he emphasized his message of good news for the poor as well as the phenomenon of his personal charisma.[67] John Gager called

64. J. Klausner, *The Messianic Idea in Israel* (London: George Allen & Unwin, 1956), p. 9.
65. Klausner, *Messianic Idea*, pp. 10-11.
66. N. Cohn, *The Pursuit of the Millennium* (London: Maurice Temple Smith, rev. edn, 1970), pp. 1-9, and 'Medieval Millenarism: Its Bearing on the Contemporary Study of Millenarian Movements', in S. Thrupp (ed.), *Millennial Dreams in Action: Essays in Comparative Study* (Comparative Studies in Society and History, Supp. 2; The Hague: Mouton, 1962), pp. 31-43. Cohn shows that the hope for an earthly kingdom of the saints was taken up by a number of Christian writers (*Pursuit*, pp. 10-14).
67. S.R. Isenberg, 'Millenarism in Greco–Roman Palestine', *Rel* 4 (1974), pp. 20-46. Isenberg made use of the work of Kenelm Burridge which is considered below.

millenarianism a 'consensus model' for research and he spoke about the problem of 'cognitive dissonance' (the awareness of differentials) which motivated early Christianity.[68] Robert Jewett showed that Paul's churches in Thessalonia were influenced by millenarian convictions which had issued in the refusal of some to engage in their daily routines.[69] Paul answered them by insisting that the Day of the Lord was yet to appear (1 Thess. 5.2) and by warning that it would be heralded by a period of tribulation (2 Thess. 2.3-12). The approach to early Christian eschatology is mentioned with approval also by A.Y. Collins in her work on the book of Revelation.[70]

All discussion of Christian millenarianism must begin with the issue of the preaching of Jesus. There are difficulties in this subject because of the difficult nature of the sources, but it is possible to reconstruct at least a broad outline of what Jesus believed about the future. Jesus proclaimed the imminence of the kingdom of God (Mk 1.15). The kingdom as Jesus preached it was connected with the theme of the eschatological fulfilment of Israel. Jesus believed that the time of consummation had come, and he did as well as said a number of things which symbolized the fact that the kingdom was near. The Journey to Jerusalem (Mk. 9–10 and parr.) symbolized the regathering of the tribes; the Triumphal Entry (Mk 11.1-10 and parr.) was a messianic entrance into Jerusalem; the Cleansing of the Temple (Mk 11.15-18 and parr.) symbolized the imminent replacement of the Temple by God; and the Last Supper (Mk 14.12-31 and parr.) was anticipatory of the kingdom's inaugural banquet. Jesus and his disciples apparently used to think about him as a king, and there was an element of secrecy about this belief. This is suggested both by the 'messianic secret' as a literary device in the Gospels and also by the fact that the Jewish authorities had to bribe Judas to discover the precise details of what Jesus and his disciples believed.[71] This suggests that Jesus

68. *Kingdom and Community* (Englewood Cliffs, NJ: Prentice-Hall, 1975), pp. 20-36.
69. R. Jewett, *The Thessalonian Correspondence: Pauline Rhetoric and Millenarian Piety* (Philadelphia: Fortress Press, 1986), esp. pp. 161-78. Jewett cites the earlier study of S. Sharot, *Messianism, Mysticism and Magic: A Sociological Analysis of Jewish Religious Movements* (Chapel Hill: University of North Carolina Press, 1982), esp. pp. 18-19. Jewett's book contains a good introduction to scholarly views about millenarianism (pp. 162-65).
70. *Crisis and Catharsis*, pp. 104-107.
71. This understanding of the betrayal was proposed by Albert Schweitzer and it is accepted by Sanders (see his *Jesus*, p. 309).

3. *The Setting of the Ascension of Isaiah*

did see himself as Israel's king of the end-time but also that he thought this belief must remain the secret of his band of followers until the kingdom finally came.

What Jesus taught about the future has been the subject of a protracted dispute. This has centred on the authenticity of the so-called 'Son of Man' sayings in the Gospels.[72] This strand of material (which is far from homogeneous) describes a figure called the 'Son of Man' who in some contexts seems to be identical with Jesus but who in others is presented as a heavenly redeemer and distinct from Jesus.[73] It is beyond doubt that the early church identified *Jesus* as the Son of Man who would return for judgment,[74] but this does not necessarily mean that Jesus thought about *himself* in this way. Some of the 'Son of Man' sayings in the Gospels do not obviously refer to Jesus. An example of this is Mt. 16.27 (cf. Mt. 19.28) where Jesus says that the Son of Man would come in the glory of his Father and that he would give each person the due reward of his or her deeds. This Matthean version of the tradition lacks any reference to the need for a response towards Jesus, which is the theme of the Markan parallel (Mk 9.37-38).[75] This raises the possibility (and it is no more than that) that Jesus did speak about 'the Son of Man' as a heavenly mediator distinct from himself, although it is a different question again whether he identified himself with that figure. If Jesus did think that the Son of Man was a heavenly redeemer, we ought to insist that such a view is in no way incompatible with the possibility that he also thought about *himself* as Israel's designated king of the end-time. It would appear impossible at this remove to reach a definite answer to the question of whether it was Jesus or the post-Easter church which first identified Jesus with the Son of Man.

The kingdom as Jesus preached it was thus to be an earthly entity. It might or might not be introduced by a heavenly mediator. It would be governed by Jesus himself and by his disciples (see Mt. 19.28). It would involve a new and perfect Temple, the regathering of the tribes and

---

72. Among recent contributions to the debate, see J.D. Crossan, *The Historical Jesus: The Life of a Mediterranean Jewish Peasant* (Edinburgh: T. & T. Clark, 1991), pp. 239-59; and E.P. Sanders, *The Historical Figure of Jesus* (London: Penguin Books, 1993), pp. 246-48. Earlier studies include Hooker, *Son of Man*; Borsch, *Son of Man*; and the literature which I cited in Chapter 2.

73. For an example of the former see Mk 2.10, 28; for the latter Mt. 16.27.

74. This is evident from the Gospels and from other isolated hints such as Acts 7.56.

75. This is noticed by Sanders, *Jesus*, p. 143.

probably the inclusion of the Gentiles as well. There is nothing in the tradition which says how long the kingdom would last or that the righteous might expect a subsequent heavenly destiny like that envisaged by *Asc. Isa.* 4.18 and chs. 9–11. The nearest that Jesus comes to this assertion is in Mk 12.25 and parallels, where he is made to say that the resurrected will be 'like the angels in heaven'. This, however, is probably to be understood as a comment on the irrelevance of present distinctions in the resurrection state, and possibly even on the celibacy of that state.[76] Jesus taught no cosmological view to match the seven-storied universe of the *Ascension of Isaiah*. His interest lay rather with the hope for the restoration of Israel in which the biblical promises would at last be fulfilled.

Pauline Eschatology

The emergence of Christianity after the death of Jesus was apparently unexpected by his disciples. They had deserted Jesus at his arrest (Mk 14.50), and the discovery of the empty tomb did not immediately lead them to suppose that he had been raised from the dead (see esp. Mk 16.8). The disciples came to believe in the resurrection after reflection on the resurrection appearances, which led them to the understanding that Jesus was a divine being in heaven.[77] Almost in the same breath they began to worship him as divine (see Phil. 2.9-11). This belief in his divinity led to a fundamental reconsideration of the problem of eschatology. Jesus had preached that the kingdom was near. His death must have caused people initially to think that this hope had been wrong. Belief in his resurrection meant that the hope for the kingdom was taken up anew and interpreted in the light of the belief that Jesus was the Lord. It began to be assumed that Jesus would return from heaven to achieve the eschatological climax which the Hebrew Bible had anticipated that God would accomplish.[78] Both the worship of Jesus and this reworking

---

76. If a reference to celibacy is implicit in this passage, that would mean that Jesus must himself be distanced from later Christian millenarian views which anticipated procreation there.

77. The evidence of Paul in Gal. 1.15-16 and 1 Cor. 15.8 is significant in this connection. These passages suggest mystical experience of the heavenly Christ (as does Rev. 1.13-14).

78. This view is expressed as an established conviction by the early passage 1 Thess. 3.13 (cf. 2 Thess. 1.7). The origin of this belief is examined by J.A.T. Robinson, *Jesus and His Coming* (London: SPCK, 1957); and by A.L. Moore, *The*

3. *The Setting of the Ascension of Isaiah*

of eschatology belong to the very earliest period of Christianity.

The earthly focus of the kingdom as preached by Jesus provided the framework for subsequent Christian eschatology. Paul's eschatology is difficult to interpret, like that of Jesus, in this case because he is an occasional writer rather than a systematic theologian. Much has to be reconstructed from what Paul says about the future and is not made explicit in the literature. It is sobering to recall that it was only because the Thessalonians and Corinthians asked him questions about the resurrection that we have a record of Paul's teaching in this area. Much of what Paul says in the context of these letters is about *resurrection* rather than about eschatology more generally. As with Jesus, however, it is possible to draw some broad conclusions about Paul's teaching in this area.

Paul evidently entertained a millenarian eschatology throughout his career. There is early evidence for millenarianism in the Thessalonian correspondence. 1 Thess. 4.13-18 offers assurance about the resurrection to readers who feared that the deaths of their friends before the parousia meant that they would miss out on eschatological benefits.[79] Paul makes early use in this passage of his major argument that the death and resurrection of Jesus meant that Christians too would rise if they died (4.14). He explains that the Lord will descend from heaven (4.16), that the Christian dead will rise at this point (4.17), and that the living and the resurrected together will be caught up 'in the clouds' to meet the Lord 'in the air' (4.17). This last phrase has been understood in more than one way. It has been held to mean, both that Paul originally thought that the kingdom of God would take place 'in the air', and also that this 'rapture' was an act of homage to Jesus as Lord whom the Christians would escort back to earth where his reign would begin.[80] It is not easy to decide between these alternatives. The later Pauline eschatology (for

Parousia in the New Testament (NovTSup, 13; Leiden: Brill, 1966).

79. See the exegesis of this passage by J. Plevnik, 'The Parousia as Implication of Christ's Resurrection: An Exegesis of 1 Thess. 4.13-18', in *idem*, (ed.), *Word and Spirit: Essays in Honor of David Martin Stanley* (Willowdale, Ont.: Regis Books, 1975), pp. 199-277.

80. See P. Hoffmann, *Die Toten in Christus* (Münster: Aschendorff, 1966), pp. 207-31; and P. Ellingworth, 'Which Way are We Going? A Verb of Movement especially in 1 Thess. 4.14b', *BT* 25 (1974), pp. 426-31. Studies of Paul's eschatology include G. Vos, *The Pauline Eschatology* (Grand Rapids: Eerdmans, 1952); and C.L. Mearns, 'Early Eschatological Development in Paul: The Evidence of I and II Thessalonians', *NTS* 27 (1980–81), pp. 137-57.

example 1 Cor. 15) leaves no doubt that Paul thought the kingdom of Christ would be an earthly one. It is tempting to conform 1 Thess. 4.17 to this pattern, but that may be too easy an answer to the problem. Paul *may* have thought at first that the kingdom would be aerial but revised this view later in his career. On the balance of probability I think that 1 Thessalonians 4 does describe an act of homage to the returning Jesus, so that the kingdom was to be an earthly one even in Paul's early understanding. The ambiguities of interpretation which surround this passage must however be duly acknowledged.

Paul's early eschatology is further evident in 2 Thessalonians. Paul says in this letter that the returning Jesus will exact vengeance upon those who had refused to 'acknowledge God' and to 'obey the gospel' of Jesus. Such people will be excluded from his presence when he comes to be adored on earth by his followers (1.9-10). This passage anticipates an earthly judgment and implies that the exclusion will be earthly, but nothing is said to indicate in detail what it will involve. Chapter 2 cautions against too imminent a view of the parousia and specifies a sequence of events which must take place before the parousia happens. A 'man of lawlessness' will appear who will rise up against all gods and take his seat in the Jerusalem Temple (2.1-4). Paul says that the 'mystery of lawlessness' is now at work but that God has restrained it (2.5-7). The coming of this wicked man will be a work of Satan and it will be attended by satanic miracles (2.9). God will even allow people to believe his lies (2.11-12). Nevertheless, Paul insists that Jesus *will* come (1.7) and that those who have accepted the Gospel will be glorified when he does (1.9-10). Here again we find the view that the kingdom was to be an earthly phenomenon which would be inaugurated by the returning Jesus. This early text shows that the delay of the parousia constitutes a problem for *all* New Testament literature and not just for its later strands.

The whole of 1 Corinthians 15 contains eschatological teaching. Paul there responds to questions about the resurrection, and initially to the assertion that there would be no resurrection at all (15.12). He answers this by insisting on the reality of the resurrection of Jesus as the centre of Christian theology (15.13-19). 15.20-28 describes the context in which the resurrection of believers will occur. Paul states that Christ has already been brought to life and that Christians in turn will be brought to life at his coming (15.23). His 'coming' (that is, from heaven to earth) will represent 'the end' (15.24). Christ will then abolish every dominion, authority and power and hand the kingdom to God the Father (15.25).

The last enemy to be abolished in this way will be death (15.26). When everything has been subjected, the Son will himself be made subject to the Father (15.28). This reference, which embarrassed many later exegetes, enshrines a subordinationist Christology which is a fundamental aspect of Paul's understanding of the messiah's future reign.

After three minor arguments (1 Cor. 15.30-34), Paul turns to the question of what form the resurrection body will take (15.35-49). This passage acknowledges the fact that the physical body must decay (15.35-38) and that God will clothe the dead 'with a body of his choice' (15.38). The resurrection body will be an imperishable one (15.42) and what Paul calls a 'spiritual body' (15.44). He defines the meaning of the 'spiritual body' in 15.45-49 where he states that it will have a heavenly origin, which includes the thought of immortality. Finally, 15.50-57 presents a summary of Paul's overall argument. The basic theme of this section is that not everyone will die but that the living and the dead alike must be transformed. The living will not be excepted just because they have not been resurrected: 'We shall not all sleep, but we shall all be changed' (15.51). The trumpet will sound, the dead will rise immortal, and the living will acquire immortality (15.52). Death will then be swallowed up by immortality (15.54) which will be offered to all. The immortality which is described by 15.51 is that which will be conferred by the spiritual or heavenly body of 15.44.

This passage represents Paul's most detailed exposition of eschatology. Its thought is relatively clear even if individual points of exegesis are disputed. Paul insists that the Christian resurrection hope must find its place within a wider scheme of eschatology. He was writing for a situation in which not everyone was expected to die. This belief determines his argument because even those who were alive at the parousia were expected to undergo transformation. This would result in the acquisition of immortality by mortal human beings. The eschatological future which Paul envisaged was thus, as in the preaching of Jesus, an earthly one. He expected that the living and the dead would enjoy a transformed and imperishable existence after the destruction of death. Nothing is said to indicate the possibility of any vacation of the human world to match the eschatology of *Asc. Isa.* 4.17. The hope that God will be 'all in all' (15.28) probably even signifies the apocalyptic removal of the distinctions between heaven and earth in which God became an accessible deity and which rendered such translation redundant.

Chapter 15 is not the only place in 1 Corinthians where Paul advances a millenarian eschatology. Earlier in the letter (1 Cor. 6.2-3) he expresses the belief that the 'saints' will judge the world, even that they will judge angels. This reference to the eschatological assize in which 'the world' will be put on trial again suggests an earthly judgment which falls within the sequence of events that will be inaugurated by the parousia. There is an interesting correspondence between this passage and what is said about the role of the twelve in Mt. 19.28, which anticipates that in the eschaton they will judge the tribes of Israel. It was evidently an important aspect of Paul's eschatology that *Christians* were to participate in the judgment, as if they were expected to be the leaders of the restored Israel. This judgement was expected to take place within an earthly context after the return of Jesus from heaven.

Paul develops the theme of the resurrection body in 2 Corinthians 5. There he explains in more detail how the 'spiritual' or 'heavenly' body will relate to the present mortal body. This passage reflects the distinctive Jewish horror of death which is presented under the image of nakedness (5.2; cf. 1 Cor. 15.37). Even if believers died, Paul promises that God has prepared for them a resurrection body, which he calls 'a house not made with hands, eternal in the heavens'. The thought is that God will provide the resurrection body from heaven and that this will be offered to believers when they are resurrected on earth. This agrees with the focus of 1 Corinthians 15 that the resurrection will take place within the transformed context of the earthly order.

We find a mature statement of Paul's eschatology in Rom. 8.18-25. This passage too has a 'this-worldly' dimension. It extends the realm of eschatological restoration to the natural order as well as to those who are called 'the children of God'. Paul states that the created universe waits with eager longing for God's children to be revealed (8.19). Although it has been subjected to futility by God's will (8.20), it will soon be freed from the shackles of mortality (8.21).[81] This passage offers a broader eschatological view than the Thessalonian and Corinthian correspondence, which arose perhaps from the apostle's further meditation on the subject. The mature Paul believed that the natural order would be restored to its pristine condition under Jesus the messiah. A form of primaeval expectation undergirds his hopes at this point which

---

81. There is a study of this strand by M.J. Harris, *Raised Immortal* (London: Marshall, Morgan & Scott, 1983), pp. 165-71.

might have emerged from his thinking about Adam at different points in his letters.

A millenarian eschatology is found also in Philippians, for which I assume a Roman origin and take to be Paul's last letter. Paul insists that the Lord was at hand (4.6). He includes a passage which shows that he had not abandoned parousia hopes even at the end of his career. 3.20-21 contains the assertion that Christians are 'citizens of heaven'. This evidently means that the authorities whom Christians acknowledge are heavenly ones: God and the Lord Jesus. It does *not* mean that Christians are destined for a heavenly immortality after death. Paul gives his view, which agrees with what he had said in earlier letters, that 'the Lord Jesus Christ' will appear from heaven to transform mortal human bodies so that they resemble his heavenly body (3.21). My conclusion, which is based on the evidence of Philippians, is that not even at the end of his life did Paul lose this hope for earthly transformation. To judge from Romans 8, he *extended* it to include the whole of creation as well as human beings within the sphere of the expected divine action.

The Eschatology of Other New Testament Documents
Eschatology is an important feature of the letter to the Hebrews. It is often thought that Hebrews uses Platonic categories to distinguish between heaven as the 'ideal' world and earth as the inferior copy of this pure form. Those who take this view believe that the eschatology of Hebrews has a characteristically 'Greek' dimension in which notions of the parousia and earthly kingdom have been replaced by the hope for a heavenly or transcendent immortality.

This exegesis of the epistle was challenged in an important article by C.K. Barrett in the Dodd *Festschrift*.[82] A starting point for such a challenge is provided by Heb. 10.37, which clearly reflects the common Christian eschatological hope: 'For yet a little while, and the coming one shall come and shall not tarry.' This reveals the same kind of future hope which Paul expressed, in which Jesus was expected to return from heaven to earth. The phrase 'appear a second time' is specifically used in this letter to reinforce this conviction about eschatology (9.28). This understanding of eschatology sets the rest of the letter in perspective,

---

82. 'The Eschatology of the Epistle to the Hebrews', in W.D. Davies and D. Daube (eds.), *The Background of the New Testament and its Eschatology: Studies in Honour of C.H. Dodd* (Cambridge: Cambridge University Press, 1954), pp. 363-93.

especially the language that is used about the heavenly Jerusalem in 12.22-29. The author tells his readers that they 'stand before Mount Zion' (12.22). This does not mean that they are heavenly beings already. The thought is rather that, as in Phil. 3.20, the source of their authority lies in heaven and, as in Gal. 4.26, that they await the heavenly Jerusalem which will shortly appear on earth. The context of this statement is the wider Christian belief that the restoration of Israel would involve the appearance of the new Jerusalem from heaven (for which there are parallels in Jewish apocalyptic literature). The 'apocalyptic' aspect of the letter consists in the disclosure of the future mysteries which are stored in heaven, to which Jesus has penetrated in his ascension (4.14) and about which the author claims to offer authoritative knowledge.

This orientation of Hebrews' eschatology explains why the author dwells in some detail on the heroes of faith in ch. 11. These are all people who expected a city which they could not see (and which they never saw). That city was expected within the context of their human experience. The same expectation is enjoined to the readers of Hebrews. They too are told to expect a city. The difference from the Old Testament heroes is that this hope is expected to be fulfilled in their lifetime (11.40), when the city is revealed from heaven. When seen in this light, Hebrews must be said to share the millenarian hopes of other New Testament literature in that earth is the focus of eschatological activity, even if much of the language and imagery is distinctive to the author. This point must not be obscured through a Platonizing reading of the text.

In this context we must consider the meaning of the term 'rest' in Hebrews.[83] This term is used some nine times in chs. 3 and 4. The source for it is the partial citation of Psalm 95 in Heb. 3.7-11. This citation concludes with the divine assertion that those who have rebelled against God will not enter his rest (3.11). The author uses this motif to criticize the unbelievers of his own day. 'Rest' is a soteriological term in Heb. 4.9-10. It denotes the sabbath rest which the author identifies with the eschatological climax. As such the 'rest' finds its meaning in the hope for earthly transformation. Readers are promised the opportunity to

---

83. On this idea see O. Hofius, *Katapausis: Die Vorstellung vom endzeitlichen Ruheort im Hebraërbrief* (WUNT, 11; Tübingen: Mohr, 1970). Hofius sees the Letter's understanding of 'rest' as signifying eschatological entry into the heavenly Temple. The meaning of the term in Hebrews is examined also by Attridge, *Hebrews*, pp. 126-28, who notes a variety of interpretations.

3. *The Setting of the Ascension of Isaiah*

share in the final rest of God from which only their repudiation of Christianity can debar them.

Another New Testament work whose eschatology has provoked debate is the book of Revelation. Revelation embodies the literary form of an apocalypse.[84] The phenomenon of 'apocalyptic' in Judaism included eschatological ideas, but the preponderance of eschatology in this text is due as much to Christian influence as to the wider characteristics of the apocalypse genre. Early Christianity *was* an eschatological movement, and Revelation is no exception in this. A pressing issue of interpretation, on which I have commented already, is the question of whether Revelation's eschatology achieved its form because of the event of a Domitianic persecution. We have seen that this theory is now increasingly challenged. It is by no means certain that Domitian called *himself* 'Lord and God', and the external evidence for Roman persecution of *Christians* at the end of the first century is slight. It was only fifteen years later, in the situation which is documented by Pliny, that the Romans once again persecuted the Christians as had happened in 64 CE. This is the situation to which the *Ascension of Isaiah* was addressed. The preponderance of eschatology in Revelation thus cannot be attributed to persecution either. As I said, it reflects the wider eschatological orientation of the Christian movement. The particular form of eschatology that we find in Revelation derives from the author's wrestling with the fact of social tension and from his reworking of traditional apocalyptic symbolism.

The eschatology of Revelation has more in common with the rest of the New Testament than is sometimes acknowledged. This is true even of the work's attitude to the Roman government. Parts of Revelation portray Rome in demonic terms and anticipate its final destruction. Chapters 13 and 17 are examples of this. This material is often contrasted with Paul's support for the emperor in Romans 13 (and with the attitude that is attributed to Jesus in Mk 12.17 and parallels), but this contrast demands further definition. *All* first-century references to civil obedience must be evaluated with reference to the early Christian conviction that 'the form of this world is passing away' (1 Cor. 7.31). The New Testament as a whole expects that the earthly kingdom of Christ will soon replace the existing order. This belief determined Christian attitudes to the state in that respect was offered to existing rulers under the belief that they would soon be set aside by God, which made opposition to

---

84. For a description of the literary genre see Collins (ed.), *Apocalypse*.

them redundant and perhaps even blasphemous given the expected divine intervention. Revelation agrees with other New Testament literature in offering no support for militaristic action against the Roman government. Its author shares the conviction that God alone will act and he presents the parousia of Jesus (22.20) as the decisive intervention. The symbolic language which is distinctive to Revelation must not lead to the conclusion that its eschatology is substantially different from what is found in other early Christian literature. The nature of its future hope is by contrast similar to what is found there.

This affinity to other literature is true especially of the work's millenarianism. Rev. 20.4 is the 'classic' New Testament millenarian passage. It anticipates the resurrection of those who had been martyred (the text says 'beheaded') for the sake of Jesus and their reign on earth with him for a thousand years. It is from this thousand-year period that the term 'millenarian' is formally derived, although the use to which this term is now put has changed somewhat. Revelation 20 offers a distinctive eschatological view in the New Testament in that it anticipates *two* resurrections. The first is to be that of the martyrs (20.4) and the second will be that of the rest of the dead (20.12). In this work's symbolic imagery there is to be a 'second death' (20.14-15) in which death and Hades will perish. This is analogous to Paul's expectation of the destruction of death in 1 Cor. 15.55. The implication of this chapter from Revelation is that the second resurrection will confer an immortality which the powers of death cannot touch. The rest of the dead will then join the martyrs in their transformed bliss.

This future hope provides the context in which the description of the new heaven and the new earth in ch. 21 is set. The author hopes that the recreation of the physical environment will signify the removal of death (21.4) and the appearance of the heavenly Jerusalem (cf. Heb. 12.22-24). Those who take their part in this new order will reign there 'for evermore' (22.5). This brings the eschatology of Revelation close again to Paul and to the view which is expressed in Romans 8. This is one in which the physical creation is to be transformed as the problems of mortality and corruption which belong to the present order are overcome by the introduction of a new state of being. As with Paul, there is no expressed hope for translation to heaven after the millenarian kingdom. The thought is rather that people will live in a redefined creation which has affinities with the present life despite being radically different from it. This is the future view on which the eschatology of Revelation is based.

3. The Setting of the Ascension of Isaiah

This analysis shows that the eschatology of Revelation 20–21 cannot be held to be exhausted by the 'millenarianism' of 20.4. The resurrection of the martyrs is only *part* of the author's eschatological programme, which also includes the hope for the renewal of all creation. The goal of Revelation's eschatology is thus the replacement of the present creation by a divinely-generated counterpart in which God and the Lamb become accessible beings (21.22). This is to be an earthly kingdom in which the saints reign with their messiah.

The New Testament literature thus offers a 'millenarian' eschatology throughout its different strands. By this I mean that the different authors present earth as the sphere of redemption and expect Jesus to return from heaven to begin his reign among the saints. This hope is a consistent theme in the literature despite the different language which is used to describe it. It is significant that this theme is not confined to the one text which embodies the literary genre of apocalypse. It is a theme of the Gospels and Epistles too. First-century Christian eschatology had a prominent 'this-worldly' orientation. This was a development of the preaching of Jesus which itself had roots in Jewish eschatology.

Millenarian Beliefs in Later Christian Writers

The Christian millenarian tradition did not die out with the first century but continued in a variety of writers for a considerable time. Early non-canonical evidence for millenarianism comes from Papias of Hierapolis, whose views are reported by Irenaeus (*Adv. Haer.* 5.33) and Eusebius (*Hist. Eccl.* 3.39).[85] If, as is generally supposed, Papias wrote in the reign of Hadrian, this makes him a near contemporary of the *Ascension of Isaiah* (according to my date for the apocalypse). Papias's importance lies in the fact that he was a 'hearer' of John the Elder and a friend of Polycarp, the bishop of Smyrna. He himself later became bishop of Hierapolis in Asia Minor.

In crucial respects Papias's eschatology must be distinguished from that of the *Ascension of Isaiah*, despite the fact that the two authors were near contemporaries. His work reportedly contained a saying of Jesus which had been handed down by John to the effect that vines would produce in prodigious proportions in the eschatological age. This

---

85. See further Bietenhard, 'Millennial Hope', pp. 13-14; and Daniélou, *Jewish Christianity*, pp. 380-81. The significance of Papias as an early tradent of first-century material is noticed by Hengel, *Johannine Question*, pp. 16-23.

represents a close parallel to *2 Bar*. 29.5, and one may perhaps suspect Jewish influence in the development of this expectation.[86] In addition, Papias thought that there would be harmony in the animal kingdom (see Irenaeus, *Adv. Haer.* 5.3.3), an idea which can be traced back to Isa. 11.6-9. Eusebius records Papias as teaching that, following the resurrection of the dead, there would be a thousand-year period when Christ's kingdom would be established 'in a material order on this earth'. This perhaps reflects early use of the book of Revelation, which would be natural given the fact that Papias worked in Asia Minor, to which the Apocalypse had been addressed.[87] The importance of Papias for this study lies in his hope for the material prosperity of creation, in which the hope for a heavenly immortality after the millenarian kingdom is expressed (4.17).

Barn. 15.3-9 extracts from the Genesis creation story the symbolic meaning that the history of the world would last for 6,000 years (on the grounds that, according to Ps. 90.4, one day was like a thousand years for God).[88] God's partaking of rest on the seventh day meant for Barnabas that in the eschatological future the Son of God would destroy the age of the lawless one. He would then judge the ungodly and transform the elements, and enter his rest. This would be followed by the eighth day which was to be the beginning of a new world. Here the notion of rest, which features also in 2 Thess. 1.7, Hebrews 3–4 and in *Asc. Isa.* 4.15 (and, as we shall see, in the Gnostic literature), is linked with sabbatarian conceptions within a scheme that is dominated by speculation about the ages of creation.

Millenarianism was reportedly held by some of the Jewish-Christian sectarians. According to Eusebius (*Hist. Eccl.* 3.28.2), who based his report on a book by one Caius, Cerinthus taught that after the resurrection Christ's kingdom would be established on earth and that in Jerusalem the flesh would enjoy feasting and other pleasures. At this time there would be a marriage feast which would last a thousand years.

---

86. Cf. Amos 9.13-14.
87. The *Ascension of Isaiah* by contrast makes no use of Rev. 20.4. I shall argue in Chapter 4 that we cannot be *certain* that the author of the author of the *Ascension of Isaiah* knew the New Testament Apocalypse. Contrast between Papias and the *Ascension of Isaiah* thus makes an interesting test case for the earliest use of the book of Revelation.
88. See Bietenhard, 'Millennial Hope', pp. 12-13; and Daniélou, *Jewish Christianity*, pp. 396-400.

3. The Setting of the Ascension of Isaiah

The reliability of this report has been questioned by Klijn and Reininck, who advocate caution against supposing that *Cerinthus* taught this view.[89] Yet Eusebius probably does report a variety of millenarianism which circulated in second-century Christianity, even if Cerinthus was not its true exponent. This report is significant for the history of Christian eschatology since it reveals precisely that criticism which Jerome would later make of the Christian millenarians, that they understood things 'in a Jewish way'. We have met this tendency already in Papias. The notions of an earthly kingdom and of feasting and fecundity have their roots in the Hebrew prophetic literature. We should note that, although this future view can claim partial support in the eschatology of Paul, what is said in Romans 8 is programmatic rather than fully descriptive, and the elements of feasting and procreation were probably inserted into the Christian eschatological tradition from a Jewish ambience. In other respects, they go against what was taught by Paul, especially when we consider his insistence on the need for transformation and the spiritual body in 1 Corinthians 15 and elsewhere.

Jerome says that the Ebionites held a millenarian eschatology (*Comm. in Is.* 66.20).[90] He complains that 'they understood all the delights of the thousand years in a literal sense'. This implies that they applied to the millennium the same paradisal speculation as did Papias of Hierapolis. Again, we cannot be sure that the *Ebionites* held this view. Evidence from the *Clementine Recognitions*, however, supports the view that such beliefs did circulate in Jewish-Christian circles. This text describes how Caiaphas tried to impugn the teaching of Jesus by emphasizing his belief in earthly rewards, such that those who fulfilled righteousness would be 'satisfied with meat and drink' (*Rec. Clem.* 1.61). The Christian additions to the *Testament of Isaac* also interpret the dominical sayings about feasting in a literal sense.[91] This very 'physical' orientation of the future hope undoubtedly helped to secure the demise of millenarianism at a later date.

89. *Patristic Evidence*, pp. 3-19.
90. See further Klijn and Reininck, *Patristic Evidence*, pp. 19-43.
91. See Bietenhard, 'Millennial Hope', p. 14; and the translation of W.F. Stinespring in Charlesworth (ed.), *Old Testament Pseudepigrapha*, I, p. 911: 'Whatever person has manifested mercy in the name of my beloved Isaac, behold I will give him to you in the kingdom of heaven and he shall be present with them at the first moment of the millennial banquet to celebrate with them in the everlasting light in the kingdom of our Master and our God and our king and our Savior, Jesus the Messiah.' The *Testament of Isaac* comes from the second century CE.

Justin Martyr shows the hold which millenarianism continued to exercise in the mid second century CE. Justin admits to knowing Christians who were contemptuous of the idea (and who believed in the soul's immediate ascension to heaven). He defended the traditional hope against these detractors (*Dial.* 80).[92] Prominent in Justin's eschatology was the belief that the resurrected would live for a thousand years in the rebuilt Jerusalem (*Dial.* 80.4). He based this idea on biblical prophecy. Justin used Ps. 90.4 to support the idea that the millennium would last for a thousand years (*Dial.* 81.3-4) and he said that Adam did not live a thousand years because of his sin.[93] Justin's eschatology is somewhat imprecise. According to *Dialogue* 81 the millenarian kingdom was the prelude to Christ's final judgment. *Dialogue* 113, however, implies that it was to be the eternal possession of the saints after the resurrection. In any event, Justin insists that the reward of the saints will be 'incorruption and fellowship' with God (*1 Apol.* 10) and immortality (*1 Apol.* 21; *Dial.* 45).

Irenaeus devotes substantial space to millenarianism in his *Adversus Haereses*.[94] Millenarianism is combined there with his theory of 'recapitulation'. Irenaeus outlines his anthropological scheme in *Adv. Haer.* 4.38.3. This passage states that the human person must recover from sin and proceed through glorification to the vision of God. At the same time Irenaeus is concerned to refute the Gnostic view that the resurrection

---

92. Trypho asked Justin: 'Do you really admit that this place, Jerusalem, shall be rebuilt; and do you expect your people to be gathered together, and make joyful with Christ and the patriarchs, and the prophets?' Justin replied: 'I and many others are of this opinion...but, on the other hand, I signified to you that many who belong to the pure and pious Christian faith, and are true Christians, think otherwise.' Justin continued: 'If you have fallen with some who are called Christians...who say that there is no resurrection of the dead, and that their souls, when they die, are taken to heaven do not imagine that they are Christians...I and others, who are right-minded Christians on all points are assured that there will be a resurrection of the dead, and a thousand years in Jerusalem, which will then be built, adorned, and enlarged [as] the prophets Ezekiel and Isaiah and others declare' (*Dial.* 80; Anti-Nicene Christian Library translation). On Justin's millenarianism see further L.W. Barnard, *Justin Martyr* (Cambridge: Cambridge University Press, 1967), pp. 157-68, esp. pp. 164-66; Bietenhard, 'Millennial Hope', pp. 14-15; and Daniélou, *Jewish Christianity*, pp. 393-94.

93. This draws on the exegesis of the Genesis creation story which is found in *Jub.* 4.29-30.

94. See the description of the material by Lawson, *Saint Irenaeus*, pp. 279-91.

was a past event.[95] He explains that human souls will be separated from their bodies and will go to the place of the dead (*Adv. Haer.* 5.31.2). In this context he upholds the hope for the resurrection of the body. This for him was a realistic and fleshly concept (cf. *Adv. Haer.* 5.2.2). *Adv. Haer.* 5.1-15 is a wide-ranging defence of the physicality of the Christian resurrection hope against its detractors. Irenaeus states that human bodies will rise in a transformed and spiritual form (5.7-8). It is in this context that he defends millenarianism. Irenaeus states that the history of the world will last for 6,000 years (*Adv. Haer.* 5.28.3) and he identifies the seventh millennium with the messianic kingdom (5.30.4) which has not yet arrived. When it comes the Antichrist will reign on earth for three and a half years (5.25.3) before being destroyed by Christ and cast into the lake of fire (5.30.4). The general resurrection will then take place, which Irenaeus affirms against the Gnostic denial of this event (5.33.1). This will be followed by the judgment (5.32.1). The creation will then be freed from its bondage to decay (5.32.1) and the earth will produce its fruits, in the citation which Irenaeus makes from Papias (5.33.3). The millennial banquet will take place on earth where the righteous will have a table prepared for them by God (5.33.2). This kingdom is the preparation for the final partaking of the divine nature: it will be the place where the saints grow more accustomed to beholding the vision of God (5.7.2). For Irenaeus the millennium is a process in which the resurrected grow up into the glory of the new creation through their experience of fellowship with Christ (5.32.1; cf. 5.35.1). They will reign during this time in Jerusalem, which is the type of the heavenly Jerusalem (5.32.1).

This analysis shows that for Irenaeus the millenarian kingdom is not so much an end in itself as a stage in the process of redemption. Irenaeus calls it 'the commencement of incorruption, by means of which Kingdom those who shall be worthy are accustomed gradually to partake of the divine nature' (*Adv. Haer.* 5.32.1). The righteous will grow progressively more accustomed to the vision of the divine glory and will enjoy communion with the holy angels (5.35.1). They will 'ascend through the Spirit to the Son, and through the Son to the Father' (5.36.2), and will finally 'see the face of the Lord' and 'rejoice with joy unspeakable' (5.7.2). There are important parallels with the *Ascension of Isaiah* in this view, not least with the suggestion of *Asc. Isa.* 7.23 that the Spirit functions as a psychopomp who conducts the righteous towards God and the Beloved One, although of course Irenaeus has nothing to match our

---

95. Cf. 2 Tim. 2.18 from earlier in the second century.

work's seven-storied cosmology. The *Ascension of Isaiah* also agrees with Irenaeus in that it allows the millenarian kingdom to precede the final vision of God, although once again the language which the two authors use is rather different. The *Ascension of Isaiah* seems to anticipate elements of the thought of Irenaeus, but in language which is distinctive to the apocalypse and which lacks such a developed anthropology.

One of the reasons why Irenaeus wrote as he did was to meet the challenge of the Gnostic assault on Christian eschatology. Gnosticism offered a pessimistic view of life in the flesh, which it held to be the result of an unfortunate and pre-mundane accident. Gnosticism understood salvation in terms of the repatriation of human souls as light-particles to the *pleroma* from which they had fallen.[96] The Gnostics used Jewish apocalyptic language to describe the end of the physical world (see *Paraph. Shem* 44.11), but the fate of individuals is not so clearly distinguished in their literature.[97] There is nothing for instance to match the hope for the resurrection of the *flesh* which is found in Irenaeus. The *Treatise on Resurrection* positively rejects this view and substitutes for it the conviction that resurrection is the 'entry into the wisdom of those who have known the Truth' (46.30-32; 47.2-12). The Gnostics thought about the body as a prison (*Apoc. John* 30.25-31.4) and they for the most part anticipated only the redemption of the soul (see for example *1 Apoc. Jas* 33.2–36.1). Indeed, one suspects that it was because of the Gnostic controversy and through the corrective influence of Irenaeus that quite literal notions of the resurrection were preserved in the church beyond their natural life. Irenaeus's presentation of eschatology has a defensive quality in this respect.

Tertullian defended the millenarian hope against Marcion, whose views about the Demiurge as the inferior creator had led him to deny the possibility of a future earthly transformation.[98] Tertullian expected that at the end God would restore the Jews to Palestine where the messianic kingdom ould be established (*Adv. Marc.* 3.24). He believed that Christians too had an earthly hope and that after the resurrection they would dwell for a thousand years in Jerusalem. Tertullian even said that in one part of Asia Minor the new Jerusalem had been seen in the sky for forty days. With reference to the messianic banquet, he stated that

96. Gnostic eschatology is described by Rudolph, *Gnosis*, pp. 171-204.
97. See further below.
98. Marcion's significance in early Christianity is examined by E.C. Blackman, *Marcion and his Influence* (London: SPCK, 1948).

3. *The Setting of the Ascension of Isaiah* 237

Christians would be rewarded in the place where they had engaged in struggle, and firmly rejected any allegorical interpretation of the biblical language (*Adv. Marc.* 4.31). Tertullian took up Revelation's idea of the two resurrections in this respect and thought that these would be interposed by the millennium at the end of the age (*De resurrectione carnis* 19).

Tertullian's comment about the vision of the heavenly Jerusalem calls to mind the Montanist eschatology. The Montanists expected that the heavenly Jerusalem would descend in Pepuza, a city of Asia Minor.[99] The Montanists agreed in this with other second-century Christians. Montanism was rejected by mainstream Christians because of its view of prophetic inspiration, the activity of its female ministers, and for the immediate rather than the earthly aspect of its eschatology.

Further evidence for Christian millenarianism can be stated more briefly since it lies beyond the second century. Questions about the authenticity of the book of Revelation featured strongly in the millenarian controversy.[100] Gaius of Rome was among the first to criticize the New Testament Apocalypse. A more moderate position was held by Dionysius of Alexandria, who denied that John the Evangelist had written the text. Hippolytus, who reports Gaius,[101] fused a literal interpretation of Revelation together with a positive acceptance of the continuing world order. He placed the millenarian hope within a scheme of 7,000 years in which he claimed that Christ had appeared in the year 5,500. This allowed him to present the millennium as a yet-future event.

Millenarianism was also challenged by the allegorical exegesis of the Alexandrian school under Clement and Origen, and especially by the latter.[102] Origen despised the millenarians for their literal understanding of the Bible. He states (*De Princ.* 2.11.2) that they anticipated the

---

99. The key sources are Epiphanius, *Adv. Haeres.*, 48; Hippolytus, *Haer.* 8.19; 10.25; Eusebius, *Hist. Eccl.* 5.16.18, and several of the writings of Tertullian. Tertullian's Montanist sympathies are examined by T.D. Barnes, *Tertullian* (Oxford: Clarendon Press, 1971), pp. 130-42; see also the article by R.E. Heine, 'Montanus, Montanism', in Freedman *et al.* (eds.), *Anchor Bible Dictionary*, IV, pp. 898-902.

100. See Bietenhard, 'Millennial Hope', pp. 18-20.

101. In Fragment VII of his work against Gaius. Theodoret (*Haereticarum Fabularum Compendium* 2.3) says that Hippolytus wrote a work against Cerinthus.

102. See Origen, *De Princ.* 2.11.2-3; *Comm. in Matt.* 17.35; and R.P.C. Hanson, *Allegory and Event* (London: SCM Press, 1959), pp. 333-56, esp. pp. 344-46; J.W. Trigg, *Origen* (London: SCM Press, 1985), pp. 113-15; and C. Bigg, *The Christian Platonists of Alexandria* (Oxford, 1886), pp. 53, 144, 146, 192, 354.

rebuilding of the earthly Jerusalem, and he cites 1 Cor. 15.44 against them. He accused them of interpreting the Scriptures 'in a Jewish way'. The messianic banquet for Origen was to occur in a strictly mental or spiritual sense, and he insisted that it must not be confused with the pleasurable feasting of which the millenarians had spoken.

Origen was opposed to a point by Methodius of Olympus, who repeated the literalism of Rev. 20.4;[103] and more strongly by Nepos of Arsinoe, who revived a thoroughgoing millenarianism (which Eusebius reported as advocating 'sensual luxury on this earth'). A similar view was held later by Apollinaris of Laodicea, who is reported by Epiphanius and Basil, and who taught that in the millennium the believer would have the same form of life as at present and that Christians would retain the Old Testament Law and even the practice of circumcision.

Jerome was another opponent of millenarianism. He criticized those who advanced such beliefs (like the Ebionites) on the grounds that they drew on Jewish ideas (*Comm. in Is.* 18). Jerome offered a spiritual interpretation of the book of Revelation and denied the possibility of any millenarian kingdom and the future restoration of Jerusalem and of Judaism (*Comm. in Jer.* book 4; *Ad. Jer.* 19.10-11). Jerome even re-edited Victorinus's commentary on Revelation to remove its support for millenarianism.

Millenarianism persisted longer in the Western Church than it did in the East. The followers of Vitalius were the last Eastern millenarians.[104] In the West Commodian opined that the history of the world would last 7000 years. He expected the heavenly Jerusalem to appear and he thought that people would marry and have children in the millennium.[105] Lactantius introduced further arguments which were based on the *Sibylline Oracles* and the belief, which he derived from Ps. 81.16 and Joel 4.18, that honey would pour from the rocks and wine and milk flow in the streams.[106] He criticized the poets for setting the golden age in the past when he thought that it belonged to the future; and he denied that the biblical promises should be spiritualized or seen as already fulfilled.

This crude approach to the millennium could not be sustained for ever. The millenarian hope was strongly criticized by Augustine after his

103. *Symposion* 9.
104. This is reported by Gregory of Nyssa, *Ep.* 102 to Cleodonius.
105. *Instructionum* 2.39; *Carmen apologeticum* 45.791.
106. See esp. his *Div. Inst.* 8.24.

3. *The Setting of the Ascension of Isaiah*

exchange of letters with Tyconius.[107] Tyconius insisted that the church was already living in the millennial age: he interpreted the first resurrection as the birth from sin to righteousness. The rule of Christ in his view was thus present rather than future: in the church and not in an ideal kingdom. Tyconius combined this view with a thoroughgoing parousia hope which he expected to come to fruition in the year 380. Augustine, who admits that he had once held millenarian views (*Sermones* 259.2), came to reject them as crude literalism. Like Tyconius, the mature Augustine referred the thousand years of Rev. 20.4 to the present and not to a transformed future (see his *De civ. D.*, 20.7).

The Eschatology of the Gnostic Literature

We must examine the eschatology of the Gnostic literature in a little more detail since it bears on the interpretation of the *Ascension of Isaiah*. Gnosticism adopted a pessimistic attitude towards the present life, which issued in the comparison of the human body with 'a prison' found in the *Apocryphon of John*. Salvation for the Gnostic consisted in the repatriation of the soul with the heavenly world, which raised the problem of the need to circumvent the opposition of the heavenly warders who tried to prevent the ascending soul from repatriation in this way. This problem was addressed by a complicated system of passwords, so that magical elements made their way into the Gnostic religion.[108]

The eschatological benefits are described allusively in the Gnostic literature, but enough is said there to indicate that they were held to constitute a form of 'reintegration'. The word 'rest' appears more than once in the literature. The sense in which it is used can be seen from the *Authoritative Teaching*. The soul which achieved knowledge of God

> came to rest in the one who is rest; she reclined in the bridal chamber; she ate of the meal for which she had hungered; she partook of the immortal food. She found what she had looked for. She received rest from her labours, while the light that shines over her does not shrink (VI. 3.34.32–35.18).[109]

Here we find the concept of rest, which was to be a feature of the

---

107. Tyconius was a Donatist theologian who wrote a commentary on Revelation (which is now extant only in fragments). For a summary of his thought see Bietenhard, 'Millennial Hope', pp. 28-30.
108. See Rudolph, *Gnosis*, pp. 172-75; and cf. Irenaeus, *Adv. Haer.* 1.21.5.
109. Translation reproduced from Rudolph, *Gnosis*, p. 189.

millenarian kingdom according to *Asc. Isa.* 4.15, applied to a celestial destiny in what represents a quite different ambience from the thought of the apocalypse.

The *Authoritative Teaching* shows what the Gnostics understood by the concept of 'resurrection'. This was essentially a spiritual phenomenon in which the body had no part to play. It is true that Paul's teaching about the 'spiritual body' (1 Cor. 15.44) is ambiguous, but the key difference between Paul and the Gnostics was that Paul believed that the resurrected would take their part in the messiah's earthly kingdom. This interpretation of eschatology goes against the fundamental principles of Gnosticism, for which the present world was something that must be left behind and for which salvation was entirely a matter of the heavenly or aeonic realm.

The Gnostic writings from Nag Hammadi do in fact contain a 'physical' interpretation of the resurrection (the *Treatise on Resurrection*, which is sometimes called the *Letter to Rheginos*, is an example of this), but this is always in a context in which the 'spiritual' resurrection is seen as the crucial one. Despite the contradictions which remain when this view is pressed, the notion of a physical resurrection seems to represent 'an attempt on the part of the gnostic understanding of resurrection to grapple with that of the belief of the Christian community'.[110] The *Treatise on Resurrection* does this by asserting two levels of resurrection: one on earth and the other after death, so that no resurrection is expected at the end of the world (NHC 14.44.30-33).

There is also material in the Gnostic writings which resembles some of the eschatological ideas found in Jewish apocalyptic literature. An example of this is the Nag Hammadi text called the *Concept of our Great Power*. This text offers a quite impressionistic view of the end of history which anticipates a sequence of aeons that are terminated by a catastrophic judgment in which only the souls of the righteous will be saved. It also anticipates natural disasters, of the kind which are familiar also from the Christian eschatological tradition, and its author expects the salvation of the Gnostic souls before the universal conflagration. This again represents a significant difference from the *Ascension of Isaiah*, in which the millenarian kingdom is interspersed between the period of tribulation (4.1-13) and the heavenly translation of the elect (4.19). It is evident from material such as this that any interpretation of the

---

110. Rudolph, *Gnosis*, p. 191.

3. *The Setting of the Ascension of Isaiah*

Ascension of Isaiah's eschatology must reckon with some significant differences from the Gnostic literature as well as with points of contact.

Millenarian Belief in the Ascension of Isaiah

The evidence for the millenarian hope in the *Ascension of Isaiah* is brief (4.14-18), but this does not mean that it is insignificant. The evidence is, on the contrary, most important and it suggests that the apocalypse stands at a crucial point in the history of Christian doctrine. The *Ascension of Isaiah* preserves a form of millenarianism which the author had inherited from the first century. Yet it also *modifies* the millenarian tradition by the inclusion of the hope for heavenly immortality (4.17; 9–11) which has parallels with Jewish martyrological beliefs and which holds themes in common with Irenaeus and with the Gnostics. This combination of ideas in the apocalypse must be examined in more detail.

The author of the *Ascension of Isaiah* was an early exegete of the New Testament literature. This exegetical interest determines his understanding of eschatology as much as of other aspects of Christian belief. I have argued that he used 2 Thess. 1.7 and perhaps other Pauline passages to frame his understanding of eschatology (but significantly there is no evidence that he used Rev. 20.4). We saw when examining the Christology that he used the New Testament material to create a new and more coherent picture which he believed was relevant to the needs of the second century. This is true also of his use of eschatological material. This author forged out a new understanding of the future hope which was bound up with explaining the relation between the hope for the millenarian kingdom, which he retained in company with other Christians (cf. Justin, *Dial.* 80), and the acquisition of heavenly immortality in the context of his teaching about martyrdom.

4.17 and much of the material in the Second Vision indicates that the saints will pass to a glorious heavenly immortality once their earthly reign has been concluded. This hope for heavenly immortality looks back to passages such as Dan. 12.2-3, *4 Macc.* 7.3 (cf. 9.22; 14.5-6) and *Jub.* 23.27-31. The closest parallels for this future view in post-apostolic literature are with Irenaeus, but the seven-storied cosmology separates the author of the apocalypse from the heresiologist and the device permits a more precise distinction between heaven and earth than is found in Irenaeus. Irenaeus implies that the vision of the divine glory will be granted to people on earth, so that the *Ascension of Isaiah* represents a somewhat different (and chronologically earlier) view, which draws on

Jewish martyrological beliefs, in which the ascension of the righteous to heaven is an important idea. The *Ascension of Isaiah* introduces a cosmological perspective into the Christian eschatological tradition, but it significantly retains the millenarianism which links the apocalypse with other Christian texts.

We must conclude from this information that the *Ascension of Isaiah* preserves the Christian millenarian hope only in a qualified form. As in Paul, human death is said not to be a barrier to participation in the kingdom. Readers are offered assurance that those who have died are in the seventh heaven already. These are expected to assume human bodies once again and to reign on earth with the messiah (4.16; cf. ch. 9). The difference from Paul is that this earthly reign is expected to be a *preparation* for the life of the seventh heaven, which is to be the final destiny of the righteous and an incorporeal state.[111] The author expects that human bodies will be left behind in the world (4.17), just as Isaiah and the righteous of ch. 9 overcame their fleshly limitations when they ascended to the seventh heaven (cf. 9.1). It perhaps an open question how far the angelomorphic state which is anticipated by the *Ascension of Isaiah* coheres with the 'spiritual body' expected by Paul. There may not in fact be a vast difference between the two ideas, except of course that the *Ascension of Isaiah* ultimately rejects the belief that earth could be the sphere of salvation. This is the crucial feature of the work's eschatology, which represents a difference from the Pauline eschatology.

The evidence for the development of Christian thought in the early second century is scanty (Ignatius certainly does not provide a complete picture), but the possibility remains that, as with his Christology, this author made his own mark on the Christian eschatological tradition. His apocalypse presumably mirrors a wider ambience in which an interest in the heavenly world had come to assume prominence, but it also contains sufficient evidence of independent thought (for instance the use of the 'Beloved One' title) to recommend the conclusion that the author was capable of original ideas in this area. There is not much external evidence to indicate that what he says was 'typical' of what the majority of Christians believed at the time. The evidence of Justin suggests, on the contrary, that it was not altogether typical, particularly in our author's assertion that the millenarian kingdom was *not* the final destiny of the

---

111. R.G. Hall is thus right to comment on the prominence of the immortality theme in the Second Vision; see his 'Isaiah's Ascent to See the Beloved: An Ancient Jewish Source for the Ascension of Isaiah', *JBL* 111.3 (1994), pp. 475-83.

3. The Setting of the Ascension of Isaiah 243

saints and in his introduction of the seven-storied cosmology. This form of eschatology must in all probability be seen as the author's own creation.

The question arises of why the author should have found it necessary to qualify the Christian millenarian tradition in this way. The answer seems to lie in the observation that the seven-storied cosmology was introduced to negate the power of the human (and the aerial) opponents whom he thought were arraigned against him. Besides the immediate crisis of 4.1-13, we must consider the material which indicates that this person was feeling marginalized by Jews and by fellow Christians, to which he responded by denying the basis of their religious authenticity. Social alienation was evidently a long-standing issue, which was exacerbated by the sense of impending conflict with the Romans. This observation does much to explain the author's development of Christian eschatology. Judaism had long asserted that martyrs passed to a heavenly reward. This idea was repeated by Paul and Ignatius (see above). Our author took up this view and interpreted it with reference to the Christian millenarian tradition to yield the form of belief that is found in the *Ascension of Isaiah*. There was doubtless a desire for compensation in this reworking of the tradition. Readers were promised a swift reward for their perseverance, and a greater reward than a transformed earthly state could offer. The author's attitude to this world as the scene of conflict led him to redefine the status of earthly life as the mere preliminary to the life of the seventh heaven. This had the effect of denying the acquisition of eschatological benefits to his more powerful opponents.

As with many features of the *Ascension of Isaiah*, we do not know the precise combination of circumstances which led the author to frame his eschatology in this way. The author may additionally have been reacting against enthusiastic tendencies in his own community. This is suggested by the caution against voluntary martyrdom which I have detected in 5.13. Those who sought martyrdom would presumably have anticipated heavenly immortality. Against these people the author counselled that those who were glorified in this way must once again assume human bodies to participate in the millenarian kingdom (4.16), and that the failure to experience martyrdom did not mean the loss of heavenly benefits. 4.14-18 may thus be a *defence* of the Christian millenarian hope against detractors in the author's circle quite as much as the second half of this passage qualifies that tradition when viewed against its other exponents.

The author's redefinition of the millenarian tradition is set in relief by a comparison with the millenarianism of Papias (and indeed with that millenarianism of Irenaeus, who cites Papias). The significance of this comparison lies in the fact that Papias worked around the same time that the *Ascension of Isaiah* was written. If the author of the apocalypse knew the ideas which Papias entertained, he would presumably have rejected them as crude in a way which anticipates the later Christian intellectual repudiation of millenarianism. The description of the millenarian kingdom which is found in *Asc. Isa.* 4.14-18 is remarkable both for its restraint and for its lack of detailed information about the future. There is no reference to earthly fecundity or to the restoration of the present order, nor even to the appearance of the heavenly Jerusalem which was a major theme of other first- and second-century Christian texts. That the author disagreed with such views about the renewal of the earth can be deduced from the fact that he makes the seventh heaven the final home of the righteous, and anticipates terrestrial destruction without the promise of recreation (4.18). This author thus anticipates those later writers who criticized the Christian millenarians for thinking 'in a Jewish way', despite his own millenarianism; but he does so in a context in which the millenarian kingdom is *distinguished* from the present life and not presented as the period of the church, so that affinities remain with the earlier view.

The question of the relationship between the *Ascension of Isaiah* and the Gnostic literature is worth pursuing a little further in this context. One of the conclusions of recent scholarship on Gnosticism is the conviction that it arose in an environment in which social alienation and the desire to move on from one's roots were prominent features. I cite the following summary from Birger A. Pearson:

> The Gnostic attitude to Judaism, in short, is one of alienation and revolt, and though the Gnostic hermeneutic can be characterized in general as a revolutionary attitude vis-à-vis established tradition, the attitude exemplified in the Gnostic texts, taken together with the massive utilization of Jewish traditions, can in my view only be explained as part of a process of religious self-redefinition. The Gnostics, at least in the earliest stages of the history of the Gnostic movement, were people who can aptly be designated as 'no longer Jews'.[112]

---

112. 'The Development of Gnostic Self-Definition', in *Gnosticism, Judaism and Egyptian Christianity*, p. 130.

3. The Setting of the Ascension of Isaiah

Pearson combines this assessment with his acceptance of Friedländer's assertion that Gnosticism was a pre-Christian phenomenon which developed on Jewish soil,[113] and his belief that 'early in the history of Gnosticism, the expansion of Christianity resulted in the appropriation of Christian theologoumena into Gnosticism as well as Gnostic theologoumena into Christianity—and Gnostic Christian groups were created'.[114]

Pearson's summary shows the sense in which it is appropriate to describe Gnosticism as a 'protest religion'. This is because it was formed by people who wanted to distance themselves from a religious affiliation which had once possessed them. At some stage in its evolution Gnosticism became intermingled with Christian ideas and it also attracted people who wished to disaffiliate themselves from Christianity, as we know from the controversies which took place between Gnostic and the Great Church theologians in the second century and beyond. Christianity entered the Gnostic equation because it had emerged as a Jewish sect and probably because many people who wished to distance themselves from Judaism joined the Christian movement, in which suspicion of Judaism was actively encouraged. Christianity in turn came to be rejected by the Gnostics because it was seen as a dominant force that was insufficiently different from Judaism, no doubt in part through the emergence of institutional structures of the kind which are criticized in the *Ascension of Isaiah* and then again in the Gnostic literature.

Perhaps the specifically Christian contribution to the development of fully-fledged Gnosticism in the mid second century has been overlooked by scholars in their desire to research the Jewish origins of Gnosticism.[115] The *Ascension of Isaiah* may in fact represent an important piece of this jigsaw which explains how the phenomenon of an incipient Gnosticism, by which I mean the complex of religious traditions and ideas which existed in the first and in the early second century, came to yield the first Gnostic apocalypses around the middle of the second century CE.

---

113. 'Alexandrian Judaism and Gnostic Origins', in the same volume, pp. 10-28. He cites M. Friedländer, *Der vorchristliche jüdische Gnosticismus* (Göttingen, 1898). Pearson comments on Friedländer's work: 'Although much of the detail of Friedländer's argument is open to question, he has been vindicated in his basic contention, that Gnosticism is a pre-Christian phenomenon that developed on Jewish soil' (p. 28).

114. 'The Development of Gnostic Self-Definition', p. 134.

115. Cf. Pétrement, *Separate God*, p. 211: 'It is not true that Gnosticism cannot be explained on the basis of Christianity.'

This happened as people who had become disillusioned with Judaism also became disillusioned with alternative expressions of Judaism which were known to be different from the mother religion but which retained many of its key concepts, albeit in a transformed way. The *Ascension of Isaiah* demonstrates the beginnings of this disillusionment with established religion but not, as I have shown, the final breach with Christianity and the church. Where the *Ascension of Isaiah* marks a significant difference from other Christian literature is in its assertion that the church leaders, and with them the majority of Christians, had distanced themselves from the apostolic example which the prophets alone maintained (3.21-31; cf. 4.9). This constitutes the acknowledgment that institutional Christianity was as flawed a religion as institutional Judaism. It also demonstrates the belief that the way to deal with this recognition about institutional Christianity was to create a sense of distance from it, in support of which the belief in the Beloved One's descent and the hope for heavenly immortality were introduced. These ideas 'explained' to people who shared the author's position why the majority of Christians could no longer be accepted as religiously authentic and why readers must stand their distance from them to preserve the truth of their religion. With reference to eschatology, this sense of distance also supported the assertion that earth was *not* the place of final salvation which the author added to the traditional understanding of the millenarian kingdom.

The *Ascension of Isaiah* stands at a sufficient distance from developed Gnosticism to suggest that it may have something to say about the question of Gnostic origins. I have already considered this matter in respect of the work's Christology (in Chapter 2), where I suggested that the motif of the Beloved One's descent was further developed in Gnosticism and the citation from Isaiah 45 deliberately recast to yield a different meaning. If the Gnostics used the *Ascension of Isaiah* (as we know from Epiphanius that they did), they must have found it in many respects a much too 'Christian' text. That would explain why many of its ideas were revamped. Yet the point must be made that the author has already begun to articulate some of the feelings of social alienation which were crucial for the emergence of developed Gnosticism a generation or so later. The need to establish a distance from *all* other religious groups had been voiced by this Christian author. This was a significant thing for people who were looking for ways to distinguish themselves from Judaism and for whom Christianity had initially provided a religious alternative.

3. *The Setting of the Ascension of Isaiah*

Where the author of the *Ascension of Isaiah* presented the majority of Christians as flawed, but upheld the value of the apostolic gospel which he claimed to preserve (3.21), Gnosticism presented Christianity itself as flawed by caricaturing its beliefs and by mutilating what the Christians believed about Jesus and about salvation.

This analysis confirms my suggestion that the *Ascension of Isaiah* stands at an intermediate stage between New Testament Christianity and Gnosticism. The apocalypse shows the development of a Christian mediatorial interest in a climate that was fuelled by feelings of social alienation. It confirms that Christian literature may reveal something about Gnostic origins even when the hypothesis that Gnosticism was also a Jewish deviation is accepted. Perhaps the most significant conclusion to be drawn from the study of Gnostic origins, and one on which most scholars comment, is that this was an extremely complex matter which cannot be reduced to a simple equation. The *Ascension of Isaiah* must certainly feature in further study of this problem. Its evidence for its author's growing sense of isolation in the second-century religious world, and his hostility towards institutional Christianity, are significant factors which recommend further work on this aspect of the apocalypse.

Millenarianism in Sociological Perspective

One of the more interesting developments in New Testament scholarship over the past decade has been the recognition that social scientific research can help to illuminate the character and distinctive concerns of early Christianity. I want now to develop my approach to the *Ascension of Isaiah*, which has been concerned so far with its place in the history of ideas, by asking whether some of the theoretical approaches which have been adopted towards millenarianism can help to exegete the apocalypse.

There is the ever-present danger in work of this kind of establishing a paradigm which is then held to 'explain' certain features of a given example. My aim in what follows is not to create a matrix of interpretation but simply to ask whether the wider study of millenarianism has any bearing on our text. This will involve examination of a variety of scholarly theories and also critical reflection about whether these constitute relevant material for the exegesis of the apocalypse.

Scholars have often discussed what causes millenarianism. Norman Cohn sees it as embracing any religious movement with a phantasy of salvation which is to be collective (enjoyed by the righteous as a group), terrestrial, imminent, total (utterly transforming life on earth, not merely to improve but to perfect) and accomplished by agencies which are consciously regarded as supernatural.[116]

A similar description is offered by K. Mannheim.[117] He insists that the driving force is what he calls 'ecstatic-orgiastic' energies, by which he means human reactions which transcend the limits of ordinary conscious reality.[118] Mannheim identifies the essence of millenarianism as belief in the present as the moment of possibility which contrasts with earlier feelings of hopelessness and despair. This point is vital to his definition. Millenarianism for Mannheim is the breach through which ecstatic feelings burst out and try to transform the world. It produces the conviction that things could be different.[119] Millenarian ideology, by contrast, is often confused and inconsistent.[120] This is because seizing the present is generally more important for millenarians than cataloguing or analysing the future benefits, which are often articulated only in an imprecise form. Millenarianism on Mannheim's definition involves the recognition that change is possible, and it sets about organizing people's lives according to that truth.

Peter Worsley argues that millenarianism is the reaction of poor or dispossessed people against the prevailing social and political order. He sees it as a 'religion of the lower orders'[121] which begins from 'a situation of dissatisfaction with existing social conditions and...yearnings for a happier life'.[122] Worsley identifies certain situations in which

---

116. Cohn, 'Medieval Millenarism', p. 32.
117. *Ideology and Utopia* (ET London: Routledge, new edn, 1991).
118. *Ideology*, p. 192.
119. *Ideology*, p. 193.
120. Cf. Mannheim's comment, *Ideology*, p. 193: 'The essential feature of Chiliasm is its tendency always to dissociate itself from its own images and symbols. It is precisely because the driving force of this utopia does not lie in the form of its external expression that a view of the phenomenon based on the mere history of ideas fails to do it justice.'
121. *The Trumpet Shall Sound: A Study of 'Cargo' Cults in Melanesia* (London: MacGibbon & Kee, 2nd edn, 1968), pp. 233-35. The influence of Karl Marx on Worsley is impossible to miss. Another Marxist understanding of millenarianism is offered by V. Lanternari, *The Religions of the Oppressed: A Study of Modern Messianic Cults* (London: MacGibbon & Kee, 1963), pp. 301-15.
122. *Trumpet*, p. 251.

3. The Setting of the Ascension of Isaiah

millenarianism characteristically occurs. These are: among people who are divided into small, separate and isolated social units;[123] in the agrarian, and especially the feudal, state;[124] and in a society with differentiated political institutions that is fighting for its existence by military and political means.[125] Concomitantly Worsley offers a portrait of Jewish and Christian millenarianism as appealing to people who were engaged in the struggle for liberation, particularly liberation from the yoke of Rome:

> Christianity itself, of course, as recent interpretations of the Dead Sea Scrolls emphasize, derived its *élan* from the millenarist traditions of the Essenes and similar sectaries at the beginning of the Christian era. These people looked for the establishment of an actual earthly kingdom of the Lord which would free the Jews from Roman oppression. Later, this doctrine commended itself as a message of hope to the downtrodden of the Roman Empire.[126]

Worsley's approach to millenarianism (as indeed to early Christianity) has been criticized or refined in several ways. I shall argue in a moment that he has made a very one-sided presentation of the early Christian movement as a revolutionary body. Secondly, Cohn points out that not all millenarians come from the deprived classes. Both the medieval 'Spirituals' and Thomas Müntzer, for instance, show that affluent people have been attracted by this type of religion.[127] Thirdly, it has been objected that the notion of 'deprivation' by itself is insufficient to explain a millenarian reaction. Sylvia Thrupp observes that deprivation often expresses itself in a non-millenarian way and that many deprived people never resort to it.[128] This leads David Aberle to speak of *'relative deprivation'* as a more exact cause of the phenomenon.[129] 'Relative deprivation' on his definition is the belief that something is left

---

123. *Trumpet*, p. 235.
124. *Trumpet*, pp. 236-38.
125. *Trumpet*, p. 238.
126. *Trumpet*, p. 234.
127. Cohn, 'Medieval Millenarism', p. 35. A similar point is made by Collins in her *Crisis and Catharsis*, pp. 105-106.
128. In her edited collection, *Millennial Dreams*, p. 26; see also K. Burridge, 'Reflections on Prophecy and Prophetic Groups', *Semeia* 21 (1981), pp. 99-100; and M. Barkun, *Disaster and the Millennium* (New Haven: Yale University Press, 1974), p. 36.
129. 'A Note on Relative Deprivation Theory as Applied to Millenarian and Other Cult Movements', in Thrupp (ed.), *Millennial Dreams*, pp. 209-14.

unsatisfied in the expectations of a human community whatever their status and resources.

Fourthly, Charles Y. Glock has criticized studies of 'deprivation' which focus on the economic aspect to the detriment of other manifestations of deprivation.[130] Glock notes some wider areas for consideration in this respect. Among these, 'social' deprivation is the inability to experience the same cultural and related benefits as other people enjoy. 'Organismic' deprivation is the sense of being cut off from the source of one's own well-being. This is often found among alcoholics and psychiatric patients. 'Ethical' deprivation is the sense of alienation which is experienced when the values of the dominant society no longer represent acceptable ideals. This is relatively independent of the other types since it mainly derives from a glut of economic or social satisfaction. 'Psychic' deprivation is the loss of meaning and philosophical coherence which takes place when the guiding principles of society are perverted or repressed in a way which a group or individual holds misguided; it is 'primarily a consequence of severe and unresolved social deprivation'.[131]

We should certainly question Worsley's interpretation of early Christianity as a quest for *political* freedom in the narrow sense. Although the Christian belief in the future divine kingdom meant by implication that all human authorities would be subordinated to the lordship of Christ (cf. 1 Cor. 15.24), this is not to say that liberation hopes dominated the agenda which Jesus and his followers established. Jesus was not a Zealot.[132] The Christians evidently distanced themselves from militaristic engagement with the Romans. Their hope for the kingdom embodied the hope for divine action and for the fulfilment of the biblical promises. This rendered their own intervention redundant and perhaps even blasphemous, because the task of introducing the kingdom belonged to God alone.

Another major treatment of millenarianism is that of Kenelm Burridge. Burridge thinks that millenarians anticipate a process of 'redemption' or change in which the decisive moment is the emergence

---

130. C.Y. Glock, 'The Role of Deprivation in the Origin and Evolution of Religious Groups', in R. Lee and M.E. Marty (eds.), *Religion and Social Contact* (New York: Oxford University Press, 1964), pp. 24-36.

131. Glock, 'The Role of Deprivation', p. 29.

132. On this point see J.P.M. Sweet, 'The Zealots and Jesus', C.F.D. Moule and E. Bammel (eds.), *Jesus and the Politics of his Day* (Cambridge: Cambridge University Press, 1984), pp. 1-9.

3. The Setting of the Ascension of Isaiah

of a 'prophet'.[133] A prophet in Burridge's understanding is a charismatic or exceptional figure who moulds diverse hopes for change into cohesion:

> A prophet is generally believed to have access to a source of inspiration that transcends man's ordinary wits. He either symbolizes the new man in himself, or he is the vehicle by means of which the lineaments of the new man may become known. He imposes certainty on a situation characterized by doubts. He must articulate thoughts and aspirations and emotions that are immanent in the community to which he speaks.[134]

Two features of Burridge's work demand attention in the context of this study. Burridge divides a typical 'millenarian movement' into three distinct 'phases',[135] and he identifies 19 prominent characteristics within it.[136] Of his three phases, the first is an attempt to understand the fact of disenfranchisement, which involves the desire for greater 'integrity' ('integrity' being a qualitative measurement in which one person or group's standing is compared with another's).[137] The second phase takes action to resolve this situation. It articulates the problems and their solution and often emphasizes the economic issue.[138] Burridge's third phase is the aftermath, in which the new ideals and assumptions are firmly established. This leads not infrequently to a resurgence of the first stage, so that there is an element of circularity in the process.[139]

Summarizing some of Burridge's 19 characteristics, within a generally permissive political régime there may arise (competing sets of assumptions about power, in which (new beginnings are predicated, and a prophet appears to articulate the community's new assumptions.[140] These new assumptions are expressed within the existing cultural idiom, and look to the rebirth of a new person. Burridge also insists that the objectives of millenarianism cannot be judged narrowly within the

---

133. *New Heaven, New Earth* (Oxford: Basil Blackwell, 1969), pp. 11-12, 153-63.
134. *New Heaven*, p. 155.
135. *New Heaven*, pp. 105-16.
136. *New Heaven*, pp. 97-99.
137. *New Heaven*, pp. 105-107.
138. *New Heaven*, pp. 107-12. Notice how the economic aspect is to the fore in this analysis.
139. *New Heaven*, pp. 112-15.
140. *New Heaven*, p. 97.

confines of a particular movement but must be examined on a larger scale to evaluate their success or failure.

Burridge's analysis is based on his study of nineteenth-century Polynesian and Melanesian millenarian movements. As with Worsley's assessment, elements of his study are useful, but the methodology must not be imported uncritically into the description of early Christianity. This is because Burridge's paradigm reflects a particular cultural idiom, which makes it problematic to apply in detail to different situations, even when some broad similarities with early Christianity are acknowledged. This sense of caution is important especially in relation to the *nature* of the response which Burridge describes. Many of his examples are 'activist' movements: movements which set out to change the world through force, and through force of arms if necessary.[141] It would be wrong to assume that millenarianism leads only to this form of expression. Pacifism was in fact more typical of millenarian groups in first-century Judaism. An example of this is recorded by Josephus who says that, at the height of the siege of Jerusalem, a crowd of six thousand Jews, including women and children, gathered in the Temple at the instigation of a 'false prophet' and stood by to await their deliverance. They were all burnt to death.[142] The Zealots, who tried to force God's hand, were in the minority at the time of the First Revolt.[143] Any suggestion that early Christianity was an 'activist' movement of this kind does little justice to the evidence and makes too little allowance for the *divine* hand in the expected intervention.

The role of 'the prophet' is an influential feature of Burridge's research. This has obvious attraction as a way of describing both Jesus

141. For example the *Hauhau* movement which is described in some detail by Burridge, *New Heaven*, pp. 15-22 (there is a further discussion of it by M. Adas, *Prophets of Rebellion: Millenarian Protest Movements against European Colonial Order* (Cambridge: Cambridge University Press, 1979), pp. 11-19). This Maori uprising came together under a man called Te Ua and attacked the British soldiers who had taken control of their territory. Following a few minor victories they surrendered and the movement was put down. A sect then emerged called the *Ringatau*, founded by a *Paimarire* convert called Te Kooti, which fused together Christian and Maori elements and which apparently still survives.

142. Josephus, *War*, 6.283-85. This passage is noted by M. Goodman, *The Ruling Class of Judaea: The Origins of the Jewish Revolt against Rome AD 66–70* (Cambridge: Cambridge University Press, 1987), pp. 90-91.

143. See M. Hengel, *The Zealots* (ET Edinburgh: T. & T. Clark, 1989), pp. 369-76.

3. The Setting of the Ascension of Isaiah

and the Teacher of Righteousness (as Isenberg noticed). It might have a superficial attraction for exegetes of the *Ascension of Isaiah* given the fact that the apocalypse seems to come from a prophetic community, or at least from an author who valued prophecy highly. Yet this aspect was significantly qualified by Worsley, who distinguished between prophets and leaders.[144] Worsley observed that prophets are often retiring individuals who are given to visionary experience but not always gifted with organizational ability. In many cases, Worsley notes, a prophet is less important than a leader or organizer who gives a movement its shape and coherence. Each individual village or unit, too, may have its own leader, so that a plurality of leaders can be involved. One should therefore beware of assuming that a *single* figure is needed to bring a millenarian movement to cohesion, and also that the decisive people are necessarily 'prophets'. The case of early Christianity and of the Essenes provides an example of this. Although both the Teacher and Jesus were exceptional figures who possessed great charisma, the success of the movements which they founded is inconceivable without the internal organization and politics which the Scrolls and the New Testament reveal. In both cases it is true to say that a significant figure supplied the initial impetus, but to this must be added the recognition that others built on that foundation and produced a movement which underwent change and development in the process.

In the situation revealed by the *Ascension of Isaiah* we find precisely the 'routinization of charisma' which was described by Max Weber. The apocalypse indicates that institutional leaders were displacing the prophets, who now felt out of place in a world in which they had once had great authority. It is tempting to see the author as a 'prophet' in Burridge's sense, especially on the basis of 3.31, but we do not actually know what role he discharged among his readers. Although I have spoken about 'the author' in the singular as a convenient shorthand, it is likely that the *Ascension of Isaiah* was the product of a community and, therefore, that a history of reflection stands behind the apocalypse. This inevitably qualifies the sense in which the material can be assigned to a single prophet. Nor is it certain that the authors as prophets formed a community which was separate from Christian churches generally. Hall's model of regular meetings of individual prophets is more likely to be correct. There is no evidence that an absolute sectarianism like that of the earlier Qumran community had been adopted. I see 2.7-11 (in which

---

144. *Trumpet*, pp. 271-72.

the prophets are presented as isolated figures) as a projection of future displacement rather than as a description of the circle's present condition. We must therefore beware of imposing Burridge's model in its entirety on the *Ascension of Isaiah*. The broader model proposed by Worsley is more flexible and has greater potential for explaining the spread of Christianity in its early period. The emergence of formal structures of leadership, however much the author of the *Ascension of Isaiah* claimed to dislike them, was a necessary part of its process of expansion.

Another issue to emerge from Burridge's book is the problem of what happens to a millenarian movement when it outgrows its ideology. An example of this from modern history is the case of the Jehovah's Witnesses. The Witnesses revise their chronology to accommodate the fact of eschatological disappointment.[145] That this can be done without the demise of the sect demonstrates the point that judgments about the 'success' or otherwise of a millenarian movement cannot be made by examining ideology alone. The means of expression is generally less important for millenarians than the recognition that the present provides the moment of opportunity. It does not necessarily matter that a particular expression of belief has only limited application, whether this limitation is temporal or situational.[146] We must examine the new assumptions about power which emerge from the expression of protest to understand a reaction of this kind. This demonstrates the need to examine the real level of human conflict and response and not just what Marx called the 'phrases and fantasies' which are used by their participants to describe them.

Another interpretation of millenarianism, which has implications on the psychological level, has been proposed by Anthony F.C. Wallace.[147]

---

145. See further L. Festinger *et al.*, *When Prophecy Fails: A Social and Psychological Study of a Modern Group that Predicted the Destruction of the World* (New York: Harper & Row, 1956), and Beckford's study (see n. 156).

146. Cf. Burridge's comment on the *Hauhau* movement (*New Heaven*, p. 21): 'Whether we conceive of the time perspective as spread over a period of weeks, years or generations, we ought to think of a millenarian movement as having (possible) political antecedents and sectarian consequences.'

147. 'Mazeway Disintegration: The Individual's Perception of Socio-Cultural Disorganization', *Human Organization* 16 (1957), pp. 23-27; 'Mazeway Resynthesis: A Bio-Cultural Theory of Religious Inspiration', *Transactions of the New York Academy of Sciences* 18 (1956), pp. 626-38; 'Revitalization Movements', *American Anthropologists* 58 (1956), pp. 264-81. There is a summary of Wallace's thought in Barkun, *Disaster*, pp. 37-41.

3. The Setting of the Ascension of Isaiah 255

Wallace believes that 'stress' is the cause of millenarian feelings. He defines stress as 'a condition in which some part, or the whole of the social organism is threatened with more or less serious damage'.[148] When faced with this threat, Wallace argues, people use a process called 'revitalization'.[149] Revitalization is the return to stability which he explains with reference to 'the mazeway'. The mazeway is 'Nature, society, culture, personality, and body image as seen by one person'.[150] Usually the mazeway is a healthy organism which reduces stress and produces satisfaction. When this function breaks down, Wallace believes that the conditions are right for 'revitalization' to occur. He posits a series of stages in which a society moves from stability through crisis to revitalization and back to a 'steady state'. Mazeway reformulation as Wallace understands it is generally undertaken by a prophet. The prophet receives a vision which provides the basis for a new perception of the world, as he does in Burridge's paradigm. Converts repeat the process of transformation in their own experience. They often join together to articulate the new ideals. Millenarianism is presented in Wallace's analysis as an ecstatic return to the sense of well-being which is adopted because other expressions have been found inappropriate or impossible.

Some questions about this interpretation have been raised by Michael Barkun. Barkun questions Wallace's shifting understanding of 'stress' and observes that he thinks first of individual but then also of social pathology.[151] Moreover, Barkun asks what kind of stress is at issue, how great it has to be to create a millenarian movement, and what percentage of the population must be involved to make the mazeway reformulation successful. Barkun himself sees millenarianism as the response of vulnerable and oppressed people to the experience of disaster 'Millenarian movements almost always occur in times of upheaval, in the wake of cultural contact, economic dislocation, revolution, war, and natural catastrophe.'[152] Any kind of disaster can produce

---

148. 'Revitalization Movements', p. 265.
149. 'Mazeway Resynthesis', pp. 626-38.
150. 'Revitalization Movements', p. 266.
151. *Disaster*, p. 39.
152. *Disaster*, p. 45. Barkun includes a footnote reference to the work of A.J.F. Köbben, 'Prophetic Movements as an Expression of Social Protest', *International Archives of Ethnography* 49.1 (1960), pp. 117-64, which is a helpful study.

social change,[153] but Barkun believes that there are four situations from which millenarianism is *not* likely to arise. These are those which leave a substantial proportion of the primary environment intact; those in which environmental damage is quickly repaired; those which are indefinitely prolonged within the same social unit; and those which occur in the absence of any ideas about future change.[154] Barkun interestingly argues that rural dwellers are particularly prone to millenarianism.[155] This is because, while the city state or conurbation is sufficiently diverse to absorb a disaster, smaller and self-sufficient communities are less able to cope and respond in a millenarian way because they lack the means to channel their feelings in other (no doubt more rational) directions.

Other interpretations of millenarianism must also be mentioned. Lofland and Stark and Beckford examine social tension, particular kinds of religious disposition and the dynamics of recruitment as possible causes.[156] Adas looks at social and political institutions, their inability to channel feelings of protest in more conventional avenues, and the phenomenon of accelerated change.[157] Mary Douglas argues for a relation between religious belief and mechanisms of social control. She sees millenarianism as appealing to those who feel the need to break their social ties.[158] Her book raises a host of questions about access to power in a human society, who makes the rules, and how far the disenfranchised feel able to challenge the structures of the dominant group.

Much of this research identifies the phenomenon of social change as a primary cause of millenarianism. Whether this represents the response to a crisis or the growing awareness of inequality, millenarianism is by

153. *Disaster*, p. 52.
154. *Disaster*, p. 64.
155. *Disaster*, p. 69. He disagrees with a comment by E.J. Hobshawm, 'There is no a priori reason why they should not be urban'; see Hobshawm's book, *Primitive Rebels: Studies in Archaic Forms of Social Movements in the Nineteenth and Twentieth Centuries* (Manchester: Manchester University Press, 1959), p. 65. Worsley, too, sees millenarianism as a rural phenomenon.
156. J. Lofland and R. Stark, 'Becoming a World-Saver: A Theory of Conversion to a Deviant Perspective', *American Sociological Review* 30 (1965), pp. 862-75; J. Lofland, *Doomsday Cult: A Study of Conversion, Proselytization, and Maintenance of Faith* (Englewood Cliffs, NJ: Prentice-Hall, 1966); J.A. Beckford, *The Trumpet of Prophecy: A Sociological Study of Jehovah's Witnesses* (Oxford: Basil Blackwell, 1975).
157. *Prophets*, pp. 183-89.
158. *Natural Symbols* (Harmondsworth: Penguin Books, 1978).

3. The Setting of the Ascension of Isaiah

general consent bound up with articulating the need for change and with the insistence that change is possible in a situation determined by the perception of inequality. This is often expressed in terms of the hope for society's complete reordering, generally through supernatural intervention, rather than for the removal of specific kinds of oppression. Deprivation too has been seen as a cause of millenarianism. The factor of 'relative deprivation' which was proposed by David Aberle seems analytically more appropriate than absolute deprivation as a projected cause. Aberle presents millenarianism as the response of people who *feel themselves* to be deprived in some way. He leaves open the questions of their relative place in society and the precise nature of their deprivation. This point is supported by Glock's observation that 'deprivation' cannot be restricted to economic categories but that other manifestations are important too.

What emerges from this survey is the conviction that millenarianism must be set in a broad framework of interpretation if justice is to be done to the subject. It cannot be presented exclusively as the reaction of the dispossessed, of those longing for political liberation or of those threatened by disaster (although all of these factors may be relevant). The situation and interests which prompt a particular outburst of millenarianism can be determined only by a careful analysis of the source material. There is thus a balance to be maintained when one example of millenarianism is compared with another. Certain generalities emerge, such as those I have mentioned here. These may recur in different movements, but the existence of generalities must not be allowed to obscure the individual and internal features which give a particular movement its shape and which are distinctive to that movement alone. These are in many ways analytically more interesting because they demonstrate the causes of concern which brought that movement into existence and reveal its distinctive character.

At the same time the study of millenarianism must examine the relevant issues on a broad as well as a local scale. Justice cannot be done to one example by ignoring the wider context from which it emerged and of which there may be recurrent instances at different periods of time. I am mindful here of Burridge's point that there is an element of circularity in the millenarian process. This is because the access to power which emerges from the expression of protest is often a restricted one which does little to remove the actual differentials that exist between people. Continued experience of disenfranchisement in this case leads to renewed expression of millenarianism because the inequality which prevents a different kind of response has not been removed. For instance, the feelings of disenfranchisement which sustained early Christianity were not confined to the period of Jesus but continued into the history of the early church. For this reason one must not minimize how real the hopes of the parousia were for the early Christians. Divine intervention was seen as the remedy for the impasse that existed on the human and historical level. The hope for a direct divine intervention must have seemed just as relevant when the *Ascension of Isaiah* was written as it did a century earlier.

Early Christianity must therefore be made the subject of a careful and responsible study across all its strata to achieve a balanced understanding of the nature and convictions of its eschatology. That can hardly be done by presuming that any single paradigm based on remote examples is necessarily appropriate, or by offering a restricted study of a single text which fails to take account of the wider convictions expressed in early Christian literature. The long-term perspective is likely to be significant since this sets the distinctive features of Christianity in perspective which in turn determines the matrix within which a particular text can be interpreted. These considerations may now be applied to the specific case of the *Ascension of Isaiah*.

Millenarianism in the Ascension of Isaiah

Conflict is a powerful theme in the *Ascension of Isaiah*. We have seen that the author was aware of difficulties in his relations with Jews, with fellow Christians and with the Romans, especially the latter. He tended to erect barriers against *everyone* who was not of his persuasion. This was a defence against the profound feelings of isolation which are revealed in the apocalypse. As a Christian exegete he was probably in conflict with Jewish religious teachers, and he must have been criticized by them for his attitude towards the Torah. As a prophet he felt displaced in the world of Christianity, in which the prophets' authority had been eroded by the emergence of the leaders. This erosion of power was exacerbated by the fear that most Christians would compromise in the sacrifice test (4.9) to leave only the prophets as the authentic representatives of Christianity (cf. 3.21). The immediate cause of the *Ascension of Isaiah* was the belief that persecution of the Christians by the Romans was impending in Syria. The apocalypse thus reveals a broadly-based set

3. *The Setting of the Ascension of Isaiah* 259

of feelings of social alienation in which the new situation with the Romans had exacerbated existing discontent.

My belief is that this specific situation was responsible for the form of eschatology in the apocalypse, which represents a response to fears about martyrdom and to the belief that many Christians would compromise over the issue of the sacrifice test and thus escape punishment from the Romans. The *Ascension of Isaiah* breathes the hope that the current situation was to be the forum for the divine intervention (4.13-14; cf. 11.37-38). This strikes an echo for readers of Mannheim, for whom the essence of millenarianism is the recognition of the present as the moment when a hopeless situation gains the potential for transformation. Our author's insistence that the intervention was imminent betrays his need to find change which was related to his isolated position in the world. Circumstances had no doubt convinced him that he lacked the power to determine his own destiny in view of the social change which had taken place in recent history.

Feelings of alienation also explain the introduction of the seven-storied cosmology (which is an eccentricity in early Christian literature) and the work's thoroughgoing dualism. The cosmology on the fictional level is a demonstration of the Beloved One's superiority to Beliar. On the author's social and political level it demonstrates his wish to believe that his circle were more powerful than those who oppressed them, especially of course the Romans. That the transformation was expected to be a divine act compensated for the fact that readers were unable to ward off Roman harassment by themselves. The material which recommends marginalization (4.13 and elsewhere) is related to this belief in that it advocates the acceptance of displacement until the promised intervention. The First Vision emphasized the gulf between Beliar and the Beloved One in connection with the hope for the Beloved One's parousia which was expected to result in the demon's destruction and the introduction of the millenarian kingdom.

It is by no means insignificant that the author reworked the Christian millenarian tradition to emphasize the hope for heavenly immortality (4.17). This is a feature of the Second Vision too. This development probably relates to a wider intellectual climate, in terms of the first assembly of the ideas which would later surface in the Gnostic apocalypses, but again it reflects the author's experience of social isolation. The impression is that the promise of earthly reward was considered insufficient compensation for the struggles of those who had maintained their Christian faith, and that because earth was understood as a place of conflict this made it an inappropriate location for the enjoyment of eschatological benefits.

Research suggests that millenarian beliefs occur among people who feel themselves to be deprived in some way. Glock's analysis of 'deprivation' helps to set this issue in perspective. Glock argues convincingly that economic factors form only one aspect of deprivation. We do not know whether this prophetic circle were poor in the sense of being economically impoverished. The fact that 2.7-11 eulogizes poverty does not of itself mean that they were poor. It would be wrong to present them simply as the underclass of Syrian society on the basis of this evidence. The *Ascension of Isaiah* displays literary flair (within the conventions of the genre), evidence of meditation on Old and New Testament literature, interpretive interest (and ability) and perhaps even genuine mystical insight. This evidence clearly indicates that the author had received a training in apocalyptic wisdom. Such proficiency suggests at least modest resources and an activity not restricted to manual labour. He *may* have had a menial occupation, but this should not be taken to imply that he was merely an illiterate peasant: R. Hillel worked as a day-labourer despite being one of the most able scripture scholars of his day.[159] Although our author may not have been wealthy, it is a superficial treatment of the issues to present him as poor just because he was a millenarian. The real answer to the question of his economic status remains largely uncertain.

The answer depends on the interpretation of 3.25. This verse comments that many had exchanged 'the garments of the saints for the robes of those who loved money'. Relativity is a useful analytical tool here. The basis of the author's criticism is the peril of personal advancement at the price of principles (in this case, the fear that many Christians would compromise with the Roman government), and not apparently a stark contrast between rich and poor. In the context of 3.21-31 'the saints' are evidently 'the prophets'. These people are distinguished from 'those who loved money', who by implication are other Christians and especially the church leaders. The phrase 'love of money' occurs twice in this section (3.25, 28). The author used it to criticize those Christians for whom prosperity had become an ambition, not just the rich of Syrian society. The church in fact probably contained very few of the latter at

---

159. See below.

3. *The Setting of the Ascension of Isaiah*

the time.[160] The author criticized their ambition because for him it represented compromise with Beliar's domain and signified an acceptance of existing standards which were destined to be set aside at the parousia. The ascetic material (2.7-11; 4.13) finds its place in this context as an indication of the lengths to which genuine disciples of the Beloved One must go in their refusal to accept the standards of an evanescent order, by accepting what was promised to be the temporary experience of marginalization.

The author's criticism of his fellow Christians therefore has a base which is broader than economic and which reflects his wider outlook on the world. The evidence suggests, but without permitting a firm conclusion, that he was a person of modest resources who had perhaps suffered financial hardship through the erosion of prophetic authority. We know from the *Didache* that wandering prophets relied on community hospitality, and it may be that settled prophets also did so. If the prophets were opposed by the leaders, and no doubt also publicly criticized by them, it is easy to see how their support could have suffered as people became less willing to resource people who were presented as opposed to the authority structures of the Christian religion. However, this is conjecture, and we know no more about how in practice the author supported himself than we know how readers as prophets functioned as members of Christian churches at the time. The conclusion that he was a person of modest but not considerable resources is perhaps a reasonable assessment of the evidence.

Other forms of deprivation may also have been pressing concerns for the author. 'Social' deprivation (the inability to enjoy the same benefits as other people) was no doubt a problem. 'Vainglory' (which means pride in position) is attributed to other Christians besides 'love of money' in 3.28. The 'respect of persons' criticized by 3.25 reveals a desire for self-improvement on the part of some which the author connected with the emergence of the ecclesiastical hierarchy. Social deprivation is revealed in the *Ascension of Isaiah* in the development of the seven-storied cosmology, which points out the false understanding of those Christians who sought personal advancement by presenting the world as Beliar's domain (esp. in 7.9-12). This confirms that our author was troubled by the success with which the ministerial orders had magnified their position and prestige.

---

160. See the examination of the New Testament material by W.A. Meeks, *The First Urban Christians* (New Haven: Yale University Press, 1983), pp. 72-73.

Although neither 'ethical' nor 'organismic' deprivation is prominent in the *Ascension of Isaiah*, 'psychic' deprivation may have been a problem too. Loss of identity would have been the natural result of conflict with other groups. Psychic deprivation is revealed by 3.21 in the comment that most Christians had deviated from the apostolic example. The erosion of prophetic authority, when combined with the other difficulties of the situation, must have created a broadly-based sense of deprivation in which readers had begun to feel substantially threatened by the changes in the church.

In terms of a psychological interpretation, then, and without wishing to be 'reductionist', I see the apocalypse as addressed to the fact that reality as experienced by the readers was proving to be painful. The reasons for that pain have been explored in this chapter, and must be sought on at least three different fronts. The apocalypse can be seen as a *response* to the pain which it describes. There are a number of stages in this response. The *Ascension of Isaiah* first of all identifies the causes of the problem. This explains the inclusion of the historical review, whose purpose was to define the current crisis by alluding to the Christian tradition that certain events must happen before the parousia. The suggestion is made in this connection that the marginalization of the prophets and the interference of the Romans had been predicted in ancient times. This was a way of limiting the difficulties through the device of predetermination. Next, the apocalypse insists that the Beloved One has already defeated Beliar and that he will soon appear to establish the millenarian kingdom. This represents an attempt to create hope by allusion to the past activity of the heavenly patron, which is in turn made a sign of his future intervention. In this context the author makes the point that salvation is a present reality by the inclusion of the Second Vision. The message of chs. 6–11 is that the Beloved One has already defeated Beliar on the cross, so that salvation can be appropriated here and now by continued trust in his victory. The 'apocalyptic' perspective of the Second Vision emphasizes this view by insisting that Beliar's subordination to the Beloved One is a reality already fully evident in the heavens. This is the 'saving knowledge' which the second half of the *Ascension of Isaiah* discloses.

One can only imagine the effect which this material would have had on the first readers of the *Ascension of Isaiah*. It is *not* at all obvious that the apocalypse would have inspired them to reckless acts of self-sacrifice. My reading of the text sees the material about prophetic

3. The Setting of the Ascension of Isaiah

withdrawal, and especially 5.13, as a warning against voluntary martyrdom, as if the author were deliberately trying to avoid this kind of self-immolation. I see the desire to preserve the prophetic office as a not insignificant factor in this caution. The position that the author adopts towards martyrdom is thus what we should call a moderate one in which the promise of the millenarian kingdom and *subsequent* immortality is used to restrain those who sought immortality through martyrdom.

The apocalypse would certainly have encouraged its readers through its insistence that the parousia was near. There is a noticeable shift between 4.13 and 4.14, which makes the point that, if dispersion happens, it will last for only a predetermined time. Readers were thereby assured that, even if persecution came and they were dispersed, they would soon gather together under the presidency of the messiah to witness the punishment of those who had oppressed them. The most obvious interpretation of this material is that readers were advised to accept the current situation, rather than to resist it or to make a spectacle of themselves during it, under the belief that it would soon be transformed by the intervention of God.

Worsley and Barkun think that millenarian feelings most often occur among rural communities. This is because such communities lack the resources of the conurbation to survive disaster. Were the author and his friends country people? We cannot make a firm judgment on this issue either. The author's interest in the agrarian lifestyle looks like the extolling of an ideal, as if retreat from society were encouraged given the situation with the Romans; but we cannot conclude from this material that they were actually country-dwellers. On my view 2.7-11, 4.13 and 5.13 advocate a prudent distance from the Romans and so do not necessarily tell us anything about the *present* status of the prophets. One might even be inclined to suppose that the author and his friends were connected with major centres like Antioch given the fact that they had experienced repression from the leaders (3.31). I find much sympathy with Hall's model of the readers as a prophetic circle who gathered periodically to sustain the authority and prestige of their office. Most of the details of their identity, however, remain speculative and we must work with ambiguous evidence.

This study of the *Ascension of Isaiah* shows that wider research in millenarianism can illuminate the social character of early Christianity by identifying the factors of social change and relative deprivation as analytically important. It also confirms that care must be taken not to allow these generalities to displace the need for the study of individual points of detail, both in terms of the text as a discrete unit and of the wider phenomenon of Christianity as a new religious movement in the ancient world. Both aspects are important and contribute to the exegesis of the apocalypse. Further research in this area will doubtless produce an approach to second-century Christianity in which historical, sociological and psychological insights are blended to yield a fruitful union of ideas. This could in turn profitably reflect on the study of the *Ascension of Isaiah*, in which readers' experience of the decline of prophecy and their fear of persecution are significant factors.

The Social Function of the Second Vision

Now we must consider the social function of the Second Vision. Chapters 6–11 have a self-contained character in the apocalypse. They differ from the First Vision in that they lack any substantial expression of the parousia hope to match the material in 4.14-18. In the second half of the apocalypse the author looks back to what the Beloved One had already achieved rather than forward to the destruction of Beliar.

This difference between the Visions must not be overplayed. The apocalypse cannot easily be dissected into 'earlier documents'. The work was written as a whole and it addresses the same situation throughout. The Second Vision agrees with the First Vision in anticipating the heavenly immortality of the righteous, which is the distinctive feature of the *Ascension of Isaiah*'s eschatology (cf. 4.17). Nevertheless, it *is* true to say that in the Second Vision the parousia hope is by no means so prominent as in the first half of the apocalypse. The most obvious interpretation of this evidence is that a different point is being made in chs. 6–11.

My reading of the Second Vision takes the view that it offers an apocalyptic disclosure of the Beloved One's victory over Beliar, which he achieved on the cross. This constitutes a form of 'saving knowledge' through which readers were encouraged to view their situation in a different light. I may briefly repeat the substance of my argument here. The description of Isaiah's ascension involves the construction of a mythological drama which posits a cosmological problem (Beliar's arrogance) and an explanation of how this problem was redressed by God. 7.9-12 outlines the problem. It describes Beliar's striving with his

3. The Setting of the Ascension of Isaiah

angels in the firmament and identifies a correspondence between angelic and human behaviour in this respect. This relates to the situation outlined in the First Vision in which the Romans are harassing the Christians and in which social alienation is a prominent theme. The Beloved One's descent is named as the remedy for the problem established in this way (7.12).

The description of the Beloved One's commission in ch. 10 explains how the victory over Beliar is achieved and the problem rectified. There, God tells his subordinate:

> Go out and descend through all the heavens...Judge and destroy the princes and the angels and the gods of that world, and the world which is ruled by them, for they have denied me and said, 'We alone are, and there is no one besides us.' And *afterwards* you shall ascend from the gods of death to your place, and you shall not be transformed in each of the heavens, but in glory you shall ascend and sit at my right hand, *and then the princes and the powers of that world shall worship you* (10.8, 12-16).

This passage makes the point that the 'judgment and destruction' of the angels will be achieved in the descent. Although the thought is elliptical, the word 'afterwards' in 10.14 has allowed me to construct a theory about when in the Beloved One's career this judgment of Beliar happens. The author implies that it takes place before the 'ascension from gods of death', which is clearly a reference to the resurrection. This must mean that the decisive moment is the crucifixion. The Second Vision discloses the fact that the victory of the cross has made heavenly immortality possible for the readers. The author was influenced in this by an interpretation of Col. 2.15 which he set within his cosmological framework and presented in the context of an apocalyptic revelation.

The Second Vision was written to change readers' response to their situation of marginalization and persecution. It did this by insisting that the Beloved One had already destroyed Beliar and by reminding the faithful of the heavenly immortality which awaited them after the millenarian kingdom. This triumphalist façade does nothing to conceal the situation of crisis to which the *Ascension of Isaiah* was addressed. The setting of the Second Vision, like that of the First, was among a readership who needed to be reminded about Beliar's defeat precisely because the demon was able to exercise power in their world. The fact that the author offered a theoretical demonstration of Beliar's downfall is an indication of Rome's considerable power.

The Second Vision gains its effect by adopting a 'utopian' perspective. Utopianism is an expression of hope which deals with imperfections in society by prescribing a model for change. Utopian writings are often stories (as the Second Vision is).[161] Their recurrent fictional character has led some commentators to conclude that utopia is, precisely, imaginative fiction.[162] But any definition must be wider than this. The essence of utopianism lies in its attempt to identify the imperfections of society in order that they can be overcome.[163] Once again Mannheim offers a helpful definition of the subject:

> Only those orientations transcending reality will be referred to by us as utopian which, when they pass over into conduct, tend to shatter, either partially or wholly, the order of things prevailing at the time.[164]

This definition emphasizes the transformative effect which dreams about a perfect society can exercise on a social order. Utopia is an imaginative construct which helps people to change their lives by altering their perceptions of reality. This, of course, can be combined with a variety of hopes about the future and it does not necessarily imply that reality itself can easily be changed. The *transformative potential* of utopianism is the crucial thing. This operates on the level of the human imagination, where it supplies the vision which enables a change in perception to emerge.

I have called the Second Vision 'utopian' because it supplies information which the author intended to exercise just such a transformation on readers' perceptions of their situation. His mythological drama stood in marked and deliberate contrast to reality. It presented Rome in what the author thought were its true colours as a blasphemous world power. It used this knowledge to demonstrate the value of belief in the Beloved One and to justify the perseverance which the author recommended. The demonstration that the Beloved One had defeated Beliar warned against the dangers of submitting to Beliar's minions, whose true nature was revealed by the cosmology. In this sense the two Visions offer complementary perspectives on the situation addressed. The parousia

---

161. This point is made by K. Kumar in his *Utopianism* (Milton Keynes: Open University Press, 1991), pp. 20-42.

162. See for example G. Negley and J.M. Patrick, *The Quest for Utopia: An Anthology of Imaginary Societies* (New York, 1952), p. 3; cf. M.L. Berneri, *Journey through Utopia* (London: Freedom Press, 1982).

163. This theme is examined by J. Passmore, *The Perfectibility of Man* (London: Gerald Duckworth, 1972).

164. *Ideology*, p. 173.

3. *The Setting of the Ascension of Isaiah* 267

hope is not set aside in the Second Vision. It rather sets the agenda to which the utopianism of chs. 6–11 is addressed. The Second Vision encourages readers to persevere until the parousia by reminding them that the decisive victory over Beliar has *already* been secured on the cross.

We should especially note the 'apocalyptic' force of the Second Vision. This material gains its impact through the construction of a mythological drama which discloses the *true meaning* of Beliar's descent from the firmament. In its first appearance (ch. 4) the motif of the demon's descent represents a heightening of tension for the Christians. The Second Vision offers a different perspective on the crisis by showing that it was really the final grasp at power by a demon who had been unmasked in the heavens despite what might appear from his power on earth. Beliar's true status as an insubordinate demon is presented in chs. 6–11 as an item of 'revealed knowledge' which only the readers could know. The progress of thought in the apocalypse deliberately emphasizes the value of this revealed knowledge as the author corrects a false perspective by introducing a new one.

The question arises of whether chs. 6–11 represent a different eschatology from that of chs. 1–5. The absence of millenarian hopes is a striking feature of the Second Vision, but I have concluded from the fact that the millenarian section is set first (4.14-18) that it supplies an eschatological programme for the whole apocalypse. On the other hand, it is true to say that the author was indeed *qualifying* a millenarian eschatology in the apocalypse. The Second Vision is a more detailed assertion that heavenly immortality was the final destiny of the righteous (see esp. ch. 9), which picks up the thought of 4.17, in which heavenly ascension is also anticipated. I conclude that 4.17 links the eschatology of the First Vision to that of the Second and that both Visions have a consistent eschatological outlook despite the differences between them.

The demonstration that the eschatology of the *Ascension of Isaiah* is not restricted to millenarianism does much to explain the popularity of the *Ascension of Isaiah* in later Christianity (especially in the form represented by L2 and S, from which the First Vision was omitted). The apocalypse contains the answer to the question of what could replace the millenarian basis of Christianity when this became redundant. This involved the creation of a more theoretical understanding in which Christ's death and enthronement were made items of doctrine. It was doctrine of this kind which appealed to later readers when millenarianism was recognized as superseded. The *Ascension of Isaiah* occupies an important place in the history of Christian thought through its eschatology, which its neglect in scholarship by no means adequately reflects.

Summary and Conclusions

My interpretation of the *Ascension of Isaiah* presents the apocalypse as the response to the fear of Roman investigation by a group of Christian prophets in the early second century CE. The apocalypse defines and limits this situation and offers assurance that readers will survive it. I have shown that the text is an important one for a number of issues, not least for the history of Christian persecution by the Romans and for the demise of prophecy in early Christianity.

I want in conclusion to tie up some 'loose ends' in this chapter. The first is the question of the author's relations with Judaism, on which I touched at the beginning. The text's vocabulary and ideas show that this person was heavily influenced by Judaism. Indeed, the repeated title 'Beloved One', which is used with a far greater frequency than in other Christian literature, suggests a desire to retain Jewish forms of thought at a time when Christianity was accommodating itself to a Graeco-Roman environment. Yet this author seems more critical of Judaism than other writers of his time. This is particularly obvious in his hostility towards the interpreters of Moses.

I have argued that the author's repudiation of Moses reveals a conflict with Jewish teachers about the norms of authority and the validity of the Christian revelation. I want now to consider the possibility that he had a connection with the Jewish scribal tradition and that this putative connection forms an important part of the background of the *Ascension of Isaiah*. His acceptance of the Prophets and Writings suggests a continuing regard for the Hebrew Bible once the question of authority had been redefined. His exegetical interest is obvious (and extends to the New Testament literature). It is hardly a new suggestion to link early Christian literature with scribal schools: Stendahl did this years ago in the case of Matthew.[165] I think that a similar background explains several features of the *Ascension of Isaiah*.

The scribes became significant figures in Judaism after 70 CE.[166] They

---

165. K. Stendahl, *The School of St. Matthew* (Lund: Gleerup, 2nd edn, 1967), pp. 20ff.

166. Such functions are well explained by J. Jeremias in his *Jerusalem in the*

3. *The Setting of the Ascension of Isaiah* 269

were the unpaid scholars and lawyers of the time; interpreters of the Scriptures and judges in legal cases.[167] Several strands of evidence suggest that our author can be seen in analogous terms. The most obvious is the work's interest in exegesis. *Asc. Isa.* 3.8-10 evidently draws on an existing scriptural comparison.[168] This author differed from his Jewish counterparts in criticizing Moses and by giving the rest of the Hebrew Bible a christological interpretation. Furthermore, his use of the Isaiah story reveals an interest in haggadah. This was another major scribal function. In this context we should note the reference to 'wisdom' and the suggested lack of it by many Christians in 3.23. 'Wisdom' in postbiblical Judaism was a quality associated with the scribes and a term used to describe their teaching.[169]

The references to the circle's (anticipated?) poverty or deprivation in 2.7-11 and 3.21-31 may be significant too (with due interpretive caution). Although a few scribes were relatively prosperous, others were poor. The young Hillel is an example of this.[170] Although our author was neither a peasant nor a destitute, the reference to 'the robes of the saints' in 3.25 (which implies a poor form of dress) could be taken to imply that he and his friends devoted their time to scriptural study rather than to more lucrative activity. *If* the author was a wandering prophet he may frequently have experienced hardship (keeping in mind all the caution noted above). This person's empathy for a tradition of poverty, combined with his interest in scriptural exegesis, suggests that he lived a manner of life not dissimilar to that of the scribes.

The reference to Isaiah 'laying his hand' (6.5) on the junior prophets also suits a scribal background. Scribes had to be ordained before they could practice or pass legal judgments.[171] The fact that there were not thought to be many true prophets (3.27), and the restrictions which are

---

Time of Jesus (ET London: SCM Press, 1969), pp. 111-15, 233-45. There is further material in E. Schürer, *The History of the Jewish People in the Age of Jesus Christ* (rev. G. Vermes *et al.*; 3 vols.; Edinburgh: T. & T. Clark, 1983–), II, pp. 314-80.

167. So Jeremias, *Jerusalem*, p. 236; Schürer, *History*, II, pp. 330-35.
168. See above.
169. See U. Wilckens, 'σοφία κτλ', in *TDNT*, VII, pp. 505-507.
170. The Mishnah and Talmud forbid scribes to receive payment. Hillel was a day-labourer (see *b. Yom.* 35b). Some scribes, though, were undoubtedly spongers—see *b. Soṭ.* 22b; Mk 12.40; *Ass. Mos.* 7.6. There is a parallel in this with the wandering prophets criticized by *Did.* 11. On this question see Jeremias, *Jerusalem*, pp. 111-17.
171. See *b. Soṭ.* 22b and Jeremias, *Jerusalem*, pp. 235-366.

placed on the reading of the apocalypse (6.17; 11.39), imply that the work came from a situation in which different teachers or schools were competing for attention.[172] The practice of ordination in the author's circle ensured that the exegesis and mysticism undertaken by junior members conformed with its philosophy and that unhelpful opinions were excluded. It also preserved the solidarity of the prophetic office at a time when this was dying out in the church.

Another argument carries considerable weight in this connection. The most important scribal function was that of guarding the esoteric tradition in Judaism.[173] The often-quoted passage *m. Ḥag.* 2.1 shows something of the apocalyptic interest in postbiblical times:

> Whoever gives his mind to four things, it were better for him if he had not come into the world—what is above? what is beneath? what was beforetime? and what will be hereafter?

This looks at first sight like a general prohibition on mystical enquiry. Evidence from the early Common Era, however, shows that well-known rabbis such as Akiba and Johanan ben Zakkai let their minds wander into precisely these areas, as if *m. Ḥag.* 2.1 should be understood as the restriction of esoteric speculation to those who were judged competent to engage in it.[174] A mystical interest stands at the heart of the *Ascension of Isaiah*. The author comments on what is above (the seven heavens, God, the Beloved One, the angels and Beliar), what is beneath (Sheol), what has happened in the past (Beliar's rebellion, Nero's persecution, the Beloved One's passion) and what will happen in the future (the parousia and acquisition of heavenly immortality). *Asc. Isa.* 6.17 recognizes that these are sensitive areas for, it is a passage in which all but the approved are excluded from the courtroom; 11.39 adds that the contents of the work are not intended for the people of Israel. The *Ascension of Isaiah* thereby conforms to the scribal practice of revealing esoteric matters only to the proficient.

These arguments do not *prove* that the author had a connection with the scribal tradition but they suggest that he may have done. His circle's combination of scriptural interpretation and mystical experience shows that their interests coincided with what some of the rabbis were doing in

---

172. See also Hall, 'The Ascension of Isaiah'.
173. This is noted by Jeremias, *Jerusalem*, pp. 237-42.
174. See the description of such activity in Rowland, *Open Heaven*, pp. 271-348.

the period between the two Jewish Revolts. I think that the model of a Christian academy, which parallels the schools which have been suggested for Matthew and John, is an appropriate one for explaining the origin of this apocalypse. It would certainly account for the author's interest in scriptural exegesis. The model also gives further definition to what is meant by calling the author's circle 'prophets'. Such an academy, if that is what it was, had a strong mystical and apocalyptic interest. This was the context in which some of the earliest documented use of the New Testament literature took place (not to mention exegesis of the Hebrew Scriptures). The circle may have contained converted rabbis, as Matthew's probably did. These people possibly continued to see themselves as members of the guild and to engage in dialogue with their Jewish counterparts in which christological interpretation of the Scriptures (like that found in *Asc. Isa.* 4.21-22) played a major part. Justin Martyr's *Dialogue with Trypho* is a later example of the arguments which were exchanged in such debate. In future discussion of this circle's identity, care must be taken to balance their interest in interpretation with their desire to achieve a more direct form of revelation from the heavenly world than exegesis could provide. These two elements stood at the heart of their prophetic self-consciousness.

Another way of probing this circle's identity is to compare them, however provisionally, with the sectarians who were opposed by the church fathers. The term 'sect' denotes a group of people who stand their distance from mainstream beliefs, a distance which they maintain through the use of ideological defences.[175] We do not what happened to readers after the *Ascension of Isaiah* was written. *Asc. Isa.* 3.21-31 suggests that they were still in contact with the mainstream church at the time of writing. It does however seem that all the conditions necessary for the subsequent formation of a sect had been created by this time even if sectarianism had not yet emerged. The text's thoroughgoing dualism, its sense of distance from other groups and rejection of

---

175. 'Sect' is thus a neutral term without the pejorative overtones found in popular speech. This point is made by B.R. Wilson, *The Social Dimensions of Sectarianism* (Oxford: Clarendon Press, 1990), p. 2. Other studies of sectarianism include E. Troeltsch, *The Social Teaching of the Christian Church* (2 vols.; ET London: George Allen & Unwin, 1931); P.L. Berger, 'The Sociological Study of Sectarianism', *Social Research* 21 (1954), pp. 467-87; and B. Johnson, 'A Critical Appraisal of the Church-Sect Typology', *American Sociological Review* 22 (1957), pp. 88-92.

compromise with 'the world' are all typical of sectarian groups. The research of Klijn and Reininck has shown that the second-century groups were not necessarily populated by people with eccentric doctrines. Social as well as doctrinal reasons must be considered for the formation of fringe groups. The emergence of institutional leadership in the second century had the effect of marginalizing certain people such as the prophets, as the *Ascension of Isaiah* makes clear. The model of 'the sect' is one possible way of explaining what happened to the author's circle in the period after the apocalypse was written. We have, of course, no sure knowledge in this area and I stop short of saying that they became sectarians of whatever persuasion (despite noting Pétrement's conclusion that they were Simonians). If they did not become sectarians they must have been subsumed in the mainstream church as the prophets died out.

I now turn to the question of the work's pseudonymous setting. There was a strong tradition of pseudepigraphy in apocalyptic literature.[176] The book of Revelation boldly departs from this convention and proclaims its author's identity as John the seer of Patmos (Hermas also lacks any pseudonymity). The *Ascension of Isaiah* retains the traditional pseudonymity, unusually perhaps in Christian literature. This was partly due to the author's desire to explain that the troubles facing readers had been predicted in ancient times so that the situation could be shown to fall within the divine plan. Hall explains the choice of Isaiah as patron for this apocalypse by observing that he had led a prophetic school (Isa. 8.16), had seen God (Isa. 6.1-4) and the Beloved (Isa. 9, 11), and had been persecuted by a rival prophetic group (the Jewish martyrdom story).[177] Isaiah's mystical prowess doubtless contributed to his selection but the prophet's social criticism must be mentioned too. Isa. 1.10 (the comparison of the Jerusalem leaders with Sodom and Gomorrah) is alluded to by *Asc. Isa.* 3.10: the apocalypse expresses discontent with those in authority which echoes the biblical Isaiah. The circle's psychology of mysticism is another possible reason for the choice (although I am not proposing a return to Wheeler Robinson's theory of 'corporate

---

176. See Russell, *Method*, pp. 127-39; J. Sint, *Pseudonymität im Altertum* (Innsbruck: Universitätsverlag Wagner, 1960); and N. Brox, *Pseudepigraphie in der heidnischen und jüdisch-christlichen Antike* (Darmstadt: Wissenschaftliche Buchgesellschaft, 1977).

177. Hall, 'The Ascension of Isaiah', p. 298.

3. The Setting of the Ascension of Isaiah

personality'[178]). Given the dangers involved in the practice of heavenly ascension it may have been felt appropriate to claim the patronage of a prophet who was known to have seen God as a way of circumventing the dangers (such as the angel opponent in 9.1) which threatened the heavenly traveller. And, given that this author interpreted the Hebrew Bible christologically (4.21-22), it probably seemed natural to issue an apocalypse in the name of a well-known prophet (cf. 2.7-11) whose book contained many significant passages. More than one reason, then, should be considered for the pseudonymous setting: but the need to find reassurance under difficulty and the willingness to stand up for religious beliefs were prominent among them.

Finally, I want to note that the 'utopian' nature of *Ascension of Isaiah* 6–11 offers an important insight into one of the likely purposes of apocalyptic literature. 'Apocalyptic' as a concept has all too often been held to be synonymous with 'eschatology'. Although the canonical apocalypses are dominated by eschatology, the equation of 'apocalyptic' with 'eschatology' runs the risk of ignoring substantial non-eschatological sections in other apocalypses which suggest that any definition of the phenomenon must be more broadly based.[179] The *Ascension of Isaiah* confirms that part of its author's purpose was to gain knowledge about the heavenly world in order to gain a measure of control over the way in which it impinged on people. This was bound up with limiting Beliar's power at a time of crisis. The seven-storied cosmology (again unusual in Christian literature) was an essential factor in this. The likely 'utopian' purpose of the apocalypses should not be neglected as a topic for research. In the interest in theodicy, heavenly dialogue and revelation which this literature displays may lie the desire to change the readers' response to an unpalatable situation. The application of this approach to other literature will, I think, help to develop our knowledge of apocalypticism in the early Common Era: not least in respect of the common assumption that it represents literature addressed to situations of crisis.

---

178. H.W. Robinson, 'The Hebrew Conception of Corporate Personality', in *Werden und Wesen des Alten Testaments* (BZAW, 66; Berlin: Alfred Töpelmann, 1936). This has been cogently criticized by J.W. Rogerson, 'The Hebrew Concept of Corporate Personality: A Re-Examination', *JTS* 21 (1970), pp. 1-16.

179. A point which is made by M.E. Stone, 'Lists of Revealed Things in Apocalyptic Literature', in F.M. Cross (ed.), *Magnalia Dei* (New York: Doubleday, 1976), pp. 414-52.

Chapter 4

THE *ASCENSION OF ISAIAH* AND THE NEW TESTAMENT LITERATURE

This book has presented the *Ascension of Isaiah* as a second-century apocalypse in which scriptural exegesis is an important activity. In terms of the author's outlook we must allow not only for his acknowledged exegesis of the Prophets and Writings (4.21-22) but also for his unacknowledged debt to the New Testament literature. The use to which the latter is put indicates that the New Testament documents had been recognized as authoritative at the time when the *Ascension of Isaiah* was written but that they had not yet been given the same canonical status as the Hebrew Bible. The author's debt to first-century material falls into two different categories. In the first place there are the traditions about Jesus which are found in 3.13-18 and 11.2-22. Secondly, there are a variety of references where knowledge of New Testament passages evidently helped the author to shape his material. I have already indicated some of these passages, but this matter must now be explored further in order to discover the extent of the author's debt to first-century Christianity.

Both the Visions contain sections which describe the life of Jesus (3.13-18; 11.2-22; the latter in the E text only). Previous scholarship has pondered the question of whether this material was gleaned from a knowledge of Matthew, or merely of the oral tradition on which Matthew also drew. This is a complex issue. The likelihood is that the author did know Matthew, given the date of the *Ascension of Isaiah* after the death of Ignatius, but this does not necessarily mean that Matthew was the source for the traditions about Jesus. The descriptions of the resurrection (3.16-17) and of the absent midwife (11.14a) show that the author's source in these two sections was wider than any of the canonical Gospels. It has been suggested that these traditions were derived from the 'kerygmatic summaries' which came from the oral tradition.[1] This oral tradition

1. By Bauckham, 'Worship of Jesus'.

4. The Ascension of Isaiah and the New Testament Literature

evidently still circulated in the early second century despite the availability of the written Gospels. If this is a correct deduction, the *Ascension of Isaiah* offers a brief glimpse of the kind of material which was lost when the oral tradition died out.

The author also alludes without acknowledgment to New Testament passages at various places in the apocalypse. The evidence of the *Ascension of Isaiah* must be set beside that of other early Christian sources in this respect. It illustrates the growing use of the New Testament materia which was typical of post-apostolic Christianity.

In this final chapter of the book I shall examine this author's use of first-century material. I shall start by asking what New Testament literature he can reasonably be assumed to have known. This will lead to a consideration of the origin of the Jesus traditions in the *Ascension of Isaiah*; thence briefly to the status of the author as exegete of Jewish traditions; and finally to the consideration of some passages in which the apocalypse makes an exegetical contribution to the New Testament literature.

Which New Testament Texts Did the Author Know?

I begin by considering the question of which New Testament texts the author evidently knew. My belief is that the *Ascension of Isaiah* was written between 112 and 138 CE. It is a reasonable assumption that most if not all of the New Testament literature had been written by this time. The one real uncertainty is 2 Peter whose date continues to be disputed. Käsemann dated 2 Peter to the middle of the second century, but this was done on the basis of a Gnosticizing interpretation of the letter which would not be accepted today.[2] Richard Bauckham is probably not far from the truth when he sets 2 Peter in the late first century.[3] The date of 2 Peter, however, is not a problem for this study because there is no convincing evidence that the author of the *Ascension of Isaiah* knew and used that letter.

No New Testament document, probably not even James or Jude which are also difficult to date, was written before 48 CE, the early date to which Galatians is sometimes assigned. I assume in what follows that Mark was written either before or just after the fall of Jerusalem and that

---

2. E. Käsemann, 'An Apologia for Primitive Christian Eschatology', in *Essays on New Testament Themes* (ET London: SCM Press, 1964), pp. 169-95.
3. Bauckham, *Jude, 2 Peter*, pp. 157-58.

Matthew and Luke originated in the 80s. To the 80s or 90s I assign Hebrews and Ephesians. Martin Hengel has recently argued that the Fourth Gospel reached its final form c. 100 CE. There are no good reasons for disagreeing with this assessment.[4] The Pastorals were probably written in the early second century around the time of the letters of Ignatius (c. 110 CE). The *Ascension of Isaiah* was thus written just after the youngest of the New Testament documents, but rather later than the majority of those documents.

Matthew

The author of the *Ascension of Isaiah* certainly knew material which is found in Matthew and he probably knew Matthew itself. The evidence for his knowledge of Matthew is wider than the issue of the Jesus traditions in the apocalypse. The question turns in part on the related question of whether the allusions to Matthew in Ignatius, the *Didache* and *Barnabas* can be regarded as allusions to Matthew himself or merely to Matthean tradition.[5] I cannot examine this matter in detail here except to say that there is a growing consensus of opinion that all three texts do contain allusions to Matthew's Gospel and not just to its sources. The argument that Ignatius and the *Didache* used Matthew is a cumulative one which is not dependent on a single passage in either text. It is less difficult to assume that the five probable allusions to Matthew in Ignatius (*Eph.* 17.1; *Smyrn.* 1.1; 6.1; *Pol.* 1.3; 2.2) reveal a knowledge of the Gospel itself and not merely its sources. If anyone knew Matthew in the early second century, some twenty years after it was written, then surely the bishop of Antioch did. In support of this view is the argument which has recently been developed by C.M. Tuckett against other

---

4. W.G. Kümmel, *Introduction to the New Testament* (ET London: SCM Press, 1975), p. 246, says that: 'The assumption that Jn was written probably in the last decade of the first century is today almost universally accepted.' Hengel adds: 'The Johannine corpus was hardly edited later than shortly after 100 and surely not very much earlier' (*Johannine Question*, p. 25).

5. On this problem see E. Massaux, *L'Influence de l'Évangile de Saint Matthieu sur la littérature chrétienne avant Saint Irénée* (Louvain: Gembloux, 1950). Massaux examines the *Ascension of Isaiah* on pp. 196-99. He concludes that the author probably knew the Gospel but that his knowledge was amplified by the use of apocryphal traditions about Jesus. The question of Early Christian knowledge of Matthew is examined further by W.-D. Köhler, *Die Rezeption des Matthäusevangeliums in der Zeit vor Irenäus* (WUNT, 24; Tübingen: Mohr, 1987).

4. *The Ascension of Isaiah and the New Testament Literature*

scholars that the Matthean allusions in the *Didache* reveal a knowledge of Matthew's Gospel.[6] This wider evidence lends a general probability to the argument that the author of the *Ascension of Isaiah* also knew Matthew. The consensus is now against dating Matthew later than 90 CE (and some would date it earlier than this). The burden of proof must therefore rest with those who *deny* that copies of Matthew were circulating in the early second century. That case must be regarded as a weak one.

The case for supposing that the author of the *Ascension of Isaiah* knew Matthew is stronger than attributing such a knowledge to Ignatius. Ignatius alluded to traditions about Jesus which can with reasonable probability be assumed to derive from Matthew. The *Ascension of Isaiah* uses material which was reported *only* by Matthew (for instance, the infancy narrative; the reference to the guard at the tomb [Mt. 27.62-66]; the allusion to Mt. 28.19 in *Asc. Isa.* 3.18). Evidence drawn from outside the Jesus traditions in the *Ascension of Isaiah* confirms that the author knew Matthew's Gospel and not just Matthew's sources.

Matthean influence is evident in ch. 5, where the story of Isaiah's martyrdom alludes to two incidents in the life of Jesus. Belchira's offer to Isaiah in *Asc. Isa.* 5.8 resembles the devil's words to Jesus in Mt. 4.8-10 (cf. Lk. 4.5-8): 'Say what I say to you, and I will turn their heart and make Manasseh, and the princes of Judah, and all Jerusalem worship you.' This allusion presupposes that the temptation narrative was sufficiently well known in the second century to be parodied in this way. *Asc. Isa.* 5.13b then records Isaiah's statement that 'for me alone the LORD has mixed the cup'. This looks back to more than one incident in the Gospels but notably to the Gethsemane story (Mt. 26.39) which records Jesus' prayer for the removal of the cup (of suffering) before his passion. References to the cup occur also in Jesus' dialogue with certain disciples in Mt. 20.22-23, where it is said that sharing the cup will lead to death. *Asc. Isa.* 5.8 reflects this cycle of material and makes Isaiah echo the words of Jesus to emphasize that the prophet's death was for Christian faith. Matthew must be regarded as the most likely source for this information, but this does not preclude the author's knowledge of the other Gospels.

---

6. 'Synoptic Tradition in the Didache', in J.-M. Sevrin (ed.), *The New Testament in Early Christianity* (Leuven: Leuven University Press, 1989), pp. 197-230. Tuckett thinks that the author of the *Didache* knew Luke as well.

Two further references support the assertion that the author of the *Ascension of Isaiah* knew Matthew. *Asc. Isa.* 1.7 (a trinitarian juristic formula) has the words 'as the Spirit which speaks in me lives'. This seems modelled on Mt. 10.20, the promise that the Spirit would speak through the disciples when they were brought to trial for the sake of Jesus. *Asc. Isa.* 9.17 states that 'many of the righteous will ascend with him'. This is similar in some respects to the strange passage about the resurrection of the saints which is found in Mt. 27.51-53 (and quite dissimilar to anything else in the New Testament). It includes those who had died before the death of Jesus within the salvation that he had secured.

A working conclusion can be drawn from this information. The date of the *Ascension of Isaiah*, combined with the internal and external evidence presented here, is a good indication that the author of the *Ascension of Isaiah* did know Matthew's Gospel. The two allusions in ch. 5 are indicative of this. They come from such different parts of Matthew that we must conclude that, if the author knew only Matthean traditions, these must have been in a form so close to Matthew itself as to make the distinction almost redundant. The author of the *Ascension of Isaiah*, in company with the *Didache* and Ignatius, is among the earliest Christian writers to use Matthew in this way.

Mark, Luke and Acts

The question of Markan influence on the *Ascension of Isaiah* is difficult to decide since, according to the generally-accepted resolution of the Synoptic Problem, Matthew incorporated large parts of Mark.[7] This makes it difficult to decide which of the two Gospels the author knew where there is an overlap between them. Mark's alleged Roman origin, however, combined with the observation that there is little in Mark which is not found in Matthew, makes it unnecessary to suppose the author's detailed knowledge of Mark; but this is not to state conclusively that he did not know Mark. It is worth observing that the phrase 'before the sabbath' in *Asc. Isa.* 3.13 is paralleled exactly in the New Testament only by Mk 15.42, although there is a near parallel in Jn 19.31. That phrase probably derived from a summary of the life of Jesus distinct from any

---

7. An article by G.M. Styler provides convincing reasons for holding Markan priority: 'The Priority of Mark', in C.F.D. Moule, *The Birth of the New Testament* (London: A. & C. Black, 1981), pp. 285-316.

4. *The Ascension of Isaiah and the New Testament Literature* 279

of the Gospels, so that Markan influence should not definitively be assumed at this point.

At one point in the *Ascension of Isaiah* we find a clear allusion to Lukan tradition. *Asc. Isa.* 4.16 says in its description of the millenarian kingdom that 'the LORD...will serve those who have kept watch in this world'. This is an allusion to Lk. 12.37b, from the parable of the Watching Servants, which states that 'he will come and serve them' (a saying for which there is no Matthean parallel). Two issues must be considered when evaluating this allusion. These are the date of the two documents and the likelihood that Lk. 12.37b itself had a history in pre-Lukan tradition.[8] Bauckham believes that the author of the *Ascension of Isaiah* knew only the *pre*-Lukan stage of the material.[9] He argues that *Asc. Isa.* 4.13 dates the apocalypse to a period when some of the original eyewitnesses of Jesus were still alive (and thus presumably to the first century).[10] My date for the *Ascension of Isaiah* (not before 112 CE) demands a different interpretation of 4.13 which makes the author's knowledge of Luke intrinsically more likely; but I take the point that 4.13 *could* have derived from a source other than the text of the Gospel. The probability of this, however, recedes the further that we set the *Ascension of Isaiah* into the second century. Why then should the author have used only Lukan tradition when the Gospel itself was available? It remains possible, I am sure, that *Asc. Isa.* 4.16 was modelled on Lk. 12.37b itself, even if we cannot be certain about this. This makes me less confident than Bauckham in his conclusion that 'it is most unlikely that the author knew the Gospel of Luke'.[11]

Some further passages in the *Ascension of Isaiah* arguably betray the influence either of Acts or at least of Lukan tradition. The description of Isaiah's martyrdom in ch. 5 contains the statement that 'his mouth spoke with the Holy Spirit until he was sawed in two' (5.14). The similarities between this account and the description of the death of Stephen in Acts 7 must be noted. Acts 7.55-56 says that at the hour of his death Stephen was filled with the Spirit and that he gazed into heaven to see God and the Son of Man. Given the likelihood of an emerging tradition of

---

8. The latter case is argued by J. Jeremias, *The Parables of Jesus* (ET London: SCM Press, 3rd edn, 1972), p. 54 n. 18: 'V. 37b is probably secondary, although pre-Lucan.'
9. 'Synoptic Parousia Parables Again', *NTS* 29 (1983), p. 130.
10. In his unpublished paper 'Gospel Traditions in the Ascension of Isaiah'.
11. 'Synoptic Parousia Parables', p. 130.

Christian martyrology (something that we see also in the *Martyrdom of Polycarp*[12]) it would have been natural for a second-century author to allude to earlier martyrdoms, particularly the death of Stephen, who was revered as the first Christian martyr. The similarities between the two passages (the martyr's possession by the Holy Spirit, his calm resolution and binitarian vision) are perhaps too great to ignore. They suggest a knowledge at least of Stephen's death as it is recorded in Acts; and possibly of the text of Acts itself.

Asc. Isa. 8.22 describes how Isaiah 'rejoiced and praised the One who has graciously given such light to those who await his promise'. The nearest New Testament analogy to this is Acts 1.4 (cf. Lk. 24.49; Acts 2.33), the command of Jesus that the disciples were to wait in Jerusalem 'for the promise of the Father' (which in that context meant the coming of the Holy Spirit). The reference in *Asc. Isa.* 8.22 is to the prophet's vision of the seventh heaven, something which 6.10-11 refers to the Spirit's activity in the case of Isaiah's ascension and 7.23 to all the righteous through the agency of the Holy Spirit. It is possible again that knowledge of the Spirit's role in Acts determined the choice of language in this passage.

The reference to the 'signs and miracles' performed by the adult Jesus in *Asc. Isa.* 11.18 (cf. the use of the same phrase about the apostles in *Asc. Isa.* 3.20) also has parallels in Acts. We have no Greek text of *Asc. Isa.* 11.18, but the Greek version of 3.20 indicates that the phrase σημεῖα καὶ τέρατα stood in the lost original. While 'signs and wonders' is a standard Old Testament phrase, which is used especially in connection with the Exodus tradition,[13] it is used some ten times in Acts, much more frequently than in other New Testament literature.[14] Indeed, of the 11 uses of τέρατα in the Greek New Testament all but three are in Luke–Acts. The distinctively Lukan colour of the phrase 'signs and wonders' must be acknowledged and reflects that author's predilection for Septuagintalisms. This suggests that *Asc. Isa.* 11.18 is, once again, an

---

12. The report of Polycarp's death contains a number of New Testament allusions. See the footnotes mentioning these in Stevenson, *New Eusebius*, pp. 18-24.

13. See for example Exod. 7.3; Deut. 4.34; 26.8; Ps. 78.43.

14. Acts 2.19, 22, 43; 4.30; 5.12; 6.8 (of Stephen); 7.36; 8.13 (signs and great miracles); 14.3 and 15.12. Paul uses the phrase in 2 Thess. 2.9; 2 Cor. 12.12 and Rom. 15.19; and John, for whom 'sign' is a technical term for 'miracle', uses the composite 'signs and wonders' only in 4.48.

allusion especially to Lukan material (although the phrase 'in the land of Israel' in this reference may have been culled from Mt. 2.20-21).

This argument from Acts is strengthened by three suggested contacts with Luke's Gospel. My exegesis of *Ascension of Isaiah* 4 accepted that two sources are fused together in the early verses of that chapter. These are Nero's identification with Beliar (which is found also in the *Sibylline Oracles*) and the myth of Beliar's descent from the firmament. I interpreted this second strand in terms of the limitation of the demon's power suggested by Lk. 10.18 and Rev. 12.7-9. It is significant that references to Satan's fall from heaven should occur *only* in Luke in the Gospel tradition. Although the presence of this idea in a text so unrelated to Luke as Revelation shows that it circulated widely, the parallel again raises the question of whether the author knew Luke (which I think is heightened by the difficulty of proving that he knew Revelation[15]). This question is raised again by the use of 'Elect One' as a title for the Beloved One in *Asc. Isa.* 8.7. This occurs in the New Testament only in Luke's Gospel (9.35; 23.35). Finally, Luke alone of the Synoptists (in their original form) records an ascension narrative (but cf. Mk 16.19). Luke does this twice, at the ending of the Gospel (24.50-52) and at the beginning of Acts (1.10-11). Although reflection about the ascension is found in earlier literature (notably 1 Pet. 3.22), on which the author of the *Ascension of Isaiah* evidently drew, the correspondence *only* with Luke in the Gospel tradition must again be noted. At the very least we must conclude that the material on which 3.18 and 11.22 were based held material in common with Luke.

I do not regard any of this material as *proof* that the author of the *Ascension of Isaiah* knew Luke but I do think that it has a certain cumulative significance. As I said, I regard this case as more open than Bauckham allows. The date of the *Ascension of Isaiah* in the early second century makes it intrinsically likely that the author knew the Synoptic Gospels. My research reveals a descending scale of probability in this as we move from Matthew through Luke to Mark.

John

The possibility that the author of the *Ascension of Isaiah* knew John is an intriguing one. Of all the Gospels, John comes closest to the *Ascension of Isaiah* in terms of its Christology. The Evangelist presents the Son of

---

15. On this point see further below.

Man as a descending-ascending mediator who became associated with Jesus (see Jn 3.13; 6.62). The similarities between the two texts must not be exaggerated. The allusions to the mediator's descent and ascent occur in some of the Johannine discourses but they do not provide an overall framework for Johannine Christology.[16] The *Ascension of Isaiah* by contrast allows the hidden descent to determine everything that is said about Jesus and it includes what I have called (in dialogue with Käsemann) a 'naïve docetism' which goes beyond anything that is found in the Fourth Gospel. The inclusion of references to heavenly descent and ascent is thus a common element in the two strands of literature, but the way in which those references are used is quite different.

The existence of tradition held in common between the texts nevertheless demands an explanation. *Asc. Isa.* 3.13 states that the Beloved One descended from heaven and transformed himself into human likeness. This is similar to the notion of the Son of Man's descent from heaven (Jn 3.13) (but the apocalypse has a seven-storied cosmology which is alien to John and the Gospel never uses the phrase 'transformation into human likeness' to describe the human Jesus). The statement of *Asc. Isa.* 3.18 that the Beloved One's ascension involved his return 'to the seventh heaven *from where he came*' is similar to the question posed by the Johannine Jesus in 6.62, 'Then what if you were to see the Son of Man ascending *where he was before*?', although not a precise verbal echo. The statement that Jesus died 'before the sabbath' (*Asc. Isa.* 3.13) can be paralleled in Jn 19.31. Jn 12.41 offers evidence for a binitarian interpretation of Isa. 6.1-4 which includes the pre-existent Christ within Isaiah's call-vision. The *Ascension of Isaiah* is apparently the earliest Christian source to interpret this passage from Isaiah in a Trinitarian sense.

The Second Vision offers further evidence of contact with John. *Asc. Isa.* 11.14b says: 'And they were all blinded concerning him; *they all knew* about him, but *they did not know* from where he was.' This passage should be compared with the statement of the Jerusalemites about Jesus in Jn 7.27: 'Yet *we know* where this man comes from; and when the Christ appears, *no one will know where he comes from.*' The two passages hold in common the statement that people *thought* that they

---

16. This point was recognized by R. Bultmann who showed that the picture of Jesus as descending and ascending constitutes a *puzzle* within the Gospel ('Die Bedeutung der neuerschlossenen mandäischen und manichäischen Quellen für das Verständnis des Johannesevangeliums', *ZNW* 24 [1925], p. 102).

4. *The Ascension of Isaiah and the New Testament Literature* 283

knew where Jesus came from and the fact that they failed to recognize his true origin in the heavenly world.[17] This very 'Johannine' touch in the *Ascension of Isaiah* poses acutely the question of the relation between the two texts.

The question must be asked whether this evidence signifies use of common tradition by the two authors or rather use of the Gospel by the author of the apocalypse. The date of the *Ascension of Isaiah* is again an important factor in this assessment. The apocalypse is at least a decade younger than John and it may be even younger than this. The venerability of John the Elder as an aged and prestigious member of the first Christian generation meant that his Gospel would have quickly acquired importance as the 'testimony' of a significant figure. We know that this happened from the evidence of the early manuscript tradition. The Rylands papyrus confirms that copies of John were circulating before the middle of the second century.[18] Papias's list of disciples (which was written between 125 and 135 CE and which is a near literary contemporary of the *Ascension of Isaiah*) also displays a knowledge of parts of John.[19]

This leads me to suggest that the author of the *Ascension of Isaiah* knew (at least a form of) John. I regard the case for his knowledge of John as analogous to that of Papias, who clearly knew at least part of the Gospel. It seems probable, given our author's knowledge of the other Gospels, that the contact with John 7 in *Asc. Isa.* 11.14b demonstrates literary allusion rather than merely use of common tradition. 11.14b seems out of place in the Jesus traditions since it supports the myth of the heavenly descent which is otherwise absent from the incorporated material about Jesus. The author has evidently inserted it from a source, and John's Gospel is a strong candidate for consideration in this respect.

---

17. *Ign. Eph.* 19 knows the tradition that Mary's virginity was hidden but significantly not that of the hidden descent. Hengel observes that Ignatius's debt to John is not one of literary dependence (*Johannine Question*, p. 15). I want to raise the question of whether this distinguishes him from the *Ascension of Isaiah*.

18. See further C.H. Roberts, *Manuscript, Society and Belief in Early Christian Egypt* (London: British Academy, 1979), pp. 12-13, 61; and K. Aland, 'Der Text des Johannes-Evangelium im 2. Jahrhundert', in W. Schrage (ed.), *Studien zum Text und zur Ethik des Neuen Testaments: Festschrift zum 80. Geburtstag von Heinrich Greeven* (*BZNW*, 47; Berlin: de Gruyter, 1986), pp. 1-10.

19. See further Hengel, *Johannine Question*, pp. 16-23. Hengel concludes that Papias's list is 'late-Johannine' and that it is 'based on the first and last chapters of the Fourth Gospel' (p. 21).

This conclusion, if it is accepted, means that the author of the *Ascension of Isaiah* ranks with Papias among the earliest documented students of John. It is interesting to observe that this contact with John should be with a christological passage in which the messiah's heavenly origin is made a cause for comment. This confirms the point which I have made that the author regarded New Testament Christology as an important topic for development, and that he was interested particularly in passages which described the messiah's heavenly origin.

We cannot be certain about this issue, but I regard the likelihood that the author of the *Ascension of Isaiah* used John as not much less than the likelihood that he used Matthew and on a par with my suggestion that he used Luke. This conclusion is significant when the status of the *Ascension of Isaiah* mid-way between the New Testament and the Gnostic literature is considered. The apocalypse would then offer evidence of how John was used in a proto-Gnostic environment which contrasts with how John was interpreted in *developed* Gnostic circles.[20] This is a matter which could profitably be explored on another occasion, and which clearly bears on the problem of Gnostic origins.

The New Testament Epistles and Revelation

The author of the *Ascension of Isaiah* also knew New Testament literature beyond the Gospels. This point is easier to prove because much of this literature was written before the Gospels and it thus had longer to circulate. Unlike the Jesus traditions in the *Ascension of Isaiah*, allusions to other New Testament literature in the apocalypse are not so obvious. The author offers a more subtle and reflective meditation on this literature which he incorporates into his own story of salvation.

A good place to begin this further study is to reiterate what I take to be the virtual certainty that the author knew and used 1 Pet. 3.22. The verbal allusion to that passage in the Ethiopic text of 1.3 is reinforced by the observation that the ascension narrative (*Asc. Isa.* 11.23-33) is also modelled on 1 Peter 3. The texts of 1 Cor. 2.8 and Col. 2.15 were equally used by the author. 1 Cor. 2.8 supplied the idea that the 'children of Israel' did not know their victim's identity; the author of the *Ascension of Isaiah* interpreted its 'rulers of this age' as human authorities who had been inspired by Beliar. Col. 2.15 indicates that the death of Jesus

20. The question of Gnostic exegesis of the Fourth Gospel is examined by Hengel in his *Johannine Question*, pp. 8-10.

4. *The Ascension of Isaiah and the New Testament Literature* 285

had resulted in the destruction of angelic powers, so that the cross receives a special prominence in that letter. All three passages are woven into the *Ascension of Isaiah*'s soteriology in the framework which the author constructed from his belief the seven-storied cosmology and in the mediator's descent.

Of Pauline influence too is the description of the parousia and its effects in *Asc. Isa.* 4.14-18. The language used to describe the Beloved One's return derives ultimately from Zech. 14.5, but the immediate source for the *Ascension of Isaiah* at this point is the eschatology of 2 Thess. 1.7 (cf. 1 Thess. 3.13), where Paul (who cites an existing tradition) expresses his hope that the Lord Jesus will be revealed from heaven with his angels to provide 'rest' for the afflicted. *Asc. Isa.* 4.14 combines this material with the eschatological timescale of Dan. 12.12, so that (as characteristically in the *Ascension of Isaiah*) a variety of passages are used to produce a new statement of belief. This is perhaps the clearest Pauline allusion in the apocalypse and one which, like the Petrine influence in 1.3 and 11.23-33, seems impossible to deny.

This evidence represents a positive indication that the author knew 1 Corinthians, 1 and 2 Thessalonians and Colossians at least among the Pauline writings. The fact that we cannot be sure about other texts (such as Romans and Galatians) does not of course mean that the author did not know them. Indeed, it is easier to suppose that he knew a *collected* Pauline corpus (cf. 2 Pet. 3.15-16) than merely individual letters. This observation does not disguise the fact that key Pauline conceptions, such as 'justification' and the state of being 'in Christ', are absent from the *Ascension of Isaiah*. The author's use of Paul was a selective one and many of his ideas are quite different from Paul's. He also used material that has connections with Matthew and John, so that he cannot be considered a 'Paulinist' in any exclusive sense.

The issue of whether the author knew Hebrews is difficult to decide. Heb. 11.37 makes a brief allusion to Isaiah's death but Pesce has shown that more than one legend about this event circulated in the first century. This makes the author's (exclusive) dependence on Hebrews an unnecessary hypothesis. The two texts probably drew independently on the same complex of traditions. There is an interesting correspondence between them in their understanding of the ascension as the moment when the mediator was acknowledged in the heavenly world (see Heb. 4.14; 10.19-20). This however was a common Christian view (cf. 1 Pet. 3.22) and again does not prove dependence on Hebrews. Since Hebrews was known to the author of *1 Clement* (see *1 Clem.* 17; 36.2-6) our author's knowledge of it is not impossible; but I can find no firm evidence that it influenced his thought.

The Pastorals contain some interesting points of correspondence with the *Ascension of Isaiah*. I put this down to the fact that they emerged at around the same time as the apocalypse, although of course the Pastorals are 'ecclesiastical' texts and the *Ascension of Isaiah* has an 'anti-ecclesiastical' perspective. The belief that there would be a decline in moral standards in the last days (see for example 2 Tim. 3.1-9) is part of a wider stock found in Jewish literature,[21] and it is unnecessary to suppose that the author derived 3.21-31 directly from the Pastorals. This section of the apocalypse is much better explained as his own account of contemporary Christianity, which is set in traditional apocalyptic language and makes the point that the prophets were being repressed at the time of writing. On the other hand, there is a very strong correspondence between the *Ascension of Isaiah* and the christological formulae in 1 Timothy (notably those found in 1 Tim. 1.15; 3.16). These are among the most 'mythological' of all the christological summaries in the New Testament and they presuppose the fact of Christ's heavenly origin as an established item of belief. These summaries evidently had a substantial history before their inclusion in the Pastorals, and 1 Tim. 3.16 in particular is only loosely related to its present context. This observation means that the correspondence between the *Ascension of Isaiah* and these christological formulae does not prove that the author of the apocalypse knew the Pastorals. The matter of dating suggests that he did not.

It is likely that the author knew Ephesians. His interest in this letter would doubtless have been stimulated by its references to 'the heavenly places' (see for example Eph. 2.6). Specific evidence of contact with Ephesians is provided by the notion of opposition from aerial powers in that letter. Ephesians more than once describes aerial opposition to Christians (2.2; 6.12). I suspect that this view helped the author of the *Ascension of Isaiah* to create the notion of Beliar as a malevolent angel who was excluded from the heavens, which he set within the context of his seven-storied cosmology. The *Ascension of Isaiah* develops the notion of 'aerial powers' from Ephesians in the way which 7.9-12 shows. *Asc.*

---

21. See for example 1QpHab 2.5-10; Philo, *Sacr.* 32; 2 Pet. 1.5-7; cf. B.S. Easton, 'New Testament Ethical Lists', *JBL* 51 (1932), pp. 1-12; and H.A. Fischel, 'The Uses of Sorites (*Climax, Gradatio*) in the Tannaitic Period', *HUCA* 44 (1973), pp. 119-51.

4. *The Ascension of Isaiah and the New Testament Literature* 287

Isa. 7.9-12 stands much closer to Ephesians than to the later Gnostic literature. It is worth noting that, besides the Fourth Gospel, Ephesians contains the only other passage in the New Testament (4.8-9) where heavenly descent is mentioned explicitly as an actuality.[22] This motif, as we have seen, takes on a new significance in the *Ascension of Isaiah*, whose author introduces the notion of the mediator's transformation into human form.

Revelation has obvious points of contact with the *Ascension of Isaiah*, notably its shared interest in the heavenly world (Rev. 4.1), the use of enthronement imagery (cf. Rev. 5.6), the speculative angelology (esp. Rev. 19.10; 22.8-9) and the material about Nero (Rev. 13.11-18). Yet there are important differences between the texts which should not be ignored. Foremost among these is the fact that worship is addressed to the pre-existent Beloved in the *Ascension of Isaiah* but to the exalted Christ in Rev. 1.13-14. The Nero material is used in a different way in the *Ascension of Isaiah* and links the reappearance of the emperor with the descent of Beliar from the firmament. The notion of Satan's ejection from heaven (Rev. 12), which is held in common with Lk. 10.18, is the subject of exegetical development in the *Ascension of Isaiah*. This may, however, have been derived from a knowledge of Luke rather than of Revelation. It is odd that, because of the similarity of genre and the traditional nature of apocalyptic language and imagery, it is difficult to be sure whether the author of the *Ascension of Isaiah* used Revelation. Use of Revelation would have been natural in our author's circle given their interest in prophecy and their likely use of the Fourth Gospel. One could certainly imagine that they would have been attracted by Revelation had they known the text. Yet the author of the *Ascension of Isaiah* does not take up the precise form of Revelation's millenarianism (20.4) nor its view about the new creation in which the heavenly world is revealed on earth (Rev. 21–22). The author's knowledge of Revelation should thus be judged an open question.

This study has shown that the author of the *Ascension of Isaiah* knew a variety of New Testament literature. The date of the apocalypse has been an important factor in this assessment. Its origin in the second century suggests intrinsically that its contact with the New Testament represents an early use of that literature rather than merely mutual use of common tradition. A text which was written in Syria after Ignatius cannot seriously be presumed to have had less knowledge of the New

---

22. Rom. 10.6-8 seems to me to be a hypothetical allusion.

Testament than Ignatius did.[23] The reference in the concluding verses of 2 Peter (3.15-16) to collections of the Pauline literature shows that copies of the New Testament epistles were available by the early second century. The Antiochene church, as a major centre of Christianity, would have had copies of these. The Gospels too were church documents and these would have been collected and treasured in the same way. We must presume that the author's knowledge of 1 Peter was derived from a process of collection analogous to that which prompted the collection of the Pauline correspondence. The *Ascension of Isaiah* thus contains important evidence for the earliest history of the canon. It is interesting to observe that neither of the two 'disputed' texts—Hebrews and Revelation—can be *proved* to have been available to the author of the apocalypse.

The Jesus Traditions in the Ascension of Isaiah

I have shown that the question of how the author acquired his knowledge of the traditions about Jesus is formally distinct from the question of which New Testament writings he knew. The *Ascension of Isaiah* gives a strong indication that its author knew Matthew, but the Jesus traditions cannot be explained on the basis of Matthew (or of any other canonical Gospel) alone. This is because they incorporate passages, such as the description of the resurrection (3.16-17) and of the absent midwife (11.14a), which are not found in any of the Gospels. We must consider a source wider than the present form of the New Testament literature for the information about Jesus that is recorded in *Asc. Isa.* 3.13-18 and 11.2-22.

This problem has generally been resolved by the suggestion that the author drew on 'kerygmatic summaries' of the life of Jesus which derived from the oral tradition and which the New Testament writers also used. These summaries contained a variety of information about Jesus, as we can see from some of the speeches in Acts. The *Ascension of Isaiah* shows something of their nature if this theory is accepted. It does indeed seem to be the best explanation of the evidence. This theory is adopted here without being made the subject of detailed investigation. It should be repeated that the author's use of these summaries does not preclude the possibility that he *also* included material about Jesus which

---

23. Cf. the allusions to 1 Cor. 1.10 in *Ign. Eph.* 3; to 2 Tim. 1.1 in *Magn.* 11; to 1 Cor. 4.4 in *Rom.* 5; and to Rom. 1.3-4 in *Smyrn.* 1.

4. *The Ascension of Isaiah and the New Testament Literature* 289

he derived from the Gospels. This is suggested by his use of John in 11.14b, which appears to be an interpolation into the incorporated Jesus traditions. We are thus faced with the interesting possibility that this second-century author used *both* the oral tradition *and* the written records of the life of Jesus. He is unlikely to have been exceptional in this procedure.

The Author as Exegete of Jewish Literature

Besides his use of the New Testament literature, the author of the *Ascension of Isaiah* used other Jewish material. This book would be incomplete without some account of his activity in this area. In the first place the author expanded Jewish legends about Isaiah to suit his purpose in the apocalypse. Charles believed that the work's narrative portions were culled from a text called 'the Martyrdom of Isaiah', but Pesce has much more convincingly referred this material to Jewish oral tradition.[24] The author's use of this material shows that its present form has a definite Christian purpose.

Chapter 5 is an example of this. Despite its Jewish parallels, this description of Isaiah's death was written to prove the point that Isaiah died for *Christian* faith. Isaiah is presented throughout the apocalypse as the recipient of both a binitarian and a Trinitarian vision: never of an exclusively monotheistic one. The Christian orientation of the apocalypse appears as early as ch. 1, where the two summaries of visionary experience confirm the Christian purpose of the narrative by their christological content. To Pesce's demonstration that the Isaiah legend was derived from Jewish tradition must be added the recognition that the whole of the *Ascension of Isaiah* speaks with a Christian voice. This includes the narrative sections as much as the apocalyptic visions.

The author's understanding of the Hebrew Bible appears from 4.21-22. He gives no sign that he regards the Torah as authentic prophecy about the Beloved One. I have argued that this is a polemical view of contemporary Judaism and that it anticipates a later Gnostic motif. The author does however maintain that the Prophets and Writings spoke about the Beloved One. This belief allows him to use that literature in an exegetical way. The licence which he takes in interpretation can be seen from his exegesis of Isaiah 52–53 in 4.21, which (against the sense of the original) he understands with reference to the Beloved One's descent to

---

24. See Chapter 1.

Sheol. Much can be learned by comparing this use of the Hebrew Bible with the *pesher* exegesis in the writings of the Qumran community. *Pesher* was a method of interpretation which understood the interpreter's circumstances as realizing the meaning of the biblical text.[25] Our author was conscious of standing within an exegetical tradition that was shaped by the history of his own circle (as well as by Christianity more generally). The way in which he used Scripture suggests his consciousness of belonging to a group that was experiencing marginalization and which turned to the resources of the Hebrew Bible to explain the circumstances of this experience.

In its use of the Hebrew Bible the *Ascension of Isaiah* represents an important bridge between the New Testament literature and the writings of Justin Martyr, in which scriptural exegesis assumes a central significance. Such brief glimpses as we have of our author's approach indicate that he saw whole passages rather than short words or phrases as foretelling events connected with the Beloved One. Thus Isaiah 52–53 supports the descent to Sheol in *Asc. Isa.* 4.21 and the reference to the 'vision of Babylon' (Isa. 13) predicts the demise of the Romans in 4.20. The *Ascension of Isaiah* supplies only the barest glimpse into what must have been the substantial exegetical activity of the author's circle. The material is however probably typical of their work. It is most unfortunate that we cannot discern with confidence the different stages in their history and exegetical activity.

Gruenwald has advanced the suggestion that the Second Vision of the *Ascension of Isaiah* draws on a Jewish *Urtext*.[26] This is in some ways an attractive hypothesis but it falls down on the impossibility, as with the projected 'Martyrdom of Isaiah', of distilling a satisfactory Jewish original from the present, quite indelibly Christian, apocalypse. This book has shown that the myth of the hidden descent was derived in essentials from Jewish angelology. Both John's Gospel and 1 Tim. 3.16 among the

---

25. On this method see W.H. Brownlee, 'Biblical Interpretation among the Sectaries of the Dead Sea Scrolls', *BA* 14 (1951), pp. 54-76; G.J. Brooke, 'Qumran Pesher: Towards the Redefinition of a Genre', *RevQ* 10 (1979–80), pp. 483-503; *idem*, *Exegesis at Qumran*: 4QFlorilegium in its Jewish Context (JSOTSup, 29; Sheffield: JSOT Press, 1985), pp. 36-44.

26. *Apocalyptic*, p. 61 n. 119: 'There are good reasons to believe that the book as a whole is of Jewish origin and that all the clear Christian references belong to a later editor or interpolator.' He adds that 'it is difficult to decide whether everything from ix, 11ff. belongs to him or whether one has even here to try to distinguish between the Jewish origin and the Christian additions'.

4. *The Ascension of Isaiah and the New Testament Literature* 291

literature of first-century Christianity reveal belief in the mediator's descent (but without providing an exact analogy to the *Ascension of Isaiah*). There must have been something in the Syrian Christian environment which made the author's development of such ideas conducive. Perhaps this was the recognition, which also touches the Gospel infancy narratives, that God sometimes communicated through angelic revelation. The *Prayer of Joseph* indicates that non-Christian circles also engaged in speculation about the connection between a human being and a heavenly mediator. This is a significant comparison if the reference to 'the words of the righteous Joseph' in *Asc. Isa.* 4.22 refers to that apocryphon. It would confirm the point that the author of the *Ascension of Isaiah* found himself attracted by Jewish mediatorial speculation of this kind. The view that the work's Christology has antecedents in Jewish angelology, but without the theory of a Jewish *Urtext*, seems the best explanation of the evidence in the present state of research.

The New Testament Literature from a Second-Century Perspective

The observation that the *Ascension of Isaiah* makes early exegetical use of the New Testament literature makes it desirable to look back on the New Testament from the vantage point of the apocalypse and to ask whether it can help with the exegesis of the canonical material. The rest of this chapter is devoted to a selected reading of certain New Testament passages which confirms the point that the *Ascension of Isaiah* is an important but neglected source for the study of early Christianity and that it can indeed benefit the reader of the New Testament in this way. The restrictions of space make what follows a very arbitrary selection of New Testament material which hardly does full justice to the subject (and which for this reason does not try to do so). Yet it is important to establish that the apocalypse has much to offer scholars by attempting preliminary work of this kind. Others will find opportunities to use the *Ascension of Isaiah* in their own exegetical work. In many cases this is being done already.

There is a particular correspondence between the *Ascension of Isaiah*'s infancy material and Matthew's early chapters. I outlined this correspondence in Chapter 1. The point is that the author of the *Ascension of Isaiah* seems to be aware of the Matthean story but that he adds to it the notion of Mary's Davidic ancestry and the fact of her *virginitas post partum*. The apocalypse thereby shows the way in which Matthean traditions were developed in the early second century. The material which I reproduced in Chapter 2 from the *Epistula Apostolorum* and the Eighth *Sibylline Oracle* provides evidence of a slightly later development of the same material. The *Ascension of Isaiah* stands near the root of a Mariology which flowered in later Christianity.[27]

A notable feature of Matthew's Gospel is the way in which it establishes a typology between Jesus and Moses in which the Jewish Lawgiver is seen as inferior to the Christian Saviour.[28] A similar downgrading of Moses is found in other early Christian writings, notably John's Gospel (6.46), Paul (2 Cor. 3.7-8) and Hebrews (3.3).[29] The *Ascension of Isaiah* takes a more radical view of this issue for which I have found parallels in the later Gnostic literature. *Asc. Isa.* 3.8-10 prefers the mysticism of Isaiah 6 to the prohibition of Exod. 33.20b, in a context in which it is implied that those who appealed to Moses to deny the value of Christian theology were misguided. The author excludes the Torah by his silence from the list of inspired writings which he mentions in 4.21-22 and never makes a positive comment about Moses in the entire apocalypse. This

---

27. On this subject see Buck, '"Ascension of Isaiah" and "Odes of Solomon"'; Kelly, *Doctrines*, pp. 490-99; W. Delius, *Texte zur Geschichte der Marienverehung und Marienverkündigung in der alten Kirche* (Berlin: de Gruyter, 1956); idem, *Geschichte der Marienverehung* (Munich/Basel: Ernst Reinhardt, 1963); H.C. Graef, *Mary: A History of Doctrine and Devotion* (2 vols.; London and New York: Sheed & Ward, 1963). There is interesting material also in R.E. Brown, K.P. Donfried, J.A. Fitzmyer and J. Reumann (eds.), *Mary in the New Testament* (Philadelphia: Fortress Press, 1978).

28. Some scholars have seen a fivefold division in the Gospel whereby the teaching of Jesus constitutes a new Pentateuch. This approach is advocated by B.W. Bacon, *Studies in St Matthew* (London: Constable & Co., 1930); G.D. Kilpatrick, *The Origins of the Gospel according to St Matthew* (Oxford: Clarendon Press, 1946); and P. Benoit, *L'Évangile selon Saint Matthieu* (Paris: Cerf, 1972). Caution towards it is advocated by D. Hill, *The Gospel of Matthew* (NCB; London: Oliphants, 1972), pp. 38-39, who cites W.D. Davies, *The Setting of the Sermon on the Mount* (Cambridge: Cambridge University Press, 1964) to the effect that the 'new Moses' image is used there only with considerable restraint.

29. On the Johannine evidence see Meeks, *Prophet King*, pp. 286-319; on Paul, C.K. Stockhausen, *Moses' Veil and the Glory of the New Covenant* (AnBib, 16; Rome: Pontifical Biblical Institute, 1989); and L.L. Belleville, *Reflection of Glory: Paul's Polemical Use of the Moses-Doxa Tradition in 2 Corinthians 3.1-18* (JSNTSup, 52; Sheffield: JSOT Press, 1991).

4. *The Ascension of Isaiah and the New Testament Literature* 293

represents an important difference from Matthew, who confers upon Moses an authority which is surpassed only by that of Jesus (see Mt. 5.18-22). Even in John's Gospel, which was allegedly written by a Christian author who found it problematic that his circle had been excluded from the synagogue, Moses is still regarded as a religious authority (see Jn 7.19). We should not forget that the author of the *Ascension of Isaiah* has a tendency to polemicize against *everyone* who is not of his own persuasion, which I think reflects his isolated position in the world. The *Ascension of Isaiah* must be seen as an exceptional example of the Christian response towards Judaism which was developed in some other second-century circles. It demonstrates the dissatisfaction with established religion which a little later yielded the Gnostic apocalypses.

There are certain eschatological similarities between the *Ascension of Isaiah* and the Synoptic Gospels. The historical review in *Ascension of Isaiah* 3–4 should be compared with the Synoptic eschatological discourse (Mt. 24 and parallels). It is often believed that Matthew drew on Mark 13, but this theory is not universally accepted.[30] We should probably think in terms of a cycle of early Christian eschatological material rather than of a uniform portrait (as the evidence of 2 Thess. 2, with its differences from the Synoptists, implies). Mt. 24.4-5 anticipates the emergence of many false messiahs (cf. 24.23-37) and 24.9-14 a period of tribulation.[31] Mt. 24.15-22 refers to an act of religious desecration when the 'Abomination of Desolation' will stand in the Holy Place.[32] There will be signs in the sun and moon (24.29). All of this is to herald the coming of the Son of Man who will arrive on the clouds of heaven to gather in his elect (24.30-31).

This eschatology is less situation-specific than the *Ascension of Isaiah*'s author's fears about Rome (*Asc. Isa.* 4), but there is a degree of

---

30. Thus G.R. Beasley-Murray, in his book *Jesus and the Future* (London: Macmillan, 1956), pp. 227-30, argues against Matthew's use of Mark. Another disputed issue is whether this chapter contains material inserted from a source—the so-called 'Little Apocalypse' theory—and thus does not go back to Jesus himself (see the comments of Hill, *Matthew*, pp. 316-17). A recent study of what Jesus taught on this issue is D.L. Tiede, *Jesus and the Future* (Cambridge: Cambridge University Press, 1990).

31. Mt. 24.4-5 is paralleled by Mk 13.5-6 and by Lk. 21.8. There is a subsequent reference to the emergence of false prophets in Mt. 24.11 where Matthew stands on his own.

32. This idea looks back ultimately to Dan. 11.31; 12.11.

similarity between the texts. This indicates that the *Ascension of Isaiah* was influenced by the wider eschatological tradition, which the author developed in his own way. The apocalypse shares Matthew's belief that the future will bring a time of testing (ch. 4). It augments this view by the device of the historical review which the author derived from the apocalyptic tradition (probably from Daniel). *Asc. Isa.* 4.5, 10 claims that Nero-Beliar will perform spurious miracles to deceive the elect, including unnatural portents in sun and moon.[33] *Asc. Isa.* 4.6 presents Beliar as a false messiah in language that is drawn from Isaiah 45; *Asc. Isa.* 4.13 (the expectation of flight to the desert) can be compared with Mt. 24.16 (the passage about flight to the mountains). Matthew's comment in 24.20 about God shortening the period of tribulation agrees in spirit with the imminent eschatology of *Asc. Isa.* 4.12, 14, but without placing a specific date on the eschaton (see esp. Mt. 24.26). The eschatological similarities between the two texts thus include: (1) the expectation that things will get worse before they get better; (2) a general apostasy (Mt. 24.10; cf. *Ascension of Isaiah* 4.9); (3) the emergence of false prophets; (4) a specific moment of conflict followed by tribulation and displacement; and (5) the sudden coming of the Son of Man or the Beloved One to emancipate the elect.

I have explained these contacts in terms of our author's knowledge of the Christian eschatological tradition. The point at issue is that this tradition was evidently sufficiently flexible to permit interpretation of this kind. In the *Ascension of Isaiah* this reinterpretation included the introduction of Daniel's 'four age' scheme, the identification of the *Romans* as the eschatological opponents, the assertion that present circumstances would produce the eschatological climax, and the importation of the eschatological timescale from Dan. 12.12. The author also introduced the notion of heavenly immortality (4.17; cf. the Second Vision), which I have suggested represents an attempt to free Christian eschatology from a totally 'this-worldly' view in a context in which the traditional language about the parousia is nevertheless retained. The *Ascension of Isaiah* represents an interesting position in second-century Christian eschatology, anticipating Gnostic developments but retaining the traditional millenarianism. It is an important text for study of the millenarian question in second-century Christianity.

---

33. For this planetary reaction cf. *Sib. Or.* 3.63-65 and *4 Ezra* 5.4.

4. *The Ascension of Isaiah and the New Testament Literature* 295

Johannine Literature

The *Ascension of Isaiah* holds several ideas in common with John's Gospel. There is an obvious development between Jn 12.41 and the *Ascension of Isaiah* in the sense that John's binitarian interpretation of Isa. 6.1-4 is interpreted in a Trinitarian direction. The *Ascension of Isaiah* also makes the mediator's descent and ascent the *framework* for its christological portrait, while in John it is merely a theme which recurs sporadically in the Gospel (see for example Jn 3.13; 6.62). This was achieved through the introduction of the language about the Beloved One's transformation into human likeness which determines the way in which the Jesus traditions are used in the apocalypse. My conclusion from this evidence is that the *Ascension of Isaiah* can be read as a development of the Johannine Christology, as of other first-century ideas about Jesus.

This identification of a shift in emphasis between John and the *Ascension of Isaiah* prompts reflection about the 'docetic' basis of Johannine Christology which was proposed by Käsemann.[34] Käsemann thought that the Evangelist offered a portrait of Jesus in which the tensions between the heavenly mediator and the human person had yet to be addressed. It is true to say that the 'Son of Man' strand in the Gospel raises questions about the relationship of the heavenly mediator to Jesus which John never satisfactorily answers. This however must not be taken as an indication that the Gospel 'reduces' the humanity of Jesus through the conviction of his divinity. Johannine Christology if anything tends in an *anti*-docetic direction through the insistence that Jesus really died on the cross (19.34).[35] There is a clear difference between John and the *Ascension of Isaiah* in this. The apocalypse describes an abnormally short pregnancy (11.6-7) and hints that the Beloved One's suckling was undertaken to protect the secret of the mediator's identity (11.17). Both elements are absent from the Gospel. This makes the *Ascension of Isaiah* more obviously docetic than John. I have argued that Käsemann's term 'naïve docetism' is in fact more appropriate as a description of the *Ascension of Isaiah*'s Christology than of the Johannine. The apocalypse illustrates the shift in understanding which took place in the christological tradition when the theme of the mediator's descent was allowed to determine a presentation of Christology. Even in the *Ascension of Isaiah*, however, it is necessary to speak of an *anti*-docetic perspective given the

---

34. *Testament*, pp. 26, 66, 70.
35. See also Hengel, *Johannine Question*, pp. 68-72.

fact that the author insists on the reality of the Beloved One's birth and death. Fully-fledged docetism is not reached in the *Ascension of Isaiah* despite these differences from John. This advocates further caution against the use of the term 'docetic' as a description of the Johannine Christology.

Pauline Literature
The issue of whether Paul thought about the messiah as a pre-existent heavenly being is one of the most vexed areas of New Testament research. The *Ascension of Isaiah* does not settle the matter either way.[36] On the other hand the apocalypse *does* contain the themes of the messiah's commission, descent and transformation into a human being, which those who argue for a 'pre-existence' interpretation of Phil. 2.5-11 and other passages by implication find reflected there in an attenuated form. The difference between first- and second-century literature in this respect is an important one. The fact that this information is found explicitly in the *Ascension of Isaiah* but not in Paul shows the extent to which such ideas have to be *assumed* in the exegesis of Pauline Christology. This is not to deny that Paul thought about the heavenly Christ in this way. I simply make the point that considerable exegetical caution is needed over this issue given the fact that a process of development can be demonstrated between first- and second-century Christology. The explicit nature of the *Ascension of Isaiah*, together with the fact that its date can be fixed with relative precision, makes it an important text to cite in connection with the exegesis of Pauline Christology, and of Phil. 2.5-11 in particular.

At one point Paul alludes to the theme of the descent to hell which plays a prominent role in the *Ascension of Isaiah* and in other second-century literature. Rom. 10.6-8 mentions a putative heavenly ascension to bring Christ down and a descent to Sheol to bring him up from there. The context of this reference is a citation and elaboration of Deut. 30.11-14.[37] That passage said that God's commandment was not far off but near the Israelites and that it was possible for them to obey it. Paul used this reference to ascent and descent to state that God's righteousness

---

36. See my discussion of this issue in Chapter 2.
37. See J. Heller, 'Himmel- und Höllenfahrt nach Römer 10.6-7', *EvT* 32 (1972), pp. 478-86; and M.J. Suggs, 'The Word is Near You: Rom. 10.6-10 within the Purpose of the Letter', in W.R. Farmer (ed.), *Christian History and Interpretation* (Cambridge: Cambridge University Press, 1967), pp. 289-312.

had been made available in Christ. Despite the problems which Rom. 10.6-8 raises, Paul does imply in hypothetical terms that Christ journeyed to the place of the dead. This idea is not prominent in the New Testament—I do not think that it can be inferred from either 1 Pet. 3.19 or 4.6 despite the fact that some have seen it there—but it is found in three passages in the *Ascension of Isaiah* (4.21; 9.16 [by implication]; and 10.10). The first of these describes a descent to Sheol, evidently as the last stage of the Beloved One's descent. The third, in ch. 10, distinguishes Sheol, which is visited, from Haguel, which in this context signifies the place of ultimate perdition, and which is not visited. The second passage speaks of the mediator 'plundering' the angel of death before his resurrection and it mentions the fact that 'many of the righteous would ascend with him' after that time (9.17). The L2 and S texts of 9.17 include a reference to the Beloved 'seizing the prince of death' and 'crushing' all his powers, which is evidently a development from the E text and reflects the growing interest in this subject in the patristic period. The thought of E is that those who had died before the Beloved's advent had been freed from their confinement in that region.[38] In the other two passages the less ornate assertion which is found in Romans, that Christ journeyed to the place of the dead, is retained. The frequent presence of this theme in the *Ascension of Isaiah* shows how the motif was developed from quite slender New Testament roots and increasingly regarded as an important item of belief in the second century.

Other second-century texts also offer evidence of an increased interest in the doctrine of Christ's descent to hell. The *Apocryphon of Jeremiah*, which is preserved by Justin (*Dial.* 72.4), and by Irenaeus (*Adv. Haer.* 3.20.4 and other references), refers this journey to the evangelization of those who had died before the coming of Christ. This view is found also in the *Gospel of Peter* 41–42. Hermas (*Sim.* 9.16.5-7) has a strange view of the descent in which the *apostles* descended to hell to accomplish this task (no doubt because they were believed to be the emissaries of Christ). *T. Levi* 4.1 says that hell was despoiled through the passion of Jesus and its author refers this achievement to the cross.[39] The *Ascension of Isaiah*

---

38. This reference casts light on the presence of the antediluvian righteous in the seventh heaven earlier in the same chapter. It seems that the *Ascension of Isaiah* views the pre-Flood generation as translated to heaven while the later dead descend to Sheol, apart from the martyrs who ascend to heaven, as suggested by 4.16.

39. For a discussion of these texts see Daniélou, *Jewish Christianity*, pp. 233-48.

thus stands within a wider context of belief in its notion of the descent to hell. This wider material must be considered in exegesis of Rom. 10.6-8, whose unornate character it reveals.

Turning now to 1 Cor. 2.8, I want briefly to disagree with Conzelmann's interpretation of the *Ascension of Isaiah*, which he mentions in connection with that passage. Conzelmann notes the similarity between the two texts but unfortunately misrepresents the provenance of the apocalypse:

> That he [i.e. Christ] is hidden from the powers of the world is again a view that is common both to wisdom and to apocalyptic. For in his descent through the cosmos he has disguised himself.[40]

To this comment he appends the following footnote:

> This motif has a part to play in Gnosticism: *Asc. Isa.* 10; Epiph. *Haer.* 21.2.4; *Pist.Soph.* 7; *Ev.Phil.* 26; Ign. *Eph.* 19; cf. also *Ep.Ap.* 13 (24).[41]

This note ranks the *Ascension of Isaiah* as a work of (developed) Gnosticism alongside texts like the *Pistis Sophia* and the *Gospel of Philip*; Conzelmann implies that it is *distinguished* in this way from Pauline Christianity with its apocalyptic outlook. This conclusion about the *Ascension of Isaiah* cannot be allowed to stand (nor indeed can the view that Ignatius was a Gnostic writer). The differences between the *Ascension of Isaiah* and the Gnostic literature which I mentioned in Chapter 2 tell against this suggestion. The *Ascension of Isaiah* has a substantial background in Jewish apocalyptic, as does Paul, despite the fact that its author has 'worked up' the cosmology and emphasized the concept of heavenly mediation. My argument in this book has been that the idea of the Beloved One's descent was modelled on an angelophany and not on a form of the Gnostic 'redeemer myth'. This in turn sheds light on a 'Gnosticizing' interpretation of 1 Corinthians. If the *Ascension of Isaiah*, which contains some rather more obvious 'Gnosticizing' tendencies than Paul (and which is of course significantly later), cannot be presented as a Gnostic apocalypse then one ought to demur at presenting Paul in Gnostic terms. Paul's intention in 1 Cor. 2.8 is rather to present an 'apocalyptic' or a 'revealed' understanding of the crucifixion in which the divine nature of Jesus is held to have escaped the attention of his tormentors. We find a similar understanding of the cross in the

---

40. H. Conzelmann, *1 Corinthians* (Philadelphia: Fortress Press, 1975), p. 63.
41. Conzelmann, *1 Corinthians*, p. 63 n. 65.

4. The Ascension of Isaiah and the New Testament Literature

Ascension of Isaiah, which gives signs that its author was influenced in this matter by reflection on earlier literature, and in a context in which the hidden descent determines the presentation of the Christology.

The identity of the ἄρχοντες τοῦ αἰῶνος τούτου in 1 Cor. 2.8 has long puzzled commentators.[42] Three different views have been proposed to explain who they are. Everling believes that they are suprahistorical beings or aerial powers;[43] Schniewind and Munck see them as human potentates responsible for the crucifixion;[44] and Cullmann offers a 'mixed' hypothesis which holds that they are both human and suprahistorical agents and that demonic beings stand behind the human actors.[45] The *Ascension of Isaiah* confirms that the third of these views was known in the early second century with its account of how 'the Adversary' provoked the Jews to betray Jesus (11.19), with which should be compared the story of Beliar, who incarnates himself as Nero in *Asc. Isa.* 4.1-13. The context in 1 Corinthians 2 is more ambiguous than that of the *Ascension of Isaiah*. Paul does not say that the ἄρχοντες are wicked angels and it makes good sense of this passage to see them merely as human beings. Given that the *Ascension of Isaiah*

---

42. See the discussion in Carr, *Angels and Principalities*, pp. 118-20; *idem*, 'The Rulers of This Age—1 Corinthians II.6-8', *NTS* 23 (1976-77), pp. 20-35. See also G. Miller, 'ARXONTWN TOY AIWNOS TOYTOY—A New Look at 1 Corinthians 2:6-8', *JBL* 91 (1972), pp. 522-28.

43. O. Everling, *Die paulinische Angelologie und Dämonologie* (Göttingen, 1888), pp. 11-14. This interpretation is supported by R. Bultmann, *The Theology of the New Testament* (2 vols.; ET; London: SCM Press, 1952), II, p. 147; G. Delling, 'ἄρχων', in *TDNT*, I, p. 489; C.K. Barrett, 'Christianity at Corinth', *BJRL* 46 (1963), p. 281; and H. Schlier, *Principalities and Powers in the New Testament* (ET; London: Burns & Oates, 1961), pp. 45-46. In patristic exegesis it featured in the work of Origen (*De Princ.* 3.2) and in Marcion (according to Tertullian, *Adv. Marc.* 5.6).

44. J. Schniewind, 'Die Archonten dieses Äons: 1 Kor. 2,6-8', in *Nachgelassene Reden und Aufsätze* (Berlin: Töpelmann, 1951), pp. 104-109; J. Munck, *Paul and the Salvation of Mankind* (ET London: SCM Press, 1959), p. 156.

45. O. Cullmann, *The State in the New Testament* (ET London: SCM Press, 1956), pp. 62-64. Other scholars holding this interpretation include M. Dibelius, *Die Geisterwelt im Glauben Paulus* (Göttingen, 1909), pp. 88-99; R. Leivestad, *Christ the Conqueror* (London: SPCK, 1954), p. 106; J. Wendland, *Die Briefe an die Korinther* (Göttingen: Vandenhoeck & Ruprecht, 1946), p. 19; G. Dehn, 'Engel und Obrigkeit: ein Beitrag zum Verständnis von Röm. 13.1-7', in E. Wolf (ed.), *Theologische Aufsätze für Karl Barth zum 50. Geburtstag* (Munich: Chr. Kaiser Verlag, 1936), p. 104; and Caird, *Principalities and Powers*, pp. 16-17.

seems to betray knowledge of 1 Cor. 2.8 (esp. in 11.19), its author evidently interpreted the Pauline text in Cullmann's sense. The apocalypse thus reveals the early interpretation of Paul but not necessarily Paul's original meaning.

The New Testament has a strong tradition of supernatural opposition to the Christians. The 'ruler' or 'king of this world' makes his first appearance in the New Testament in 2 Cor. 4.4. He reappears in the Fourth Gospel and then again in the *Ascension of Isaiah* where he is identified as Beliar (ch. 4). Paul says in 2 Corinthians that the 'god of this age' had blinded the minds of unbelievers to prevent them from understanding the Gospel. A.F. Segal has shown that this negative portrayal of the figure in Christian literature is quite opposed to his high evaluation in Judaism, where he functions as the leader of the heavenly chorus.[46] This difference occurs as early as Paul, but we must note a significant difference between Paul and the two later Christian sources. 2 Cor. 4.4 does not identify the 'god of this world' with any specific human opponent. He is however identified with the Jews in John and with all social groups opposed to the author in the *Ascension of Isaiah*. The *Ascension of Isaiah* evidently *develops* the perspective of earlier literature and heightens the shift between readers and others which is implicit in John, a shift which I have referred to the author's social isolation. It shows a second-century Christian interpretation of an important New Testament theme.

2 Corinthians 12 relates a heavenly ascension similar to that described in *Ascension of Isaiah* 6–9. Paul claims to have known a man in Christ who, fourteen years earlier, had been caught up to the third heaven. Most scholars take this as an autobiographical reference.[47] The passage mirrors an experience which is described in both Jewish and Christian apocalyptic literature. Paul mentions it in the context of his repudiation of the Corinthians' boasting about their spiritual prowess. The circumlocutionary nature of the report suggests that he was loth to do so

---

46. 'Ruler of this World', p. 251.

47. For discussion of this possibility see R.P. Martin, *2 Corinthians* (Waco: Word Books, 1986) p. 399. The passage is examined also by J.W. Bowker, 'Merkabah Visions and the Visions of Paul', *JJS* 16 (1971), pp. 157-73; A.T. Lincoln, 'Paul the Visionary: The Setting and Significance of the Rapture to Paradise in 2 Corinthians 12.1-10', *NTS* 25 (1979), pp. 204-20; Rowland, *Open Heaven*, pp. 380-86; and R.P. Spittler, 'The Limits of Ecstasy: An Exegesis of 2 Corinthians 12.1-10', in G.F. Hawthorne (ed.), *Current Issues in Biblical and Patristic Interpretation* (Grand Rapids: Eerdmans, 1975), pp. 259-66.

4. *The Ascension of Isaiah and the New Testament Literature* 301

(perhaps because of the esoteric nature of the experience), but the secrecy also suggests that it was more common than he admits. Gal. 1.15-16 alludes to an earlier apocalyptic experience at the beginning of Paul's Christian activity (and 1 Cor. 15.8 is suggestive of this as well). Such experiences were valued because they permitted a more direct disclosure of the divine will than was offered by scriptural exegesis. Scholarship must concede that at this remove it has little chance of discovering precisely how common these experiences were and what they contributed to Paul's developing understanding of religion. Nevertheless, we should observe that *Ascension of Isaiah* 6 offers a rare glimpse into the practice of apocalyptic experience in the ancient Christian world. In company with the Jewish mystical text called *Hekhaloth Rabbati*, the *Ascension of Isaiah* offers a relatively sustained description of how mystical ascension was undertaken. Although ch. 6 may have been worked over in the course of transmission, and then abbreviated in the form represented by L2 and S, and although it doubtless conforms to a particular literary convention, it is possible to reconstruct from it a picture of visionary ascension of this kind. The apocalypse suggests that this was a mental or psychological phenomenon in which the mystic's body remained inert on the ground, apparently in a cataleptic trance, while in his imagination he thought that he wandered through the heavens.[48]

This information sheds light on Paul's enigmatic comment in 2 Cor. 12.3: εἴτε ἐν σώματι εἴτε χωρὶς τοῦ σώματος οὐκ οἶδα, ὁ θεὸς οἶδεν. Our work's suggestion of extra-bodily experience raises the possibility that Paul, too, entered a trance in which normal functions were suspended and which he found difficult to describe in writing although it made a profound impact on him. The *Ascension of Isaiah* thus represents a valuable exegetical aid for 2 Corinthians 12. It confirms, in company with Rev. 4.1, that Paul does not describe an isolated or unique experience in terms of Christian religious praxis. *Asc. Isa.* 2.7-11, which has parallels in the book of Daniel, indicates that asceticism and perhaps the eating of certain herbs were preparations for this type of experience in at least some Christian circles. One wonders, but without the evidence to answer the question, whether this was true of Paul as well.

An important issue of cosmology arises from comparing 2 Corinthians

---

48. See further Wapnick, 'Mysticism and Schizophrenia'; and cf. J. Cheek, 'Paul's Mysticism in the Light of Psychedelic Experience', *JAAR* 38 (1970), pp. 381-89.

12 with the *Ascension of Isaiah* in this way.[49] Paul describes his ascension to the third heaven and to paradise (which may represent a higher region), but the *Ascension of Isaiah* mentions seven heavens. Seven is the number of heavens found in much apocalyptic and rabbinic cosmology.[50] This was not the case in early Christian literature, however. The book of Revelation mentions only one heaven, as do Hebrews and John's Gospel. I think that the notion of a single-storied universe which pervades most New Testament writings reflects the Christian belief that God had been made accessible through Jesus, which made further cosmological speculation inappropriate (cf. esp. Jn 3.13 in this connection). Both 2 Corinthians 12 and the *Ascension of Isaiah* are exceptions to this wider tendency and reflect, I think, that desire to find a 'higher wisdom though revelation' which Martin Hengel has identified as a religious characteristic of late antiquity, and which was deemed appropriate to the context of both documents.[51] Paul's reference to the three heavens constitutes proof (however reluctantly offered) of his mystical prowess in a context in which certain Corinthians had been boasting of their accomplishments and denigrating his.[52] On this view Paul introduced a more complicated cosmology than he used elsewhere—but still not the full seven heavens—to support his claim to authority. He was content elsewhere with the simpler view that is found in most New Testament literature.

This comparison emphasizes the exceptional nature of the *Ascension of Isaiah*'s cosmology in the context of early Christian literature. My belief is that its author deliberately introduced this theme from Jewish apocalyptic and that he did so to support his apocalyptic disclosure of salvation (especially in the Second Vision). The work's cosmology has the social function of contrasting Beliar's position in the firmament with that of the Beloved One in the seventh heaven. This was a way of limiting the Romans' authority by explaining that they were inspired by a demon who had been defeated by the Beloved One and who was even excluded from the heavens. It bolstered the hopes of fretful Christian

---

49. Jewish and Christian cosmology is examined by Bietenhard, *Himmlische Welt*.

50. According to *b. Ḥag* 12b. This passage records a dispute about the matter between R. Judah and Resh Lakish.

51. Hengel, *Judaism and Hellenism*, I, pp. 210-18.

52. There is an important parallel with *2 En.* 8.1 which locates Paradise in the third heaven.

prophets by offering them information about their promised heavenly immortality. The significance of the *Ascension of Isaiah* for students of the New Testament lies in its explicit description of heavenly ascension and the social use to which apocalyptic revelation is put in the text. Future research might like to consider the possibility that the *Ascension of Isaiah* has in part the status of a mystical manual whose purpose was an accomplished mystic's offering instructions to the junior prophets about how this experience could be achieved in a climate in which religious experience of this kind was discouraged by the church authorities. Such an approach to the text is not inappropriate given the way in which the *Ascension of Isaiah* seems to encourage the preservation of prophetic activity.

Other New Testament Literature
The thought-world of Ephesians has significant parallels with that of the *Ascension of Isaiah*. The most obvious of these is the belief that opposition to Christians stemmed from the activity of aerial powers (Eph. 2.2; 6.12). The author of the *Ascension of Isaiah* probably knew Ephesians and developed its demonology by introducing the seven-storied cosmology and by linking its aerial powers with human opponents in the manner suggested by ch. 4 and by 7.9-12.

Comparison between Ephesians and the *Ascension of Isaiah* draws attention to the significance of the eschatology of Ephesians. Ephesians displays a perceptible lack of interest in the parousia hope despite the fact of its first-century origin. The text concentrates on Christ's finished achievement and on the enthronement of believers with him in what are called 'the heavenly places' (see for example Eph. 2.6). This perspective is often called a 'realized eschatology'. By this is meant that the letter demonstrates the conviction that the full eschatological benefits are available in the present in a way which tends to detract from the need to emphasize the future consummation of salvation. This is no doubt a question of perspective, grounded in the pastoral need to emphasize the full accessibility of these benefits, and it had the effect of diverting attention from the problem of the delayed parousia. In this context we must note that Ephesians is not *devoid* of references to a future consummation (see 1.14; 2.7; 4.30; 5.5; 6.8, 13), even if in practice this is not emphasized in the text. 'Realized eschatology' is perhaps a difficult term because it fails adequately to acknowledge the two different axes, spatial and temporal, on which early Christian eschatology operated. Ephesians concentrates on the spatial axis and offers hope and assurance by distinguishing between earth, the air and heaven; but the temporal axis is not completely absent from the letter. I see in Eph. 2.6 one of the clearest calls to a 'utopian' perspective in the New Testament. The notion of the believers' heavenly enthronement is an ideal view which seems intended to transform readers' perspectives on their situation; as Christians they may have felt quite isolated in their social world. Comparison with the *Ascension of Isaiah* helps to isolate the significance of the references to 'heavenly places' in Ephesians. The apocalypse shows how that letter's perspective was refined by the introduction of the seven-storied cosmology.

Ephesians is an important text for students of Christian doctrine because it is an early example of the attempt to construct an understanding of salvation within a perspective that is determined by cosmology. Cosmology was an essential element in primitive Christian belief because of the nature of the views about God's existence and his relation with the world which pertained at the time. God was understood in Judaism and early Christianity as a heavenly being. Heaven was believed to be above the sky, which was in turn superimposed above the earth. Speculation about God thus meant speculation about the heavenly world. This made it inevitable that the language of heavenly descent should be introduced into Christian theology given the way in which Christology developed the belief that Jesus was divine. The belief that salvation had been provided came to involve the story (we might say 'the narrative') of how God had sent a mediator who became involved with the human Jesus. This is what is found in Eph. 4.8-9, which we examined in Chapter 2, and for which I think that the 'incarnational' interpretation is the correct one. The author of the *Ascension of Isaiah* again developed this first-century view by increasing the number of the heavens and by introducing the themes of the mediator's *hidden* descent and his transformation into human likeness. His understanding of salvation in terms of the distinction between heaven and earth had first-century roots, as we can see from Ephesians. The importance of Ephesians within first-century literature, which provides a link with the second-century *Ascension of Isaiah*, lies in its creation of a mythological realm which is held to be of importance for the construction of the emerging Christian understanding of Christ.

We are almost bound to consider a relationship between the *Ascension of Isaiah* and 1 Tim. 3.16 given the extent of the overlap between them.

4. *The Ascension of Isaiah and the New Testament Literature* 305

The opening line of the hymn cited there ('He was manifested in the flesh') recalls the epiphanic Christology of the apocalypse. The Second Vision of the *Ascension of Isaiah* in many ways looks like an expansion and explanation of this christological summary, as if the author knew it and developed its thought to yield a new and more detailed form of belief.

1 Tim. 3.16 has a chiastic structure whose precise nature has been disputed.[53] There is no doubt more than one way of reading the material. Arrangement according to the pattern 'AABAAB', in which 'A' indicates events connected with the human Jesus and 'B' indicates events connected with his ascension to heaven, yields a form of belief that is strikingly close to the thought of the Second Vision:

ἐφανερώθη ἐν σαρκί, (A)
ἐδικαιώθη ἐν πνεύματι, (A)
ὤφθη ἀγγέλοις, (B)

ἐκηρύχθη ἐν ἔθνεσιν, (A)
ἐπιστεύθη ἐν κόσῳ, (A)
ἀνελήμφθη ἐν δόξῃ. (B)

This arrangement would allow for a hymn of two stanzas (perhaps one excerpted from a longer original), both of which describe two events connected with the earthly Jesus followed by a reference to the ascension. If the ὤφθη ἀγγέλοις in the first stanza is taken to designate the same event as the ἀνελήμφθη ἐν δόξῃ of the second then we have a close correspondence with *Asc. Isa.* 11.23-33 (and also with 1 Pet. 3.22). Other elements of 1 Tim. 3.16 are also echoed in the apocalypse. The ἐφανερώθη ἐν σαρκί describes an earthly appearance similar to that envisaged by the *Ascension of Isaiah*, where a divine being is held to have assumed human form; and in a context moreover in which this descent is subsequently followed by an ascension.[54] The *Ascension of Isaiah* also knows the tradition of universal evangelism (3.18), which in both texts is set *before* the ascension in what seems to be a strange order. The sequence of events in the second stanza of 1 Tim. 3.16

---

53. E. Schweizer identified a chiasmus which runs according to the pattern AB/BA/AB ('πνεῦμα, πνευματικός', *TDNT*, VI, p. 414). My pattern is based on a view of how the passage was read by the author of the *Ascension of Isaiah* and it is not intended as a comment on the sense of the original.

54. On the problem of whether pre-existence is presupposed here, see M. Dibelius, *The Pastoral Epistles* (ET; Philadelphia: Fortress Press, 1972), p. 63, and H. Windisch, 'Zur Christologie der Pastoralbriefe', *ZNW* 34 (1935), p. 222.

(ἐκηρύχθη–ἐπιστεύθη–ἀνελήμφθη) agrees precisely with the thought of *Asc. Isa.* 3.18 ('they will teach...those who believe...his ascension'). This evidence makes the author's knowledge of the material in 1 Tim. 3.16 a strong possibility. This, as I said, indicates that the authors of the apocalypse and of the Pastorals were resourced by the same stock of liturgical material.

1 Peter 3.18-22
It has been argued throughout this book that 1 Pet. 3.18-22 was a key passage for the author of the *Ascension of Isaiah*. The author used it to construct his description of the ascension which is found in 11.23-33. There is a general consensus that 1 Pet. 3.18-22 comes from a pre-Petrine fragment which has been incorporated in that letter. The passage describes how Christ was brought to life in the Spirit and how he preached to 'imprisoned spirits' before seating himself at the right hand of God's throne.[55] The passage by general consent also contains a number of difficulties.[56] One of these in particular can be alleviated with reference to the *Ascension of Isaiah*. This is the identity of the 'imprisoned spirits' who are mentioned in v. 19. Four different interpretations have been proposed to explain who these 'spirits' are. Ephraem and Hippolytus referred the passage to Christ's descent to the dead, which

---

55. Almost all who have commented on this passage have agreed about its pre-Petrine origin: see, for instance, R. Bultmann, 'Bekenntnis und Liedfragmente im ersten Petrusbriefe', in *Exegetica* (Tübingen: Mohr, 1967) pp. 285-97; C.H. Huntzinger, 'Zur Struktur des Christus-Hymnen in Phil. 2 und 1 Pet. 3', in E. Lohse (ed.), *Der Ruf Jesu und die Antwort der Gemeinde* (Göttingen: Vandenhoeck & Ruprecht, 1970), pp. 142-56; J. Jeremias, 'Zwischen Karfreitag und Ostern', *ZNW* 42 (1949), pp. 194-201; and M.E. Boismard, *Quatre hymnes baptismales dans la Première Épître de Pierre* (Paris: Cerf, 1961), pp. 57-109.

56. There is a readable, popular statement of the problems in W.A. Grudem, *1 Peter* (Leicester: Inter-Varsity Press, 1988), pp. 157-58. There are two detailed scholarly treatments of 1 Pet. 3.18-22, Reicke's *Disobedient Spirits* and Dalton's *Christ's Proclamation*. In addition to these, see C.E.B.Cranfield, 'The Interpretation of 1 Peter iii.19 and iv.6', *ExpTim* 69 (1957–58), pp. 369-72; W.J. Dalton, 'The Interpretation of 1 Peter 3,19 and 4–6: Light from 2 Peter', *Bib* 60.4 (1979), pp. 347-55; A.T. Hanson, 'Salvation Proclaimed: 1 Peter 3.18-22', *ExpTim* 93 (1982), pp. 100-15; S.E. Johnson, 'The Preaching to the Dead (1 Pet. 3,18-22)', *JBL* 79 (1960), pp. 48-51; K. Shimada, 'The Christological Credal Formula in 1 Peter 3, 18-22—Reconsidered', *Annual of Japanese Biblical Institute* 5 (1979), pp. 154-76; and the bibliography detailing these and other studies in J.R. Michaels, *1 Peter* (Waco: Word Books, 1988), p. 194.

4. *The Ascension of Isaiah and the New Testament Literature* 307

they thought took place between his crucifixion and resurrection.[57] Augustine, following his correspondence with Evodius,[58] saw the 'spirits' as antediluvian humans whom Christ addressed on earth through the mouthpiece of Noah. A third interpretation, which is found principally in post-Enlightenment scholarship,[59] links the 'spirits' of 3.19 with the Fallen Watchers of Genesis 6.[60] Genesis 6 describes how these Watchers

---

57. See Reicke, *Disobedient Spirits*, pp. 21-22. The relevant passages are Ephraem, *Carmina Nisibena*, 35.75-90 and a fragment of Hippolytus preserved in Syriac; see K. Geschwind, *Die Niederfahrt Christi in die Unterwelt: Ein Beitrag zur Exegese des Neuen Testaments und zur Geschichte des Taufssymbols* (Münster, 1911), pp. 45-46. The Syriac text of this can be found in P. de Lagarde, *Analecta Syriaca* (Leipzig, 1858), pp. 88-89. There is a Greek translation in H. Achelis, *Hippolytus' kleinere exegetische und homiletische Schriften* (Leipzig, 1897), pp. 286-87, while Reicke has an English translation. Dalton (*Christ's Proclamation*, p. 16) comments on this interpretation that: 'This is the view which is by far the most strongly represented among the early fathers and writers of the Church up to the time of St Augustine'; Clement of Alexandria was its earliest exponent (in his *Strom.* 6.6.38-39, *PG* 9.268a). Among recent scholars it is supported by C.E.B. Cranfield, *The First Epistle of Peter* (London: SCM Press, 1950), pp. 86-88.

58. Evodius pointed out to Augustine that Christ could hardly be held to have preached an unsuccesful sermon to the spirits in hell: '*Qui sunt illi spiritus, de quibus in Epistola sua ponit Petrus testimonium de Domino dicens; hoc inserens quod in inferno fuerunt, et descendens Christus omnibus evangelizavit, omnesque a tenebris et poenis per gratiam liberavit?*' (*PL* 33, pp. 708-16). Augustine replied that he must therefore have addressed sinners through the mouthpiece of Noah (see his *De Haeresibus* 79 [*PL* 42, p. 45B], *Ep.* 164.14-17, and Dalton, *Christ's Proclamation*, pp. 34-36).

59. F. Spitta, *Christ Predigt an die Geister* (Göttingen: Vandenhoeck & Ruprecht, 1890); but cf. the criticism of his interpretation in Dalton, *Christ's Proclamation*, p. 36. Later scholars agreed with Spitta's approach but set the preaching in the context of the descent to hell; see for example W. Bousset, *Kyrios Christos* (Göttingen: Vandenhoeck & Ruprecht, 1921), pp. 32-40; 'Zur Hadesfahrt Christi', *ZNW* 19 (1919–20), pp. 50-66; and Jeremias, 'Karfreitag', pp. 194-201. Geschwind (*Niederfahrt*, pp. 97-144) makes the ascension the moment that Christ addressed the angels.

60. Gen. 6.1-4 raises a number of problems, many of which are addressed by E.G. Kraeling, 'The Significance and Origin of Gen. 6.1-4', *JNES* 6 (1947), pp. 193-208. Kraeling suggests a Phoenician origin for this legend. The discovery of Hittite texts containing Hurrian material may also affect the exegesis of the passage. E.A Speiser sees them as the ultimate source for later Phoenician and Greek speculation (see his *Genesis* [AB; Garden City, NY: Doubleday, 1947], p. 46). He cites H.G. Güterbock, 'The Hittite Version of the Hurrian Kumarbi Myths: Oriental Forerunners of Hesiod', *AJA* 52 (1948), pp. 123-34, and Pope, *El in the Ugaritic*

descended from heaven in rebellion against God. Their punishment was a favourite topic in postbiblical literature. Fourthly, Michaels suggests that the 'spirits' in 1 Pet. 3.19 are not the Watchers themselves but the Giants who emerged from their union with the women and who wreaked havoc on earth.[61]

All but the third of these interpretations cause problems. The descent to hell was a popular theme in Christian writers of the second century (for instance the *Ascension of Isaiah*), but 1 Pet. 3.19 was never cited in connection with it before the time of Clement of Alexandria (who died c. 215 CE).[62] This observation casts doubt on the attempt to see that background reflected in first-century literature.[63] Moreover, the progress of thought in vv. 18-19 creates an obstacle to setting Christ's 'proclamation' before his resurrection. The phrase πορευθεὶς ἐκήρυξεν (3.19) occurs only after the ζῳοποιηθεὶς of 3.18, which is clearly a reference to the resurrection.[64] This means that the journey and preaching are seen as post-resurrectional events. Augustine's interpretation raises difficulties too. Kelly asks why Noah's contemporaries should have been singled out to hear the gospel, and he observes that the phrase 'in prison' on this interpretation must bear the metaphorical sense 'imprisoned *in sin*',

---

Texts, pp. 4-5. On the Watchers in Jewish literature, see Hengel, *Judaism and Hellenism*, I, pp. 231-34; Russell, *Method*, pp. 249-54; Urbach, *The Sages*, I, pp. 167-69; and Ginzberg, Legends, I, pp. 147-51.

61. Michaels, *1 Peter*, pp. 207-209.

62. This point is made by Dalton, *Christ's Proclamation*, p. 16. The first clear reference to it is Clement, *Strom*. 6.6.38-39 (*PG* 9.268a). Irenaeus discusses the descent apart from 1 Pet. 3.19 in his *Adv. Haer*. 4.22.1; 4.27.2; 5.31.1 (see Dalton's n. 5 on p. 16). See further Dalton, *Christ's Proclamation*, pp. 32-34.

63. This idea can hardly be found in 1 Pet. 4.6 either although that passage has often been held to support it. 1 Pet. 4.6 says εἰς τοῦτο γὰρ καὶ νεκροῖς εὐηγγελίσθη. The context is a reference to Christ as one who judged the living and dead (so 4.5) and the passage seems to designate those Christians who had perished before the parousia (cf. 1 Thess. 4.13-18). On its problems of interpretation see Dalton, *Christ's Proclamation*, pp. 263-77; and E. Schweizer, '1 Petrus 4, 6' *TZ* 8 (1952), pp. 152-54.

64. The verb generally indicates the resurrection in early Christian usage; see BAGD, p. 342. This sense is accepted by Bultmann, in *TDNT*, 'ζῳοποιέω', II, p. 875; but we should note that H. Windisch and H. Preisker, *Die Katholischen Briefe* (Tübingen: Mohr, 1951), p. 71, try to distinguish 'being made alive' here from 'being raised from the dead' in v. 22. This interpretation seems very forced and it is rightly criticized by Michaels, *1 Peter*, pp. 203-204.

4. *The Ascension of Isaiah and the New Testament Literature* 309

which is by no means obvious in the text.[65] Failure to supply an adequate understanding of 'imprisonment' must be levelled against the fourth interpretation as well, as Michaels himself notes. The Giants are nowhere said to be punished by imprisonment in Jewish tradition. Imprisonment, however, stands at the heart of the text. This makes the identification of the Spirits with the offspring of the Watchers unlikely.

This process of elimination leaves the third interpretation of 1 Pet. 3.19 as the most promising exegesis. Speculation about the Watchers and about their punishment is commonly found in apocalyptic literature.[66] According to *1 En.* 10.13 the Watchers were banished 'into the bottom of the fire—and in torment—in the prison [where] they will be locked up forever'.[67] This sentence is reconfirmed by *1 En.* 13.2: [Enoch to Azazel] 'They will put you in bonds, and you will not have [an opportunity] for rest and supplication, because you have taught injustice and because you have shown to the people deeds of shame, injustice and sin.' There was an alternative view of their fate in which the angels were held to have been confined to the lower heavens. This is found in *2 Enoch* 7:

> And those men took me up to the second heaven. And they set me down on the second heaven. And they showed me prisoners under guard, in measureless judgment. And there I saw the condemned angels, weeping. And I said to the men who were with me, 'Why are they tormented?'. The men answered me, 'They are evil rebels against the LORD, who did not listen to the voice of the LORD, but they consulted their own will' (2 En. 7.1-3, A recension).[68]

The identification of the 'spirits' with the Watchers of Genesis 6 makes good sense of Peter's notion of imprisonment. On this view the spirits were imprisoned in the air or in some other remote region and addressed by Christ after his resurrection. This interpretation gains plausibility from the observation that the Greek text of *1 Enoch* 1–32 often calls the

---

65. J.N.D. Kelly, *A Commentary on the Epistles of Peter and Jude* (London: A. & C. Black, 1982), p. 153.
66. See for example the Qumran *Gen. Apoc.* 2.1-25; 1QM 14.15; CD 2.15-20; and the text published by J.M. Allegro, 'Some Unpublished Fragments of Pseudepigraphal Literature from Qumran's Fourth Cave', *Annual of the Leeds University Oriental Society* 4 (1962–63), pp. 3-5; and cf. *Jub.* 4.22; 5.1-11; 7.21-35; 8.3.
67. Translation of *1 Enoch* by E. Isaac in Charlesworth (ed.), *Old Testament Pseudepigrapha*, I, p. 18.
68. Translation by F.I. Andersen in Charlesworth (ed.) *Old Testament Pseudepigrapha*, I, pp. 113-15.

Watchers πνεύματα (10.15; 13.6; many times in ch. 15). On this interpretation 1 Pet. 3.19-22 describes how Christ addressed rebellious angels in his ascension to the throne of God.

Verses 20-21 have often been seen as a digression in the passage, one which was suggested by the reference to the spirits in v. 19 and which led the author to comment on Noah and then on the significance of salvation through water (namely baptism). If this is so, and the author inserted his own material in the middle part of the hymn, v. 22 would have directly followed v. 19 in the lost original. This would have associated Christ's preaching to the spirits with his entry into heaven (cf. the 'seen by angels' of 1 Tim. 3.16 in this connection). This identification creates an obvious parallel with *Asc. Isa.* 11.23-33 where the Beloved One's identity is revealed as he ascends through the firmament.[69] This is the moment when the firmament angels acknowledge him as 'our Lord' and worship him. The *Ascension of Isaiah*, whose author knew 1 Peter, preserves the sequence of thought which 1 Peter's insertion has obscured and allows us to see more clearly the thought of the original hymn. This is because the two authors share a mutual understanding of the ascension as the demonstration of Christ's glory which involved the subordination of the angel world.

Reicke has identified the presence of a typology between Jesus and Enoch in 1 Peter 3 through which the author made Jesus achieve more than his antediluvian counterpart. 1 Pet. 3.22 describes how the angels submit to Jesus as he ascends to heaven. This contrasts with the material from the early chapters of *1 Enoch* which makes Enoch a mediator between God and the Fallen Watchers. The difference in the Christian text is that Jesus is a divine being who receives the angelic submission. The *Ascension of Isaiah* further develops this understanding by making the angels *worship* the Beloved One in his ascension. The likelihood that 1 Pet. 3.19-22 is founded on Jewish mythology confirms that speculation about Enoch and the Watchers probably stands behind the *Ascension of Isaiah*'s mythology too. *Asc. Isa.* 7.9-12 can very helpfully be exegeted on this basis. 7.12 comments that the angelic rebellion had stemmed from the creation of the world. This statement supports the view that the author was thinking about antediluvian times. The *Ascension of Isaiah* reads back this angelic rebellion to the *moment* of creation, in what

---

69. The contact between 1 Peter and the *Ascension of Isaiah* is surprisingly not explored in most scholarship on this passage except for a short comment by Dalton, *Christ's Proclamation*, p. 237.

might be read as a reaction against the suggestion of 1 Pet. 3.19 that it took place in primaeval history but *later* than the event of creation itself. Gnosticism would further develop this idea by asserting the idea of a *pre*-mundane fall. The suggestion that early Christian belief about the aerial powers emerged from Jewish apocalyptic speculation of the kind represented by *1 Enoch* 1–36 and *2 Enoch* 7 is, I think, a helpful one.

Revelation
Finally, we must note that several themes unite the *Ascension of Isaiah* with the book of Revelation. I have argued that we cannot be certain that the author of the *Ascension of Isaiah* knew Revelation. It is conceivable that the material that the two apocalypses hold in common was derived from a wider ambience which they used in their own ways. Certainly, it would be out of keeping with the author's other use of New Testament material to suggest that the Nero material (ch. 4) represents a detailed exegesis of Revelation. The differences between the two apocalypses in many ways outstrip the similarities. It would be an interesting research project to explore these differences, by which ostensibly similar motifs are used in different ways in the two strands of literature.

These differences can briefly be explored here. First of all, there is the vision of the throne of God which is an important feature of both works and which lies at the heart of all Jewish mysticism. Such a vision is found in Revelation 4–5 and in *Ascension of Isaiah* 9–11. The difference between the texts is that the Beloved One in the *Ascension of Isaiah* is worshipped by the angels *before* his appearance as Jesus (9.27-42), whereas Christ in Revelation is the counterpart of the risen and ascended Jesus (1.13-14; 5.6). This is a most interesting difference given that there is perhaps only twenty years between the texts and in view of the fact that other first-century sources (notably the Fourth Gospel) are willing to countenance a heavenly antecedent to the ministry of Jesus. Trinitarianism is another area of difference. The Spirit in Revelation is the mediator of apocalyptic revelation, and Rev. 22.17 names him in company with the Bride. In the *Ascension of Isaiah* the angel of the Holy Spirit receives *worship* from the angels (9.35-36), in what represents a second-century development in Christian theology.

The use of the Nero material is also significant. Both apocalypses allude to the myth of Nero's return, but the ways in which the motif is used are quite different. Revelation 13 presents Nero as the second beast which comes up from the earth and gives him the cheirogram '666'.

The *Ascension of Isaiah* by contrast fuses the myth of Nero's return with the notion of Beliar's descent from the firmament to criticize the Romans for their persecution of the Christians after 112 CE (ch. 4). In both Revelation and the *Ascension of Isaiah* Nero is a symbolic figure who has passed from the arena of history. He symbolizes Roman oppression on the basis of what was remembered about his reign, which served as a typical instance of Roman arrogance. The *Ascension of Isaiah* shows how mythology about Nero was developed in Christian circles in the early second century to meet a new phase of relations with Rome when persecution had become a contentious issue.

Finally, there is the millenarian eschatology which the two works hold in common. It is important to make the points that this links the *Ascension of Isaiah* not just with Revelation but with all the New Testament literature; and that the specific figure 'a thousand years' is not mentioned by *Asc. Isa.* 4.14-18. The case which I have argued is that the author of the *Ascension of Isaiah* modified the first-century millenarian picture by his introduction of the notion of *heavenly* immortality after the millenarian kingdom (4.17). The difference in this between Revelation and the *Ascension of Isaiah* ought not to be underestimated. It is not least one of cosmology and of the extent to which cosmology is allowed to determine a presentation of soteriology; and the standpoint of the *Ascension of Isaiah*, as I have argued, represents a step towards the Gnostic eschatology which is absent from Revelation.

Summary and Conclusions

At the end of the book I must summarize the ground that has been covered and restate my major conclusions.

I have taken the view that the *Ascension of Isaiah* is a second-century apocalypse which was written in Syria to address the threat of impending persecution by the Romans after 112 CE but before the death of Hadrian in 138 CE. This dating of the text has determined the conclusions about the various areas of research which the book has addressed. Chapter 2 argued the case that the *Ascension of Isaiah* embodies an angelomorphic Christology in which the Beloved One is presented as a divine being who receives worship from the angels, but in imagery which derives from Jewish angelology. I identified the development of an exalted angel in apocalyptic literature and the notion of the angelophany as important sources in this respect. Angelomorphic language was a feature both of

4. *The Ascension of Isaiah and the New Testament Literature* 313

first-century Christology and of the Christology of literature which was written after the *Ascension of Isaiah*. It must be distinguished from 'angel-Christology', which I take to be the portrayal of Christ quite literally as an angel. The significance of the *Ascension of Isaiah* lies in the way in which it develops first-century Christology by the introduction of the notions of the hidden descent and of the mediator's transformation into human likeness. This results in the work's docetic tendencies, as 11.2-22 (E text) shows.

Chapter 3 examined the work's setting in second-century Christianity. I have set the material about Rome in 4.1-13 at the centre of my analysis, although other scholars have seen this passage as an insertion into the apocalypse. I mentioned the problems of opposition from the Jews and from the church leaders as subsidiary factors which led the author to write as he did. The *Ascension of Isaiah* is of particular interest for the history of prophecy in early Christianity. It illustrates the time when prophetic influence was on the wane in the church but when it had not yet died out. The signs are that the emergence of the ministerial orders was an important factor in the demise of prophecy. I argued that the situation which the apocalypse addressed was the threat of persecution after 112 CE. The author responded to this threat by offering a qualified version of the Christian millenarian tradition. This asserted the reality of the Beloved One's imminent return from heaven and the establishment of his earthly kingdom (4.14-16), but promised a subsequent heavenly immortality (4.17) which is discussed in greater detail in the Second Vision. This reworking of the Christian millenarian tradition represents a transitional stage between the New Testament and the Gnostic literature. The *Ascension of Isaiah* is an important text for the study of Gnostic origins in Christian literature.

Chapter 4 argued from the fact of the work's second-century origin that the author knew texts such as the letters of Paul and at least some of the Gospels; but I made the point that he probably derived the Jesus traditions in chs. 3 and 11 from a source that was similar to the 'kerygmatic summaries' which also influenced the author of Acts. I noticed how he incorporated, but without acknowledgement, New Testament literature alongside other Jewish material in shaping his apocalypse, and allowed the framework of the Beloved One's descent and ascent to determine the way in which this earlier material was used. The *Ascension of Isaiah* is an important source for students of the New

Testament literature. Its evidence can profitably be incorporated into scholarly discussion of a variety of passages.

Future scholarship will be dominated by the new critical edition, but I think that the areas of research which I have presented here—the work's Christology, its social setting and contact with the New Testament literature—will continue to be important ones now that text has appeared. The next decade, I hope, will see a growing interest in the apocalypse and perhaps a consensus concerning its major lines of interpretation. This will be to the good of research into early Christianity as a whole.

BIBLIOGRAPHY

Aberle, D., 'A Note on Relative Deprivation Theory as Applied to Millenarian and Other Cult Movements', in Thrupp (ed.), *Millennial Dreams in Action*, pp. 209-14.
Abramowski, L., 'Sprache und Abfassungszeit der Oden Salomos', *OrChr* 68 (1984), pp. 80-90.
Acerbi, A., 'La Visione di Isaia nelle vicende dottrinali del catarismo lombardo', *CrSt* 1 (1980), pp. 59-74.
—*Serra Lignea: Studi sulla Fortuna della Ascensione di Isaia* (Rome: Editrice AVE, 1984).
—*L'Ascensione di Isaia: Cristologia e Profetismo in Siria nei primi decenni del II Secolo* (Milan: Vita e Pensiero, 1989).
Achelis, H., *Hippolytus' kleinere exegetische und homiletische Schriften* (Leipzig, 1897).
Adas, M., *Prophets of Rebellion: Millenarian Protest Movements against European Colonial Order* (Cambridge: Cambridge University Press, 1979).
Aland, K., *Synopsis Quattuor Evangeliorum: locis parallelis evangeliorum et Patrum adhibitis* (Stuttgart: Württembergische Bibelanstalt, 1979).
—'Der Text des Johannes-Evangeliums im 2. Jahrhundert', in W. Schrage (ed.), *Studien zum Text and zur Ethik des Neuen Testaments: Festschrift zum 80. Geburtstag von Heinrich Greeven* (Berlin: de Gruyter, 1986), pp. 1-10.
Alexander, P.S., 'The Targumim and Early Exegesis of "Son of God" in Genesis 6', *JJS* 28 (1977), pp. 156-60.
Allegro, J.M., 'Some Unpublished Fragments of Pseudepigraphal Literature from Qumran's Fourth Cave', *Annual of the Leeds University Oriental Society* 4 (1962–63), pp. 3-5.
Aptowitzer, V., *Kain und Abel in der Agada, den Apokryphen, der hellenist., christlich. und muhammed. Literatur* (Kohut Memorial Foundation, 1922).
Attridge, H., *Hebrews* (Philadelphia: Fortress Press, 1989).
Audet, J.P., *La Didaché* (Paris: Lecoffre, 1958).
Aune, D.E., *Prophecy in Early Christianity and the Mediterranean World* (Grand Rapids: Eerdmans, 1983).
Avis, P. (ed.), *The Resurrection of Jesus* (London: Darton, Longman & Todd, 1993).
Bacon, B.W., *Studies in St Matthew* (London: Constable & Co., 1930).
Bakker, A., 'Christ an Angel? A Study of Early Christian Docetism', *ZNW* 32 (1933), pp. 255-65.
Balz, H.R., *Methodische Probleme der Neutestamentliche Christologie* (Neukirchen–Vluyn: Neukirchener Verlag, 1967).
Bammel, E., 'Versuch zu Kol. 1.15-20', *ZNW* 52 (1961), pp. 88-95.

Barbel, J., *Christos Angelos: Die Anschauung von Christus als Bote und Engel in der gelehrten und volkstümlichen Literatur des christlichen Altertums* (Theophaneia, 3; Bonn: Peter Hanstein, 1941).
Bardy, G., 'Cérinthe', *RB* 30 (1921), pp. 341-73.
Barkun, M., *Disaster and the Millennium* (New Haven: Yale University Press, 1974).
Barnard, L.W., *Justin Martyr* (Cambridge: Cambridge University Press, 1967).
Barnes, T.D., *Tertullian* (Oxford: Clarendon Press, 1971).
Barrett, C.K., 'The Eschatology of the Epistle to the Hebrews', in W.D. Davies and D. Daube (eds.), *The Background of the New Testament and its Eschatology: Studies in Honour of C.H. Dodd* (Cambridge: Cambridge University Press, 1954), pp. 363-93.
—'Christianity at Corinth', *BJRL* 46 (1963), pp. 269-97.
Barton, J., 'The Ascension of Isaiah', in H.F.D. Sparks (ed.), *The Apocryphal Old Testament* (Oxford: Clarendon Press, 1984), pp. 775-812.
Barton, S., and G.N. Stanton, (eds.), *Resurrection: Essays in Honour of Leslie Houlden* (London: SPCK, 1994).
Basset, R., *Les apocryphes éthiopiens traduits en français* (Paris, 1893).
Bauckham, R.J., 'Gospel Traditions in the Ascension of Isaiah' (unpublished manuscript).
—'The Worship of Jesus in Apocalyptic Christianity', *NTS* 27 (1980–81), pp. 332-41.
—*Jude, 2 Peter* (Waco: Word Books, 1982).
—'Synoptic Parousia Parables Again', *NTS* 29 (1983), pp. 129-33.
Bauer, W., *Orthodoxy and Heresy in Earliest Christianity* (ET; London: SCM Press, 1972).
Baumeister, T., *Die Anfänge der Theologie des Martyriums* (MBT, 45; Münster: Aschendorff, 1980).
Beasley-Murray, G.R., *Jesus and the Future* (London: Macmillan, 1956).
Beckford, J.A., *The Trumpet of Prophecy: A Sociological Study of Jehovah's Witnesses* (Oxford: Basil Blackwell, 1965).
Belleville, L.L., *Reflections of Glory: Paul's Polemical Use of the Moses-Doxa Tradition in 2 Corinthians 3.1-18* (JSNTSup, 52; Sheffield: JSOT Press, 1991).
Benoit, P., *L'Évangile selon Saint Matthieu* (Paris: Cerf, 1972).
Berger, P.L., 'The Sociological Study of Sectarianism', *Social Research* 21 (1954), pp. 467-87.
Berger, P., and T. Luckmann, *The Social Construction of Reality* (Garden City, NY: Doubleday, 1966).
Berneri, M.L., *Journey through Utopia* (London: Freedom Press, 1982).
Betz, H.D., *Galatians* (Philadelphia: Fortress Press, 1979).
Bianchi, U., 'L'*Ascensione di Isaia!*: Tematiche soteriologiche di *descensus/ascensus*', in Pesce (ed.), *Isaia, il Diletto e la Chiesa*, pp. 155-83.
Bianchi, U. (ed.), *Le Origini dello Gnosticismo* (Leiden: Brill, 1967).
Bietenhard, H., *Die himmlische Welt im Urchristentum und Spätjudentum* (WUNT, 2; Tübingen: Mohr, 1951).
—'The Millennial Hope in the Early Church', *SJT* 6 (1953), pp. 12-30.
Bigg, C., *The Christian Platonists of Alexandria* (Oxford, 1886).
Black, M., 'The Son of Man in Recent Research and Debate', *BJRL* 45 (1962–63), pp. 305-18.

—'The Throne-Theophany Prophetic Commission and the Son of Man', in R.G. Hamerton-Kelly and R. Scroggs (eds.), *Jews, Greeks, and Christians: Religious Culture in Late Antiquity* (Leiden: Brill, 1976), pp. 57-73.

Blackman, E.C., *Marcion and his Influence* (London: SPCK, 1948).

Blinzler, J., *Die Brüder und Schwestern Jesu* (SBS, 21; Stuttgart: Katholisches Bibelwerk, 1967).

Boismard, M.E., *Quatre hymnes baptismales dans la Premiere Épître de Pierre* (Paris: Cerf, 1961).

Boor, C. de., 'Weiteres zur Chronik des Skylites', *Byzantinischer Zeitschrift* 14 (1905), pp. 425-33.

Borgen, P., 'God's Agent inthe Fourth Gospel', in Neusner (ed.), *Religions in Antiquity*, pp. 137-48.

—*Bread from Heaven* (NovTSup, 10; Leiden: Brill, 1975).

—*Logos was the True Light* (Leiden: Brill, 1983).

—'Logos was the True Light: Contributions to the Interpretation of the Prologue of John', *NovT* 14 (1972), pp. 115-30.

Bori, P.C., 'L'estasi del profeta: *Ascensio Isaiae* 6 e l'Antico Profetismo Cristiano', *CrSt* 1 (1980), pp. 367-89.

—'L'esperienza profetica nell'*Ascensione di Isaia*', in Pesce, (ed.), *Isaia*, pp. 133-54.

Boring, M.E., 'What are we Looking For? Towards a Definition of the Term "Christian Prophet"', in G.W. Macrae (ed.), *SBL 1973 Seminar Papers* (Missoula: Scholars Press), II, p. 147.

—'Prophecy (Early Christian)', in Freedman *et al.* (eds.), *The Anchor Bible Dictionary*, V, pp. 495-502.

Borsch, F.H., *The Son of Man in Myth and History* (London: SCM Press, 1967).

—*The Christian and Gnostic Son of Man* (SBT, 14; London: SCM Press, 1970).

Bousset, W., *The Antichrist Legend* (ET; London: Hutchinson, 1896).

—*Die Religion des Judentums im Neutestamentlichen Zeitalter* (Berlin: Reuther & Reichard, 1903).

—'Zur Hadesfahrt Christi', *ZNW* 19 (1919–20), pp. 50-66.

—*Kyrios Christos* (Göttingen: Vandenhoeck & Ruprecht, 1921).

—*Der Himmelsreise der Seele* (repr.; Darmstadt: Wissenschaftliche Buchgesellschaft, 1971).

Bowker, J.W., 'Merkabah Visions and the Visions of Paul', *JJS* 16 (1971), pp. 157-73.

Brandon, S.G.F., *The Fall of Jerusalem and the Christian Church: A Study of the Effects of the Jewish Overthrow of AD 70 on Christianity* (London: SPCK, 1951).

—*Jesus and the Zealots* (Manchester: Manchester University Press, 1967).

Brandt, W., *Elchesai: Ein Religionsstifter und sein Werk* (Leipzig, 1912).

Brooke, G.J., 'Qumran Pesher: Towards the Redefinition of a Genre', *RevQ* 10 (1979–80), pp. 483-503.

—*Exegesis at Qumran: 4QFlorilegium in its Jewish Context* (JSOTSup, 29; Sheffield: JSOT Press, 1985).

Brooks, S.H., *Matthew's Community: The Evidence of his Special Sayings Material* (JSNTSup, 16; Sheffield: JSOT Press, 1987).

Brown, R.E., *The Birth of the Messiah* (London: Geoffrey Chapman, 1977).

Brown, R.E., with K.P. Donfried, J.A. Fitzmyer and J. Reumann (eds.), *Mary in the New Testament* (Philadelphia: Fortress Press, 1978).

Brownlee, W.H., 'Biblical Interpretation among the Sectaries of the Dead Sea Scrolls', *BA* 14 (1951), pp. 54-76.
—'The Cosmic Role of Angels in 11Q Targum of Job', *JSJ* 8 (1977), pp. 83-84.
Brox, N., *Pseudepigraphie in der heidnischen und jüdisch-christlichen Antike* (Darmstadt: Wissenschaftliche Buchgesellschaft, 1977).
Buck, F., 'Are the "Ascension of Isaiah" and the "Odes of Solomon" Witnesses to an Early Cult of Mary?', in *De primordiis cultu Mariani* (Rome: Pontificia Academia Mariana Internationalis, 1970), IV, pp. 371-99.
Bühner, J.-A., *Der Gesandte und sein Weg im vierten Evangelium* (WUNT, 2; Tübingen: Mohr, 1977).
Bultmann, R., 'Die Bedeutung der neuerschlossenen mandäischen und manichäischen Quellen für das Verständnis des Johannesevangeliums', *ZNW* 24 (1925), pp. 100-46.
—*The Theology of the New Testament* (ET; 2 vols.; London: SCM Press, 1952).
—'Bekenntnis und Liedfragmente im ersten Petrusbriefe', in *Exegetica* (Tübingen: Mohr, 1967), pp. 285-97.
Burch, V., 'The Literary Unity of *Ascensio Isaiae*', *JTS* 20 (1919), pp. 17-23.
—'Material for the Interpretation of *Ascensio Isaiae*', *JTS* 21 (1920), pp. 249-65.
Burchard, C., *Untersuchungen zu Joseph und Aseneth* (WUNT, 8; Tübingen: Mohr, 1965).
Burger, C., *Jesus als Davidssohn* (Göttingen: Vandenhoeck & Ruprecht, 1970).
Burkitt, F.C., *Jewish and Christian Apocalypses* (London: British Academy, 1914).
Burridge, K., *New Heaven, New Earth* (Oxford: Basil Blackwell, 1969).
—'Reflections on Prophecy and Prophetic Groups', *Semeia* 21 (1981), pp. 99-102.
Caird, G.B., *Principalities and Powers* (Oxford: Clarendon Press, 1956).
—*A Commentary on the Revelation of St John the Divine* (London: A. & C. Black, 1966).
Caquot, A., 'Bref Commentaire du Martyre d'Isaïe', *Sem* 23 (1973), pp. 65-93.
Caragounis, C.C., *Son of Man* (WUNT, 38; Tübingen: Mohr, 1986).
Carmignac, J., 'Le Document de Qumran sur Melkisédeq', *RevQ* 7 (1970), pp. 343-78.
Carr, A.W., 'The Rulers of This Age—1 Corinthians II.6-8', *NTS* 23 (1976–77), pp. 20-35.
—*Angels and Principalities* (SNTSMS, 42; Cambridge: Cambridge University Press, 1981).
Casey, P.M., 'The Use of the Term "Son of Man" in the Similitudes of Enoch', *JSJ* 7 (1976), pp. 11-29.
Charles, R.H., *The Ascension of Isaiah* (London: A. & C. Black, 1900).
—*The Apocrypha and Pseudepigrapha of the Old Testament* (Oxford: Oxford University Press, 1913).
—*A Critical and Exegetical Commentary on the Book of Daniel* (Oxford: Oxford University Press, 1929).
Charlesworth, J.H., 'The Portrait of the Righteous as an Angel', in G.W. Nickelsburg and J.J. Collins (eds.), *Ideal Figures in Ancient Judaism* (Chico, CA: Scholars Press, 1980), pp. 135-51.
—'Christian and Jewish Self-Definition in Light of the Christian Additions to the Apocryphal Writings', in E.P. Sanders (ed.), *Jewish and Christian Self-Definition* (London: SCM Press, 1985), II, pp. 27-55.

Bibliography

—*The Pseudepigrapha and Modern Research* (Missoula: Scholars Press, 2nd edn with Supplement, 1981).
Charlesworth, J.H. (ed.), *The Old Testament Pseudepigrapha* (2 vols.; London: Darton, Longman & Todd, 1983, 1985).
Cheek, J., 'Paul's Mysticism in the Light of Psychedelic Experience', *JAAR* 38 (1970), pp. 381-89.
Chernus, I., 'Visions of God in Merkabah Mysticism', *JSJ* 13 (1982), pp. 123-46.
—*Mysticism in Rabbinic Judaism* (Studia Judaica, 11; Berlin: de Gruyter, 1982).
Chilton, B.D., 'The Transfiguration: Dominical Assurance and Apostolic Vision', *NTS* 27 (1981), pp. 115-24.
Christ, F., *Jesus Sophia: Die Sophia-Christologie bei den Synoptikern* (ATANT, 57; Zürich: Zwingli-Verlag, 1950).
Clemen, C., 'Die Himmelfahrt des Jesaja, ein ältestes Zeugnis für das römische Martyrium des Petrus', *ZWT* (1896), pp. 388-415.
—'Nochmals der Märtyrtod des Petrus in der *Ascensio Jesaiae*', *ZWT* (1897), pp. 455-65.
Cohn, N., 'Medieval Millenarism: Its Bearing on the Contemporary Study of Millenarian Movements', in Thrupp (ed.), *Millennial Dreams in Action*, pp. 31-43.
—*The Pursuit of the Millennium* (London: Maurice Temple Smith, rev. edn, 1970).
Collins, A.Y., *Crisis and Catharsis: The Power of the Apocalypse* (Philadelphia: Westminster Press, 1984).
Collins, J.J., *The Sibylline Oracles of Egyptian Judaism* (SBLDS, 13; Missoula: Scholars Press, 1974).
—*The Apocalyptic Vision of the Book of Daniel* (HSM, 16; Missoula: Scholars Press, 1977).
—*Daniel: A Commentary on the Book of Daniel* (Philadelphia: Fortress Press, 1993).
Collins, J.J. (ed.), *Apocalypse: Morphology of a Genre* (*Semeia* 14 , 1979).
Colonna, M.E., *Gli Storici bizantini dal IV al XV secolo, I: Storici profani* (Naples: Casa Editrice Armani, 1956).
Colson, F.H., and G.H. Whittaker, *et al.*, *Philo* (LCL; Cambridge, MA: Harvard University Press, 1929–53).
Conzelmann, H., *1 Corinthians* (Philadelphia: Fortress Press, 1975).
Cothenet, E., 'Isaïe (L'Ascension de)', *Catholicisme* 6 (1963), pp. 144-46.
Cranfield, C.E.B., *The First Epistle of Peter* (London: SCM Press, 1950).
—'The Interpretation of 1 Peter iii.19 and iv.6', *ExpTim* 69 (1957–58), pp. 369-72.
—*Mark* (Cambridge: Cambridge University Press, 1959).
Crossan, J.D., *The Historical Jesus: The Life of a Mediterranean Jewish Peasant* (Edinburgh: T. & T. Clark, 1991).
Culianu, I.P., 'La Visione di Isaia e la tematica della Himmelsreise', in Pesce (ed.), *Isaia, il Diletto e la Chiesa*, pp. 95-116.
Cullmann, O., *The State in the New Testament* (ET; London: SCM Press, 1956).
—*The Christology of the New Testament* (ET; London: SCM Press, 2nd edn, 1963).
Dalton, W.J., *Christ's Proclamation to the Spirits: A Study of 1 Peter 3.18-4.6* (Rome: Pontifical Biblical Institute, 1965).
—'The Interpretation of 1 Peter 3,19 and 4–6: Light from 2 Peter', *Bib* 60.4 (1979), pp. 347-55.
Daniélou, J., 'Trinité et angélologie dans la théologie judéo-chrétienne', *RSR* 45 (1957), pp. 5-41.

—*The Theology of Jewish Christianity* (ET; London: SCM Press, 1964).
Davies, S.L., *The Gospel of Thomas and Christian Wisdom* (New York: Seabury, 1983).
Davies, W.D., *The Setting of the Sermon on the Mount* (Cambridge: Cambridge University Press, 1964).
Deane, W.J., *Pseudepigrapha* (Edinburgh, 1891).
Dehandschutter, B., *Martyrium Polycarpi: een literair-kritische studie* (Leuven: Leuven University Press, 1979).
Dehn, G., 'Engel und Obrigkeit: Ein Beitrag zum Verständnis von Röm. 13.1-7', in E. Wolf (ed.), *Theologische Aufsätze für Karl Barth zum 50. Geburtstag* (Munich: Chr. Kaiser Verlag, 1936), pp. 90-109.
Deichgräber, R., *Gotteshymnus und Christushymnus in der frühen Christenheit* (SUNT, 5; Göttingen: Vandenhoeck & Ruprecht, 1967).
Delcor, M.L., 'Melchizedek from Genesis to the Qumran Texts and the Epistles to the Hebrews', *JSJ* 2 (1971), pp. 115-35.
—'L'Ascension d'Isaïe à travers le predication d'un évêque cathare en Catalogne au quatorzième siècle', *RHR* 184 (1973), pp. 157-78.
Delius, W., *Texte zur Geschichte der Marienverehung und Marienverkündigung in der alten Kirche* (Berlin: de Gruyter, 1956).
—*Geschichte der Marienverehung* (Munich/Basel: Ernst Reinhardt, 1963).
Denis, A.-M., *Fragmenta Pseudepigraphorum Graeca* (PVTG, 3; Leiden: Brill, 1970).
—*Introduction aux Pseudepigraphes grecs d'Ancien Testament* (SVTP, 1; Leiden: Brill, 1970).
Dibelius, M., *Die Geisterwelt im Glauben Paulus* (Göttingen: Vandenhoeck & Ruprecht, 1909).
—*The Pastoral Epistles* (ET; Philadelphia: Fortress Press, 1972).
Dillmann, C.F.A., *Ascensio Isaiae* (Leipzig, 1877).
Dix, G., 'The Seven Archangels and the Seven Spirits', *JTS* 28 (1927), pp. 233-50.
Dodd, C.H., *The Apostolic Preaching and its Development* (London: Hodder & Stoughton, 1936).
—*According to the Scriptures* (London: Nisbet & Co., 1952).
Doran, R., 'The Martyr: A Synoptic View of the Mother and her Seven Sons', in J.J. Collins and G.W. Nickelsburg (eds.), *Ideal Figures in Ancient Judaism* (Chico, CA: Scholars Press, 1980), pp. 189-221.
Douglas, M., *Natural Symbols* (Harmondsworth: Penguin Books, 1978).
Dunn, J.D.G., *Christology in the Making* (London: SCM Press, 1980).
Easton, B.S., 'New Testament Ethical Lists', *JBL* 51 (1932), pp. 1-12.
Ehrhardt, A., 'Judaeo-Christians in Egypt', in F.L. Cross (ed.), *Studia Evangelica* (TU, 68; Berlin: Akademie Verlag, 1964), III, pp. 360-82.
Eichrodt, W., *The Theology of the Old Testament* (2 vols.; ET; London: SCM Press, 1967).
Ellingworth, P., 'Which Way are We Going? A Verb of Movement Especially in 1 Thess. 4.14b', *BT* 25 (1974), pp. 426-31.
Emerton, J.A., 'The Origin of the Son of Man Imagery', *JTS* 9 (1958), pp. 225-42.
—'Melchizedek and the Gods: Fresh Evidence for the Jewish Background of John 10.34-36', *JTS* 17 (1966), pp. 399-401.
Epp, E.J., 'Wisdom, Torah, Word: The Johannine Prologue and the Purpose of the Fourth Gospel', in G.F. Hawthorne (ed.), *Current Issues in Biblical and Patristic*

Interpretation: Studies in Honour of M.C. Tenney (Grand Rapids: Eerdmans, 1975), pp. 128-46.

Epstein, I., *The Babylonian Talmud* (London: Soncino Press, 1936).

Erbetta, M., 'Ascensione di Isaia 4, 3 e la testimonia più antica del martirio di Petro', *Euntes Docete* 19 (1966), pp. 427-36.

Esler, P.F., *The First Christians in their Social Worlds: Social-Scientific Approaches to New Testament Interpretation* (London: Routledge, 1994).

Everling, O., *Die paulinische Angelologie und Dämonologie* (Göttingen, 1888).

Fabricius, J.A., *Codex Pseudepigraphanus Veteris Testamenti* (1722).

Fantis, A. de., *Opera nuper in lucem prodeuntia* (Venice, 1522).

Ferch, A., *Daniel 7* (Berrien Springs: Andrews University Press, 1979).

Festinger, L., *et al.*, *When Prophecy Fails: A Social And Psychological Study of a Modern group that Predicted the Destruction of the World* (New York: Harper & Row, 1956).

Festugière, A.J., 'A Propos des arétalogies d'Isis', *HTR* 42 (1949), pp. 209-34.

Feuillet, A., *Le Christ Sagesse de Dieu d'après les épîtres Pauliniennes* (Paris: Lecoffre, 1966).

Fischel, H.A., 'The Uses of Sorites (*Climax, Gradatio*) in the Tannaitic Period', *HUCA* 44 (1973), pp. 119-51.

Fischer, J., 'Der davidische Abkunft der Mutter Jesu: biblische-patristische Untersuchung', *Weidenauerstudien* 4 (1911), pp. 1-115.

Fitzmyer, J.A., 'Further Light on Melchizedek from Qumran Cave 11', *JBL* 86 (1967), pp. 25-41.

Flusser, D., 'The Apocryphal Book of *Ascensio Isaiae* and the Dead Sea Sect', *IEJ* 3 (1953), pp. 30-47.

Foerster, W., *Gnosis* (2 vols.; Oxford: Clarendon Press, 1972–74).

Ford, J.M., 'Mary's *Virginitas post Partum* and Jewish Law', *Bib* 54 (1951), pp. 94-101.

—'Millennium', in Freedman *et al.* (eds.), *The Anchor Bible Dictionary*, IV, pp. 832-34.

Forsyth, N., *The Old Enemy* (Princeton, NJ: Princeton University Press, 1987).

Fossum, J-A., *The Name of God and the Angel of the Lord: Samaritan and Jewish Concepts of Intermediation and the Origin of Gnosticism* (WUNT, 36; Tübingen: Mohr, 1985).

Francis, F.O. (ed.), *Conflict at Colossae* (SBS, 4; Missoula, MT: Scholars Press, 1973).

Frank, T. (ed.), *An Economic Survey of Ancient Rome* (5 vols. and index; Baltimore: The Johns Hopkins University Press, 1933–40).

Freedman, D.N. *et al.* (eds.), *The Anchor Bible Dictionary* (6 vols.; Garden City, NY: Doubleday, 1992).

Frend, W.H.C., *Martyrdom and Persecution in the Early Church* (Oxford: Basil Blackwell, 1965).

Friedländer, M., *Der vorchristliche jüdische Gnosticismus* (Göttingen, 1898).

Friedrich, G., 'Prophets in the Early Church', *TDNT*, VI, pp. 856-61.

Fuchs, H., *Der geistige Widerstand gegen Rom in der antiken Welt* (Berlin: de Gruyter, 1938).

Fuller, R.H., *The Foundations of New Testament Christology* (London: Fount Paperbacks, new edn, 1979).

Gager, J.G., *Kingdom and Community* (Englewood Cliffs, NJ: Prentice-Hall, 1975).
—*The Origins of Anti-Semitism* (Oxford: Oxford University Press, 1985).
Gärtner, B., *The Temple and the Community in Qumran and the New Testament* (SNTSMS, 1; Cambridge: Cambridge University Press, 1965).
Gebhardt, O. von., 'Die Ascensio Isaiae als Heilegenlegende', *ZWT* 21 (1878), pp. 330-53.
Geschwind, K., *Die Niederfahrt Christi in die Unterwelt: Ein Beitrag zur Ezegese des Neuen Testaments und zu Geschichte des Taufssymbols* (NTAbh, 2; Münster: Aschendorff, 1911).
Giambelluca Kossova, A., 'Osservazioni sulla tradizione paleoslava della Visione di Isaia: coincidenze e divergenze con la tradizione testuale dell'*Ascensione di Isaia*' (unpublished paper).
Giblin, G.H., 'Three Monotheistic Texts in Paul', *CBQ* 37 (1975), pp. 527-47.
Gieseler, J.C.L., *Programma quo Academiae Georgiae Augustae prorector et senatus sacra pentecostalia anni MDCCCXXXII pie concelebranda indixerunt* (Göttingen, 1832).
Ginzberg, L., *The Legends of the Jews* (7 vols.; Philadelphia: Jewish Publication Society of America, 1947).
Glasson, T.F., *The Second Advent: The Origin of the New Testament Doctrine* (London: Epworth Press, 1963).
—*Moses in the Fourth Gospel* (SBT, 40; London: SCM Press, 1963).
Glock, C.Y., 'The Role of Deprivation in the Origin and Evolution of Religious Groups', in R. Lee and M.E. Marty (eds.), *Religion and Social Contact* (New York: Oxford University Press, 1964), pp. 24-36.
Gnoli, G., 'Questioni comparative sull'*Ascensione de Isaia*: la tradizione iranica', in Pesce (ed.), *Isaia, il Diletto e la Chiesa*, pp. 117-32.
Goodenough, E.R., *By Light, Light: The Mystic Gospel of Hellenistic Judaism* (New Haven: Yale University Press, 1935).
—*An Introduction to Philo Judaeus* (Oxford: Basil Blackwell, 1962).
Goodman, M., *The Ruling Class of Judaea: The Origins of the Jewish Revolt against Rome AD 66–70* (Cambridge: Cambridge University Press, 1987).
Goulder, M.D., 'Did Jesus of Nazareth Rise from the Dead?', in S. Barton and G.N. Stanton (eds.), *Resurrection: Essays in Honour of Leslie Houlden* (London: SPCK, 1994), pp. 58-68.
Gourgues, M., *A la Droite de Dieu: Résurrection de Jésus et actualisation du Psaume 110.1 dans le Nouveau Testament* (Paris: Lecoffre, 1978).
Gowan, D.E., *Eschatology in the Old Testament* (Philadelphia: Fortress Press, 1986).
Graef, H.C., *Mary: A History of Doctrine and Devotion* (2 vols.; London and New York: Sheed & Ward, 1963).
Grant, R.M., *Gnosticism and Early Christianity* (New York: Columbia University Press, 1959).
Grässer, E., 'Hebraer 1.1-4: Ein exegetisch Versuch' (EKKNT, Vorarbeiten, 3, 1971), pp. 55-91.
Grelot, P., 'Deux toséphtas targoumiques inédites sur Isaïe LXVI', *RB* 79 (1972), pp. 511-43.
Grenfell, B.P., and A.S. Hunt, *The Amherst Papyri...Part 1: The Ascension of Isaiah and Other Theological Fragments* (London: Oxford University Press, 1900).
Grillmeier, A., *Christ in Christian Tradition* (ET London: Mowbrays, 2nd edn, 1975).

Grudem, W.A., *1 Peter* (Leicester: Inter-Varsity Press, 1988).
Gruenwald, I., *Apocalyptic and Merkabah Mysticism* (Leiden: Brill, 1980).
Güterbock, H.G., 'The Hittite Version of the Hurrian Kumarbi Myths: Oriental Forerunners of Hesiod', *AJA* 52 (1948), pp. 123-34.
Habermann, J., *Präexistenzaussagen im Neuen Testament* (Frankfurt: Peter Lang, 1990).
Hahn, F., *The Titles of Jesus in Christology: Their History in Early Christianity* (ET; London: Lutterworth, 1969).
Hall, R.G., 'The Ascension of Isaiah: Community Situation, Date, and Place in Early Christianity', *JBL* 109.2 (1990), pp. 289-306.
—'Isaiah's Ascent to See the Beloved: An Ancient Jewish Source for the Ascension of Isaiah', *JBL* 111.3 (1994), pp. 463-84.
Halperin, D., *The Merkabah in Rabbinic Literature* (New Haven: American Oriental Society, 1980).
Hamerton-Kelly, R.G., *Pre-Existence, Wisdom, and the Son of Man: A Study in the Idea of Pre-Existence in the New Testament* (SNTSMS, 21; Cambridge: Cambridge University Press, 1973).
Hammershaimb, E., 'Das Martyrium Esajas', in W.G. Kümmel *et al.* (eds.), *Jüdische Schriften aus hellenistisch-römische Zeit* (Gütersloh: Gerd Mohn, 1973), II, pp. 15-34.
—*De Gammeltestamentlige Pseudepigrapher* (Copenhagen: Gads Forlag, 1976).
Hanson, A.T., *Jesus Christ in the Old Testament* (London: SPCK, 1965).
—'Salvation Proclaimed: 1 Peter 3.18-22', *ExpTim* 93 (1982), pp. 100-15.
Hanson, P.D., *The Dawn of Apocalptic* (Philadelphia: Fortress Press, 1975).
Hanson, R.P.C., *Allegory and Event* (London: SCM Press, 1959).
Harnack, A. von, *Geschichte der altchristlichen Literatur* (Leipzig, 1893).
Harper, G.M., 'Village Administration in the Roman Province of Syria', *Yale Classical Studies* 1 (1928), pp. 105-68.
Harris, M.J., *Raised Immortal* (London: Marshall, Morgan & Scott, 1983).
Harrison, P.N., *Polycarp's Two Epistles to the Philippians* (Cambridge: Cambridge University Press, 1936).
Hay, D.M., *Glory at the Right Hand* (Nashville: Abingdon Press, 1973).
Hegermann, H., *Die Vorstellung vom Schöpfungsmittler im hellenistischen Judentum und Urchristentum* (TU, 82; Berlin: Akademie Verlag, 1961).
Heichelheim, F.M., 'Roman Syria', in Frank (ed.), *An Economic Survey of Ancient Rome*, IV, pp. 231-45.
Heine, R.E., 'Montanus, Montanism', in Freedman *et al.* (eds), *The Anchor Bible Dictionary*, IV, pp. 898-902.
Heller, J., 'Himmel- und Höllenfahrt nach Römer 10.6-7', *EvT* 32 (1972), pp. 478-86.
Hellholm, D. (ed.), *Apocalypticism in the Mediterranean World and the Near East* (Tübingen: Mohr, 1983).
Helmbold, A.K., 'Ascension of Isaiah', in M.C. Tenny, (ed.), *Zonderman Pictorial Encyclopedia of the Bible* (Grand Rapids: Eerdmans, 1975), pp. 248-50.
—'Gnostic Elements in the Ascension of Isaiah', *NTS* 18 (1972), pp. 222-27.
Hengel, M., *Judaism and Hellenism* (2 vols.; ET; London: SCM Press, 1974).
—*The Son of God* (ET; London: SCM Press, 1976).
—'Messianische Hoffnung und politischer "Radikalismus" in der "jüdisch-hellenistischen Diaspora" ', in Hellholm (ed.), *Apocalypticism*, pp. 665-86.
—*The Cross of the Son of God* (ET; London: SCM Press, 1986).

—*The Johannine Question* (London: SCM Press, 1989).
—*The Zealots* (ET Edinburgh: T. & T. Clark, 1989).
— *Studies in Early Christology* (Edinburgh: T. & T. Clark, 1995).
Hennecke, E., with W. Schneemelcher and R.McL. Wilson (eds.), *New Testament Apocrypha* (ET; London: SCM Press, 1963–65).
Hermisson, H.J., *Studien zur israelitischen Spruchweisheit* (Neukirchen–Vluyn: Neukirchener Verlag, 1968).
Heussi, K., 'Die *Ascensio Isaiae* und ihr vermeintliches Zeugnis für ein römisches Martyrium des Apostels Petrus', *Wissenschaftliche Zeitschrift der Friedrich-Schiller-Universität Jena* 12 (1983), pp. 269-74.
Hill, D., 'The Ascension of Isaiah', in Hennecke *et al.* (eds.), *New Testament Apocrypha*, II, pp. 642-63.
—*The Gospel of Matthew* (NCB; London: Oliphants, 1972).
—*New Testament Prophecy* (London: Marshall, Morgan & Scott, 1979).
Hindley, J.C., 'Towards a Date for the Similitudes of Enoch', *NTS* 14 (1968), pp. 551-65.
Hobshawm, E.J., *Primitive Rebels: Studies in Archaic Forms of Social Movements in the Nineteenth and Twentieth Centuries* (Manchester: Manchester University Press, 1959).
—*Bandits* (London: Weidenfeld & Nicolson, 1969).
Hoffmann, P., *Die Toten im Christus* (NTAbh, n.s. 2; Münster: Aschendorff, 1966).
Hofius, O., *Katapausis: Die Vorstellung vom endzeitlichen Ruheort im Hebräerbrief* (WUNT, 11; Tübingen: Mohr, 1970).
—*Der Vorhang vor dem Thron Gottes: Eine exegetische-religionsgeschichtliche Untersuchung zu Hebräerbrief 6,19f. und 10,19f.* (WUNT, 14; Tübingen: Mohr, 1972).
Holladay, C.R., 'The Portrait of Moses in Ezekiel the Tragedian', in G.W. Macrae (ed.), *SBL 1976 Seminar Papers* (Missoula, MT: Scholars Press, 1976), pp. 447-52.
—*Theios Aner in Hellenistic Judaism* (SBLDS, 40; Missoula, MT: Scholars Press, 1977).
—'New Testament Christology: A Consideration of Dunn's *Christology in the Making*', *Semeia* 30 (1984), pp. 64-82.
Holtz, T., *Die Christologie der Apokalypse des Johannes* (Berlin: Akademie Verlag, 1962).
Hooker, M.D., *The Son of Man in Mark* (London: SPCK, 1967).
—*Jesus and the Servant: The Influence of the Servant Concept of Deutero-Isaiah in the New Testament* (London: SPCK, 1959).
Horbury, W., '1 Thess. ii.3 as Rebutting the Charge of False Prophecy', *JTS* 33 (1982), pp. 492-508.
Hornschüh, M., *Studien zur Epistula Apostolorum* (Berlin: de Gruyter, 1965).
Horsley, R.A., 'The Background of the Confessional Formula in 1 Cor. 8.6', *ZNW* 69 (1978), pp. 130-34.
—'Popular Prophetic Movements at the Time of Jesus, their Principal Features and Social Origins', *JSNT* 26 (1986), pp. 3-27.
Horst, P. van der, 'Moses' Throne-Vision in Ezekiel the Dramatist', *JJS* 34 (1983), pp. 21-29.
Horton, F.L., *The Melchizedek Tradition* (SNTSMS, 30; Cambridge: Cambridge University Press, 1976).

Huntzinger, C.H., 'Zur Struktur des Christus-Hymnen in Phil. 2 und 1 Petr. 3', in E. Lohse (ed.), *Der Ruf Jesus und die Antwort der Gemeinde* (Göttingen: Vandenhoeck & Ruprecht, 1970), pp. 142-56.

Hurtado, L.W., *One God, One Lord* (London: SCM Press, 1988).

Isenberg, S.R., 'Millenarism in Greco–Roman Palestine', *Rel* 4 (1974), pp. 20-46.

Ivanov, J., *Bogomilski knigi i legendi* (Sofia, 1925).

Jacobson, H., 'Mysticism and Apocalyptic in Ezekiel's *Exagoge*', *Illinois Classical Studies* 6 (1981), pp. 272-93.

—*The Exagoge of Ezekiel* (Cambridge: Cambridge University Press, 1983).

Jefford, C.N., *The Sayings of Jesus in the Teaching of the Twelve Apostles* (Leiden: Brill, 1989).

Jeremias, J., 'Zwischen Karfreitag und Ostern', *ZNW* 42 (1949), pp. 194-201.

—*Theophanie: Die Geschichte einer alttestamentlichen Gattung* (Neukirchen–Vluyn: Neukirchener Verlag, 1965).

—*Jerusalem in the Time of Jesus* (ET; London: SCM Press, 1969).

—*The Parables of Jesus* (ET; London: SCM Press, 3rd edn, 1972).

Jewett, R., *The Thessalonian Correspondence: Pauline Rhetoric and Millenarian Piety* (Philadelphia: Fortress Press, 1986).

Johnson, B., 'A Critical Appraisal of the Church-Sect Typology', *American Sociological Review* 22 (1957), pp. 88-92.

Johnson, S.E., 'The Preaching to the Dead (1 Pet. 3.18-22)', *JBL* 79 (1960), pp. 48-51.

Käsemann, E., 'Kritische Analyse zu Phil. 2, 5-11', *ZTK* 47 (1950), pp. 313-60. Reprinted in *Exegetische Versuche und Besinnung: Erste Band* (Göttingen: Vandenhoeck & Ruprecht, 1960), pp. 51-95.

—'An Apologia for Primitive Christian Eschatology', in his *Essays on New Testament Themes* (ET; London: SCM Press, 1964), pp. 169-95.

—*The Testament of Jesus* (ET; London: SCM Press, 1966).

Katz, E., 'Das Martyrium Isaias', *Communio Viatorum* 11 (1968), pp. 169-74.

Kautsch, E., *Die Apokryphen und Pseudepigraphen des Altens Testaments* (2 vols.; Tübingen, 1900).

Kee, H.C., *The Community of the New Age: Studies in Mark's Gospel* (London: SCM Press, 1977).

Kelly, J.N.D., *Early Christian Creeds* (London: Longmans, Green, 3rd edn, 1972).

—*Early Christian Doctrines* (London: A. & C. Black, 5th edn, 1977).

—*A Commentary on the Epistles of Peter and Jude* (London: A. & C. Black, 1982).

Kilpatrick, G.D., *The Origins of the Gospel according to St Matthew* (Oxford: Clarendon Press, 1946).

Kim, S., *The Origin of Paul's Gospel* (WUNT, 4; Tübingen: Mohr, 1981).

Klausner, J., *The Messianic Idea in Israel* (London: George Allen & Unwin, 1956).

Klijn, A.F.J., and G.J. Reininck, *Patristic Evidence for Jewish-Christian Sects* (NovTSup, 36; Leiden: Brill, 1973).

Klinzing, G., *Die Umdeutung des Kultus in der Qumrangemeinde und in Neuen Testament* (SUNT, 7; Göttingen: Vandenhoeck & Ruprecht, 1971).

Knibb, M.A., The Date of the Parables of Enoch', *NTS* 25 (1978–79), pp. 345-59.

—'The Ascension of Isaiah', in Charlesworth (ed.), *The Old Testament Pseudepigrapha*, II, pp. 143-76.

Knight, J.M., *The Ascension of Isaiah* (GAP, 2; Sheffield: Sheffield Academic Press, 1995).
Knox, W.L., 'The Divine Wisdom', *JTS* 38 (1937), pp. 230-37.
—*St Paul and the Church of the Gentiles* (Cambridge: Cambridge University Press, 1939).
Köbben, A.J.F., 'Prophetic Movements as an Expression of Social Protest', *International Archives of Ethnography*, 49.1 (1960), pp. 117-64.
Köhler, W.-D., *Die Rezeption des Matthäusevangeliums in der Zeit vor Irenäus* (WUNT, 24; Tübingen: Mohr, 1987).
Kolenkow, A.B., 'The Angelology of the Testament of Abraham', in G.W.E. Nickelsburg (ed.), *Studies on the Testament of Abraham* (SBLSCS; Missoula, MT: Scholars Press, 1976), pp. 153-62.
Kozak, E., 'Bibliographische Übersicht der biblisch-apokryphen Literatur bei den Slaven', *Jahrbücher für Protestantischer Theologie* 18 (1892), pp. 127-58.
Kraeling, E.G., 'The Significance and Origin of Gen. 6.1-4', *JNES* 6 (1947), pp. 193-208.
Kretschmar, G., *Studien zur frühchristlichen Trinitätstheologie* (BHT, 21; Tübingen: Mohr, 1956).
Küchler, M., *Frühjüdische Weisheitstraditionen: Zum Fortgang weisheitlichen Denkens im Bereich des frühjüdischen Jahweglaubens* (Göttingen: Vandenhoeck & Ruprecht, 1979).
Kumar, K., *Utopianism* (Milton Keynes: Open University Press, 1991).
Kümmel, W.G., *Introduction to the New Testament* (ET; London: SCM Press, 1975).
Labriolle, P., *La Crise Montaniste* (Paris: Fondation Tiers, 1913).
Lacau, P., 'Fragments de l'Ascension d'Isaïe en copte', *Le Muséon* 59 (1946), pp. 453-67.
Lagarde, P. de., *Analecta Syriaca* (Leipzig, 1858).
Lampe, G.W.H., 'AD 70 in Christian Reflection', in C.F.D. Moule and E. Bammel (eds.), *Jesus and the Politics of his Day* (Cambridge: Cambridge University Press, 1984), pp. 153-71.
Lang, B., *Frau Weisheit: Deutung einer biblischen Gestalt* (Düsseldorf: Patmos Verlag, 1978).
Langen, F., *Das Judenthum im Palästina* (Freiburg, 1866).
Lanne, E., 'Chérubim et Séraphim', *RSR* 43 (1955), pp. 524-35.
Lanternari, V., *The Religions of the Oppressed: A Study of Modern Messianic Cults* (London: MacGibbon & Kee, 1963).
Larkin, K.J.A., *The Eschatology of Second Zechariah: A Study of the Formation of a Mantological Wisdom Anthology* (Kampen: Kok Pharos, 1994).
Laurence, R., *Ascensio Isaiae Vatis* (Oxford, 1819).
Lawson, J., *The Biblical Theology of St Irenaeus* (London: Epworth Press, 1948).
Lefort, L.T., 'Coptica Lovaniensia', *Le Muséon* 51 (1938), pp. 24-30.
—'Fragments d'apocryphes en copte-akhmîmique', *Le Muséon* 52 (1939), pp. 7-10.
Leivestad, R., *Christ the Conqueror* (London: SPCK, 1954).
—'Exit the Apocalyptic Son of Man', *NTS* 18 (1971-72), pp. 243-67.
Lentzen-Deis, F., *Die Taufe Jesu nach den Synoptikern* (FThSt, 4; Frankfurt: Josef Knecht, 1970).
Leonardi, C., 'Il testo dell'AI nel Vat. lat. 5750', *CrSt* 1 (1980), pp. 59-74.

Lincoln, A.T., 'Paul the Visionary: The Setting and Significance of the Rapture to Paradise in 2 Corinthians 12.1-10', *NTS* 25 (1979), pp. 204-20.
—*Ephesians* (Dallas: Word Books, 1990).
Lofland, J., *Doomsday Cult: A Study of Conversion, Proselytization, and Maintenance of Faith* (Englewood Cliffs, NJ: Prenctice-Hall, 1966).
Lofland, J., and R. Stark, 'Becoming a World-Saver: A Theory of Conversion to a Deviant Perspective', *American Sociological Review* 30 (1965), pp. 862-75.
Logan, A.H.B., and A.J.M. Wedderburn, *The New Testament and Gnosis* (Edinburgh: T. & T. Clark, 1983).
Lohmeyer, E., *Kyrios Jesus: Eine Untersuchung zu Phil 2.5-11* (Heidelberg: Carl Winter, 1928).
Longenecker, R., *The Christology of Early Jewish Christianity* (SBT, 17; London: SCM Press, 1970).
Lorenz, R., *Arius Ioudaizans?* (Göttingen: Vandenhoeck & Ruprecht, 1980).
Lossky, V., *The Mystical Theology of the Eastern Church* (Cambridge: James Clarke, 1973).
Lüdtke, W., 'Beiträge zu slavischen Apokryphen', *ZAW* 31 (1911), pp. 218-35.
Luecken, W., *Michael* (Göttingen, 1898).
Mack, B.L., *Logos und Sophia: Untersuchungen zur Weisheitstheologie im hellenistischen Judentum* (Göttingen: Vandenhoeck & Ruprecht, 1983).
McKane, W., *Wisdom in Proverbs* (London: SCM Press, 1970).
Macrae, G.W., 'Some Elements of Jewish Apocalyptic and Mystical Tradition and their Relation to Gnostic Literature' (PhD dissertation, University of Cambridge, 1966).
Mai, A., *Collectio Nova Scriptorum Veterum* (Rome, 1828).
Maier, J., *Vom Kultus zu Gnosis* (Salzburg: Otto Müller, 1964).
Mannheim, K., *Ideology and Utopia* (ET; London: Routledge, new edn, 1991).
Markschies, C., *Valentinus Gnosticus? Untersuchungen zur valentinianischen Gnosis mit einem Kommentar zu den Fragmentem Valentins* (WUNT, 65; Tübingen: Mohr, 1992).
—' "*Sessio ad dexteram*": Bemerkungen zu einem altchristlichen Bekenntnismotiv in der christologischen Diskussion altkirchlichen Theologen', in M. Philonenko (ed.), *Le Trône de Dieu* (WUNT, 69; Tübingen: Mohr, 1993), pp. 252-317.
Marshall, I.H., *The Gospel of Luke* (Exeter: Paternoster Press, 1978).
Martin, R.P., *Carmen Christi* (Grand Rapids: Eerdmans, 2nd edn, 1983).
—*2 Corinthians* (Waco: Word Books, 1986).
Martyn, J.L., *History and Theology in the Fourth Gospel* (New York: Harper & Row, 1968).
Marucchi, O., *Le catacombe romane* (Rome: Libreria dello Stato, 1933).
Massaux, E., *L'Influence de l'Évangile de Saint Matthieu sur la littérature chrétienne avant Saint Irénée* (Louvain: Gembloux, 1950).
Mearns, C.L., 'Early Eschatological Development in Paul: The Evidence of I and II Thessalonians', *NTS* 27 (1980-81), pp. 137-57.
Meeks, W.A., *The Prophet King* (NovTSup, 14; Leiden: Brill, 1967).
—'Moses as God and King', in Neusner (ed.), *Religions in Antiquity*, pp. 324-77.
—'The Man from Heaven in Johannine Sectarianism', *JBL* 91 (1972), pp. 44-72.
—*The First Urban Christians* (New Haven: Yale University Press, 1983).
—'Social Functions of Apocalyptic Language in Pauline Christianity', in Hellholm (ed.), *Apocalypticism*, pp. 687-705.

Meeks, W.A., and R. Wilken, *Jews and Christians at Antioch in the First Four Centuries of the Common Era* (Missoula, MT: Scholars Press, 1978).
Meslin, M., *Les ariens d'occident 335–430* (Coll. Patristica Sorbonensia, 8; Paris: Du Seuil, 1967).
Metzger, B.M., *The Early Versions of the New Testament* (Oxford: Oxford University Press, 1977).
Meyer, R., 'Himmelfahrt und Martyrium des Jesaja', in K. Galling (ed.), *Die Religion in Geschichte und Gegenwart* (Tübingen: Mohr, 3rd edn, 1965).
Michaels, J.R., *1 Peter* (Waco: Word Books, 1988).
Michaelis, W., *Zur Engelchristologie im Urchristentum* (Basel: Heinrich Majer, 1942).
Milik, J.T., *Ten Years of Discovery in the Wilderness of Judaea* (ET; London: SCM Press, 1959).
Miller, G., 'ARXONTWN TOY AIWNOS TOUTOU—A New Look at 1 Corinthians II:6-8', *JBL* 91 (1972), pp. 522-28.
Miller, M.P., 'The Function of Isaiah 61.1-2 in 11Q Melchizedek', *JBL* 88 (1969), pp. 467-69.
Moore, A.L., *The Parousia in the New Testament* (NovTSup, 13; Leiden: Brill, 1966).
Moore, G.F., 'Christian Writers on Judaism', *HTR* 14 (1921), pp. 197-254.
—'Intermediaries in Jewish Theology', *HTR* 15 (1922), pp. 41-79.
—'Apocrypha', *JewEnc*, II (1902), pp. 1-60.
Moravcsik, *Byzantinoturcica I* (Budapest, 2nd edn, 1958).
Morgan, D., *Wisdom in Old Testament Traditions* (Oxford: Basil Blackwell, 1981).
Moule, C.F.D., *The Origin of Christology* (Cambridge: Cambridge University Press, 1977).
—*The Holy Spirit* (London: Mowbrays, 1978).
Moule, C.F.D., and E. Bammel (eds.), *Jesus and the Politics of his Day* (Cambridge: Cambridge University Press, 1984).
Mowinckel, S., *He That Cometh* (ET; Oxford: Basil Blackwell, 1956).
Moxnes, H., 'God and his Angel in the Shepherd of Hermas', *ST* 28 (1974), pp. 49-56.
Müller, U., *Prophetie und Predigt im Neuen Testament* (Gütersloh: Gerd Mohn, 1975).
Munck, J., *Paul and the Salvation of Mankind* (ET; London: SCM Press, 1959)
Murphy-O'Connor, J., 'Christological Anthropology in Phil. ii 6-11', *RB* 83 (1976), pp. 25-50.
—'Redactional Angels in 1 Tim. 3,16', *RB* 91 (1984), pp. 178-81.
Negley, G., and J.M. Patrick, *The Quest for Utopia: An Anthology of Imaginary Societies* (New York, 1952).
Neusner, J. (ed.), *Religions in Antiquity: Essays in Memory of Erwin Ramsdell Goodenough* (Leiden: Brill, 1968).
Nickelsburg, G.W.E., *Resurrection, Immortality and Eternal Life in Inter-Testamental Judaism* (HTS, 26; Cambridge, MA: Harvard University Press, 1972).
—*Jewish Literature between the Bible and the Mishnah* (Philadelphia: Fortress Press, 1981).
—'Social Aspects of Palestinian Jewish Apocalypticism', in Hellholm, (ed.), *Apocalypticism*, pp. 641-54.
Niditch, S., 'The Visionary', in J.J. Collins and G.W. Nickelsburg (eds.), *Ideal Figures in Ancient Judaism* (SCS, 12; Chico, CA: Scholars Press, 1980), pp. 153-79.
Nitzsch, I., 'Nachweisung zweier Bruchstücke einer alten lateinischen Übersetzung vom Anabatikon Esaiou', *Theologische Studien und Kritiken* 3 (1830), pp. 209-46.

Norden, E., *Agnostos Theos* (repr.; Darmstadt: Wissenschaftliche Buchgesellschaft, 1956).

Norelli, E., 'La resurrezione di Gesù nell'*Ascensione di Isaia*', *CrSt* 1 (1980), pp. 315-66.

—'Il Martyrio di Isaia come *testimonium* antiguidaico?', *Henoch* 2 (1980), pp. 35-57.

—'Sulla pneumatologia dell'*Ascensione di Isaia*', in Pesce (ed.), *Isaia, il Diletto e la Chiesa*, pp. 211-76.

—'Collazione del testo della Leggenda greca pubblicata ds O.v. Gebhardt dal ms. Paris Gr. 1534 con il testo del ms. Vat.Pal. Gr.27' (unpublished manuscript).

—'Studio sul rapporto tra i. mss. etiopici di AI, limitamente ai capp. 1-5' (unpublished manuscript).

—'Studio sui rapporti tra testo etiopico, frammento greco, antica versione latina, versione copta sahidica, con esame e critica delle testi di Charles sulla storia del testo di AI 1-5' (unpublished manuscript).

Odeberg, H., *III Enoch or the Hebrew Book of Enoch* (Cambridge: Cambridge University Press, 1928).

Pagels, E., *The Gnostic Gospels* (London: Weidenfeld & Nicolson, 1979).

Pannenberg, W., *Jesus: God and Man* (ET; London: SCM Press, 1968).

Passmore, J., *The Perfectibility of Man* (London: Gerald Duckworth, 1972).

Pearson, B.A., 'Hellenistic–Jewish Wisdom Speculation and Paul', in Wilken, (ed.), *Aspects of Wisdom in Judaism and Christianity*, pp. 43-66.

—'The problem of "Jewish Gnostic" Literature', in C.W. Hedrick and R. Hodgson (eds.), *Nag Hammadi, Gnosticism and Early Christianity* (Peabody, MA: Hendrickson, 1985), pp. 15-35.

—*Gnosticism, Judaism and Egyptian Christianity* (Minneapolis: Fortress Press, 1990).

Percy, E., *Die Probleme der Kolosser- und Epheserbriefe* (Lund: Gleerup, 1946).

Perdue, L.G., *Wisdom and Cult* (Missoula, MT: Scholars Press, 1977).

Perrone, L., 'Note critiche (e "autocritiche") sull'edizione del testo etiopico dell'*Ascensione di Isaia*', in Pesce (ed.), *Isaia, il Diletto e la Chiesa*, pp. 77-93.

Pesce, M., *Paolo e gli arconti a Corinto* (Brescia: Paideia, 1977).

—'Presupposti per l'utilazzione storica dell'*Ascensione di Isaia*: Formazione e tradizione del testo; genere letterario; cosmologia angelica', in *idem* (ed.), *Isaia, il Diletto e la Chiesa*, pp. 13-76.

—'Tradizioni giudaiche utilizzate in A1 1-5 e il genere letterario di AI' (unpublished paper).

Pesce, M. (ed.), *Isaia, il Diletto e la Chiesa* (Brescia: Paideia, 1983).

Peterson, E., 'Die Spiritualität des griechischen Physiologos', *BZ* 47 (1954), pp. 70ff.

Pétrement, S., *A Separate God: The Christian Origins of Gnosticism* (ET; London: Darton, Longman & Todd, 1991).

Philonenko, M., *Pseudépigraphes de l'Ancien Testament et Manuscripts de la Mer Morte* (Paris, 1967).

Piper, R.A., *Wisdom in the Q Tradition: The Aphoristic Teaching of Jesus* (SNTSMS, 61; Cambridge: Cambridge University Press, 1989).

Plevnik, J., 'The Parousia as Implication of Christ's Resurrection: An Exegesis of 1 Thess. 4.13-18', in *idem* (ed.), *Word and Spirit: Essays in Honor of David Martin Stanley* (Willowdale, Ont.: Regis Books, 1975), pp. 199-277.

Plumpe, J.S., 'Some Little-Known Early Witnesses to Mary's *Virginitas in Partu*', *TS* 9 (1948), pp. 567-77.

Pope, M.H., *El in the Ugaritic Texts* (VTSup, 2; Leiden: Brill, 1955).
Popov, A., *Opsianie rukopisei i katalog knigi tserkovnoi pechati biblioteki A.I. Khludova* (Moscow, 1872).
Proksch, O., 'Die Berüfungsvision Hezekiels', *BZAW*, 34 (1920), pp. 141ff.
Rad, G. von., *Old Testament Theology* (2 vols.; ET; London: SCM Press, 1961).
—*Wisdom in Israel* (ET; London: SCM Press, 1972).
Ramsey, A.M., *The Glory of God and the Transfiguration of Christ* (London: Longmans, Green, 1945).
Reicke, B., *The Disobedient Spirits and Christian Baptism* (Lund: Ejnar Munksgaard, 1946).
Reid, B.E., *The Transfiguration: A Source- and Redaction-Critical Study of Luke 9.28-36* (Paris: Gabalda, 1993).
Renoux, C., 'Note sur l'Ascension d'Isaïe dans la tradition liturgique hiérosolymitaine', *CrSt* 2 (1981), pp. 367-70.
Riesenfeld, H., *Jésus transfiguré: L'arrière-plan du récit évangelique de la Transfiguration de Nôtre-Seigneur* (ASNU, 16: Copenhagen: Munksgaard, 1947).
Riessler, P., *Altjüdisches Schrifttum ausserhalb der Bibel* (Heidelberg: F.H. Kerle, 2nd edn, 1966).
Roberts, C.H., *Manuscript, Society and Belief in Early Christian Egypt* (London: British Academy, 1979).
Robinson, H.W., 'The Hebrew Conception of Corporate Personality', in *Werden und Wesen des Alten Testaments*, BZAW, 66; Berlin: Töpelmann, 1936).
Robinson, J.A., 'Ascension of Isaiah', in J.H. Hastings (ed.), *A Dictionary of the Bible* (Edinburgh: T. & T. Clark, 1900), II, pp. 499-501.
Robinson, J.A.T., *Jesus and His Coming* (London: SPCK, 1957).
—*Redating the New Testament* (London: SPCK, 1975).
Robinson, J.M. (ed.), *The Nag Hammadi Library in English* (Leiden: Brill, 1977).
Rogerson, J.W., 'The Hebrew Concept of Corporate Personality: A Re-Examination', *JTS* 21 (1970), pp. 1-16.
Ronchey, S., *Indagine sul Martirio di San Policarpo: critica storica e fortuna agiografica di un caso giudiziario in Asia Minore* (Rome: Istituto Palazzo Borromini, 1990).
Rost, L., *Einleitung in die alttestamentlich Apokryphen und Pseudepigraphen einschliesslich der grossen Qumran Handschriften* (Heidelberg: Quelle & Meyer, 1971).
Rowland, C.C., 'Visions of God in Apocalyptic Literature', *JSJ* 10 (1979), pp. 137-54.
—'The Vision of the Risen Christ in Rev. i.13ff.: The Debt of an Early Christology to an Aspect of Jewish Angelology', *JTS* 31 (1980), pp. 1-11.
—*The Open Heaven* (London: SPCK, 1982).
—*Christian Origins* (London: SPCK, 1985).
—'A Man Clothed in Linen: Daniel 10.5-6 and Jewish Angelology', *JSNT* 24 (1985), pp. 99-110.
—*Radical Christianity* (Oxford: Polity Press, 1988).
Rudolph, K., *Gnosis* (ET; Edinburgh: T. & T. Clark, 1983).
Russell, D.S., *The Method and Message of Jewish Apocalyptic* (London: SCM Press, 1964).
Sachmatov, A.A., and P.A. Lavrov, *Sbornik XII věka Moskovskago Uspenskago Sobora* (Moscow, 1899).

Ste Croix, G. de., 'Why were the Early Christians Persecuted?', *Past and Present* 26 (1963), pp. 6-38.
—'Why were the Early Christians Persecuted? A Rejoinder', *Past and Present* 27 (1964), pp. 28-33.
Sánchez, J.M.C., 'San José en los libros apocrifos del Nuevo Testamento', *Cahiers de Joséphologie* 19 (1971), pp. 123-49.
Sanders, E.P., *Paul and Palestinian Judaism* (London: SCM Press, 1981).
—*Jesus and Judaism* (London: SCM Press, 1985).
—*The Historical Figure of Jesus* (London: Penguin Books, 1993).
Sanders, E.P. (ed.), *Jewish and Christian Self-Definition* (3 vols.; London: SCM Press, 1980–83).
Schaberg, J., *The Father, the Son and the Holy Spirit: The Triadic Phrase in Matthew 28.19b* (SBLDS, 61; Chico, CA: Scholars Press, 1982).
Schäfer, P., *Rivalität zwischen Engeln und Menschen* (Berlin: de Gruyter, 1975).
Schillebeeckx, E., *Jesus: An Experiment in Christology* (London: Collins, 1969).
—*Christ: The Christian Experience in the Modern World* (London: SCM Press, 1980).
Schlier, H., *Christus und die Kirche im Epheserbrief* (Tübingen: Mohr, 1930).
—*Principalities and Powers in the New Testament* (ET; London: Burns & Oates, 1961).
Schmid, H.H., *Wesen und Geschichte der Weisheit* (Berlin: Töpelmann, 1966).
Schmidt, C., *Gespräche Jesu mit seinen Jungern nach der Auferstehung* (TU, 43; Berlin: Hinrichs, 1919).
Schnabel, E.J., *Law and Wisdom from Ben Sira to Paul* (WUNT, 16; Tübingen: Mohr, 1985).
Schniewind, J., 'Die Archonten dieses Äons: 1 Kor. 2,6-8', in *Nachgelassene Reden und Aufsätze* (Berlin: Töpelmann, 1951), pp. 104-109.
Schoedel, W.R., *Ignatius of Antioch* (Philadelphia: Fortress Press, 1985).
Schoeps, H.J., *Theologie und Geschichte des Judenchristentums* (Tübingen: Mohr, 1949).
Scholem, G., *Major Trends in Jewish Mysticism* (London: Thames & Hudson, 1955).
—*Jewish Gnosticism, Merkabah Mysticism and Talmudic Tradition* (New York: Jewish Theological Seminary of America, 1960).
Schottroff, L., *Der glaubende und die feindliche Welt: Beobachtungen zum gnostitche Dualismus und seiner Bedeutung für Paulus und der Johannesevangelium* (WMANT, 37; Neukirchen–Vluyn: Neukirchener Verlag, 1970).
Schürer, E., *The History of the Jewish People in the Age of Jesus Christ* (rev. G. Vermes *et al.*; 3 vols.; Edinburgh: T. & T. Clark, 1983–87).
Schweinburg, K., 'Die ursprüngliche Form des Kedrenechronik', *Byzantinischer Zeitschrift* 30 (1929–30), pp. 68-77.
Schweizer, E., '1 Petrus 4, 6', *TZ* 8 (1952), pp. 152-54.
—'Zum religionsgeschichtlichen Hintergrund der "Sendungsformel" Gal. 4.4f., Rom. 8.3f., John 3.16f., 1 John 4.9', *ZNW* 57 (1966), pp. 199-21.
Scott, M., *Sophia and the Johannine Jesus* (JSNTSup, 71; Sheffield: JSOT Press, 1992).
Segal, A.F., *Two Powers in Heaven* (Leiden: Brill, 1978).
—'Heavenly Ascent in Hellenistic Judaism, Early Christianity and their Environments', *ANRW* II.23.2, pp. 1333-94.
—'Ruler of this World: Attitudes about Mediator Figures and the Importance of Sociology for Self-Definition', in Sanders (ed.), *Jewish and Christian Self-Definition*, II, pp. 245-68.

Sevrin, J.-M. (ed.), *The New Testament in Early Christianity* (Leuven: Leuven University Press, 1989).

Sharot, S., *Messianism, Mysticism and Magic: A Sociological Analysis of Jewish Religious Movements* (Chapel Hill: University of North Carolina Press, 1982).

Sherwin-White, A.N., 'Early Persecutions and Roman Law Again', *JTS* 3 (1952), pp. 199-213.

—'Why were the Early Christians Persecuted?—an Amendment', *Past and Present* 27 (1964), pp. 23-27.

Shimada, K., 'The Christological Credal Formula in 1 Peter 3, 18-22—Reconsidered', *Annual of Japanese Biblical Institute* 5 (1979), pp. 154-76.

Simonetti, M., *La crisi ariani nel IV secolo* (Rome: Institutum Patristicum Augustinianum, 1975).

—'Note sulla cristologia dell'*Ascensione di Isaia*', in Pesce (ed.), *Isaia, il Diletto e la Chiesa*, pp. 185-209.

Sint, J., *Pseudonymität im Altertum* (Innsbruck: Universitätsverlag Wagner, 1960).

Sjøberg, E., *Der Menschensohn in dem Äthiopischen Henochbuch* (Lund: Gleerup, 1946).

Smallwood, E.M., *The Jews under Roman Rule* (Leiden: Brill, 1976).

Smith, J.P., *Proof of the Apostolic Preaching* (London: Longmans, Green, 1952).

Smith, J.Z., 'The Prayer of Joseph', in Neusner (ed.), *Religions in Antiquity* (Leiden: Brill, 1968), pp. 253-94.

Sparks, H.F.D., *The Apocryphal Old Testament* (Oxford: Clarendon Press, 1984).

Speiser, E.A., *Genesis* (AB; Garden City, NY: Doubleday, 1947).

Spitta, F., *Christ Predigt an die Geister* (Göttingen: Vandenhoeck & Ruprecht, 1980).

Spittler, R.P., 'The Limits of Ecstasy: An Exegesis of 2 Corinthians 12.1-10', in G.F. Hawthorne (ed.), *Current Issues in Biblical and Patristic Interpretation* (Grand Rapids: Eerdmans, 1975), pp. 259-66.

Stead, G.C., 'The Origins of the Doctrine of the Trinity, I', *Theology* 77 (1974), pp. 508-17.

Stendahl, K., *The School of St Matthew* (Lund: Gleerup, 2nd edn, 1967).

Stenger, W., 'Der Christushymnus in 1 Tim. 3,16: Aufbau-Christologie-Sitz im Leben', *TTZ* 78 (1969), pp. 33-48.

Stevenson, J., *A New Eusebius* (London: SPCK, 1957).

Stier, F., *Gott und sein Engel im Alten Testament* (Münster: Aschendorff, 1935).

Stockhausen, C.K., *Moses' Veil and the Glory of the New Covenant* (ABI, 16; Rome: Pontifical Biblical Institute, 1989).

Stojanovic, L.V., 'Stare srpske hrisovulje, akti, biographie, letopesi, tipici, pomenici, zapisi i dr', in *Spomenik Sprkse Kraljevske Akademije* (Belgrade, 1890), III, pp. 190-93.

Stone, M.E., 'The Concept of the Messiah in 4 Ezra', in J. Neusner, (ed.), *Religions in Antiquity*, pp. 295-312.

—'Lists of Revealed Things in Apocalyptic Literature', in F.M. Cross (ed.), *Magnalia Dei* (New York: Doubleday, 1976), pp. 414-52.

Strecker, G., 'Jewish Christianity', in W. Bauer, *Orthodoxy and Heresy in Earliest Christianity* (ET; London: SCM Press, 1972), Appendix, pp. 241-85.

Strugnell, J., 'The Angelic Liturgy at Qumran: 4Q Serek Širôt 'Olat Haššabāt', in G.W. Anderson *et al.* (eds.) (VTSup, 7; Leiden: Brill, 1960), pp. 318-45.

Stuckenbruck, L., *Angel Veneration and Christology: A Study in Early Judaism and in the Christology of the Apocalypse of John* (WUNT, 70; Tübingen: Mohr, 1995).
Styler, G.M., 'The Priority of Mark', in C.F.D. Moule, *The Birth of the New Testament* (London: A. & C. Black, 1981), pp. 285-316.
Suggs, M.J., 'The Word is Near You: Rom. 10.6-10 within the Purpose of the Letter', in W.R. Farmer (ed.), *Christian History and Interpretation* (Cambridge: Cambridge University Press, 1967), pp. 289-312.
—*Wisdom, Christology and Law in Matthew's Gospel* (Cambridge, MA: Harvard University Press, 1970).
Sweet, J.P.M., 'The Zealots and Jesus', in Moule and Bammel (eds.), *Jesus and the Politics of his Day*, pp. 1-9.
Székely, S., *Bibliotheca Apocrypha: Introductio historico-critica in libros apocryphos utriusque Testamenti cum explicatione argumenti et doctrinare*, I (Freiburg: Herder, 1913).
Talbert, C.H., 'The Myth of the Descending-Ascending Redeemer in Mediterranean Antiquity', *NTS* 22 (1976), pp. 418-40.
Talbert, C.H., *What is a Gospel? The Genre of the Canonical Gospels* (Philadelphia: Fortress Press, 1977).
Talmon, Y., 'The Pursuit of the Millennium: The Relations between Religions and Social Change', *Archives Européennes de Sociologie* 3 (1962), pp. 125-48.
—'Millenarian Movements', *Archives Européennes de Sociologie* 7 (1966), pp. 159-200.
—'Millenarism', in D.L. Sills (ed.), *International Encylopedia of the Social Sciences* (New York: Macmillan, Free Press, 1968), X, pp. 349-62.
Taylor, L.R., *The Divinity of the Roman Emperor* (Philological Monographs, I; Middletown, CT: American Philological Association, 1931).
Theisohn, J., *Der auserwählte Richter* (Göttingen: Vandenhoeck & Ruprecht, 1975).
Thiele, E.R., *The Mysterious Numbers of the Hebrew Kings* (Grand Rapids: Eerdmans, 1983).
Thompson, L.L., *The Book of Revelation: Apocalypse and Empire* (Oxford and New York: Oxford University Press, 1990).
Thrupp, S. (ed.), *Millennial Dreams in Action: Essays in Comparative Study* (Comparative Studies in Society and History, Supp. 2; The Hague: Mouton, 1962).
Tidball, D., *An Introduction to the Sociology of the New Testament* (Exeter: Paternoster Press, 1984).
Tiede, D.L., *Jesus and the Future* (Cambridge: Cambridge University Press, 1990).
Tisserant, E., *Ascension d'Isaïe* (Paris: Letouzey et Ané, 1909).
Tödt, H.E., *The Son of Man in the Synoptic Tradition* (London: SCM Press, 1965).
Trakatellis, D., *The Pre-Existence of Christ in Justin Martyr* (Missoula: Scholars Press, 1976).
Trigg, J.W., *Origen* (London: SCM Press, 1985).
Trites, A.A., *The Transfiguration of Christ: A Hinge of Holy History* (Hantsport: Lancelot Press, 1994).
Troeltsch, E., *The Social Teaching of the Christian Church* (2 vols.; ET; London: George Allen & Unwin, 1931).
Tuckett, C.M., 'Synoptic Tradition in the Didache', in Sevrin (ed.), *The New Testament in Early Christianity*, pp. 197-230.

Turdeanu, E., 'Apocryphes bogomiles et apocryphes pseudo-bogomiles', *RHR* 69 (1950), pp. 213-18.
—*Apocryphes slaves et roumaines de l'Ancien Testament* (SVTP, 5; Leiden: Brill, 1981).
Ullendorff, E., *Ethiopia and the Bible* (London: British Academy, 1968).
Urbach, E.E., *The Sages: Their Concepts and Beliefs* (Jerusalem: Magnes Press, 1975).
Vaillant, A., 'Un apocryphe pseudo-bogomile: La Vision d'Isaïe', *Révue des Études Slaves* 42 (1963), pp. 109-21.
—*Textes Vieux-slaves* (Institut d'Études slaves; Paris: Imprimerie Nationale, 1968).
VanderKam, J.C., *Enoch and the Growth of an Apocalyptic Tradition* (Washington: Catholic Biblical Association of America, 1984).
Verheyden, J., 'L'Ascension d'Isaïe et l'Évangile de Matthieu', in Sevrin (ed.), *The New Testament in Early Christianity*, pp. 247-74.
Vermes, G., *The Dead Sea Scrolls in English* (Harmondsworth: Penguin Books, 1975).
Vos, G., *The Pauline Eschatology* (Grand Rapids: Eerdmans, 1952).
Wallace, A.F.C., 'Mazeway Resynthesis: A Bio-Cultural Theory of Religious Inspiration', *Transactions of the New York Academy of Sciences* 18 (1956), pp. 626-38.
—'Revitalization Movements', *American Anthropologists* 58 (1956), pp. 264-81.
—'Mazeway Disintegration: The Individual's Perception of Socio-Cultural Disorganization', *Human Organization* 16 (Summer 1957), pp. 23-27.
Wapnick, K., 'Mysticism and Schizophrenia', in R. Woods (ed.), *Understanding Mysticism* (London: Athlone Press, 1980), pp. 321-37.
Weber, F., *System der altsynagogen palästinischen Theologie aus Targum, Midrash und Talmud dargestellt* (Leipzig, 1880).
Weigandt, P., 'Doketismus im Urchristentum', (PhD dissertation, University of Heidelberg, 1961).
Weiser, A., *The Psalms* (London: SCM Press, 1962).
Weiss, J., *Earliest Christianity* (2 vols.; ET; New York: Harper & Row, 1957, 1959).
Wendland, J., *Die Briefe an die Korinther* (Göttingen: Vandenhoeck & Ruprecht, 1946).
Werner, M., *Die Entstehung des christlichen Dogmas* (Bern: Verlag Paul Haupt, 2nd edn, 1954). *The Formation of Christian Dogma* (trans. S.G.F. Brandon; London: A. & C. Black, 1955).
Whiteley, D.E.H., *The Theology of St Paul* (Oxford: Basil Blackwell, 1964).
Whybray, R.N., *Wisdom in Proverbs* (London: SCM Press, 1965).
Wilckens, U., *Weisheit und Torah* (Tübingen: Mohr, 1959).
Wilken, R.L. (ed.), *Aspects of Wisdom in Judaism and Christianity* (Notre Dame: University of Notre Dame Press, 1975).
Wilson, B., 'A Typology of Sects', in R. Bocock and K. Thompson (eds.), *Religion and Ideology* (Manchester: Manchester University Press, 1985), pp. 297-311.
—*The Social Dimensions of Sectarianism* (Oxford: Clarendon Press, 1990).
Wilson, R.McL., *The Gnostic Problem* (London: Mowbrays, 1958).
—*Gnosis and the New Testament* (Oxford: Basil Blackwell, 1968).
—*Hebrews* (Basingstoke: Marshall, Morgan & Scott, 1987).
Windisch, H., 'Zur Christologie der Pastoralbriefe', *ZNW* 34 (1935), pp. 213-38.
Windisch, H., and H. Preisker, *Die Katholischen Briefe* (Tübingen: Mohr, 1951).
Wolfson, H.A., *Philo: Foundations of Religious Philosophy in Judaism, Christianity and Islam* (Cambridge, MA: Harvard University Press, 1947).

Worsley, P.M., *The Trumpet Shall Sound: A Study of 'Cargo' Cults in Melanesia* (London: MacGibbon & Kee, 2nd edn, 1968).
Woude, A.S. van der, and M. de Jonge, 'Melchizedek and the New Testament', *NTS* 12 (1965–66), pp. 301-306.
Yamauchi, E., *Pre-Christian Gnosticism* (London: Tyndale Press, rev. edn, 1983).
Zeller, E., 'Die Märtyrtod des Petrus', *ZWT* (1896), pp. 558-68.
Zimmerli, W., *Ezechiel* (2 vols.; Neukirchen–Vluyn: Neukirchener Verlag, 1979).

INDEXES

INDEX OF REFERENCES

OLD TESTAMENT

Genesis		21.23	126	44.1	154
1.1	161	26.8	280	45.6	101
2.21	194	30.11-14	296	68.18	137
4.4-5	110	32.39	178	78.43	280
5.24	99, 100	34.6	100, 105	81.16	238
6	132, 307			82	108
6.1-4	307	*Joshua*		90.4	232
14.18-24	109	5.13-15	112	95	228
16	162	5.14	162	98.6-8	159
16.7-14	112			110	130
16.13	112	*Judges*		110.1	69, 90,
18	113, 125	2.1	112		127, 160
	159, 162	13	125		
18.1-15	112			*Proverbs*	
18.2	113	*1 Kings*		1.20-33	96
18.17	113	17.2-5	51	3.19	95, 129
19	44	19.1-8	42	8.22	95, 96,
19.24	159	22.19	100		98, 129
28.11	98			8.23-29	95
31.11-13	112	*2 Kings*		8.29	95
32.24-30	112	2.11-12	100	8.32-36	96
32.28	111	20.1-11	40		
		20.12-19	40	*Isaiah*	
Exodus		21.16	29	1.10	44, 272
3.1-6	112			3.13-18	156
7.1	108, 109	*2 Chronicles*		6	43, 75,
7.3	280	32.24	40		76, 144,
20	179	33	40		162, 191
23.20-21	159	33.11	43		192
23.20	162			6.1-4	17, 100,
24.10	105	*Job*			272, 282
33	191, 192	28.12-19	95		295
33.10	196	28.21	95	6.10	194
33.20	191, 292	28.28	95	8.7	156
				9	272
Deuteronomy		*Psalms*		9.5	156
4.34	280	110.1	130, 131	9.6	161
6.4	179	24	165	10.7	156

Index of References

11	214, 272		116, 117	10.9	120
11.2-22	156		134	11.31	293
11.6-9	214, 232	8	117, 118	12	117, 179
13	290	8.1-2	118	12.1	110
30.26	214, 217	9.2	116	12.2-3	218, 241
35	246	28.13	116	12.11	293
38	40	34	46	12.12	50, 51, 285, 294
44–47	179				
45	50, 127, 174, 175	*Daniel*		*Hosea*	
45.18	50, 174, 175, 178	4.12	14	3.5	215
		4.14	14		
52–53	289, 290	7	114, 115, 117, 119	*Joel*	
52.13–53.12	53	7.9-14	75, 101, 113	4.18	238
52.13	155	7.9-10	120		
53	53	7.9	113, 119	*Amos*	
64.4	69	7.13-14	113	9.13-15	215
65.25	214	7.13	119, 120	9.13-14	232
66.1	29	7.27	114	9.13	214, 216
		10	117-20		
Ezekiel		10.4-6	116	*Zechariah*	
1.6-7	116	10.5-6	19, 94, 116, 117, 120, 134	1.14	169
1.13	116			14.5	52, 81, 127, 285
1.24	116				
1.26-27	100,	10.7-9	147		

APOCRYPHA

Tobit		12.19	90, 91, 124, 148	*Ecclesiasticus*	
3.13	147			24	96, 124, 147
3.16-17	124, 146, 147	12.20	148	24.2	96
		14.5	217	24.8	96
5	124, 146	14.16-17	217	24.23	96
10	147			25.24	178
11	147	*Wisdom of Solomon*		45.2	107, 109
12	124, 146	7.22	96	47.11	101
12.13-15	147	8.4-6	129		
12.15-20	124	9.4	96, 97	*2 Maccabees*	
12.16	147			2.18	217
12.19-20	147				

NEW TESTAMENT

Matthew		10.20	278	19.3-9	194
2.20-21	281	11.2-22	11	19.28	61, 221, 226
3.13-18	11	11.14	12		
3.16-17	12	11.28-30	125	20.22-23	54, 277
4.8-10	277	13.41	102, 115	22.15	195
4.8-9	54	16.16	22	24	293
5.18-22	293	16.27	221	24.4-5	293
8.20	204	16.28	219	24.9-14	293
10.15	44	17.1-7	134	24.10	294

338   *Disciples of the Beloved One*

24.11	293	*Luke*		14.28	87	
24.15-22	293	1.16	44	14.30	84	
24.16	294	2.4	130	16.11	84	
24.20	294	4.5-8	277	17.4-5	140	
24.23-27	293	9.28-36	134	19	196	
24.24	50	9.35	102, 281	19.31	278, 282	
24.26	294	10.18	14, 207, 287	19.34	89, 140, 295	
24.29	293	12.37	52, 279	20.28	151	
24.30-31	293	21.8	293			
26.39	54, 277	21.20	38, 195	*Acts*		
26.50	85	22.30	61	1.4	280	
27.9	44	23.35	102, 281	1.9-11	68	
27.25	195, 196	24	133	1.10-11	281	
27.31	45	24.49	280	2	199	
27.51-53	278	24.50-52	68	2.19	280	
27.52-53	61			2.22	280	
27.62-66	45, 277	*John*		2.23-24	127	
28.19	45, 68, 80, 143, 144, 152, 178, 277	1.1-18	72	2.33	127, 280	
		1.1-14	138	2.36	127	
		1.1-2	143	2.43	280	
		1.1	143	4.30	280	
		1.14-18	138	5.12	280	
Mark		1.14	96, 138	5.17	46	
1.1	130	1.17-18	138	5.30	85	
1.11	156	1.34	102	6.8	280	
1.15	220	3.3	218	7	279	
2.10	221	3.7	88	7.36	280	
2.28	221	3.13	105, 126, 138-40, 146, 192, 282, 295, 302	7.55-56	54, 279	
9–10	220			7.56	102, 221	
9 19				8.13	280	
9.1	132			10.39	85	
9.2-8	134			14.3	280	
9.7	156			14.12	91	
9.37-38	221	3.14	140, 194	15.12	280	
11.1-10	220	3.17	139	21.38	51	
11.15-18	220	4.34	139			
12.17	229	4.48	280	*Romans*		
12.25	222	5.23	139	1.3-4	288	
12.35-37	130	6.46	105, 126, 139, 140, 292	1.3	130	
12.40	269			4.25	158	
13	293			8	233	
13.5-6	293			8.3	135	
13.20-22	50	6.62	138, 139, 282, 295	8.18-25	226	
14.12-31	220			8.19	226	
14.50	222	7	283	8.20	226	
15.42	278	7.19	293	8.21	226	
16.8	128, 222	7.25	67	8.34	131	
16.12	133, 134	7.27	282	9.29	44	
16.19	281	8.58	113, 159	10.6-8	136, 287, 296, 297	
24.50-52	281	10.1-6	196			
		12.31	84	13	229	
		12.41	282, 295			

15.19	280	*2 Corinthians*			222
		3.7-8	292	2.10	85
1 Corinthians		3.7	44	3.20-21	227
1.10	288	3.13	44	3.20	228
2.8	12, 66,	4.4	84, 300	3.21	227
	68, 79,	5	226	4.6	227
	85, 135,	5.2	226		
	191 284,	8.9	135	*Colossians*	
	298-300	12	32,	1.15-20	72, 77,
2.9	69		300-302		136, 143
4.4	288	12.3	301		173
6.2-3	226	12.12	280	1.16	58
7.31	229			2.15	12, 16,
8.6	81, 125,	*Galatians*			79, 88,
	127 129,	1.15-16	128, 222		265, 284
	151		301	2.18	77
10.4	159	1.16	133	3.1	131
10.11	70	3.8	194	1.15	125
12–14	47, 204	3.13	85, 126		
12.8	198	4.4	135	*1 Thessalonians*	
12.28	199	4.14	228	1.7	12
14.5	199	4.26	228	2.14-16	195
15	131, 224			3.13	51, 52,
	226, 233	*Ephesians*			81, 127,
15.7	128	1.5-6	154		222, 285
15.8	128, 133	1.6	143, 154	4	224
	222, 301	1.14	303	4.13-18	223, 308
15.12	224	1.20	131	4.14	223
15.13-19	224	2.2	286, 303	4.16	223
15.20-28	224	2.6	286, 303	4.17	223, 224
15.23	224		304	5.2	220
15.24-25	131	2.7	303		
15.24	224, 250	2.20	199, 202	*2 Thessalonians*	
15.25	224	4.8-9	136, 137	1.7	51, 81,
15.26	225		146, 287		127, 222
15.28	87, 225		304		232, 241
15.30-34	225	4.30	303		285
15.35-49	225	5.5	303	1.9-10	224
15.35-38	225	6.8	303	2	49, 224,
15.37	226	6.12	286, 303		293
15.38	225	6.13	303	2.1-4	224
15.42	225			2.3-12	220
15.44	225, 238	*Philippians*		2.5-7	224
	240	1.1	198	2.7	224
15.45-49	225	1.23	52, 218	2.9-10	224
15.50-57	225	2	71, 136	2.9	224, 280
15.51	225	2.5-11	71, 75,	2.11-12	224
15.52	225		127, 296		
15.54	225	2.6-11	135	*1 Timothy*	
15.55	230	2.6	77, 135	1.15	88, 138,
		2.8-9	127		286
		2.9-11	82, 174,	2.5	126

340   Disciples of the Beloved One

3.1-13	199	12.24	126		118, 120
3.16	45, 137,				134, 143
	138, 146	*James*			222 287,
	286, 290	2.1-7	46		311
	304, 305	*1 Peter*		2.10	61
	310	2.24	85	3.11	61
4.14	199	3	132, 284, 310	3.21	61
4.18	199	3.18–4.6	93	4–5	143, 311
		3.18-22	306	4	120
2 Timothy		3.18-19	308	4.1	56, 287,
1.1	288	3.18	308		301
2.18	235	3.19-22	93, 310	4.4	61
3.1-9	286	3.19	126, 297	5	120
			306-11	5.6	102, 132
Titus		3.20-21	310		287, 311
1.5-9	199	3.22	12, 16,	9.40	149
			40, 63,	1.13-14	144
Philemon			68, 69,	12	180, 287
2.9-11	143		78, 79,	12.7-12	14
			90, 125,	12.7-9	207, 281
Hebrews			126, 131	13	49, 229,
1	77		132, 144		311
1.1-4	72		151, 281	13.11-18	287
1.2	136		285, 305	17	49, 229
1.6	136		308, 310	18.2	205
2.14	136	4.5	308	19.10	59, 287
3–4	232	4.6	297, 308	20–21	231
3	228	5.4	61	20	52, 230
3.3	292	11.32-33	144	20.4	214,
3.7-11	228				230-32,
3.33	228	*2 Peter*			238, 239
4	228	1.5-7	286		241
4.9-10	228	1.19-21	199	20.12	230
4.14	125, 285	2.1-3	199	20.14-15	230
9.15	126	3	46	21–22	287
9.28	227	3.4	132	21	230
10.19-20	125, 285	3.15-16	285, 288	21.4	230
10.37	227			21.12	217
11	228	*Jude*		21.22	231
11.37	34, 285	7	44	22.5	230
11.40	228			22.8-9	59, 287
12.22-29	228	*Revelation*		22.17	311
12.22-24	230	1.1-4	149	22.20	230
12.22	228	1.13-14	19, 81,		

PSEUDEPIGRAPHA

Apocalypse of		*Apocalypse of*		*Ascension of Isaiah*	
Abraham		*Zephaniah*		1–5	14, 23,
10.9	87	9.12–10.9	59		27, 30,
11.3	119				31, 187,
16.3	178				267

Index of References

Ascension of Isaiah		3.2-5	43				44-46,
(cont.)		3.6-12	29				48, 182,
1	39	3.6-10	19, 38,				187, 197
1.1–3.12	13		39, 43,				201, 205
1.1-5	28		190				246, 260
1.1-2	29	3.6	43, 195				269, 271
1.1	22, 39	3.8-10	43, 105,				286
1.2	40, 154		190-93,	3.21			33, 37,
1.3-4	40, 78,		196, 269				41, 46,
	80		292				187, 197
1.3	79, 284,	3.10	44, 195,				201, 210
	285		272				247, 258
1.5	40, 80	3.12	21, 44				262
1.6	40, 55	3.13–4.22	14, 29,	3.23			46, 197,
1.7-13	28		30, 32,				201, 269
1.7	40, 278		177	3.24			46, 197
1.12	40	3.13–4.1	32, 187	3.25			46, 260,
2–5	22	3.13–4.4	22				261, 269
2	15, 40	3.13-31	187	3.26-28			198
2.1-15	28	3.13-20	14	3.26-27			47, 56,
2.2	41	3.13-19	26				152, 197
2.4–4.4	21	3.13-18	15, 44,				204
2.4–3.12	22		66, 71,	3.26			47, 197,
2.4	39		172, 274				201
2.5	41		288	3.27			47, 197,
2.6	41	3.13-16	43				269
2.7-11	19, 41,	3.13	19, 28,	3.28			260, 261
	42, 47,		40, 44,	3.29-30			197
	189, 197		45, 154,	3.30			47
	202, 204		191, 195,	3.31			47, 197,
	210, 253		196, 278				198, 202
	260, 261		282				253, 263
	263, 269	3.14	45	4–5			36
	273, 301	3.15	45, 111	4			33, 34,
2.7	41	3.16-18	54				36, 48,
2.8	42	3.16-17	45, 59,				54, 58,
2.9-11	42		62, 80,				92, 187,
2.12-16	43		81, 86,				189 206,
2.12	28		87, 145,				267 281,
2.13	59		153, 274				293 294,
2.14–3.13	23		288				303 311,
2.14–3.12	24	3.16	21				312
2.14	39	3.18	45, 65,	4.1-13			12, 14,
2.16	43		277, 281				20, 32,
2.24	22		282, 305				36, 44,
2.25	22		306				48, 54,
2.27	60	3.19-21	47				188, 205
2.37	22, 60,	3.19-20	44, 45				207, 240
	83, 155	3.20	280				243, 313
3–4	293	3.21–4.22	197	4.1-4			41
3	313	3.21-31	12, 14,	4.1-3			299
3.1	43, 193		19,	4.3			49, 207,

Ascension of Isaiah
(cont.)
210
4.4-12   15
4.4   49
4.5   49, 294
4.6-7   36
4.6   16, 50,
          209, 294
4.8   36, 50,
          209
4.9   37, 41,
          50, 205,
          209, 212
          246, 258
          294
4.10-11   50
4.10   294
4.11   36, 50,
          210
4.12   29, 50,
          81, 294
4.13-14   42, 259
4.13   37, 51,
          155, 189
          210, 259
          261, 263
          279, 294
4.14-18   15, 44,
          51, 81,
          186, 205
          212, 216
          241, 243
          244, 264
          267, 285
          312
4.14-16   38, 173,
          213, 313
4.14   15,
          50-52,
          80, 81,
          151, 213
          263, 285
          294
4.15-17   15
4.15   52, 213,
          232, 240
4.16   52, 173,
          179, 197
          218, 242
          243, 279
          297

4.17

4.18

4.19-21
4.19
4.20
4.21-22

4.21

4.22
5

5.1-16

5.1-14
5.1
5.2-14
5.2
5.3-6
5.8
5.9-10
5.9
5.10
5.11-12
5.13

5.14
5.15-16
6–11

15, 17,
32, 53,
60, 61,
85, 172,
173, 179
213, 225
232, 241
242, 259
264, 267
294,
312, 313
52, 53,
213, 222
244
53
205, 240
290
19, 53,
63, 80,
152, 163
191, 193
196, 271
273, 274
289, 292
53, 155,
289, 290
297
111, 291
36, 54,
210,
277-79

13, 23,
29
28
54
28
54
54
54, 277
54
54
181
54
36, 37,
54, 55,
204, 210
243, 263
277
54, 279
54
15, 20,
23, 24,

6–9
6

6.1-7
6.1-6
6.1
6.4
6.5
6.6
6.10-12
6.10-11
6.13
6.14
6.16-17
6.17

7
7.1-19
7.7-8

7.8
7.9-12

7.9
7.12
7.13-17
7.13
7.14
7.15
7.17

7.18-23
7.19
7.21

26, 30,
31, 55,
177, 187
189, 198
262, 264
267, 273
300
16, 27,
30, 48,
55, 188,
198 204,
301
187
28
22, 55
201
55, 269
56
56
280
56, 187
19, 56
56
19, 28,
270
215
23, 24
19, 56,
57, 62,
81, 86,
142, 143
152
57
15, 38,
41, 58,
150, 173
180, 212
261 264,
286, 287
303, 310
180
265, 310
82
58
58
58
17, 59,
62, 63,
143, 152
59
59
59

Index of References

Ascension of Isaiah		9.15	65, 85			83, 86,
(cont.)		9.16-17	64			142, 153
7.23	59, 62,	9.16	61, 65,			155
	87, 143,		85, 297	10.8-16	64	
	152 235,	9.17	61, 85,	10.8-11	88	
	280		155,	10.8	64, 265	
7.27	58, 215		278, 297	10.9	64	
8	82	9.18	61, 85	10.10	64, 297	
8.1	60	9.23	62, 86,	10.11	63, 64,	
8.7	60, 281		142		143	
8.8	58	9.24-26	61, 181	10.12-16	265	
8.9-10	60	9.26	65	10.12-13	16, 36,	
8.10	82	9.27-42	57, 61,		79, 88	
8.16-28	60		143, 311	10.12	64	
8.17	60	9.27-39	63	10.13	64	
8.18	60, 62,	9.27-36	57, 90	10.14-15	16	
	81, 155	9.27-34	63, 143	10.14	16, 64,	
8.22	280	9.27-28	19		65, 79,	
8.24	212	9.27	61, 85,		88, 172,	
8.25-28	60		86, 142,		265	
8.25	83, 155		143	10.15-16	79	
8.27	213	9.28-29	62	10.16–11.33	71	
9–11	71, 173,	9.29-23	61	10.16	69, 90	
	222, 241	9.29	62, 86	10.17–11.33	74, 133	
	311	9.30	62, 87,	10.24	89	
9	17, 57,		158	10.25	65	
	59, 60,	9.32	62, 85	10.27	86	
	82, 86,	9.33-36	87	10.29-31	89	
	152, 242	9.33	62, 87	10.29-30	66	
	267	9.35-36	62, 63,	10.30	86	
9.1-5	62		151, 152	11	19, 59,	
9.1	60, 82,		154, 311		66, 140,	
	87, 103,	9.36	62		313	
	242, 273	9.37-38	178	11.2-22	15, 26,	
9.2	60	9.40-42	74		27, 44,	
9.3	22, 27	9.40	63, 87,		68, 140,	
9.5	22, 60,		144 145,		148, 172	
	63, 80,		151		274, 288	
	82, 83,	9.42	62		313	
	86, 142,	10–12	215	11.2-3	67	
	151, 153	10–11	17	11.2	16	
	155	10	16, 19,	11.4-6	67	
9.6-18	213		45, 64,	11.6-7	295	
9.6	84		65, 79,	11.7-10	67	
9.7-12	60		89, 164,	11.8	89	
9.8-9	61, 84		265, 297	11.11-13	67	
9.10	61		298	11.14	67, 274,	
9.12	61, 65,	10.6-17	38		282, 283	
	84	10.6	81		288, 289	
9.13	84, 155	10.7-16	16, 38,	11.16	67	
9.14	65, 83,		87, 88	11.17	67, 89,	
	84, 155	10.7	22, 60,			91, 148,

Ascension of Isaiah (cont.)		Assumption of Moses		93.9	216
	295	7.6	269	2 Enoch	
11.18	68, 280			1.4-10	56
11.19	68, 79,	2 Baruch		7	309, 311
	191, 195	10.9	217	7.1-3	309
	196, 299	29–30	216	8.1	302
	300	29.5	216, 232	10.1-7	100
11.20	68	30.1-3	217	20.3-4	87
11.21	68, 90	30.4-5	217	22.6	59
11.22-23	68	39	217	32.2	216
11.22	90, 281	40.1	217	33.1-2	216
11.23-33	16, 40,	40.3	217		
	68, 78,	72.2	217	3 Enoch	
	79, 90,			1–12	103
	148, 284	3 Baruch		10	104
	285, 305	4.8	178	12.1	104
	306, 310			12.5	104
		1 Enoch		16	104
11.23-31	16	1–36	311	16.3	104
11.23-24	16, 90	1–32	309	16.5	104
11.23	69	10.13	309		
11.24-25	90	10.15	310	4 Ezra	
11.24	69	12–14	100	2.43-45	61
11.25	58	13.2	309	5.4	50, 294
11.32-33	16, 59,	13.6	310	7.28-36	216
	60, 62,	14	63, 118,	7.29	216
	63, 69,		134, 178	13	115
	74, 79,	14.10	110	13.3-4	115
	87, 153	14.17	110		
11.32	85, 90,	14.18-25	100	Joseph and Asenath	
	110	14.20-21	134	14	111
11.33	69, 151,	15	310	14.9	120
	152	36–71	100		
11.34-35	70, 213	42	96, 97,	Jubilees	
11.34	69		124	1.20	16
11.35	55, 60,	45.3	101	1.27	107
	173	46.1-3	114	4.17-26	100
11.36-40	70	48.10	101	4.17	100
11.37-38	259	51.3	101	4.22	309
11.38	15	51.4	101	4.29-30	234
11.39	270	55.4	101	5.1-11	309
11.41-43	70, 187	61.8	101	7.21-35	309
11.41	70	61.9-13	87	8.3	309
11.42	70	62.2-6	101	22.27-31	52
11.43	70	62.14	101	23.27-31	218, 241
12.1	215	70.27	101		
12.2	215	71	101, 129	Lives of the Prophets	
12.3	215	71.14	102, 103	17.2	16
20.4	287	90.28-29	217		
33.20	193	90.30-33	217	4 Maccabees	
8.24-5	55	91.9	217	7.3	218, 241
9.37-38	63	93	216		

Index of References

9.22	218, 241		206	*Testament of Benjamin*	
14.5-6	218, 241	3.63-65	294	9.2	217
		8.9-11	208	11.2	154
Odes of Solomon		8.54-55	208		
1.2	91	3.350-55	208	*Testament of Dan*	
19.9	12, 67	3.63-5	50	1.7	16
		4.145-48	208		
Prayer of Joseph		5.101-104	34, 48,	*Testament of Job*	
4.22	149		206	48–50	87
		5.144-46	206		
Psalms of Solomon		5.414-30	217	*Testament of Levi*	
11	217	5.416-17	208	3.8	58
17.22	217	8.456-61	164	4.1	297
17.26-34	217				
17.30	217	*Testament of Abraham*		*Testament of Moses*	
		2.4	125	3.4	217
Sibylline Oracles		11.3	100	11.16	107
3	207	12.4-5	110		
3.63-74	14, 48,	13.2-3	110		

QUMRAN

11QTemple		*1QS*		*CD*	
29.9-10	217	2.19	16	2.15-20	309
		4.7	218	16.5	16
1QM					
2.7	217	*1QpHab*		*Gen. Apoc.*	
12.10	217	2.5-10	286	2.1-25	309
13.11	16				
14.15	309				

MISHNAH

Ḥagigah		*Kelim*		*Kilaim*	
2.1	270	17.6-7	209	9.2	209

TALMUDS

B. Bat.		*b. Pes.*		*b. Yeb.*	
127	209	68	217	49b	12, 28
		b. Šab.		*b. Yom.*	
B. Meṣ.		6	218	35	269
86	113				
		b. Sanh.		*b. Zeb.*	
b. Ḥag.		103b	29	49	191, 192
12	302	44	209		
12b	41	97	218	*j. Sanh.*	
14	115	99	218	10.2	12
15	104				
		b. Soṭ.		*t. Sanh.*	
		22	269	13.10	217

MIDRASH

Gen R.		Pes. R.	
50.2	113	4.3	29

PHILO

Abr.		Gig.			
84	98	60–61	99	2.24	98
				2.67	99

Agr.
51   108

Leg. All.
1.36-37   99
1.46   98

Quaest. in Gen.
2.62   98, 99

Conf. Ling.
146   98, 152, 162

Migr. Abr.
103   98
70–85   98

Rer. Div. Her.
119   98
205   108
280   98

Congr.
79   99

Op. Mund.
143   98
20   98
36   98

Sacr.
32   286
80–83   98

Det. Pot. Ins.
54   129
161-62   108

Poster. C.
15   99
168-69   99

Somn.
1.65-67   98
1.102-14   98
1.215   108
1.239   99

Ebr.
132   98
157   98
44   99

Praem. Poen.
45   99

Vit. Mos.
1.155-6   108
1.156   108
1.158   108

Fug.
101-102   98

Quaest. in Exod.
2.13   98

CHRISTIAN AUTHORS

1 Apocryphon of James
33.2–36.1   236

2.1.30-31   172
II.1.22.21-24   194
30.25–31.4   236

Barnabas
1–2   193
15.3-9   232
16.4   195

1 Clement
17   286
23   46
36.2-6   286

Augustine
De civ.
20.7   239

Carmen
apologeticum
45.791   238

Acts of Peter
24   67

Sermones
259.2   239

Clement
Paidagogos
2.7   162

Apocryphon of John
11.18-21   50
2.1.1   172
2.1.22   172
2.1.24   172

Authoritative
Teaching VI.
3.34.32-35.18   239

Strom.
1.23.155   106

Index of References

Did.		*Gos. Pet.*		19.1	67, 85
7–15	200	39	45		
10.7	200	41–42	297	*Magn.*	
11	204, 269			8.2	201
11.7	200	Gregory of Nyssa		11	288
13	200	*Ep.*			
13.1	200	102	238	*Phld.*	
13.2	200			5.2	201
13.3	200	Hermas		7.2	201
13.4	200	*Man.*			
15	200, 202	11.5.8	199	*Pol.*	
		5.1.7	158	1.3	276
Ep. Ap.				2.2	276
13–14	163	*Sim.*		7.1	201
		5.4.4	158		
Epiph., Ev. Phil.		8.1.1-2	158	*Rom.*	
26	298	8.2.1	61	2.2	52, 218
		8.2.3	61	4.1	210
Epiph., Haer.		8.2.6	61	5 288	
21.2.4	298	9.12.7-8	158		
		9.16.5-7	297	*Smyrn.*	
Epiph., Pist. Soph.		10.3.1	157	1 288	
7 298				1.1	276
		Vis.		5.1	193
Epiphanius		5.2	157	6.1	276
Adv. Haeres.				2.1-2	203
48	237	Hippolytus		8.1	201
67.3	30	*Haer.*			
		8.19	237	*Trall.*	
Pan.		9.13.2-3	168	2.2	201
19.4.1-2	168			10.1	203
21.2.4	171	*Refutatio*			
30.14.2	169	*Omnium*		*Instructionum*	
30.16.3	169	*Haersium*		2.39	238
30.16.4	169	5.10	172		
30.18.5	169			Irenaeus	
30.2.2	169	Ignatius		*Adv. Haer.*	
30.3.1	169	*Ep.Ap.*		1.3.2	61
30.3.5-6	169	13	298	1.20.13	172
67.3	63, 154, 162	24	298	1.21.5	239
				1.23.3	171
		Eph.		1.24	66, 141
Eusebius		3 288		1.26	141, 166-68
Hist. Eccl.		17.1	276		
3.39	231	19	30, 283, 298	1.30.12	172
3.28.2	232			1.30.13	178
5.16.18	237	3.2	199	3.2.1	167
		6.1	201	3.3.4	167
Praep. Evang.		7 72		3.6.1	159
9.28-9	106	9.1	218	3.6.2	160
		18.2	60, 66, 151	3.11.2-3	160
				3.20.4	297

3.21.1	169	Justin Martyr		Contra Cels.	
4.6.7	84	*1 Apol.*		5.61	169
4.22.1	308	10	234	5.65	169
4.27.2	308	21	234	6.30-31	172
4.28.3	234	62–63	159		
4.33.4	168			*De Princ.*	
5.1-15	235	*Dial.*		2.11.2-3	237
5.1.3	169	17.1	46	1.3.4	57, 162
5.2.2	235	37–38	159	2.11.2	237
5.3.3	232	45	234	4.3.14	57, 162
5.7-8	235	45.4	66		
5.7.2	235	56–62	159	*Epistula ad Julium*	
5.25.3	235	56.11	159	*Africanum*	
5.28-3	235	56.13	72, 99, 122	9.25	12
5.30.4	235				
5.31.1	308	56.61	99	*Hom. Is.*	
5.31.2	235	56.128	99	1.2	162
5.32.1	235	58	159	4.1	162
5.33	231	60.2	159		
5.33.1	235	60.5	159	*In Joh.*	
5.33.2	235	61	122, 152, 159	2.31	53, 111, 162
5.33.3	235				
5.35.1	235	61.1	159		
5.36.2	235	72.41	297	*In libr. Jes. Nav. Com.*	
		75–86	159	6.2	162
Adv. Marc.		80	234, 241		
3.9-10	161	80.4	234	*Symposium*	
3.27	161	81	234	9 238	
		81.3-4	234		
Adv. Prax.		95	196	Ovid	
14	161	113-14	159	*Met.*	
		113	234	8.626-721	91
De Carne Christi		120.5	54		
14	161	125-29	159	*Paraph. Shem*	
		128	113, 122, 152, 159	44.11	236
Demonstratio					
10	160			*Pistis Sophia*	
84	163	Lactantius		7.12	171
		Div. Inst.			
Jerome		8.24	238	Pliny	
Ad. Jer.				*Ep.*	
19.10-11	238	Novatian		10.33	36
		De Trin.		10.96-97	34
Comm. in Is.		12	162	10.96	12, 34, 54, 209
3.6.2	162	17	162		
18	238			10.97	12, 35, 209
64.4-5	12	Origen			
64.4	26	*Comm. in Matt.*			
66.20	233	17.35	237	*Prot. Jas*	
		16.12	169	10.1	66
Comm. in Jer.					
4 238					

Rec. Clem.		Testim. Truth		Treat. Res.	
1.61	233	9.30.40-41	181	46.30-32	236
				47.2-12	236

Tertullian
Adv. Marc.
3.24   236
4.31   237

Theodoret
Haereticarum Fabularum Compendium
2.3   237

De praescr. haeret.
33.3-5   169

De resurrectione carnis
19   237

OTHER

Appian		Josephus		Tacitus	
Syr.		*War*		*Annals*	
8.50	208	6.283-85	252	15.44.2-8	210
		7.6.218	208		

Dio Cass.
64.9   34
69.12 209

Suetonius
Claud.
25.4   211

Hist.
2.8   34
2.9   34

Ezekiel the Tragedian
Exagoge II.
68-82   106

Nero
57   34

Ulpian
Dig.
50.15.3   208

INDEX OF AUTHORS

Aberle, D. 249
Abramowski, L. 67
Acerbi, A. 11-14, 24, 29, 33, 41, 46, 54, 57, 63, 69, 162, 164, 187
Achelis, H. 307
Adas, M. 252, 256
Aland, K. 283
Alexander, P. 103
Allegro, J.M. 309
Andersen, F.I. 309
Aptowitzer, V. 110
Attridge, H. 136, 228
Aune, D.E. 197
Avis, P. 128

Bacon, B.W. 292
Bakker, A. 66
Balz, H.R. 117
Bammel, E. 39, 250
Barbel, J. 75, 157, 159, 161
Bardy, G. 166
Barkun, M. 249, 254-56
Barnard, L.W. 234
Barnes, T.D. 237
Barrett, C.K. 227, 299
Barton, J. 27
Barton, S. 128
Bauckham, R.J. 11, 18, 52, 57, 73, 94, 126, 274, 275, 279
Baumeister, T. 181
Beasley-Murray, G.R. 293
Beckford, J.A. 254, 256
Beer, G. 28
Belleville, L.L. 292
Benoit, P. 292
Berger, P.L. 271
Berneri, M.L. 266
Bettiolo, P. 26
Betz, H.D. 133
Bianchi, U. 37, 38, 170, 180
Bietenhard, H. 15, 41, 143, 213, 231-34, 237, 239, 302

Bigg, C. 237
Black, M. 117
Blackman, E.C. 236
Boismard, M.E. 306
Bonwetsch, N. 25, 57
Boor, C. de 29
Borgen, P. 96, 105
Bori, P.C. 14, 26, 30, 32, 39, 47, 187
Boring, M.E. 197, 204
Borsch, F.H. 110, 114, 221
Bousset, W. 14, 73, 92, 121, 179, 307
Bowker, J.W. 300
Brandon, S.G.F. 13
Brandt, W. 167
Brooke, G.J. 290
Brown, R.E. 66, 67, 292
Brownlee, W.H. 290
Brox, N. 272
Buck, F. 66, 292
Bühner, J-.A. 72, 138
Bultmann, R. 282, 299, 306, 308
Burch, V. 16
Burchard, C. 120
Burkitt, F.C. 13, 27, 57
Burridge, K. 249, 251-54

Caird, G.B. 78, 103, 299
Caquot, A. 28, 40, 43
Caragounis, C.C. 114
Carmignac, J. 109
Carr, W.A. 78
Casey, P.M. 115
Charles, R.H. 11, 13, 22-25, 27-31, 33, 43, 45, 49, 57, 67, 117, 154, 155
Charlesworth, J.H. 11, 14, 16, 21, 22, 24, 25, 27, 33, 39, 42, 43, 45-47, 50-52, 54, 62, 64, 67, 69, 70, 83, 106, 110, 111, 119, 155, 179, 233, 309
Cheek, J. 301
Chilton, B.D. 134
Clemen, C. 49

Index of Authors

Cohn, N. 219, 248, 249
Collins, A.Y. 48, 211, 220, 249
Collins, J.J. 14, 48, 52, 177, 181, 205, 215, 229
Colonna, M.E. 29
Conzelmann, H. 298
Cranfield, C.E.B. 130, 306, 307
Cross, F.L. 163
Cross, F.M. 273
Crossan, J.D. 221
Cullmann, O. 72, 299

Dalton, W.J. 93, 125, 132, 306-308, 310
Daniélou, J. 16, 18, 32, 39, 45, 57, 59, 61, 62, 67, 79, 85, 144, 150, 158, 160, 162-65, 213, 231, 232, 234, 297
Daube, D. 227
Davies, S.L. 93
Davies, W.D. 227, 292
Deane, W.J. 176
Dehandschutter, B. 37
Dehn, G. 299
Deichgräber, R. 137
Delcor, M. 108
Delius, W. 292
Denis, A.-M. 21, 22, 24, 28
Dibelius, M. 305
Dillman, C.F.A. 11, 24
Dix, G. 147
Dodd, C.H. 131
Donaldson, J. 160
Donfried, K.P. 292
Doran, R. 181
Douglas, M. 256
Dunn, J.D.G. 18, 71, 72, 77, 91, 97, 113, 138

Easton, B.S. 286
Ehrhardt, A. 163
Ellingworth, P. 223
Emerton, J.A. 109, 114
Epp, E.J. 96
Epstein, I. 191
Everling, O. 299

Fantis, A. de 24
Farmer, W.R. 296
Ferch, A. 114
Festinger, L. 254
Festugière, A.J. 95

Fischel, H.A. 286
Fischer, J. 66
Fitzmyer, J.A. 109, 292
Flusser, D. 42, 43
Ford, J.M. 67, 213
Foerster, W. 170
Forsyth, N. 16
Fossum, J.-A. 92, 122, 145
Francis, F.O. 77
Frank, T. 208
Freedman, D.N. 197, 213, 237
Frend, W.H.C. 34-36
Friedländer, M. 245
Friedrich, G. 197, 200, 204
Fuchs, H. 207
Fuller, R.H. 72

Gager, J.G. 190, 196, 220
Gebhardt, O. von 22
Geschwind, K. 307
Giblin, G.H. 129
Gieseler, J.C.L. 24
Ginzberg, L. 12, 113, 178, 308
Glock, C.Y. 250
Goodenough, E.R. 97, 98, 105
Goodman, M. 252
Goulder, M.D. 128
Gourgues, M. 69
Gowan, D.E. 214
Graef, H.C. 292
Grant, R.M. 170
Grenfell, B.P. 21, 45, 49
Grillmeier, A. 72
Grudem, W.A. 306
Gruenwald, I. 56, 103, 104, 179, 290
Güterbock, H.G. 307

Habermann, J. 71, 135
Hahn, F. 72
Hall, R.G. 20, 29, 32, 33, 187, 188, 203, 242, 270, 272
Halperin, D. 56
Hamerton-Kelly, R.G. 72, 92, 117
Hammershaimb, E. 28
Hanson, A.T. 306
Hanson, P.D. 42
Hanson, R.P.C. 237
Harnack, A. von 25
Harper, G.M. 208
Harris, M.J. 226
Harrison, P.N. 200
Hastings, J.H. 154

Hawthorne, G.F. 96, 300
Hay, D.M. 69, 130
Hedrick, C.W. 99
Hegermann, H. 136
Heichelheim, F.M. 208
Heine, R.E. 237
Heller, J. 296
Hellholm, D. 48
Helmbold, A.K. 33, 176
Hengel, M. 18, 48, 66, 69, 72, 77, 95, 127, 128, 130, 131, 137, 138, 140, 206, 216, 231, 252, 276, 283, 284, 295, 302, 308
Hennecke, E. 27, 164
Hermisson, H.J. 94
Heussi, K. 49
Hill, D. 27, 197, 204, 292, 293
Hindley, J.C. 102
Hobshawn, E.J. 256
Hodgson, R. 99
Hoffmann, P. 223
Hofius, O. 125, 228
Hofman, J. 22
Holladay, C.R. 91, 106, 108
Holtz, T. 119
Hooker, M.D. 53, 113, 221
Horbury, W. 41
Hornschüh, M. 164
Horsley, R.A. 129, 197
Horst, P. van der 106
Horton, F.L. 109
Hunt, A.S. 21, 45, 49
Huntzinger, C.H. 306
Hurtado, L.W. 19, 73, 92, 101, 106, 107, 110, 118, 123, 126, 129

Isaac, E. 309
Isenberg, S.R. 219
Ivanov, J. 25

Jacobson, H. 106
Jefford, C.N. 200
Jeremias, J. 63, 268-70, 279, 306, 307
Jewett, R. 220
Johnson, B. 271
Johnson, S.E. 306
Jonge, M. de 108

Käsemann, E. 71, 89, 140, 275, 295
Katz, E. 28
Kautsch, E. 28
Kelly, J.N.D. 67, 309

Kilpatrick, G.D. 292
Kim, S. 92
Klausner, J. 219
Klijn, A.F.J. 166-68, 233
Knibb, M.A. 11, 13, 16, 21-25, 27, 28, 33, 39, 42, 43, 45-47, 50-52, 54, 58, 62, 64, 67, 69, 70, 82, 83, 102, 155
Knight, J.M. 11
Knox, W.L. 95
Köbben, A.J.F. 255
Köhler, W.-D. 276
Kolenkow, A.B. 110
Kozak, E. 25
Kraeling, E.G. 307
Kretschmar, G. 119
Küchler, M. 94
Kuhn, K.G. 110
Kumar, K. 266
Kümmel, W.G. 28, 276

Lacau, P. 26
Lagarde, P. de 307
Lampe, G.W.H. 38, 195
Lang, B. 94
Langen, F. 176
Lanne, E. 160
Lanternari, V. 248
Larkin, K.J.A. 42
Laurence, R. 23, 24, 33
Lavrov, P.A. 25
Lawson, J. 159, 234
Lee, R. 250
Lefort, L.T. 26
Leivestad, R. 114, 299
Lentzen-Deis, F. 133
Leornardi, C. 24
Lincoln, A.T. 137, 300
Lofland, J. 256
Logan, A.H.B. 170
Lohmeyer, E. 71
Lohse, E. 306
Longenecker, R. 18
Lorenz, R. 153
Lossky, V. 105
Lüdtke, W. 25

Mack, B.L. 95
Macrae, G.W. 106, 198
Mai, A. 24
Maier, J. 117

Index of Authors

Mannheim, K. 248, 266
Markschies, C. 69, 128, 130
Martin, R.P. 135, 300
Marty, M.E. 250
Martyn, J.L. 192
Massaux, E. 276
McKane, W. 96
Mearns, C.L. 223
Meeks, W.A. 93, 105-107, 261, 292
Metzger, B.M. 22
Michaelis, W. 75, 121
Michaels, J.R. 306, 308
Milik, J.T. 102
Miller, G. 299
Miller, M.P. 109
Moore, A.L. 222
Moore, G.F. 73, 121
Moravcsik, G. 29
Morgan, D. 94
Moule, C.F.D. 38, 101, 114, 115, 151, 250, 278
Mowinckel, S. 114
Moxnes, H. 157
Müller, U. 197
Munck, J. 299
Murphy-O'Conner, J. 71, 137

Negley, G. 266
Neusner, J. 105, 108, 111, 115
Nickelsburg, G.W.E. 52, 110, 179, 181, 218
Niebuhr, B.G. 24
Nitzsch, I. 24
Norden, E. 137
Norelli, E. 12, 21, 22, 28, 31, 45, 62, 79, 83, 145

Odeberg, H. 100, 103

Pagels, E. 178, 182
Pannenberg, W. 84
Passmore, J. 266
Patrick, J.M. 266
Pearson, B.A. 99, 125, 171, 244, 245
Percy, E. 137
Perdue, L.G. 94
Perrone, F. 23

Pesce, M. 11, 13, 16, 20-24, 26, 28, 29, 31, 33, 38, 42, 46, 47, 57, 62, 63, 67, 76, 150, 156, 180, 186, 187
Peterson, E. 165

Pétrement, S. 182, 245
Philonenko, M. 69
Piper, R.A. 92
Plevnik, J. 223
Plumpe, J.S. 67
Pope, M. 114, 307
Popov, A. 25
Preisker, H. 308
Procksch, O. 117

Rad, G. von 95, 112
Ramsey, A.M. 134
Reicke, B. 93, 132, 306, 307
Reid, B.E. 134
Reininck, G.J. 166-68, 233
Reumann, J. 292
Riesenfeld, A. 134
Riessler, P. 28
Roberts, C.H. 283
Robertson, A. 160
Robertson, R.G. 106
Robinson, H.W. 273
Robinson, J.A 154
Robinson, J.A.T. 33, 222
Robinson, J.M. 170, 181, 194
Rogerson, J.W. 273
Ronchey, S. 37
Rost, L. 28
Rowland, C.C. 57, 63, 92, 101, 103, 104, 116-20, 123, 134, 143, 270, 300
Rubinkiewicz, R. 119
Rudolph, K. 170, 171, 236, 239, 240
Russell, D.S. 100, 113, 272, 308

Sachmatov, A.A. 25
Ste Croix, G. de 35, 211
Sánchez, J.M.C. 67
Sanders, E.P. 14, 75, 84, 128, 217, 220, 221
Schaberg, J. 144
Schäfer, P. 56, 60
Schillebeeckx, E. 105
Schlier, H. 46, 137
Schmid, H.H. 94
Schmidt, C. 163

Schnabel, E.J. 93, 96
Schneemelcher, W. 27
Schniewind, J. 299
Schoedel, W.R. 85, 201
Schoeps, H.J. 166

Scholem, G. 65
Schotroff, L. 38
Schrage, W. 283
Schürer, E. 269
Schweinburg, K. 29
Schweizer, E. 44, 305, 308
Scott, M. 125
Scroggs, R. 117
Segal, A.F. 57, 68, 84, 92, 103, 123, 124, 148, 178, 300
Sevrin, J.-M. 11, 277
Sharot, S. 220
Sherwin-White, A.N. 35
Shimada, K. 306
Simonetti, M. 16, 57, 62, 76, 80, 142, 152, 155, 156
Sint, J. 272
Sjoberg, E. 101
Smallwood, E.M. 208, 209, 211
Smith, J.P. 160
Smith, J.Z. 111
Sparks, H.F.D. 27, 102
Speiser, E.A. 307
Spitta, F. 307
Spittler, R.P. 300
Stanton, G.N. 128
Stark, R. 256
Stead, G.C. 57
Stendahl, K. 268
Stenger, W. 137
Stevenson, J. 34, 280
Stier, F. 112
Stinespring, W.F. 233
Stockhausen, C.K. 292
Stone, M.E. 115, 216, 273
Stuckenbruck, L. 75
Styler, G.M. 278
Suggs, M.J. 93, 125, 296
Sweet, J.P.M. 250

Talbert, C.H. 18, 92
Taylor, L.R. 50
Theisohn, J. 101
Thiele, E.R. 40
Thompson, L.L. 50, 211
Thrupp, S. 219, 249
Tiede, D.L. 293
Tisserant, E. 22, 24, 27
Tödt, H.E. 114
Trakatellis, D. 72, 122, 158
Trigg, J.W. 237
Trites, A.A. 134

Troeltsch, E. 271
Tuckett, C.M. 277
Turdeanu, E. 25

Ullendorff, E. 22
Urbach, E.E. 100, 308

Vaillant, A. 25, 62
VanderKam, J.C. 100
Verheyden, J. 11, 22, 45, 145, 153
Vermes, G. 109, 269
Vos, G. 223

Wainwright, A.W. 79
Wallace, A.F.C. 254, 255
Wapnick, K. 56, 301
Weber, F. 73, 92, 121
Wedderburn, A.J.M. 170
Weigandt, P. 66
Weiser, A. 130
Weiss, J. 71
Wendland, J. 299
Werner, M. 13, 75-77, 121, 144
Whiteley, D.E.H. 129
Whybray, N. 95
Wilckens, U. 269
Wilken, R.L. 93, 125
Wilson, B.R. 271
Wilson, R.McL. 27, 170
Windisch, H. 305, 308
Wisse, F. 194
Wolf, E. 299
Wolfson, H.A. 97
Woods, R. 56
Worsley, P. 248, 249
Woude, A.S. van der 108

Yamauchi, E. 170

Zeller, E. 49
Zimmerli, W. 117

JOURNAL FOR THE STUDY OF THE PSEUDEPIGRAPHA
SUPPLEMENT SERIES

1   J.R. Levison, *Portraits of Adam in Early Judaism: From Sirach to 2 Baruch*
2   P. Bilde, *Flavius Josephus between Jerusalem and Rome: His Life, his Works, and their Importance*
3   P.R. Callaway, *The History of the Qumran Community: An Investigation*
4   T.W. Willet, *Eschatology in the Theodicies of 2 Baruch and 4 Ezra*
5   J.R. Mueller, *The Five Fragments of the Apocryphon of Ezekiel: A Critical Study*
6   R.G. Hall, *Revealed Histories: Techniques for Ancient Jewish and Christian Historiography*
7   G.J. Brooke (ed.), *Temple Scroll Studies: Papers Presented at the International Symposium on the Temple Scroll (Manchester, 1987)*
8   L.H. Schiffman (ed.), *Archaeology and History in the Dead Sea Scrolls: The New York University Conference in Memory of Yigael Yadin*
9   J.J. Collins & J.H. Charlesworth (eds.), *Mysteries and Revelations: Apocalyptic Studies since the Uppsala Colloquium*
10 S. Talmon (ed.), *Jewish Civilization in the Hellenistic-Roman Period*
11 M.J. Davidson, *Angels at Qumran: A Comparative Study of 1 Enoch 1–36, 72–108 and Sectarian Writings from Qumran*
12 D. Bryan, *Cosmos, Chaos and the Kosher Mentality*
13 G.M. Zerbe, *Non-Retaliation in Early Jewish and New Testament Texts: Ethical Themes in Social Contexts*
14 J.H. Charlesworth & C.A. Evans (eds.), *The Pseudepigrapha and Early Biblical Interpretation*
15 M. Wise, *Thunder in Gemini, and Other Essays on the History, Language and Literature of Second Temple Palestine*
16 R.D. Chesnutt, *From Death to Life: Conversion in Joseph and Aseneth*
17 E.M. Humphrey, *The Ladies and the Cities: Transformation and Apocalyptic Identity in Joseph and Aseneth, 4 Ezra, the Apocalypse and The Shepherd of Hermas*
18 J. Knight, *Disciples of the Beloved One: The Christology, Social Setting and Theological Context of the Ascension of Isaiah*
19 I. Fröhlich, *Time and Times and Half a Time: Historical Consciousness in the Jewish Literature of the Persian and Hellenistic Eras*
20 P. Sacchi, *Jewish Apocalyptic and Its History* (trans. W. Short)